Selected Essays of
R. P. Blackmur

Selected Essays of

R.P. BLACKMUR

Edited and with an Introduction

by Denis Donoghue

The Ecco Press

NEW YORK

Essays copyright © 1930, 1931, 1934, 1935, 1936,
1937, 1943, 1948, 1951, 1964 by R. P. Blackmur
Introduction copyright © 1985 by Denis Donoghue
First published by The Ecco Press in 1986
18 West 30th Street, New York, N.Y. 10001
Published simultaneously in Canada by
Penguin Books Canada Ltd., Ontario
Printed in the United States of America
Designed by Cynthia Krupat

Publication of this book was made possible in part
by a grant from the National Endowment for the Arts.

Library of Congress Cataloging-in-Publication Data
Blackmur, R. P. (Richard P.), 1904–1965.
Selected essays of R.P. Blackmur.
Contents: A critic's job of work—Notes on E.E.
Cummings's language—Examples of Wallace Stevens—
[etc.]
1. Literature, Modern—19th century—History and
criticism—Addresses, essays, lectures. 2. Literature,
Modern—20th century—History and criticism—Addresses,
essays, lectures. I. Donoghue, Denis. II. Title.
PN761.B525 1986   809.1   85-20541
ISBN 0-88001-083-5
ISBN 0-88001-103-3 (ppbk.)

Page 375 constitutes an extension of this page.

Contents

Introduction: *The Sublime Blackmur* 3

ONE

TWO

THREE

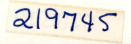

Selected Essays of

R. P. Blackmur

Introduction:

The Sublime Blackmur

In 1941 John Crowe Ransom published *The New Criticism*, an account of certain critical procedures as practised by T. S. Eliot, I. A. Richards, William Empson, Yvor Winters, and R. P. Blackmur. He did not present his critics exemplifying a school or a movement: they seemed, in his account, more different than similar. It was enough for his purpose that they exhibited loose kinship while each went about his particular business. Ransom had an interest in showing that a critic might find his sustenance, and most of his vocabulary, in supposing a privileged relation between literature and something else, some other body of preoccupations and lores. Such a body would likely be found among the social sciences, especially in psychology and history, or among the stricter concerns of philosophy, such as those of logic. Each of these critical procedures would be at best a partial affair, and each would hold out a possibility which it didn't itself fulfill—that of a complete criticism—which Ransom called for in the final chapter. Wanted: an ontological critic. Or, in the terms common to *The New Criticism* and an earlier essay, "Criticism, Inc.," Ransom wanted a critic who would assume that the writing of a poem is a desperate ontological or metaphysical manoeuvre. The poet "perpetuates in his poem an order of existence which in actual life is constantly crumbling beneath his touch." In his daily life, a poet has practical interests much the same as anyone else's: he has to live, he has to use the materials at hand. Only in poetry is he free to celebrate the natural or human object "which is real, individual, and qualitatively infinite." An ontological critic would respect the poet for this tenderness and value the poem for being a special form of discourse and embodying a special kind of attention. Ransom proposed that such a critic would think of a poem as having a logical object or universal, which might be produced as an imagined scene or story, and, in addition, "a tissue of irrelevance" from which the object would not really emerge. The tissue of irrelevance would testify to the plenitude of sentiment with which the object is suffused.

None of the five critics was sufficiently ontological, by Ransom's exacting standard in that vocabulary. But Blackmur could have protested that his interest in literature did not issue from a prior interest in something else. He was not, like Richards, a psychologist who resorted to literature merely for evidence; or a logician, like Winters, who judged literature upon its capacity to make impeccable statements. Blackmur's approach to literature was technical, it featured a concern for language and form, the adequacy of the arranged words to everything they had to do. Completeness was not, for him, the supreme value it was for Ransom. He never spoke, as Ransom often did, of the companionship of structure and texture.

But I am running ahead of myself. It is enough to say for the moment that *The New Criticism* placed Blackmur's work in company he was happy enough to keep, though in later years he repudiated the orthodoxy generally ascribed to him as a New Critic.

Blackmur's first notable steps in criticism were taken in 1927 when he became one of the editors of *Hound and Horn* and a frequent presence in its analytical pages. He reviewed T. S. Eliot, Santayana, and Wyndham Lewis. In 1928, on the occasion of the presidential election, he wrote an essay—in the form and spirit of *The Education of Henry Adams*—denouncing Herbert Hoover and recommending Al Smith. I have only circumstantial evidence for saying that, with Hoover's victory, Blackmur withdrew from overt comment on political matters and confined himself to literature, an institution he could at least hope to understand. Many years later he enlarged his survey again, pronouncing upon the social and cultural situation and the many forms of trouble-making he saw at large. But in Hoover's America he concentrated on reading literature and thought the best work he could do would be close to the page.

For the time being the only method he used was the one Eliot recommended, that of being very intelligent. High intelligence and exegetical zest amounted to the only credo he acted on.

Over a few years, Blackmur published close work on many writers, mostly modern poets but also a few prosers—Samuel Butler, Henry Adams—who caught his mind for one reason or another. Eliot was never out of his interest for long. Blackmur gradually took up the notion of writing a big book on Adams. After many years, still incomplete, it became a thorn or a burden or a broken promise. He made forays into it, published several essays on Adams, and left it unfinished upon his death; it has now been published in a form adequate to the gist of what he had to say. Henry James was a companionable figure to Adams—*Hound and Horn*, like the *Little Review* and other journals, brought out a special issue on him, and he remained exemplary to Blackmur for the rest of his life in criticism.

These and other figures inhabited Blackmur's mind, and were always available for reference and provocation. He liked to set them in relation, one to another, as he set James in relation to Adams on the consideration that James's mind was willing to let the pattern of experience emerge as the amassed record of the experience itself, while Adams insisted on having the pattern in advance. "James imagined human reality always through dramatizing the bristling sensual record of the instance—almost any instance that had a story in it—and let the pattern, the type, the *vis a tergo*, take care of itself, which under the stress of the imaginative process it commonly did." The only problem was to know, or to sense, what would make a story, or how the story would stretch all the way from its constituents to the pattern they would, taken together, manage to imply. "Adams, on the other hand, tended in a given case to depend on his feeling for human type and pattern—for history and lines of force—as the source of drama, and hence saw the individual as generalized *first*." To put it another way—and Blackmur liked putting his perceptions in several ways—"Adams's set of intellectual instruments more or less *predicted* what he would discover; James resorted to instruments only to ascertain what his sensibility had *already* discovered."

Blackmur worked such relations for all they seemed to be worth. He wanted to know what would happen in his own mind if he set Eliot in relation to Dante and really worked the relation. Stevens and Pound: Stevens and Eliot: these comparisons were rarely elaborated, Blackmur was content to catch from them a glint, a sharpened insight good for the moment. In *Anni Mirabiles 1921–1925*—lectures he gave at the Library of Congress in January 1956—he nearly turned comparison into a method, and guarded himself against the danger by making most of the instances eccentric. So he compared Faulkner and Proust, Hart Crane and Stevens, Pound and Whitman (a common comparison, this), Cummings and Dryden, Auden and Tennyson, Byron and William Carlos Williams. Sometimes he surrounded a poet with two comparative figures, setting the glints running up and down and all around the town. Hart Crane was beset with Baudelaire and Whitman, Marianne Moore with Keats and D. H. Lawrence, Henry James with Joyce and Proust.

But no procedure amounted to a method or depended upon a theory. Indeed, it is odd and therefore exhilarating that we are reading Blackmur more ardently than ever in conditions which he would have reproved. He flourished in an Age of Criticism, but he would not have borne in patience an Age of Theory in which literature and criticism are nearly dissolved in favor of the theory of each. In "A Critic's Job of Work" Blackmur compared criticism with walking, how both need a constant intricate shifting and catching of balance, and how neither is done very well. The fact that Blackmur, in his later years, walked little and that little with extreme difficulty makes the comparison the more telling. Most men in our day, he said, prefer "paved walks or some form of rapid transit—some easy theory or outmastering dogma." Not that he would have approved a hard theory; he didn't want a theory near him or pressing upon him any more than he wanted a dogma, though he accepted that some minds think themselves in need of both. Again in "A Critic's Job of Work":

For most minds, once doctrine is sighted and is held to be the completion of insight, the doctrinal mode of thinking seems the only one possible. When doctrine totters it seems it can fall only into the gulf of bewilderment; few minds risk the fall; most seize the remnants and swear the edifice remains, when doctrine becomes intolerable dogma.

If you hand your mind over to a theory—he seems to say—you have only yourself to rebuke when your theory hardens first into doctrine and then into dogma. Even if it doesn't, you can't do anything with your theory but apply it, forcing it upon your poems as if they could have no other desire than to receive such overbearing attention. No wonder Blackmur thought the best kind of mind the most provisional, and Montaigne the finest exemplar of it, revelling in mobility of perception—"La constance mesme n'est autre chose qu'un branle plus languissant," Montaigne wrote, unruefully. Poetry does not flow from thin air, Blackmur said, "but requires always either a literal faith, an imaginative faith, or, as in Shakespeare, a mind full of many provisional faiths"—the last the best kind of mind, he didn't even consider it necessary to say. When he wrote his early essays on Adams, Blackmur made him seem far more mobile than he was, assimilating him to an idiom he resorted to, with more cause, in describing Montaigne. He described Adams's skeptical intelligence as "restless but attentive, saltatory but serial, provisional in every position yet fixed upon a theme: the theme of thought or imagination conceived as the form of human energy."

It follows that Blackmur's values can be made to coincide with an attitude, a preference subjected to the mobility of mood and standing well back from a doctrine. He despised what he called "romantic egoism" and took it as asserting that "whatever I experience is real and final, and whatever I say represents what I experience." He was irritated by poems that proclaimed their spontaneity, and thought it no praise of Whitman and Pound to say that "each remained spontaneous all his life," because that condition, too, was just as congealed as dogma. He was not impressed by minds that offered "an easy vault from casual interpretation to an omnivorous world-view." Like Eliot and perhaps instructed by him, Blackmur thought that ideas as such had no place in a poem, and were a nuisance, killing the feelings they pretended to stand for.

It follows, too, that Blackmur valued literature so far as it presents experiences in forms which enable us to know them. "All his life long," he said of James, "and in all but his slightest work, he struggled to use the conventions of society, and to abuse them when necessary, to bring himself directly upon the emotion that lay under the conventions, coiling and recoiling, ready to break through." The tragic character of thought, Blackmur said, is "that it takes a rigid mold too soon" and insists upon a destiny long before it has become necessary to choose one. Hence the value of irony, which postpones destiny and keeps our minds on the stretch, so that even when we succumb to an idea we are not so besotted as to stick to it. Hence, too, the supreme value of imagination, in any of the attributes Blackmur described as rational, dramatic, or symbolic. "In poetry, and largely elsewhere," he said, "imagination is based upon the reality of words and the emotion of their joining." What precedes the words—whether we think of it as obsession, self-delusion, or plain nonsense—doesn't much matter, so long as its presence in the poet's mind is provisional and not dogmatic. Yeats's magic doesn't matter, however seriously he took it and practised it, because it became rational as it reached words and assented to their reality. Dante's imagination "enabled him to dramatize with equal ardor and effect what his doctrine blessed, what it assailed, and what, at heart, it was indifferent to."

But I am merely indicating in Blackmur a broad preference, or a working prejudice, which helped him to get his work done and kept it fresh. Between the prejudice and the sentences of his criticism as they work together in particular essays, we come upon his idiom. Some have found it an obstacle, and wished he had written the kind of prose that cats and dogs can read. He was often as lucid as anyone else. He could even be aphoristic, when he had done whatever he could to wring the perception from its conditions and now, at last, could simply release it; as when he said, having worked through several sentences on Adams's faith, that "he had no faith, but only the need of it." Or when he said of Henry James that "he began at once to cultivate what his father had planted in him, the

8]

habit of response across any barrier—the more barrier the more response." Or again of James and in excessive depreciation of *The Bostonians* and *The Princess Casamassima*, that these novels "have a strangely transformed air of protecting themselves from what they are really about." Or, finally, when he said that there is no sex anywhere in Marianne Moore's poetry—"No poet has been so chaste; but it is not the chastity that rises from an awareness—healthy or morbid—of the flesh, it is a special chastity aside from the flesh—a purity by birth and from the void"—and went on, a page or so later, to hear again the word "aside" and to say that her sensibility "constitutes the perfection of standing aside."

But there is still an obstacle; not, as a general thing, the quirky verbal play which Ransom and other readers of Blackmur have shaken their heads over, but the words and phrases which, because Blackmur uses them with an emphasis designed to be cumulative, amount in the end to his diction. Like any poet's diction, it begins to be recognisable only when its recurrence constitutes a problem. Till then, we take the words as they come.

But they come not in single file but in relations, sometimes specified, often assumed; hence the problem. Perhaps I can dispose them in categories, bringing together the words that are synonymous or nearly so.

There is, to begin with, the set of terms which refer to the "firstness" of experience, the earliest stirrings of sentient life before it knows what it is or why it is stirring. Sometimes Blackmur calls this "emotion," as in the sentence I quoted about James's use and abuse of conventions; sometimes sensation, momentum, intuition, and very often feelings or behavior, the last of which is virtually a technical term in Blackmur. "Behavior is the medium in which our lives take place"; elsewhere "the actual momentum in which the form of life is found." It is our impulse, and it is anarchy unless we want to mitigate the sentence and say, as Blackmur says in "Between the Numen and the Moha," that behavior "may merely want a different sort of order," different, that is, from any of the official sorts on offer. By any name, behavior is the cry of anything that is actual before it reaches the condition of being anything more or other. It is where all the ladders start.

The next stage—next because it has to be represented as coming after our behavior and offering to redeem it or somehow enhance it—marks our aspiration. If the first is behavior, the next is what Blackmur regularly calls manners, or "morals in action." Manners are the ideal insight, so far as it is embodied in society. Ransom associated a code of manners with the formal decency of a poem, and valued the latter as a sign in miniature of the former. Blackmur often settled for a phrase from Croce—"theoretic form"—to represent the sense we make of our feelings. "A theoretic form is a way of seeing: no more." No less, too; and what it sees is our feeling or our behavior so far as we want to make sense of it. Theoretic form is what we do to our behavior when we want to convert the actual into the real; or momentum into performance. "The great drive is in the craving of the actual to become real." We confront our behavior, and thereafter "our great fear is that our behavior may overwhelm us; our great delight is when we have transformed our aspirations into behavior; our fate is that we shall be mainly incarnations of our behavior." But our great delight can't be secured except by an act of the imagination, at once rational, dramatic, and symbolic. In some contexts Blackmur calls this achievement poetry or fiction; or, if he thinks of it in closely linguistic terms, he calls it rhythm, as in what would otherwise be merely the arrangement of syllables. Theoretic form, to try again, is how we construe our behavior when we try to make sense of it by bringing it into relation to different senses already in place: we give it a form and enact it. So in poetry: the poem is always at a remove from the feelings or the behavior that incited it. Stevens's success "is due largely to his double adherence to words and experience as existing apart from his private sensibility." His great labor has been "to allow the reality of what he felt personally to pass into the superior impersonal reality of words." What is in its natural condition mostly a torment—behavior—is transformed into the poem "where it may be rehearsed and understood in permanent form." So too in criticism: its perennial task is that of "bringing the work of art to the condition of performance." In pursuit of the theoretic form of our behavior, we resort to particular skills, which in a novelist are those of his art, and in anyone amount to what Blackmur calls the technical or executive forms.

So much for an ideal conversion of behavior into manners. If it could succeed, all our behaviors would be redeemed, our first steps would arrive, our scribbled first drafts would turn into live poems, the words vivid with the life we've given them. But in frequent practice our imaginations are incomplete or otherwise half-hearted. It would be too cynical to represent this condition as the inevitable third phase; inaccurate, too, because sometimes it doesn't obtrude at all and sometimes it has already obtruded before the act of imagination can properly get started. In a diagram it would be set aslant from the sequence of behavior and manners. But in any event it must be regarded as the perversion of manners, or their degraded form. In Blackmur's terms, the perversion involves the ousting of "morals in action" by "morals prescribed"; the congealment of forms as formulae; repetition and rote instead of performance. Here would come the ossification of feelings in the dreadful form of ideas. Reviewing Blackmur's *Language as Gesture*, Ransom took issue with him on the demeaning of ideas: "he is repudiating the ideas as ideas, and reckoning their usefulness for the poem." In Blackmur's later essays on the novel, especially those now collected in *The Lion and the Honeycomb* and *Eleven Essays on the European Novel*, he felt obliged, in Ransom's view, "to talk directly about those ideas, morals, faiths, which enter into the conduct of life," but the talk seems to me still technical and formal and never addresses itself to ideas as if they had the same substantive value inside the novel as outside. Blackmur never thought of ideas as having, within the poem or novel, the character they have outside. He always repudiated what he regarded as the rigmarole of theory, doctrine, dogma. Or, in a long-established distinction, he could not think of reason as on the same level of value as imagination. Blackmur sometimes spoke well of reason—"Reason is in substance all the living memory of the mind," he said in *Anni Mirabiles*. When he quoted a favorite phrase from Maritain, that "art bitten by poetry longs to be freed from reason," he insisted on saying that reason "is the great reminder of the constant and the grave; what sees the unity, the disparity, the permanent behavior of things." But generally he sided with Adams's prejudice in the *Education*, that "the mind resorts to reason for want of training." And he quoted Elizabeth Sewell's observation in her study of Valéry that "words are the mind's one defence against possession by thought or dreams; even Jacob kept trying to find out the name of the angel he wrestled with." Words, according to that sentiment, are the behavior of mind which thought, given its way, would domesticate. In any of these versions, reason, habit, and formula would suppress the imagination, and prescribe as order what is mere rote.

But Blackmur has a further set of terms. Assuming that the conversion of behavior into morals takes place, or that we can transform our aspirations into behavior, we haven't then come to the end of our possibilities. We have written our poem, perhaps, but there is still poetry itself as more than the sum of poems. We think of Kenneth Burke rather than of Blackmur when we take to the notion of "tracking down the implications" of our vocabularies. Burke, far more determinedly than Blackmur, proposes that we pursue the entelechy of driving our words "to the end of the line." But Blackmur, too, has a sense of ultimacy, though a more occult one than Burke's or Ransom's.

The names we have to invoke to document Blackmur's version of ultimacy are Longinus and, again, Montaigne. Longinus stands for the blow of the sublime, the height of eloquence far beyond any degree of it that could have been predicted. In "Between the Numen and the Moha" Blackmur brings Longinus and Montaigne together, on the strength of a passage which he quotes, in Zeitlin's translation, from Book I, Chapter 37 of Montaigne:

Here is a wonder: we have far more poets than judges and interpreters of poetry; it is easier to write it than to understand it. At a certain level one may judge it by rules and by art. But the true, supreme, and divine poesy is above all rules and reasons. Whoever discerns the beauty of it with assured and steady sight, he does not see it any more than the splendor of a flash of lightning. It does not seduce our judgment; it ravishes and overwhelms it.

Swayed by the last few lines, and sensing in them the tradition of the sublime which Montaigne resumes without having read Longinus, Blackmur posits an ultimacy of insight and eloquence under the auspices of imagination and not of reason. Here, he says, "we see the pride of imagination, which is confronted with reality, in the act of breaking down the pride of reason, which manipulates reality in a merely administrative rather than an understanding sense." The sublime is not the furthest reach of common sense but the ravishing of every sense. In another vocabulary it is epiphany or revelation, and in Shakespeare's vocabulary it is what Ophelia experiences so that she can say "O, to have seen what I have seen, see what I see." Blackmur thought he could at least point in its direction by calling it, in "Notes on Four Categories in Criticism," symbol, and saying that "symbol stands for nothing previously known, but for what is 'here' made known and what is about to be made known." But the common understanding of symbol is hardly enough to send it into the abyss or wherever it has to go to register the sublime and the authority beyond prediction which is its blow. At least once, Blackmur called such authority God, God "who is reality by definition: the reality yet to be." Sometimes he thought its eloquence such that it must be called silence; and he wrote an essay, "The Language of Silence," not in the hope of annotating it but of testifying to it as a ravishing possibility. Or he called it, in every honorific sense, gibberish, on Stevens's authority who wrote in *Notes toward a Supreme Fiction* of "the poet's gibberish" in its relation to "the gibberish of the vulgate." Once, Blackmur called the sublime power Numen, meaning "that power within us, greater than and other than ourselves, that moves us, sometimes carrying us away, in the end moving us forward unless we drop out, always overwhelming us." Whether the power is in Nature or in us hardly matters. If it is in Nature, we take it to ourselves or supplicate it by magic or superstition or mystery. If it is in ourselves, we recognise it, by preference, in others, and so far as possible reduce its authority in ourselves. Or we are willing to come upon it in paintings and music and literature, or hear it in Myshkin's scream in *The Idiot*— this is one of Blackmur's instances—of which Dostoevski says that in it "everything human seems obliterated and it is impossible, or very difficult, for an observer to realize and admit that it is the man himself screaming: it seems as though it were someone else screaming from within the man."

Blackmur's figure of the sublime is a phrase: to be beside oneself. To be beside oneself is to be in ecstasy, released from one's demeaning contexts—"obsessed, freed, and beside themselves," as Blackmur says of certain animals and men in Marianne Moore's poetry. In "A Burden for Critics" he refers to "those forces that operate in the arts which are greater than ourselves and come from beyond or under ourselves" and, he almost says, drive us beyond ourselves if we attend to them.

How we attend to them is a desperate question. "We have lost," Blackmur believes, "the field of common reference, we have dwindled in our ability to think symbolically, and as we look about us we see all our old unconscious skills at life disappearing without any apparent means of developing new unconscious skills." We have a plethora of new conscious skills, lodged in psychology, anthropology, and sociology, but these are useless for any purpose except that of making trouble for ourselves—they "undermine purpose, blight consciousness, and prevent decision," they promote nothing but "uncertainty, insecurity, anxiety, and incoherence." Besides, so far as they are merely conscious skills, they have no genuine but only mechanical access to the very materials they claim as their own.

Where the old unconscious skills are to be sought is a hard question. With extraordinary daring and tempting effrontery, Blackmur associates them with what he calls bourgeois humanism, but a humanism still in some degree accessible to the sublime. He writes in *Anni Mirabiles:*

Bourgeois humanism (the treasure of residual reason in live relation to the madness of the senses) is the only conscious art of the mind designed to deal with our megalopolitan mass society: it alone knows what to do with momentum in its new guise; and it alone knows it must be more than itself without losing itself in order to succeed.

If a political program is implied, it must be bourgeois humanism kept alert and uncomplacent by constant recourse to tory anarchy of spirit, so that what it speaks is a live mixture of common sense and the gibberish of the vulgate.

We can now place Blackmur's criticism, taking care never to domesticate it but to bring it into relation to our own concerns and those of his contemporaries. Blackmur's relations to James, Eliot, Ransom, Richards and Burke are well established but not, I think, well enough rehearsed. But it may be more useful to follow Blackmur in considering his relation to a critic with whom indeed he had little in common. Blackmur's review of *The Liberal Imagination*— it is in *The Lion and the Honeycomb*—discloses not only the differences between himself and Trilling but between himself and most of the high criticism written in his time. It is clear from the first paragraphs that Blackmur respects Trilling's criticism but regards it as too willingly taking its bearings from a social understanding of literature and criticism. "We see that he cultivates a mind never entirely his own, a mind always deliberately to some extent what he understands to be the mind of society, and also a mind always deliberately to some extent the mind of the old European society taken as corrective and as prophecy." The sentence is a little excessive; it doesn't say much more than that Trilling too contentedly thinks he is Matthew Arnold. But it leads to a more telling one. Trilling, according to Blackmur, "has always wanted a pattern, whether a set or a current, a pattern of relevant ideas as a vantage from which to take care of his occasional commitments." This begins to sound as if Trilling's mind and needs were akin to Adams's, needing a pattern in advance of any occasion; the unspoken consequence being that Blackmur himself corresponds to James and gains authority by the comparison. Of Blackmur, as of James, it may truly be said that he cultivates a mind entirely his own, or as nearly his own as its subjection to the syntax of prose allows. Blackmur doesn't want a pattern or a set, because he distrusts anything that offers itself as a formula, and he construes predictive capacity as merely setting limits in advance.

He has a further objection, which he merely implies. Literature best serves society by serving it only in the long run. It is under no obligation to endorse its official purposes at any moment or to sustain society's understanding of itself.

[1 5

"The true business of literature, as of all intellect, critical or creative, is to remind the powers that be, simple and corrupt as they are, of the turbulence they have to control." To which Blackmur appends this admonition: "There is a disorder vital to the individual which is fatal to society. And the other way round is also true."

If we think of Blackmur's insistence on cultivating a mind entirely his own, we find it easy to be patient with his language even when it runs to exorbitance. "It is only the language we use," he says, "which must abbreviate and truncate our full discourse"—which is not much different from Pater's reference, in the Conclusion to *The Renaissance*, to objects "in the solidity with which language invests them." The impression of stability is a compromise worked out between language and our nerves. The abbreviations and truncations of our discourse are a similar compromise worked out between languages and our biological defensiveness. So Blackmur, insisting on a mind of his own, insists equally on working his language hard, forcing it to the twist and torsion which he calls idiom.

Blackmur's meaning for us is far more active when his style is scandalous than when it is ingratiating. We are reading him at a time of rampant illiteracy and rampantly conscious skills—which he regarded as much the same thing. Criticism's recourse to psychology, politics, anthropology, philosophy, and linguistics is rarely seen for the desperate device it is: what are all or any of these but patterns set in advance, or values having as their sole destiny that they are incessantly applicable? Meanwhile our literature remains, in every sense of the word that matters, unread.

—*Denis Donoghue*

O N E

A Critic's Job of Work

[1 9 3 5]

I

Criticism, I take it, is the formal discourse of an amateur. When there is enough love and enough knowledge represented in the discourse it is a self-sufficient but by no means an isolated art. It witnesses constantly in its own life its interdependence with the other arts. It lays out the terms and parallels of appreciation from the outside in order to convict itself of internal intimacy; it names and arranges what it knows and loves, and searches endlessly with every fresh impulse or impression for better names and more orderly arrangements. It is only in this sense that poetry (or some other art) is a criticism of life; poetry names and arranges, and thus arrests and transfixes its subject in a form which has a life of its own forever separate but springing from the life which confronts it. Poetry is life at the remove of form and meaning; not life lived but life framed and identified. So the criticism of poetry is bound to be occupied at once with the terms and modes by which the remove was made and with the relation between—in the ambiguous stock phrase—content and form; which is to say with the establishment and appreciation of human or moral value. It will be the underlying effort of this essay to indicate approaches to criticism wherein these two problems—of form and value—will appear inextricable but not confused—like the stones in an arch or the timbers in a building.

These approaches—these we wish to eulogize—are not the only

ones, nor the only good ones, nor are they complete. No approach opens on anything except from its own point of view and in terms of its own prepossessions. Let us set against each other for a time the facts of various approaches to see whether there is a residue, not of fact but of principle.

The approaches to—or the escapes from—the central work of criticism are as various as the heresies of the Christian church, and like them testify to occasional needs, fanatic emphasis, special interest, or intellectual pride, all flowing from and even the worst of them enlightening the same body of insight. Every critic like every theologian and every philosopher is a casuist in spite of himself. To escape or surmount the discontinuity of knowledge, each resorts to a particular heresy and makes it predominant and even omnivorous.[1]

For most minds, once doctrine is sighted and is held to be the completion of insight, the doctrinal mode of thinking seems the only one possible. When doctrine totters it seems it can fall only into the gulf of bewilderment; few minds risk the fall; most seize the remnants and swear the edifice remains, when doctrine becomes intolerable dogma.[2] All fall notwithstanding; for as knowledge itself is a fall from the paradise of undifferentiated sensation, so equally every formula of knowledge must fall the moment too much weight is laid upon it—the moment it becomes omnivorous and pretends to be omnipotent—the moment, in short, it is taken literally. Literal knowledge is dead knowledge; and the worst bewilderment—which is always only comparative—is better than death. Yet no form, no formula, of knowledge ought to be surrendered merely because it runs the risk in bad or desperate hands of being used literally; and similarly, in our own thinking, whether it is carried to the point of formal discourse or not, we cannot only afford, we ought scrupulously to risk the use of any concept that seems propitious or helpful in getting over gaps. Only the use should be consciously provisional, speculative, and dramatic. The end-virtue of humility comes

[1] The rashest heresy of our day and climate is that exemplified by T. S. Eliot when he postulates an orthodoxy which exists whether anyone knows it or not.
[2] Baudelaire's sonnet *"Le Gouffre"* dramatizes this sentiment at once as he saw it surmounted in Pascal and as it occurred insurmountably in himself.

only after a long train of humiliations; and the chief labor of humbling is the constant, resourceful restoration of ignorance.

The classic contemporary example of use and misuse is attached to the name of Freud. Freud himself has constantly emphasized the provisional, dramatic character of his speculations: they are employed as imaginative illumination, to be relied on no more and no less than the sailor relies upon his buoys and beacons.[3] But the impetus of Freud was so great that a school of literalists arose with all the mad consequence of schism and heresy and fundamentalism which have no more honorable place in the scientific than the artistic imagination. Elsewhere, from one point of view, Caesarism in Rome and Berlin is only the literalist conception of the need for a positive state. So, too, the economic insights of Marxism, merely by being taken literally in their own field, are held to affect the subject and value of the arts, where actually they offer only a limited field of interest and enliven an irrelevant purpose. It is an amusing exercise—as it refreshes the terms of bewilderment and provides a common clue to the secrets of all the modes of thinking—to restore the insights of Freud and Fascism and Marxism to the terms of the Church; when the sexual drama in Freud becomes the drama of original sin, and the politics of Hitler and Lenin becomes the politics of the City of God in the sense that theology provides both the sanctions of economics and the values of culture. Controversy is in terms absolutely held, when the problems argued are falsely conceived because necessarily abstracted from "real" experience. The vital or fatal nexus is in interest and emotion and is established when the terms can be represented dramatically, almost, as it were, for their own sakes alone and with only a pious or ritualistic regard for the doctrines in which they are clothed. The simple, and fatal, example is in the glory men attach to war; the vital, but precarious example, is in the intermittent conception of free institutions and the persistent re-formulation of the myth of reason. Then the doctrines do not matter, since they are taken only for what they are

[3] Santayana's essay "A Long Way Round to Nirvana" (in *Some Turns of Thought in Modern Philosophy*) illustrates the poetic-philosophic character of Freud's insight into death by setting up its analogue in Indian philosophy; and by his comparison only adds to the stimulus of Freud.

worth (whatever rhetorical pretensions to the contrary) as guides and props, as aids to navigation. What does matter is the experience, the life represented and the value discovered, and both dramatized or enacted under the banner of doctrine. All banners are wrong-headed, but they make rallying points, free the impulse to cry out, and give meaning to the cry itself simply by making it seem appropriate.

It is on some analogue or parallel to these remarks alone that we understand and use the thought and art of those whose doctrines differ from our own. We either discount, absorb, or dominate the doctrine for the sake of the life that goes with it, for the sake of what is *formed* in the progressive act of thinking. When we do more—when we refine or elaborate the abstracted notion of form—we play a different game, which has merit of its own like chess, but which applied to the world we live in produces false dilemmas like solipsism and infant damnation. There is, taking solipsism for example, a fundamental distinction. Because of the logical doctrine prepared to support it, technical philosophers employ years[4] to get around the impasse in which it leaves them; whereas men of poetic imagination merely use it for the dramatic insight it contains—as Eliot uses it in the last section of *The Waste Land*; or as, say, everyone uses the residual mythology of the Greek religion—which its priests nevertheless used as literal sanctions for blood and power.

Fortunately, there exist archetypes of unindoctrinated thinking. Let us incline our minds like reflectors to catch the light of the early Plato and the whole Montaigne. Is not the inexhaustible stimulus and fertility of the Dialogues and the Essays due as much as anything to the absence of positive doctrine? Is it not that the early Plato always holds conflicting ideas in shifting balance, presenting them in contest and evolution, with victory only the last shift? Is it not that Montaigne is always making room for another idea, and implying always a third for provisional, adjudicating irony? Are not the forms of both men themselves ironic, betraying in their most intimate recesses the duplicity of every thought, pointing it out, so

---

[4] Santayana found it necessary to resort to his only sustained labor of dialectic, *Scepticism and Animal Faith*, which, though a beautiful monument of intellectual play, is ultimately valuable for its *incidental* moral wisdom.

to speak, in the act of self-incrimination, and showing it not paled on a pin but in the buff life? . . . Such an approach, such an attempt at vivid questing, borrowed and no doubt adulterated by our own needs, is the only rational approach to the multiplication of doctrine and arrogant technologies which fills out the body of critical thinking. Anything else is a succumbing, not an approach; and it is surely the commonest of ironies to observe a man altogether out of his depth do his cause fatal harm merely because, having once succumbed to an idea, he thinks it necessary to stick to it. Thought is a beacon not a life-raft, and to confuse the functions is tragic. The tragic character of thought—as any perspective will show—is that it takes a rigid mold too soon; chooses destiny like a Calvinist, in infancy, instead of waiting slowly for old age, and hence for the most part works against the world, good sense, and its own object: as anyone may see by taking a perspective of any given idea of democracy, of justice, or the nature of the creative act.

Imaginative skepticism and dramatic irony—the modes of Montaigne and Plato—keep the mind athletic and the spirit on the stretch. Hence the juvenescence of *The Tempest*, and hence, too, perhaps, the air almost of precocity in *Back to Methuselah*. Hence, at any rate, the sustaining power of such varied works as *The Brothers Karamazov*, *Cousine Bette*, and *The Magic Mountain*. Dante, whom the faithful might take to the contrary, is yet "the chief imagination of Christendom"; he took his doctrine once and for all from the Church and from St. Thomas and used it as a foil (in the painter's sense) to give recessiveness, background, and contrast. Vergil and Aristotle, Beatrice and Bertrans de Born, have in their way as much importance as St. Thomas and the Church. It was this security of reference that made Dante so much more a free spirit than were, say, Swift and Laurence Sterne. Dante had a habit (not a theory) of imagination which enabled him to dramatize with equal ardor and effect what his doctrine blessed, what it assailed, and what, at heart, it was indifferent to. Doctrine was the seed and structure of vision, and for his poems (at least to us) never more. The *Divine Comedy* no less than the *Dialogues* and the *Essays* is a true Speculum Mentis.

With lesser thinkers and lesser artists—and in the defective works of the greater—we have in reading, in criticizing, to supply the skepticism and the irony, or, as may be, the imagination and the drama, to the degree, which cannot be complete since then we should have had no prompts, that they are lacking. We have to rub the looking-glass clear. With *Hamlet*, for example, we have to struggle and guess to bring the motive out of obscurity: a struggle which, aiming at the wrong end, the psychoanalysts have darkened with counsel. With Shelley we have to flesh out the Platonic Ideas, as with Blake we have to cut away, since it cannot be dramatized, all the excrescence of doctrine. With Baudelaire we have sometimes to struggle with and sometimes to suppress the problem of belief, working out the irony implicit in either attitude. Similarly, with a writer like Pascal, in order to get the most out of him, in order to compose an artistic judgment, we must consider such an idea as that of the necessity of the wager, not solemnly as Pascal took it, but as a dramatized possibility, a savage, but provisional irony; and we need to show that the skepticisms of Montaigne and Pascal are not at all the same thing—that where one produced serenity the other produced excruciation.

Again, speaking of André Gide, we should remind ourselves not that he has been the apologist of homosexuality, not that he has become a Communist, but that he is par excellence the French puritan chastened by the wisdom of the body, and that he has thus an acutely scrupulous ethical sensibility. It is by acknowledging the sensibility that we feel the impact of the apologetics and the political conversion. Another necessity in the apprehension of Gide might be put as the recognition of similarity in difference of the precocious small boys in Dostoevski and Gide, e.g. Kolya in *Karamazov* and young George in *The Counterfeiters*: they are small, cruel engines, all naked sensibility and no scruple, demoniacally possessed, and used to keep things going. And these in turn may remind us of another writer who had a predilection for presenting the *terrible* quality of the young intelligence: of Henry James, of the children in *The Turn of the Screw*, of Maisie, and all the rest, all beautifully efficient agents of dramatic judgment and action, in that they take all things seriously for themselves, with the least prejudice of preparation, candidly, with an intelligence life has not yet violated.

Such feats of agility and attention as these remarks illustrate seem facile and even commonplace, and from facile points of view there is no need to take them otherwise. Taken superficially they provide escape from the whole labor of specific understanding; or, worse, they provide an easy vault from casual interpretation to an omnivorous world-view. We might take solemnly and as of universal application the two notions of demonic possession and inviolate intelligence in the children of Gide, Dostoevski, and James, and on that frail nexus build an unassailable theory of the sources of art, wisdom, and value; unassailable because affording only a stereotyped vision, like that of conservative capitalism, without reference in the real world. The maturity of Shakespeare and of Gertrude Stein would then be found on the same childish level.

But we need not go so far in order to draw back. The modes of Montaigne and Plato contain their own safety. Any single insight is good only at and up to a certain point of development and not beyond, which is to say that it is a provisional and tentative and highly selective approach to its field. Furthermore, no observation, no collection of observations, ever tells the whole story; there is always room for more, and at the hypothetical limit of attention and interest there will always remain, quite untouched, the thing itself. Thus the complex character—I say nothing of the value—of the remarks above reveals itself. They flow from a dramatic combination of all the skills and conventions of the thinking mind. They are commonplace only as criticism—as an end-product or function. Like walking, criticism is a pretty nearly universal art; both require a constant intricate shifting and catching of balance; neither can be questioned much in process; and few perform either really well. For either a new terrain is fatiguing and awkward, and in our day most men prefer paved walks or some form of rapid transit—some easy theory or outmastering dogma. A good critic keeps his criticism from becoming either instinctive or vicarious, and the labor of his understanding is always specific, like the art which he examines; and he knows that the sum of his best work comes only to the pedagogy of elucidation and appreciation. He observes facts and he delights in discriminations. The object remains, and should remain, itself, only made more available and seen in a clearer light. The imagination of Dante is for us only equal to what we can know of it at a given time.

Which brings us to what, as T. S. Eliot would say,[5] I have been leading up to all the time, and what has indeed been said several times by the way. Any rational approach is valid to literature and may be properly called critical which fastens at any point upon the work itself. The utility of a given approach depends partly upon the strength of the mind making it and partly upon the recognition of the limits appropriate to it. Limits may be of scope, degree, or relevance, and may be either plainly laid out by the critic himself, or may be determined by his readers; and it is, by our argument, the latter case that commonly falls, since an active mind tends to overestimate the scope of its tools and to take as necessary those doctrinal considerations which habit has made seem instinctive. No critic is required to limit himself to a single approach, nor is he likely to be able to do so; facts cannot be exhibited without comment, and comment involves the generality of the mind. Furthermore, a consciously complex approach like that of Kenneth Burke or T. S. Eliot, by setting up parallels of reference, affords a more flexible, more available, more stimulating standard of judgment—though of course at a greater risk of prejudice—than a single approach. What produces the evil of stultification and the malice of controversy is the confused approach, when the limits are not seen because they tend to cancel each other out, and the driving power becomes emotional.

The worse evil of fanatic falsification—of arrogant irrationality and barbarism in all its forms—arises when a body of criticism is governed by an *idée fixe,* a really exaggerated heresy, when a notion of genuine but small scope is taken literally as of universal application. This is the body of tendentious criticism where, since something is assumed proved before the evidence is in, distortion, vitiation, and absolute assertion become supreme virtues. I cannot help feel-

[5] . . . that when "morals cease to be a matter of tradition and orthodoxy—that is, of the habits of the community formulated, corrected, and elevated by the continuous thought and direction of the Church—and when each man is to elaborate his own, then *personality* becomes a thing of alarming importance" (*After Strange Gods*). Thus Mr. Eliot becomes one of those viewers-with-alarm whose next step forward is the very hysteria of disorder they wish to escape. The hysteria of institutions is more dreadful than that of individuals.

ing that such writers as Maritain and Massis—no less than Nordau before them—are tendentious in this sense. But even here, in this worst order of criticism, there is a taint of legitimacy. Once we reduce, in a man like Irving Babbitt, the magnitude of application of such notions as the inner check and the higher will, which were for Babbitt paramount—that is, when we determine the limits within which he really worked—, then the massive erudition and acute observation with which his work is packed become permanently available.

And there is no good to be got in objecting to and disallowing those orders of criticism which have an ulterior purpose. Ulterior is not in itself a pejorative, but only so when applied to an enemy. Since criticism is not autonomous—not a light but a process of elucidation—it cannot avoid discovering constantly within itself a purpose or purposes ulterior in the good sense. The danger is in not knowing what is ulterior and what is not, which is much the same as the cognate danger in the arts themselves. The arts serve purposes beyond themselves; the purposes of what they dramatize or represent at that remove from the flux which gives them order and meaning and value; and to deny those purposes is like asserting that the function of a handsaw is to hang above a bench and that to cut wood is to belittle it. But the purposes are varied and so bound in his subject that the artist cannot always design for them. The critic, if that is his bent, may concern himself with those purposes or with some one among them which obsess him; but he must be certain to distinguish between what is genuinely ulterior to the works he examines and what is merely irrelevant; and he must further not assume except within the realm of his special argument that other purposes either do not exist or are negligible or that the works may not be profitably discussed apart from ulterior purposes and as examples of dramatic possibility alone.

I I

Three examples of contemporary criticism primarily concerned with the ulterior purposes of literature should, set side by side, exhibit both the defects and the unchastened virtues of that approach; though they must do so only tentatively and somewhat invidiously—with an exaggeration for effect. Each work is assumed to be a representative ornament of its kind, carrying within it the seeds of its own death and multiplication. Let us take then, with an eye sharpened by the dangers involved, Santayana's essay on Lucretius (in *Three Philosophical Poets*), Van Wyck Brooks's *Pilgrimage of Henry James*, and Granville Hicks's *The Great Tradition*. Though that of the third is more obvious in our predicament, the urgency in the approach is equal in all three.

Santayana's essay represents a conversion or transvaluation of an actually poetic ordering of nature to the terms of a moral philosophy which, whatever its own responsibilities, is free of the special responsibility of poetry. So ably and so persuasively is it composed, his picture seems complete and to contain so much of what was important in Lucretius that *De Rerum Natura* itself can be left behind. The philosophical nature of the insight, its moral scope and defect, the influence upon it of the Democritan atom, once grasped intellectually as Santayana shows us how to grasp them, seem a good substitute for the poem and far more available. But—what Santayana remembers but does not here emphasize since it was beyond his immediate interest—there is no vicar for poetry on earth. Poetry is idiom, a special and fresh saying, and cannot for its life be said otherwise; and there is, finally, as much difference between words used about a poem and the poem as there is between words used about a painting and the painting. The gap is absolute. Yet I do not mean to suggest that Santayana's essay—that any philosophical criticism—is beside the point. It is true that the essay may be taken as a venture in philosophy for its own sake, but it is also true that it reveals a body of facts about an ulterior purpose in Lucretius' poem— doubtless the very purpose Lucretius himself would have chosen to see enhanced. If we return to the poem it will be warmer as the facts come alive in the verse. The re-conversion comes naturally in this instance in that, through idioms differently construed but equally imaginative, philosophy and poetry both buttress and express moral value. The one enacts or represents in the flesh what the other reduces to principle or raises to the ideal. The only precaution the critic of poetry need take is negative: that neither poetry nor philosophy can ever fully satisfy the other's purposes, though each may seem to do so if taken in an ulterior fashion. The relationship is mutual but not equivalent.

When we turn deliberately from Santayana on Lucretius to Van Wyck Brooks on Henry James, we turn from the consideration of the rational ulterior purpose of art to the consideration of the irrational underlying predicament of the artist himself, not only as it predicts his art and is reflected in it, but also, and in effect predominantly, as it represents the conditioning of nineteenth-century American culture. The consideration is sociological, the method of approach that of literary psychology, and the burden obsessive. The conversion is from literary to biographical values. Art is taken not as the objectification or mirroring of social experience but as a personal expression and escape-fantasy of the artist's personal life in dramatic extension. The point for emphasis is that the cultural situation of Henry James's America stultified the expression and made every escape ineffectual—even that of Europe. This theme—the private tragedy of the unsuccessful artist—was one of Henry James's own; but James saw it as typical or universal—as a characteristic tragedy of the human spirit—illustrated, as it happened for him, against the Anglo-American background. Brooks, taking the same theme, raises it to an obsession, an omnivorous concept, under which all other themes can be subsumed. Applied to American cultural history, such obsessive thinking is suggestive in the very exaggeration of its terms, and applied to the private predicament of Henry James the man it dramatically emphasizes—uses for all and more than it is worth—an obvious conflict that tormented him. As history or as biography the book is a persuasive imaginative picture, although clearly not the only one to be seen. Used as a nexus between James the man and the novels themselves, the book has only possible relevance and cannot be held as material. *Hamlet*, by a similar argument, could be shown to be an unsuccessful expression of Shakespeare's personality. To remain useful in the field of literary criticism, Brooks's notions ought to be kept parallel to James's novels but never allowed to merge with them. The corrective, the proof of the gap, is perhaps in the great air of freedom and sway of mastery that pervades the Prefaces James wrote to his collected edition. For

James art was enough because it molded and mirrored and valued all the life he knew. What Brooks's parallel strictures can do is to help us decide from another point of view whether to choose the values James dramatized. They cannot affect or elucidate but rather—if the gap is closed by will—obfuscate the values themselves.

In short, the order of criticism of which Brooks is a masterly exponent, and which we may call the psycho-sociological order, is primarily and in the end concerned less with the purposes, ulterior or not, of the arts than with some of the ulterior *uses* to which the arts can be appropriately put. Only what is said in the meantime, by the way—and does not depend upon the essence of argument but only accompanies it—can be applied to the arts themselves. There is nothing, it should be added, in Brooks's writings to show that he believes otherwise or would claim more; he is content with that scope and degree of value to which his method and the strength of his mind limit him; and his value is the greater and more urgent for that.

Such tacit humility, such implicit admission of contingency, are not immediate characteristics of Granville Hicks's *The Great Tradition*, though they may, so serious is his purpose, be merely virtues of which he deliberately, for the time being and in order to gain his point, deprives himself of the benefit. If that is so, however expedient his tactics may seem on the short view they will defeat him on the long. But let us examine the book on the ground of our present concern alone. Like Brooks, Hicks presents an interpretation of American literature since the Civil War, dealing with the whole body rather than single figures. Like Brooks he has a touchstone in an obsessive idea, but where we may say that Brooks *uses* his idea—as we think for more than it is worth—we must say that Hicks is victimized by his idea to the point where the travail of judgment is suspended and becomes the mere reiteration of a formula. He judges literature as it expressed or failed to express the economic conflict of classes sharpened by the industrial revolution, and he judges individual writers as they used or did not use an ideology resembling the Marxist analysis as prime clue to the clear representation of social drama. Thus Howells comes off better than Henry James, and Frank Norris better than Mark Twain, and, in our own day, Dos Passos is stuck on a thin eminence that must alarm him.

Controversy is not here a profitable exercise, but it may be said for the sake of the record that although every period of history presents a class struggle, some far more acute than our own, the themes of great art have seldom lent themselves to propaganda for an economic insight, finding, as it happened, religious, moral, or psychological—that is to say, interpretative—insights more appropriate impulses. If *Piers Plowman* dealt with the class struggle, *The Canterbury Tales* did not, and Hicks would be hard put, if he looked sharp, to make out a better case of social implication in Dostoevski than in Henry James.

What vitiates *The Great Tradition* is its tendentiousness. Nothing could be more exciting, nothing more vital, than a book by Hicks which discovered and examined the facts of a literature whose major theme hung on an honest, dramatic view of the class struggle—and there is indeed such a literature now emerging from the depression. And on the other hand it would be worth while to have Hicks sharpen his teeth on all the fraudulent or pseudo art which actually slanders the terms of the class and every other struggle.

The book with which he presents us performs a very different operation. There is an initial hortatory assumption that American literature ought to represent the class struggle from a Marxist viewpoint, and that it ought thus to be the spur and guide to political action. Proceeding, the point is either proved or the literature dismissed and its authors slandered. Hicks is not disengaging for emphasis and contemporary need an ulterior purpose; he is not writing criticism at all; he is writing a fanatic's history and a casuist's polemic, with the probable result—which is what was meant by suggesting above that he had misconceived his tactics—that he will convert no one who retains the least love of literature or the least knowledge of the themes which engage the most of life. It should be emphasized that there is no more quarrel with Hicks's economic insight as such than there was with the insights of Santayana and Van Wyck Brooks. The quarrel is deeper. While it is true and good that the arts may be used to illustrate social propaganda—though it is not a great use—you can no more use an economic insight as your chief critical tool than you can make much out of the Mass by submitting the doctrine of transubstantiation to chemical analysis.

These three writers have one great formal fact in common, which they illustrate as differently as may be. They are concerned with the separable content of literature, with what may be said without consideration of its specific setting and apparition in a form; which is why, perhaps, all three leave literature so soon behind. The quantity of what can be said directly about the content alone of a given work of art is seldom great, but the least saying may be the innervation of an infinite intellectual structure, which, however valuable in itself, has for the most part only an asserted relation with the works from which it springs. The sense of continuous relationship, of sustained contact, with the works nominally in hand is rare and when found uncommonly exhilarating; it is the fine object of criticism: as it seems to put us in direct possession of the principles whereby the works move without injuring or disintegrating the body of the works themselves. This sense of intimacy by inner contact cannot arise from methods of approach which hinge on seized separable content. We have constantly—if our interest is really in literature—to prod ourselves back, to remind ourselves that there was a poem, a play, or a novel of some initial and we hope terminal concern, or we have to falsify facts and set up fictions[6] to the effect that no matter what we are saying we are really talking about art after all. The question must often be whether the prodding and reminding is worth the labor, whether we might not better assign the works that require it to a different category than that of criticism.

I I I

Similar strictures and identical precautions are necessary in thinking of other, quite different approaches to criticism, where if

---

[6] Such a fiction, if not consciously so contrived, is the fiction of the organic continuity of all literature as expounded by T. S. Eliot in his essay, "Tradition and the Individual Talent." The locus is famous and represents that each new work of art slightly alters the relationships among the whole order of existing works. The notion has truth, but it is a mathematical truth and has little relevance to the arts. Used as Eliot uses it, it is an experimental conceit and pushes the mind forward. Taken seriously it is bad constitutional law, in the sense that it would provoke numberless artificial and insoluble problems.

there are no ulterior purposes to allow for there are other no less limiting features—there are certainly such, for example, for me in thinking of my own. The ulterior motive, or the limiting feature, whichever it is, is a variable constant. One does not always know what it is, nor what nor how much work it does; but one always knows it is there—for strength or weakness. It may be only the strength of emphasis—which is necessarily distortion; or it may be the worse strength of a simplifying formula, which skeletonizes and transforms what we want to recognize in the flesh. It may be only the weakness of what is unfinished, undeveloped, or unseen—the weakness that follows on emphasis; or it may be the weakness that shows when pertinent things are deliberately dismissed or ignored, which is the corresponding weakness of the mind strong in formula. No mind can avoid distortion and formula altogether, nor would wish to; but most minds rush to the defense of qualities they think cannot be avoided, and that, in itself, is an ulterior motive, a limiting feature of the mind that rushes. I say nothing of one's personal prepossessions, of the damage of one's private experience, of the malice and false tolerance they inculcate into judgment. I know that my own essays suffer variously, but I cannot bring myself to specify the indulgences I would ask; mostly, I hope, that general indulgence which consists in the task of bringing my distortions and emphases and opinions into balance with other distortions, other emphases, and better opinions.

But rather than myself, let us examine briefly, because of their differences from each other and from the three critics already handled, the modes of approach to the act of criticism and habits of critical work of I. A. Richards, Kenneth Burke, and S. Foster Damon. It is to characterize them and to judge the *character* of their work— its typical scope and value—that we want to examine them. With the objective validity of their varying theories we are not much here concerned. Objective standards of criticism, as we hope them to exist at all, must have an existence anterior and superior to the practice of particular critics. The personal element in a given critic— what he happens to know and happens to be able to understand—is strong or obstinate enough to reach into his esthetic theories; and as most critics do not have the coherence of philosophers it seems doubtful if any outsider could ever reach the same conclusions as the critic did by adopting his esthetics. Esthetics sometimes seems only as implicit in the practice of criticism as the atomic physics is present in sunlight when you feel it.

But some critics deliberately expand the theoretic phase of every practical problem. There is a tendency to urge the scientific principle and the statistical method, and in doing so to bring in the whole assorted world of thought. That Mr. Richards, who is an admirable critic and whose love and knowledge of poetry are incontestable, is a victim of the expansiveness of his mind in these directions, is what characterizes, and reduces, the scope of his work as literary criticism. It is possible that he ought not to be called a literary critic at all. If we list the titles of his books we are in a quandary: *The Foundations of Aesthetics, The Meaning of Meaning* (these with C. K. Ogden), *The Principles of Literary Criticism, Science and Poetry, Practical Criticism, Mencius on the Mind,* and *Coleridge on Imagination.* The apparatus is so vast, so labyrinthine, so inclusive—and the amount of actual literary criticism is so small that it seems almost a by-product instead of the central target. The slightest volume, physically, *Science and Poetry,* contains proportionally the most literary criticism, and contains, curiously, his one obvious failure in appreciation—since amply redressed—, his misjudgment of the nature of Yeats's poetry. His work is for the most part *about* a department of the mind which includes the pedagogy of sensibility and the practice of literary criticism. The matters he investigates are the problems of belief, of meaning, of communication, of the nature of controversy, and of poetic language as the supreme mode of imagination. The discussion of these problems is made to focus for the most part on poetry because poetry provides the only great monuments of imagination available to verbal imagination. His bottom contention might I think be put as this: that words have a synergical power, in the realms of feeling, emotion, and value, to create a reality, or the sense of it, not contained in the words separately; and that the power and the reality as experienced in great poetry make the chief source of meaning and value for the life we live. This contention I share; except that I should wish to put on the same level, as sources of meaning and value, modes of imagination that have no medium in words—though words may call on them—and are not susceptible of verbal re-formulation: the modes of great acting, architecture, music, and painting. Thus I can assent to Mr. Richards' positive statement of the task of criticism, because I can add to it positive tasks in analogous fields: "To recall that poetry is the supreme use of language, man's chief coordinating instrument, in the service of the most integral purposes of life; and to explore, with thoroughness, the intricacies of the modes of language as working modes of the mind." But I want this criticism, engaged in this task, constantly to be confronted with examples of poetry, and I want it so for the very practical purpose of assisting in pretty immediate appreciation of the use, meaning, and value of the language in that particular poetry. I want it to assist in doing for me what it actually assists Mr. Richards in doing, whatever that is, when he is reading poetry for its own sake.

Mr. Richards wants it to do that, too, but he wants it to do a great deal else first. Before it gets to actual poetry (from which it is said to spring) he wants literary criticism to become something else and much more: he wants it to become, indeed, the master department of the mind. As we become aware of the scope of poetry, we see, according to Mr. Richards, that "the study of the modes of language becomes, as it attempts to be thorough, the most fundamental and extensive of all inquiries. It is no preliminary or preparation for other profounder studies. . . . The very formation of the objects which these studies propose to examine takes place through the processes (of which imagination and fancy are modes) by which the words they use acquire their meanings. Criticism is the science of these meanings. . . . Critics in the future must have a theoretical equipment which has not been felt to be necessary in the past. . . . But the critical equipment will not be *primarily* philosophical. It will be rather a command *of the methods of general linguistic analysis.*"[7] I think we may take it that *Mencius on the Mind* is an example of the kind of excursion on which Mr. Richards would lead us. It is an excursion into multiple definition, and it is a good one if that is where you want to go and are in no hurry to come back: you learn

[7] All quoted material is from the last four pages of *Coleridge on Imagination.*

the enormous variety and complexity of the operations possible in the process of verbally describing and defining brief passages of imaginative language and the equal variety and complexity of the result; you learn the practical impossibility of verbally ascertaining what an author means—and you hear nothing of the other ways of apprehending meaning at all. The instance is in the translation of Mencius, because Mr. Richards happens to be interested in Mencius, and because it is easy to see the difficulties of translating Chinese; but the principles and method of application would work as well on passages from Milton or Rudyard Kipling. The real point of Mr. Richards' book is the impossibility of understanding, short of a lifetime's analysis and compensation, the mechanism of meaning in even a small body of work. There is no question of the exemplary value and stimulus of Mr. Richards' work; but there is no question either that few would care to emulate him for any purpose of literary criticism. In the first place it would take too long, and in the second he does not answer the questions literary criticism would put. The literal adoption of Mr. Richards' approach to literary criticism would stultify the very power it was aimed to enhance—the power of imaginative apprehension, of imaginative co-ordination of varied and separate elements. Mr. Richards' work is something to be aware of, but deep awareness is the limit of use. It is notable that in his admirable incidental criticism of such poets as Eliot, Lawrence, Yeats, and Hopkins, Mr. Richards does not himself find it necessary to be more than aware of his own doctrines of linguistic analysis. As philosophy from Descartes to Bradley transformed itself into a study of the modes of knowing, Mr. Richards would transform literary criticism into the science of linguistics. Epistemology is a great subject, and so is linguistics; but they come neither in first nor final places; the one is only a fragment of wisdom and the other only a fraction of the means of understanding. Literary criticism is not a science— though it may be the object of one; and to try to make it one is to turn it upside down. Right side up, Mr. Richards' contribution shrinks in weight and dominion but remains intact and preserves its importance. We may conclude that it was the newness of his view that led him to exaggerate it, and we ought to add the probability that had he not exaggerated it we should never have seen either that it was new or valuable at all.

From another point of view than that of literary criticism, and as a contribution to a psychological theory of knowledge, Mr. Richards' work is not heretical, but is integral and integrating, and especially when it incorporates poetry into its procedure; but from our point of view the heresy is profound—and is far more distorting than the heresies of Santayana, Brooks, and Hicks, which carry with them obviously the impetus for their correction. Because it is possible to apply scientific methods to the language of poetry, and because scientific methods engross their subject matter, Mr. Richards places the whole burden of criticism in the application of a scientific approach, and asserts it to be an implement for the judgment of poetry. Actually, it can handle only the language and its words and cannot touch—except by assertion—the imaginative product of the words which is poetry: which is the object revealed or elucidated by criticism. Criticism must be concerned, first and last—whatever comes between—with the poem as it is read and as what it represents is felt. As no amount of physics and physiology can explain the *feeling* of things seen as green or even certify their existence, so no amount of linguistic analysis can explain the *feeling* or existence of a poem. Yet the physics in the one case and the linguistics in the other may be useful both to the poet and the reader. It may be useful, for example, in extracting the facts of meaning from a poem, to show that, whether the poet was aware of it or not, the semantic history of a word was so and so; but only if the semantics can be resolved into the ambiguities and precisions created by the poem. Similarly with any branch of linguistics; and similarly with the applications of psychology—Mr. Richards' other emphasis. No statistical description can either explain or demean a poem unless the description is translated back to the imaginative apprehension or feeling which must have taken place without it. The light of science is parallel or in the background where feeling or meaning is concerned. The Oedipus complex does not explain *Oedipus Rex*; not that Mr. Richards would think it did. Otherwise he could not believe that "poetry is the supreme use of language" and more, could not convey in his comments on T. S. Eliot's *Ash Wednesday* the actuality of his belief that poetry is the supreme use.

It is the interest and fascination of Mr. Richards' work in reference to different levels of sensibility, including the poetic, that has given him both a wide and a penetrating influence. No literary critic can escape his influence; an influence that stimulates the mind as much as anything by showing the sheer excitement as well as the profundity of the problems of language—many of which he has himself made genuine problems, at least for readers of poetry: an influence, obviously, worth deliberately incorporating by reducing it to one's own size and needs. In T. S. Eliot the influence is conspicuous if slight. Mr. Kenneth Burke is considerably indebted, partly directly to Mr. Richards, partly to the influences which acted upon Mr. Richards (as Bentham's theory of Fictions) and partly to the frame of mind which helped mold them both. But Mr. Burke is clearly a different person—and different from anyone writing today; and the virtues, the defects, and the élan of his criticism are his own.

Some years ago, when Mr. Burke was an animating influence on the staff of *The Dial*, Miss Marianne Moore published a poem in that magazine called "Picking and Choosing" which contained the following lines.

> and Burke is a
> psychologist—of acute raccoon-
> like curiosity. *Summa diligentia;*
> to the humbug, whose name is so amusing—very young and very
>
> rushed, Caesar crossed the Alps 'on the top of a
> diligence'. We are not daft about the meaning, but this familiarity
> with wrong meanings puzzles one.

In the index of Miss Moore's *Observations*, we find under Burke that the reference is to Edmund, but it is really to Kenneth just the same. There is no acuter curiosity than Mr. Burke's engaged in associating the meanings, right and wrong, of the business of literature with the business of life and vice versa. No one has a greater awareness—not even Mr. Richards—of the important part wrong meanings play in establishing the consistency of right ones. The writer of whom he reminds us, for the buoyancy and sheer remarkableness of his speculations, is Charles Santiago Saunders Peirce; one is enlivened by them without any *necessary* reference to their truth; hence they have truth for their own purposes, that is, for their own uses. Into what these purposes or uses are it is our present business to inquire.

As Mr. Richards in fact uses literature as a springboard or source for a scientific method of a philosophy of value, Mr. Burke uses literature, not only as a springboard but also as a resort or home, for a philosophy or psychology of moral possibility. Literature is the hold-all and the persuasive form for the patterns of possibility. In literature we see unique possibilities enacted, actualized, and in the moral and psychological philosophies we see the types of possibility generalized, see their abstracted, convertible forms. In some literature, and in some aspects of most literature of either great magnitude or great possibility, we see, so to speak, the enactment of dramatic representation of the type or patterns. Thus Mr. Burke can make a thrilling intellectual pursuit of the subintelligent writing of Erskine Caldwell: where he shows that Caldwell gains a great effect of humanity by putting in *none himself,* appealing to the reader's common stock: i.e., what is called for so desperately by the pattern of the story must needs be generously supplied. Exactly as thrilling is his demonstration of the great emotional role of the outsider as played in the supremely intelligent works of Thomas Mann and André Gide. His common illustrations of the pervasive spread of symbolic pattern are drawn from Shakespeare and from the type of the popular or pulp press. I think that on the whole his method could be applied with equal fruitfulness either to Shakespeare, Dashiell Hammett, or Marie Corelli; as indeed he does apply it with equal force both to the field of anarchic private morals and to the outline of a secular conversion to Communism—as in, respectively, *Toward a Better Life* and *Permanence and Change.*

The real harvest that we barn from Mr. Burke's writings is his presentation of the types of ways the mind works in the written word. He is more interested in the psychological means of the meaning, and how it might mean (and often really does) something else, than in the meaning itself. Like Mr. Richards, but for another purpose, he is engaged largely in the meaning of meaning, and is therefore much bound up with considerations of language, but on the plane of emotional and intellectual patterns rather than on the emotional plane; which is why his essays deal with literature (or other writings) as it dramatizes or unfolds character (a character is a pattern of emotions and notions) rather than with lyric or meditative poetry which is Mr. Richards' field. So we find language containing felt character as well as felt co-ordination. The representation of character, and of aspiration and symbol, must always be rhetorical; and therefore we find that for Mr. Burke the rightly rhetorical is the profoundly hortatory. Thus literature may be seen as an inexhaustible reservoir of moral or character philosophies in action.

It is the technique of such philosophies that Mr. Burke explores, as he pursues it through curiosities of development and conversion and duplicity; it is the technique of the notions that may be put into or taken out of literature, but it is only a part of the technique of literature itself. The final reference is to the psychological and moral possibilities of the mind, and these certainly do not exhaust the technique or the reality of literature. The reality in literature is an object of contemplation and of feeling, like the reality of a picture or a cathedral, not a route of speculation. If we remember this and make the appropriate reductions here as elsewhere, Mr. Burke's essays become as pertinent to literary criticism as they are to the general ethical play of the mind. Otherwise they become too much a methodology for its own sake on the one hand, and too much a philosophy at one remove on the other. A man writes as he can; but those who use his writings have the further responsibility of re-defining their scope, an operation (of which Mr. Burke is a master) which alone uses them to the full.

It is in relation to these examples which I have so unjustly held up of the philosophical, the sociological or historical, the tendentious, the semasiological, and the psychological approaches to criticism that I wish to examine an example of what composes, after all, the great bulk of serious writings about literature: a work of literary scholarship. Upon scholarship all other forms of literary criticism depend, so long as they are criticism, in much the same way that architecture depends on engineering. The great editors of the last century—men such as Dyce and Skeat and Gifford and Furness—performed work as valuable to the use of literature, and with far less complement of harm, as men like Hazlitt and Arnold and Pater. Scholarship, being bent on the collection, arrangement, and scrutiny of facts, has the positive advantage over other forms of criticism that it is a co-operative labor, and may be completed and corrected by subsequent scholars; and it has the negative advantage that it is not bound to investigate the mysteries of meaning or to connect literature with other departments of life—it has only to furnish the factual materials for such investigations and connections. It is not surprising to find that the great scholars are sometimes good critics, though usually in restricted fields; and it is a fact, on the other hand, that the great critics are themselves either good scholars or know how to take great advantage of scholarship. Perhaps we may put it that for the most part dead critics remain alive in us to the extent that they form part of our scholarship. It is Dr. Johnson's statements of fact that we preserve of him as a critic; his opinions have long since become a part of that imaginative structure, his personality. A last fact about scholarship is this, that so far as its conclusions are sound they are subject to use and digestion not debate by those outside the fold. And of bad scholarship as of bad criticism we have only to find means to minimize what we cannot destroy.

It is difficult to find an example of scholarship pure and simple, of high character, which can be made to seem relevant to the discussion in hand. What I want is to bring into the discussion the omnipresence of scholarship as a background and its immediate and necessary availability to every other mode of approach. What I want is almost anonymous. Failing that, I choose S. Foster Damon's *William Blake* (as I might have taken J. L. Lowes's *Road to Xanadu*) which, because of its special subject matter, brings its scholarship a little nearer the terms of discussion than a Shakespeare commentary would have done. The scholar's major problem with Blake happened to be one which many scholars could not handle, some refused to see, and some fumbled. A great part of Blake's meaning is not open to ordinarily well-instructed readers, but must be brought out by the detailed solution of something very like an enormous and enormously complicated acrostic puzzle. Not only earnest scrutiny of the poems as printed, but also a study of Blake's reading, a reconstruction of habits of thought, and an industrious piecing together into a consistent key of thousands of clues throughout the work, were necessary before many even of the simplest appearing poems could be explained. It is one thing to explain a mystical poet, like Crashaw, who was attached to a recognized church, and difficult enough; but it is a far more difficult thing to explain a mystical poet like Blake, who was so much an eclectic in his sources that his mystery as well as his apprehension of it was practically his own. All Mr. Damon had to go on besides the texts, and the small body of previous scholarship that was pertinent, were the general outlines of insight to which all mystics apparently adhere. The only explanation would be in the facts of what Blake meant to mean when he habitually said one thing in order to hide and enhance another; and in order to be convincing—poetry being what it is—the facts adduced had to be self-evident. It is not a question here whether the mystery enlightened was worth it. The result for emphasis is that Mr. Damon made Blake exactly what he seemed least to be, perhaps the most intellectually consistent of the greater poets in English. Since the chief weapons used are the extended facts of scholarship, the picture Mr. Damon produced cannot be destroyed even though later and other scholarship modifies, re-arranges, or adds to it with different or other facts. The only suspicion that might attach is that the picture is too consistent and that the facts are made to tell too much, and direct, but instructed, apprehension not enough.

My point about Mr. Damon's work is typical and double. First, that the same sort of work, the adduction of ultimately self-evident facts, can be done and must be done in other kinds of poetry than Blake's. Blake is merely an extreme and obvious example of an unusually difficult poet who hid his facts on purpose. The work must be done to the appropriate degree of digging out the facts in all orders of poetry—and especially perhaps in contemporary poetry, where we tend to let the work go either because it seems too easy or because it seems supererogatory. Self-evident facts are paradoxically the hardest to come by; they are not evident till they are seen; yet the meaning of a poem—the part of it which is intellectually formulable—must invariably depend on this order of facts, the facts about the meanings of the elements aside from their final meaning in combination. The rest of the poem, what it is, what it shows, its final value as a created emotion, its meanings, if you like, *as* a poem, cannot in the more serious orders of poetry develop itself to the full without this factual or intellectual meaning to show the way. The other point is already made, and has been made before in this essay, but it may still be emphasized. Although the scholarly account is indispensable it does not tell the whole story. It is only the basis and perhaps ultimately the residue of all the other stories. But it must be seen to first.

My own approach, such as it is, and if it can be named, does not tell the whole story either; the reader is conscientiously left with the poem with the real work yet to do; and I wish to advance it—as indeed I have been advancing it *seriatim*—only in connection with the reduced and compensated approaches I have laid out; and I expect, too, that if my approach is used at all it will require its own reduction as well as its compensations. Which is why this essay has taken its present form, preferring for once, in the realm of theory and apologetics, the implicit to the explicit statement. It is, I suppose, an approach to literary criticism—to the discourse of an amateur—primarily through the technique, in the widest sense of that word, of the examples handled; technique on the plane of words and even of linguistics in Mr. Richards' sense, but also technique on the plane of intellectual and emotional patterns in Mr. Burke's sense, and technique, too, in that there is a technique of securing and arranging and representing a fundamental view of life. The advantage of the technical approach is I think double. It readily admits other approaches and is anxious to be complemented by them. Furthermore, in a sense, it is able to incorporate the technical aspect, which always exists, of what is secured by other approaches—as I have argued elsewhere that so unpromising a matter as T. S. Eliot's religious convictions may be profitably considered as a dominant element in his technique of revealing the actual. The second advantage of the technical approach is a consequence of the first; it treats of nothing in literature except in its capacity of reduction to literary fact, which is where it resembles scholarship, only passing beyond it in that its facts are usually further into the heart of the literature than the facts of most scholarship. Aristotle, curiously, is here the type and master; as the *Poetics* is nothing but a collection and explanation of the facts of Greek poetry, it is the factual aspect that is invariably produced. The rest of the labor is in the effort to find understandable terms to fit the composition of the facts. After all, it is only the facts about a poem, a play, a novel, that can be reduced to tractable form, talked about, and examined; the rest is the product of the facts, from the technical point of view, and not a product but the thing itself from its own point of view. The rest, whatever it is, can only be known, not talked about.

But facts are not simple or easy to come at; not all the facts will appear to one mind, and the same facts appear differently in the light of different minds. No attention is undivided, no single approach sufficient, no predilection guaranteed, when facts or what their arrangements create are in question. In short, for the arts, *mere* technical scrutiny of any order is not enough without the direct apprehension—which may come first or last—to which all scrutinies that show facts contribute.

It may be that there are principles that cover both the direct apprehension and the labor of providing modes for the understanding of the expressive arts. If so, they are Socratic and found within, and subject to the fundamental skepticism as in Montaigne. There must be seeds, let us say—seeds, germs, beginning forms upon which I can rely and to which I resort. When I use a word, an image, a notion, there must be in its small nodular apparent form, as in the peas I am testing on my desk, at least prophetically, the whole future growth, the whole harvested life; and not rhetorically nor in a formula, but stubbornly, pervasively, heart-hidden, materially, in both the anterior and the eventual prospect as well as in the small handled form of the nub. What is it, what are they, these seeds of understanding? And if I know, are they logical? Do they take the processional form of the words I use? Or do they take a form like that of the silver backing a glass, a dark that enholds all brightness? Is every metaphor—and the assertion of understanding is our great metaphor—mixed by the necessity of its intention? What is the mixture of a word, an image, a notion?

The mixture, if I may start a hare so late, the mixture, even in the fresh use of an old word, is made in the pre-conscious, and is by hypothesis unascertainable. But let us not use hypotheses, let us not desire to ascertain. By intuition we adventure in the preconscious; and there, where the adventure is, there is no need or suspicion of certainty or meaning; there is the living, expanding, *prescient* substance without the tags and handles of conscious form. Art is the looking-glass of the preconscious, and when it is deepest seems to participate in it sensibly. Or, better, for purposes of criticism, our sensibility resumes the division of the senses and faculties at the same time that it preens itself into conscious form. Criticism may have as an object the establishment and evaluation (comparison and analysis) of the modes of making the preconscious *consciously* available.

But this emphasis upon the preconscious need not be insisted on; once recognized it may be tacitly assumed, and the effort of the mind will be, as it were, restored to its own plane—only a little sensitive to the tap-roots below. On its own plane—that is the plane where almost everything is taken for granted in order to assume adequate implementation in handling what is taken for granted by others; where because you can list the items of your bewilderment and can move from one to another you assert that the achievement of motion is the experience of order;—where, therefore, you must adopt always an attitude of provisional skepticism; where, imperatively, you must scrutinize and scrutinize until you have revealed, if it is there, the inscrutable divination, or, if it is not, the void of personal ambition; where, finally, you must stop short only when you have, with all the facts you can muster, indicated, surrounded, detached, somehow found the way demonstrably to get at, in pretty conscious terms which others may use, the substance of your chosen case.

Notes on

E. E. Cummings' Language

[1 9 3 0]

In his four books of verse, his play, and the autobiographical
Enormous Room,[1] Mr. Cummings has amassed a special vocabulary and has developed from it a special use of language which these
notes are intended to analyze and make explicit. Critics have commonly said, when they understood Mr. Cummings' vocabulary at
all, that he has enriched the language with a new idiom; had they
been further interested in the uses of language, they would no doubt
have said that he had added to the general sensibility of his time.
Certainly his work has had many imitators. Young poets have found
it easy to adopt the attitudes from which Mr. Cummings has written, just as they often adopt the superficial attitudes of Swinburne
and Keats. The curious thing about Mr. Cummings' influence is
that his imitators have been able to emulate as well as ape him;
which is not so frequently the case with the influence of Swinburne
and Keats. Mr. Cummings is a school of writing in himself; so that
it is necessary to state the underlying assumptions of his mind, and
of the school which he teaches, before dealing with the specific
results in poetry of those assumptions.

It is possible to say that Mr. Cummings belongs to the anti-
culture group; what has been called at various times vorticism,

[1] As of 1930. There would seem little modification of these notes necessary because of *Eimi*
or the subsequent volumes of verse.

futurism, dadaism, surrealism, and so on.[2] Part of the general dogma of this group is a sentimental denial of the intelligence and the deliberate assertion that the unintelligible is the only object of significant experience. These dogmas have been defended with considerable dialectical skill, on the very practical premise that only by presenting the unintelligible as viable and actual *per se* can the culture of the *dead intelligence* (Brattle Street, the Colleges, and the Reviews) be shocked into sentience. It is argued that only by denying to the intelligence its function of discerning quality and order, can the failures of the intelligence be overcome; that if we take things as they come without remembering what has gone before or guessing what may come next, and if we accept these things at their face value, we shall know life, at least in the arts, as it really is. Nothing could be more arrogant, and more deceptively persuasive to the childish spirit, than such an attitude when held as fundamental. It appeals to the intellect which wishes to work swiftly and is in love with immediate certainty. A mind based on it accepts every fragment of experience as final and every notion as definite, yet never suffers from the delusion that it has learned anything. By an astonishing accident, enough unanimity exists among these people to permit them to agree among themselves; to permit them, even, to seem spiritually indistinguishable as they appear in public.

The central attitude of this group has developed, in its sectaries, a logical and thoroughgoing set of principles and habits. In America, for example, the cause of the lively arts has been advanced against the ancient seven; because the lively arts are necessarily immediate in appeal and utterly transitory. Thus we find in Mr. Cummings' recent verse and in his play *Him* the side show and the cabaret set up as "inevitable" frames for experience. Jazz effects, tough dialects, tough guys, slim hot queens, barkers, fairies, and so on, are made into the media and symbols of poetry. Which is proper enough in Shakespeare where such effects are used ornamentally or for pure play. But in Cummings such effects are employed as substance, as the very mainstay of the poetry. There is a continuous effort to escape the realism of the intelligence in favor of the realism

[2]The reader is referred to the late numbers of *transition* for a serial and collaborative expression of the latest form which this group has assumed: the Battle of the Word. [As of 1930.]

of the obvious. What might be stodgy or dull because not properly worked up into poetry is replaced by the tawdry and by the fiction of the immediate.

It is no great advantage to get rid of one set of flabby generalities if the result is merely the immersion of the sensibility in another set only superficially less flabby. The hardness of the tough guy is mostly in the novelty of the language. There is no hardness in the emotion. The poet is as far from the concrete as before. By denying the dead intelligence and putting on the heresy of unintelligence, the poet only succeeds in substituting one set of unnourished conventions for another. What survives, with a deceptive air of reality, is a surface. That the deception is often intentional hardly excuses it. The surface is meant to clothe and illuminate a real substance, but in fact it is impenetrable. We are left, after experiencing this sort of art, with the certainty that there was nothing to penetrate. The surface was perfect; the deceit was childish; and the conception was incorrigibly sentimental: all because of the dogma which made them possible.

If Mr. Cummings' tough-guy poems are excellent examples of this sentimentality, it is only natural that his other poems—those clothed in the more familiar language of the lyric—should betray even more obviously, even more perfectly, the same fault. There, in the lyric, there is no pretense at hardness of surface. We are admitted at once to the bare emotion. What is most striking, in every instance, about this emotion is the fact that, in so far as it exists at all, it is Mr. Cummings' emotion, so that our best knowledge of it must be, finally, our best guess. It is not an emotion resulting from the poem; it existed before the poem began and is a result of the poet's private life. Besides its inspiration, every element in the poem, and its final meaning as well, must be taken at face value or not at all. This is the extreme form, in poetry, of romantic egoism: whatever I experience is real and final, and whatever I say represents what I experience. Such a dogma is the natural counterpart of the denial of the intelligence.

Our interest is not in the abstract principle, but in the results of its application in poetry. Assuming that a poem should in some sense be understood, should have a meaning apart from the poet's private life, either one of two things will be true about any poem written from such an attitude as we have ascribed to Mr. Cummings. Either the poem will appear in terms so conventional that everybody will understand it—when it will be flat and no poem at all; or it will appear in language so far distorted from convention as to be inapprehensible except by lucky guess. In neither instance will the poem be genuinely complete. It will be the notes for a poem, from which might flow an infinite number of possible poems, but from which no particular poem can be certainly deduced. It is the purpose of this paper to examine a few of the more obvious types of distortion which Mr. Cummings has practiced upon language.

The question central to such a discussion will be what kind of meaning does Mr. Cummings' poetry have; what is the kind of equivalence between the language and its object. The pursuit of such a question involves us immediately in the relations between words and feelings, and the relations between the intelligence and its field in experience—all relations which are precise only in terms themselves essentially poetic—in the feeling for an image, the sense of an idiom. Such relations may only be asserted, may be judged only tentatively, only instinctively, by what seems to be the disciplined experience, but what amounts, perhaps, only to the formed taste. Here criticism is appreciation. But appreciation, even, can take measures to be certain of its grounds, and to be full should betray the constant apprehension of an end which is the necessary consequence, the proper rounding off, of just those grounds. In the examination of Mr. Cummings' writings the grounds will be the facts about the words he uses, and the end will be apprehended in the quality of the meaning his use of these words permits.

There is one attitude toward Mr. Cummings' language which has deceived those who hold it. The typographical peculiarities of his verse have caught and irritated public attention. Excessive hyphenation of single words, the use of lower case "i," the breaking of lines, the insertion of punctuation between the letters of a word, and so on, will have a possible critical importance to the textual scholarship of the future; but extensive consideration of these peculiarities today has very little importance, carries almost no reference to the *meaning* of the poems. Mr. Cummings' experiments in typography merely extend the theory of notation by adding to the number, *not* to the *kind*, of conventions the reader must bear in mind, and are dangerous only because since their uses cannot readily be defined, they often obscure rather than clarify the exact meaning. No doubt the continued practice of such notation would produce a set of well-ordered conventions susceptible of general use. At present the practice can only be "allowed for," recognized in the particular instance, felt, and forgotten: as the diacritical marks in the dictionary are forgotten once the sound of the word has been learned. The poem, after all, only takes wing on the page, it persists in the ear.[3]

Considering typographical peculiarities for our present purposes as either irrelevant or unaccountable, there remain the much more important peculiarities of Mr. Cummings' vocabulary itself; of the poem *after* it has been read, as it is in the mind's ear, as it is on the page only for reassurance and correction.

If a reader, sufficiently familiar with these poems not to be caught on the snag of novelty, inspects carefully any score of them, no matter how widely scattered, he will especially be struck by a sameness among them. This sameness will be in two sorts—a vagueness of image and a constant recurrence of words. Since the one depends considerably upon the other, a short list of some of Mr. Cummings' favorite words will be a good preliminary to the examination of his images. In *Tulips and Chimneys* words such as these occur frequently—thrilling, flowers, serious, absolute, sweet, unspeaking, utter, gradual, ultimate, final, serene, frail, grave, tremendous, slender, fragile, skillful, carefully, intent, young, gay, untimid, incorrigible, groping, dim, slow, certain, deliberate, strong, chiseled, subtle, tremulous, perpetual, crisp, perfect, sudden, faint, strenuous, minute, superlative, keen, ecstatic, actual, fleet, delicious, stars, enthusiastic, capable, dull, bright. In listing these as

[3] It is not meant to disparage Mr. Cummings' inventions, which are often excellent, but to minimize an exaggerated contemporary interest. A full discussion of the virtues of notation may be found in *A Survey of Modernist Poetry* by Laura Riding and Robert Graves (London, Heinemann, 1927), especially in Chapter III which is labeled: "William Shakespeare and E. E. Cummings: A study in original punctuation and spelling." Their point is made by printing sonnet 129 in its original notation beside a modern version; the point being that Shakespeare knew what he was doing and that his editors did not.

favorite words, it is meant that these words do the greater part of the work in the poems where they occur; these are the words which qualify the subject matter of the poems, and are sometimes even the subjects themselves. Observe that none of them, taken alone, are very *concrete* words; and observe that many of them are the rather *abstract*, which is to say typical, *names* for precise qualities, but are not, and cannot be, as *originally important* words in a poem, very precise or very concrete or very abstract: they are middling words, not in themselves very much one thing or the other, and should be useful only with respect to something concrete in itself.

If we take Mr. Cummings' most favored word "flower" and inspect the uses to which he puts it, we should have some sort of key to the kind of poetry he writes. In *Tulips and Chimneys* the word "flower" turns up, to a casual count, forty-eight times, and in &, a much smaller volume, twenty-one times. We have among others the following: smile like a flower; riverly as a flower; steeped in burning flowers; last flower; lipping flowers; more silently than a flower; snow flower; world flower; softer than flowers; forehead a flight of flowers; feet are flowers in vases; air is deep with flowers; slow supple flower of beauty; flower-terrible; flower of thy mouth; stars and flowers; mouth a new flower; flower of silence; god's flowers; flowers of reminding; dissonant flowers; flower-stricken air; Sunday flower; tremendous flower; speaking flower; flowers of kiss; futile flowers, etc., etc. Besides the general term there is a quantity of lilies and roses, and a good assortment of daisies, pansies, buttercups, violets, and chrysanthemums. There are also many examples of such associated words as "petals" and "blooms" and "blossoms," which, since they are similarly used, may be taken as alternative to flowers.

Now it is evident that this word must attract Mr. Cummings' mind very much; it must contain for him an almost unlimited variety and extent of meaning; as the mystic says god, or at least as the incomplete mystic repeats the name of god to every occasion of his soul, Mr. Cummings in some of his poems says flower. The question is, whether or not the reader can possibly have shared the experience which Mr. Cummings has had of the word; whether or not it is possible to discern, after any amount of effort, the precise impact which Mr. Cummings undoubtedly feels upon his whole experience when he uses the word. "Flower," like every other word not specifically the expression of a logical relation, began life as a metaphor, as a leap from feeling to feeling, as a bridge in the imagination to give meaning to both those feelings. Presumably, the amount of meaning possible to the word is increased with each use, but only the meaning *possible*. Actually, in practice, a very different process goes on. Since people are occupied mostly with communication and argument and conversation, with the erection of discursive relationships, words are commonly spoken and written with the *least* possible meaning preserved, instead of the most. History is taken for granted, ignored, or denied. Only the outsides of words, so to speak, are used; and doubtless the outsides of words are all that the discursive intellect needs. But when a word is used in a poem it should be the sum of all its appropriate history made concrete and particular in the individual context; and in poetry all words act *as if* they were so used, because the only kind of meaning poetry can have requires that all its words resume their full life: the full life being modified and made unique by the *qualifications* the words perform one upon the other in the poem. Thus even a very bad poem may seem good to its author, when the author is not an acute critic and believes that there is life in his words merely because there was life (and a very different sort of life, truly) in the feelings which they represent. An author should remember, with the Indians, that the reality of a word is anterior to, and greater than, his use of it can ever be; that there is a perfection to the feelings in words to which his mind cannot hope to attain, but that his chief labor will be toward the approximation of that perfection.

We sometimes speak of a poet as a master of his words, and we sometimes say that a man's poetry has been run away with by words—meaning that he has not mastered his words but has been overpowered by his peculiar experience of certain among them. Both these notions are commonly improper, because they represent misconceptions of the nature of poetry in so far as they lay any stress upon originality, or the lack of it, in the poet's use of words. The only mastery possible to the poet consists in that entire submission to his words which is perfect knowledge. The only originality of which the poet is properly capable will be in the choice of order, and even this choice is largely a process of discovery rather than of origination. As for words running away with a poet or a poem, it would be more accurate to say that the poet's *ideas* had run away with him than his words.

This is precisely what has occurred with Mr. Cummings in his use of the word "flower" as a maid of all work. The word has become an idea, and in the process has been deprived of its history, its qualities, and its meaning. An idea, the intellectual pin upon which a thought is hung, is not transmissible in poetry as an important element in the poem and ought only to be employed to pass over, with the greatest possible velocity, the area of the uninteresting (what the poet was not interested in). That is, in a poem whose chief intent was the notation of character and yet required a descriptive setting, the poet might well use for the description such vague words as space and time, but could not use such words as goodness or nobleness without the risk of flatness. In Mr. Cummings' poetry we find the contrary; the word "flower," because of the originality with which he conceives it, becomes an idea and is used to represent the most interesting and most important aspect of his poem. Hence the center of the poem is permanently abstract and unknowable for the reader, and remains altogether without qualifications and concreteness. It is not the mere frequency of use that deadens the word flower into an idea; it is the kind of thought which each use illustrates in common. By seldom saying *what* flower, by seldom relating immitigably the abstract word to a specific experience, the content of the word vanishes; it has no inner mystery, only an impenetrable surface.

This is the defect, the essential deceit, we were trying to define. Without questioning Mr. Cummings, or any poet, as to sincerity (which is a personal attitude, irrelevant to the poetry considered) it is possible to say that when in any poem the important words are forced by their use to remain impenetrable, when they can be made to surrender nothing actually to the senses—then the poem is defective and the poet's words have so far deceived him as to become ideas merely.[4] Mr. Cummings is not so much writing poetry, as he is dreaming, idly ringing the changes of his reveries.

Perhaps a small divagation may make clearer the relation of these remarks to Mr. Cummings' poems. Any poetry which does not consider itself as much of an art and having the same responsibilities to the consumer as the arts of silversmithing or cobbling shoes—any such poetry is likely to do little more than rehearse a waking dream. Dreams are everywhere ominous and full of meaning; and why should they not be? They hold the images of the secret self, and to the initiate dreamer betray the nerve of life at every turn, not through any effort to do so, or because of any inherited regimen, but simply because they cannot help it. Dreams are like that— to the dreamer the maximal limit of experience. As it happens, dreams employ words and pictorial images to fill out their flux with a veil of substance. Pictures are natural to everyone, and words, because they are prevalent, seem common and inherently sensible. Hence, both picture and word, and then with a little stretching of the fancy the substance of the dream itself, seem expressible just as they occur—as things created, as the very flux of life. Mr. Cummings' poems are often nothing more than the report of just such dreams. He believes he knows what he knows, and no doubt he does. But he also believes, apparently, that the words which he encourages most vividly to mind are those most precisely fitted to put his poem on paper. He transfers the indubitable magic of his private musings from the cell of his mind, where it is honest incantation, to the realm of poetry. Here he forgets that poetry, so far as it takes a permanent form, is written and is meant to be read, and that it cannot be a mere private musing. Merely because his private fancy furnishes his liveliest images, is the worst reason for assuming that this private fancy will be approximately experienced by the reader or even indicated on the printed page.

---

[4]It should be confessed that for all those persons who regard poetry only as a medium of communication, these remarks are quite vitiated. What is communicated had best remain as abstract as possible, dealing with the concrete as typical only; then "meaning" will be found to reside most clearly in the realm of ideas, and everything will be given as of equal import. But here poetry is regarded not at all as communication but as expression, as statement, as presentation of experience, and the emphasis will be on what is made known concretely. The question is not what one shares with the poet, but what one knows in the poem.

But it is unfair to limit this description to Mr. Cummings; indeed, so limited, it is not even a description of Mr. Cummings. Take the *Oxford Book of English Verse*, or any anthology of poems equally well known, and turn from the poems printed therein of such widely separated poets as Surrey, Crashaw, Marvell, Burns, Wordsworth, Shelley, and Swinburne, to the collected works of these poets respectively. Does not the description of Mr. Cummings' mind at work given above apply nearly as well to the bulk of this poetry as to that of Mr. Cummings, at least on the senses' first immersion? The anthology poems being well known are conceived to be understood, to be definitely intelligible, and to have, without inspection, a precise meaning. The descent upon the collected poems of all or of any one of these authors is by and large a descent into tenuity. Most of their work, most of any poet's work, with half a dozen exceptions, is tenuous and vague, private exercises or public playthings of a soul in verse. So far as he is able, the reader struggles to reach the concrete, the solid, the definite; he must have these qualities, or their counterparts among the realm of the spirit, before he can understand what he reads. To translate such qualities from the realm of his private experience to the conventional forms of poetry is the problem of the poet; and the problem of the reader, likewise, is to come well equipped with the talent and the taste for discerning the meaning of those conventions as they particularly occur. Neither the poet's casual language nor the reader's casual interlocution is likely to be much help. There must be a ground common but exterior to each: that is the poem. The best poems take the best but not always the hardest reading; and no doubt it is so with the writing. Certainly, in neither case are dreams or simple reveries enough. Dreams are natural and are minatory or portentous; but except when by accident they fall into forms that fit the intelligence, they never negotiate the miracle of meaning between the poet and the poem, the poem and the reader.

Most poetry fails of this negotiation, and it is sometimes assumed that the negotiation was never meant, by the poet, to be made. For the poet, private expression is said to be enough; for the reader, the agitation of the senses, the perception of verbal beauty, the mere sense of stirring life in the words, are supposed sufficient. If this defense had a true premise—if the poet did express himself to his private satisfaction—it would be unanswerable; and to many it is so. But I think the case is different, and this is the real charge against Mr. Cummings: the poet does not ever express himself privately. The mind cannot understand, cannot properly know its own musing until those musings take some sort of conventional form. Properly speaking a poet, or any man, cannot be adequate to himself in terms of himself. True consciousness and true expression of consciousness must be external to the blind seat of consciousness—man as a sensorium. Even a simple image must be fitted among other images, and conned with them, before it is understood. That is, it must take a form in language which is highly traditional and conventional. The genius of the poet is to make the convention apparently disappear into the use to which he puts it.

Mr. Cummings and the group with which he is here roughly associated, the anti-culture or anti-intelligence group, persist to the contrary. Because experience is fragmentary as it strikes the consciousness it is thought to be essentially discontinuous and therefore essentially unintelligible except in the fragmentary form in which it occurred. They credit the words they use with immaculate conception and there hold them unquestionable. A poem, because it happens, must mean something and mean it without relation to anything but the private experience which inspired it. Certainly it means something, but not a poem; it means that something exciting happened to the writer and that a mystery is happening to the reader. The fallacy is double: they believe in the inexorable significance of the unique experience; and they have discarded the only method of making the unique experience into a poem—the conventions of the intelligence. As a matter of fact they do not write without conventions, but being ignorant of what they use, they resort most commonly to their own inefficient or superficial conventions—such as Mr. Cummings' flower and doll. The effect is convention without substance; the unique experience becomes a rhetorical assurance.

If we examine next, for the sake of the greatest possible contrast, one of the "tough" poems in *Is 5*, we will find a similar breach with the concrete. The use of vague words like "flower" in the lyrical poems as unexpanded similes, is no more an example of sentimental egoism than the use of vague conventions about villains. The distortion differs in terms but is essentially identical.

Sometimes the surface of the poem is so well constructed that the distortion is hard to discover. Intensity of process occasionally triumphs over the subject. Less frequently the subject itself is conceived directly and takes naturally the terms which the language supplies. The poem numbered One-XII in *Is 5* is an example in so far as the sentimental frame does not obscure the process.

> now dis "daughter" uv eve (who aint precisely slim) sim
>
> ply don't know duh meanin uv duh woid sin in
> not disagreeable contras tuh dat not exacly fat
>
> "father" (adjustin his robe) who now puts on his flat hat.

It is to be noted in this epigram, that there is no inexorable reason for either the dialect or the lapses from it into straight English. No one in particular is speaking, unless it be Mr. Cummings slumming in morals along with he-men and lady social workers, and taking it for granted that the dialect and the really refined language which the dialect exercises together give a setting. There are many other poems in *Is 5*, more sentimental and less successful, where the realism is of a more obvious sort; not having reference to an ideal so much as to a kind of scientific reality. That is, there is an effort to ground an emotion, or the facts which make the emotion, in the style of the character to whom the emotion happens. It is the reporter, the man with the good ear for spoken rhythms, who writes out of memory. The war poems and the poem about Bill and his chip (One-XVI) are examples. Style in this sense (something laid on) is only an attribute; is not the man; is not the character. And when it is substituted for character, it is likely to be sentimental and melodramatic. That is, the emotion which is named in the poem (by one of its attributes) is in excess of its established source (that same attribute). There is a certain immediate protection afforded to this insufficiency by the surface toughness, by the convention of burlesque; as if by mocking oneself one made sure there was something to mock. It is a kind of trickery resulting from eager but lazy senses; where the sensation itself is an excess, and appears to have done all the work of intuition and intelligence; where sensation seems expert without incorporation into experience. As if sensation could be anything more than the idea of sensation, so far as poetry goes, without being attached to some central body of experience, genuinely understood and *formed* in the mind.

The intrusion of science into art always results in a sentimental realism and always obfuscates form when that science is not kept subordinate to the qualitative experience of the senses—as witness the run of sociological novels. The analogues of science, where conventions are made to do the work of feeling instead of crowning it, are even more dangerous. Mr. Cummings' tough guy and his hard-boiled dialects are such analogues.

Mr. Cummings has a fine talent for using familiar, even almost dead words, in such a context as to make them suddenly impervious to every ordinary sense; they become unable to speak, but with a great air of being bursting with something very important and precise to say. "The bigness of cannon is *skillful* . . . enormous rhythm of *absurdity* . . . *slimness* of *evenslicing* eyes are chisels . . . electric Distinct face haughtily vital *clinched* in a swoon of *synopsis* . . . my friend's being continually whittles *keen* careful futile *flowers,*" etc. With the possible exception of the compound *evenslicing* the italicized words are all ordinary words; all in normal contexts have a variety of meanings both connotative and denotative; the particular context being such as to indicate a particular meaning, to establish precisely a feeling, a sensation or a relation.

Mr. Cummings' contexts are employed to an opposite purpose in so far as they wipe out altogether the history of the word, its past associations and general character. To seize Mr. Cummings' meaning there is only the free and *uninstructed* intuition. Something precise is no doubt intended; the warrant for the belief is in the almost violent isolation into which the words are thrown; but that precision can seldom, by this method, become any more than just that "something precise." The reality, the event, the feeling, which we will allow Mr. Cummings has in mind, is not sensibly in the word. It is one thing for meaning to be difficult, or abstruse—hidden in its heart, that is. "Absent thee from *felicity* a while," Blake's

[59

"Time is the *mercy* of eternity" are reasonable examples; there the mystery is inside the words. In Mr. Cummings' words the mystery flies in the face, is on the surface; because there is no inside, no realm of possibility, of essence.

The general movement of Mr. Cummings' language is away from communicable precision. If it be argued that the particular use of one of the italicized words above merely makes that word unique, the retort is that such uniqueness is too perfect, is sterile. If by removing the general sense of a word the special sense is apotheosized, it is only so at the expense of the general sense itself. The destruction of the general sense of a word results in the loss of that word's individuality; for in practice the character of a word (which is its sense) is manifest only in good society, and meaning is distinguished only by conventional association. Mr. Cummings' use of words results in a large number of conventions, but these conventions do not permeate the words themselves, do not modify their souls or change their fates; they cannot be adopted by the reader because they cannot be essentially understood. They should rather be called inventions.

If we take a paragraph from the poem beginning on page thirty in *Is 5*, we will discover another terminus of the emotional habit of mind which produced the emphasis on the word "flower" in *Tulips and Chimneys*.

the Bar. tinking luscious jugs dint of ripe silver with warmlyish wetflat splurging smells waltz the glush of squirting taps plus slush of foam knocked off and a faint piddle-of-drops she says I ploc spittle what the lands thaz me kid in no sir hopping sawdust you kiddo he's a palping wreaths of badly Yep cigars who jim him why gluey grins topple together eyes pout gestures stickily point made glints squinting who's a wink bum-nothing and money fuzzily mouths take big wobbly footsteps every goggle cent of it get out ears dribbles soft right old feller belch the chap hic summore eh chuckles skulch. . . .

Now the point is that the effect of this whole paragraph has much in common with the effect of the word "flower." It is a flower disintegrated, and the parts are not component; so that by presenting an analysis of his image Mr. Cummings has not let us into its secret:

the analysis is not a true analysis, because it exhibits, finally, what are still only the results, not the grounds, of his private conventions, his personal emotions. It is indubitable that the words are alive; they jostle, even overturn, the reader in the assurance of their vitality; but the notion of what their true vitality is remains Mr. Cummings' very own. The words remain emotive. They have a gusty air of being something, but they defeat themselves in the effort to say what, and come at last to a bad end, all fallen in a heap.

The easiest *explanation* of the passage would be to say that each separate little collection of words in it is a note for an image; an abstraction, very keen and lively in Mr. Cummings' mind, of something very precise and concrete. Some of the words seem like a painter's notes, some a philologist's. But they are all, as they are presented, notes, abstractions, ideas—with their concrete objects unknown—except to the most arbitrary guess. The guess must be arbitrary because of the quantity, not the quality, of the words employed. Mr. Cummings is not here overworking the individual words, but by heaping so many of them together he destroys their individuality. Meaning really residual in the word is not exhausted, is not even touched; it must remain abstract and only an emotional substitute for it can be caught. The interesting fact about emotional substitutes in poetry, as elsewhere, is their thinness, and the inadequacy resulting from the thinness. The thinness is compulsory because they can, so far as the poem is concerned, exist only as a surface; they cannot possess tentacular roots reaching into, and feeding on, feelings, because the feelings do not exist, are only present by legerdemain. Genuine emotion in poetry perhaps does not *exist* at all; though it is none the less real for that, because a genuine emotion does not need the warrant of existence: it is the necessary result, in the mind, of a convention of feelings: like the notion of divine grace.

In *Tulips and Chimneys* (p. 109) there is a poem whose first and last lines supply an excellent opposition of proper and improper distortion of language.

the Cambridge ladies who live in furnished souls . . .
the
moon rattles like a fragment of angry candy.

In the context the word "soul" has the element of surprise which is surprise at *justness*; at *aptness*; it fits in and finishes off the notion of the line. "Furnished souls" is a good, if slight, conceit; and there is no trouble for the reader who wishes to know what the line means: he has merely to *extend* his knowledge slightly, just as Mr. Cummings merely extended the sense of his language slightly by releasing his particular words in this particular order. The whole work that the poet here demands of his reader is pretty well defined. The reader does not have to *guess*; he is enabled to *know*. The reader is not collecting data, he is aware of a meaning.

It would be unfair not to quote the context of the second line.

> . . . the Cambridge ladies do not care, above
> Cambridge if sometimes in its box of
> sky lavender and cornerless, the
> moon rattles like a fragment of angry candy.

We can say that Mr. Cummings is putting beauty next to the tawdry; juxtaposing the dead with the live; or that he is being sentimentally philosophical in verse—that is, releasing from inadequate sources something intended to be an emotion.[5]

We can go on illustrating Mr. Cummings' probable intentions almost infinitely. What Mr. Cummings likes or admires, what he holds dear in life, he very commonly calls flowers, or dolls, or candy— terms with which he is astonishingly generous; as if he thought by making his terms general enough their vagueness could not matter, and never noticed that the words so used enervate themselves in a kind of hardened instinct. We can understand what Mr. Cummings intended by "moon" and "candy" but in the process of understanding, the meaning of the words themselves disappears. The thrill of the association of "rattles" with "moon" and "angry" with "candy" becomes useless as a guide. "Rattles" and "angry" can only be continued in the meaning of the line if the reader supplies them with a

---

[5] That is, as the most common form of sentimentality is the use of emotion in *excess* of its impetus in the feelings, here we have an example of emotion which fails by a great deal to *come up* to its impetus. It is a very different thing from understatement, where the implications are always definite and where successful disarming.

force, a definiteness of suggestion, with which Mr. Cummings has not endowed them.

The distortion is here not a release of observation so keen that commonplace language would not hold it; it is not the presentation of a vision so complete that words must lose their normal meanings in order to suggest it. It is, on the contrary, the distortion of the commonplace itself; and the difficulty about a commonplace is that it cannot be known, it has no character, no fate, and no essence. It is a substitute for these.

True meaning (which is here to say knowledge) can only exist where some contact, however remote, is preserved between the language, forms, or symbols in which it is given and something concrete, individual, or sensual which inspired it; and the degree in which the meaning is seized will depend on the degree in which the particular concreteness is realized. Thus the technique of "meaning" will employ distortion only in so far as the sense of this concreteness is promoted by it. When contrast and contradiction disturb the ultimate precision of the senses the distortion involved is inappropriate and destructive. Mr. Cummings' line about the moon and candy does not weld a contradiction, does not identify a substance by a thrill of novel association. It leaves the reader at a loss; where it is impossible to *know*, after any amount of effort and good will, what the words mean. If it be argued that Mr. Cummings was not interested in meaning then Mr. Cummings is not a serious poet, is a mere collector of sensations, and can be of very little value to us. And to defend Mr. Cummings on the ground that he is in the pretty good company of Swinburne, Crashaw, and Victor Hugo, is partly to ignore the fact that by the same argument all four also enjoy the companionship of Mr. Guest. Such defense would show a very poor knowledge of the verses of Mr. Cummings, who is nothing if not serious in the attempt to exhibit precise knowledge. His interest in words and in their real meaning is probably greater than that of most poets of similar dimensions. He has consciously stretched syntax, word order, and meaning in just the effort to expand knowledge in poetry; and his failure is because he has gone too far, has lost sight of meaning altogether—and because, perhaps, the experience which he attempts to translate into poetry remained always personal to him and was never known objectively as itself. By his eagerness Mr. Cummings' relation to language has become confused; he has put down what has meant much to him and can mean little to us because for us it is not put down—is only indicated, only possibly there. The freshness and depth of his private experience is not denied; but it is certain that, so far as its meaning goes, in the poetry into which he translated it, sentimentality, empty convention, and commonplace rule. In short, Mr. Cummings' poetry ends in ideas *about* things.

When Mr. Cummings resorts to language for the *thrill* that words may be made to give, when he allows his thrill to appear as an equivalent for concrete meaning, he is often more successful than when he is engaged more ambitiously. This is true of poets like Swinburne and Poe, Shelley and the early Marlowe: where the first pair depended almost as much upon *thrill* as Mr. Cummings in those poems where they made use of it at all, and where the second pair, particularly Marlowe, used their thrills more appropriately as ornament: where all four were most successful in their less ambitious works, though perhaps not as interesting. Likewise, today, there is the example of Archibald MacLeish, whose best lines are those that thrill and do nothing more. So that at least in general opinion Mr. Cummings is in this respect not in bad company. But if an examination of thrill be made, whether in Mr. Cummings' verse or in that of others, it will be shown that the use of thrill has at heart the same sentimental impenetrability that defeats the possibility of meaning elsewhere. Only here, in the realm of thrill, the practice is comparatively less illegitimate. Thrill, by itself, or in its proper place, is an exceedingly important element in any poem; it is the circulation of its blood, the *quickness* of life, by which we know it, when there is anything in it to know, most intimately. To use a word for its thrill, is to resurrect it from the dead; it is the incarnation of life in consciousness; it is movement.[6]

[6]Cf. Owen Barfield's *Poetic Diction* (London, Faber and Gwyer, 1928), page 202. "For what is absolutely necessary to the present existence of poetry? Movement. The wisdom which she has imparted may remain for a time at rest, but she herself will always be found to have gone forward to where there is life, and therefore movement, *now*. And we have seen that the experience of esthetic pleasure betrays the real presence of movement. . . . But without the continued existence of poetry, without a steady influx of new meaning into language, even

But what Mr. Cummings does, when he is using language as thrill, is not to resurrect a word from the dead: he more often produces an apparition, in itself startling and even ominous, but still only a ghost: it is all a thrill, and what it is that thrilled us cannot be determined. For example in *XLI Poems*, the following phrases depend considerably for their effect upon the thrill that is in them: "Prisms of sharp *mind*; where strange birds *purr*; into the *smiling* sky *tense* with *blending*; ways cloaked with *renewal*; sinuous riot; *steeped* with burning flowers; little kittens who are called *spring*; electric Distinct face haughtily vital clinched in a *swoon* of synopsis; unreal *precise* intrinsic fragment of actuality; an orchid whose *velocity* is *sculptural*; scythe takes *crisply* the *whim* of thy *smoothness*; perpendicular *taste*; wet stars," etc., etc. (The italics are mine.)

Take especially the phrase, "scythe takes *crisply* the *whim* of thy *smoothness*." We know in the poem that it is the scythe of death and that it is youth and beauty (in connection with love) that is to be cut off. So much is familiar, is very conventional; and so the conventional or dead emotion is placed before us; the educated reader receives it and reacts to it without a whimper. But Mr. Cummings must not have been content with presenting the conventional emotion in its conventional form; he felt bound to enliven it with metaphor, with overtones of the senses and the spirit: so that he substituted for the direct statement a rather indirect image combining three unusually sensed words for the sake of the *thrill* the special combination might afford. As the phrase stands there is no precision in it. There is a great suggestion of precision about it—like men going off to war: but precisely *what* is left for the reader to guess, to supply from his own heart. By themselves *whim* and *smoothness* are abstract quality words; and in order for them to escape the tensity, the dislocated strain, of abstractness and gain the intensity, the firm disposition, of concrete meaning, they should demand a particular reference.

Smoothness is probably the smoothness of the body and is used

the knowledge and wisdom which poetry herself has given in the past must wither away into a species of mechanical calculation. Great poetry is the progressive incarnation of life in consciousness." That is, we must know what thrills us; else being merely thrilled we are left gasping and aghast, like the little girl on the roller coaster.

here as a kind of metonymy; but it may be pure metaphor and represent what is really to die—the spirit—taken in its physical terms:
or it may be that all that is to be understood is a pure tautology.
And so on. Even with this possible variety of reference, *smoothness*
would not be very objectionable, were it the only word in the phrase
used in this way, or were the other words used to clarify the *smoothness*. But we have also the noun *whim* bearing directly on *smoothness* and the adverb *crisply* which while it directly modifies *takes*,
really controls the entire phrase. Taken seriously *whim*, with reference to the smoothness of either the body or the spirit or the love it
inspires, is to say the least a light word; one might almost say a
"metrical" word, introduced to stretch the measure, or because the
author liked the sound of it, or enjoyed whimsy. It diminishes without limiting the possibilities of *smoothness*. Because it is here, in
the phrase, it is inseparable from the phrase's notion of smoothness;
yet instead of assisting, tends to prevent what that notion of smoothness is from being divulged.

    Crisply is even more difficult to account for; associated with a
scythe it perhaps brings to mind the sound of a scythe in a hayfield,
which is surely not the reference here intended; it would be very
difficult for such a crispness to associate itself with death, which the
scythe represents, or *whim*, or *smoothness* in either the spiritual or
fleshly sense. If it implies merely a cleanness, a swiftness of motion
in the apparition of death, some other word would have seemed
better chosen. If this analysis be correct, the three words are unal-
terably combined by the force of *crisply* in such a way as to defeat
the only possible sense their *thrilling* use would have had. They
are, so to speak, only the notions of themselves and those selves
must remain forever unknown. All we are left with in such a phrase
as this is the strangeness which struck us on our first encounter; and
the only difference is that the strangeness is the more intensified the
more we prolong the examination. This is another test of poetry:
whether we understand the *strangeness* of a poem or not.[7]

[7] *Poetic Diction, op. cit.*, pp. 197–8: "It (strangeness) is not synonymous with wonder; for
wonder is our reaction to things which we are conscious of not quite understanding, or at
any rate of understanding less than we had thought. The element of strangeness in beauty
has the contrary effect. It arises from contact with a different kind of *consciousness* from our
own, different, yet not so remote that we cannot partly share it, as indeed, in such a connex-

E. E. Cummings

As it happens there is an exquisite example of the proper use of this strangeness, this thrill, in another poem of Mr. Cummings: where he speaks of a cathedral before whose face "the streets turn *young* with rain." While there might be some question as to whether the use of *young* presents the only adequate image, there is certainly no question at all that the phrase is entirely successful: that is, the suggestive feeling in *young* makes the juncture, the emotional conjugation, of streets and rain transparent and perfect. This may be so because there is no element of essential contradiction, in the terms of feeling, between the emotional word *young* and the factual word *streets* and *rain;* or because, positively, what happens to the context by the insertion of *young* is, by a necessary leap of the imagination, something qualified. *Young* may be as abstract a word by itself, as purely relative and notional a word, as any other; but here it is brought into the concrete, is fixed there in a proper habitation. Just because reference is not commonly made either to young streets or young rain, the combination here effected is the more appropriate. The surprise, the contrast, which lend force to the phrase, do not exist in the poem; but exist, if at all, rather in the mind of the reader who did not foresee the slight stretch of his sensibility that the phrase requires—which the phrase not only requires, but necessitates. This, then, is a *strangeness* understood by its own viableness. No preliminary agreement of taste, or contract of symbols, was necessary.

The point is that Mr. Cummings did not here attempt the impossible, he merely stretched the probable. The business of the poet who deals largely with tactual and visual images, as Mr. Cummings does, for the meat of his work, is to escape the prison of his private mind; to use in his poem as little as possible of the experience that happened to him personally, and on the other hand to employ as much as possible of that experience as it is data.

It is idle for a critic to make the familiar statement that the mind of the writer is his work, or that "the style is the man," when by mind and man is meant the private experience of the author. So far as, in this sense, the mind *is* the work, or the style *is* the man, we can understand the work or the style only through an accidental

ion, the mere word 'contact' implies. Strangeness, in fact, arouses wonder when we do not understand; esthetic imagination when we do."

[67

unanimity; and what we understand is likely to be very thin—perhaps only the terms of understanding. For the author himself, in such circumstances, can have understood very little more. He has been pursuing the impossible, when the probable was right at hand; he has been transcending his experience instead of submitting to it. And this is just what Mr. Cummings does in the phrases quoted above.

It would be ungracious to suppose that as a poet "a swoon of synopsis" did not represent to Mr. Cummings a very definite and very suggestive image. But to assent to that image would be a kind of *tour de force*; the application of such assent would imply that because the words appear, and being words contain notions, they must in this particular instance exhibit the undeniable sign of interior feeling. The proper process of poetry designs exactly what the reader will perceive; that is what is meant when a word is said to be inevitable or *juste*. But this exactness of perception can only come about when there is an extreme fidelity on the part of the poet to his words as living things; which he can discover and control— which he must learn, and nourish, and stretch; but which he cannot invent. This unanimity in our possible experience of words implies that the only unanimity which the reader can feel in what the poet represents must be likewise exterior to the poet; must be somehow both anterior and posterior to the poet's own experience. The poet's mind, perhaps, is what he is outside himself with; is what he has learned; is what he knows: it is also what the reader knows. So long as he is content to remain in his private mind, he is unknowable, impenetrable, and sentimental. All his words perhaps must thrill us, because we cannot know them in the very degree that we sympathize with them. But the best thrills are those we have without knowing it.

This essay has proceeded so far on the explicit assumption that the poems of Mr. Cummings are unintelligible, and that no amount of effort on the part of the reader can make them less so. We began by connecting Mr. Cummings to two schools, or groups, which are much the same essentially—the anti-culture group which denies the intelligence, and the group, not limited to writers, of which the essential attitude is most easily defined as sentimental egoism or romantic idealism. Where these schools are most obviously identical is in the poetry they nourish: the avowed interest is the relentless pursuit of the actual in terms of the immediate as the immediate is given, without overt criticism, to the ego. Unintelligibility is a necessary consequence of such a pursuit, if by the intelligible we mean something concrete, qualified, permanent, and public. Poetry, if we understand it, is not in immediacy at all. It is not given to the senses or to the free intuition. Thus, when poetry is written as if its substance were immediate and given, we have as a result a distorted sensibility and a violent inner confusion. We have, if the poet follows his principles, something abstract, vague, impermanent, and essentially private. When every sensation and every word is taken as final and perfect, the substance which sensations report and for which words must stand remains inexplicable. We can understand only by accident.

Of course there is another side to the matter. In a sense anyone can understand Mr. Cummings and his kind by the mere assertion that he does understand. Nothing else is needed but a little natural sympathy and a certain aptness for the resumption of a childish sensibility. In much the same way we understand a stranger's grief— by setting up a private and less painful simulacrum. If we take the most sentimental and romantic writers as they come, there will be always about their works an excited freshness, the rush of sensation and intuition, all the ominous glow of immediacy. They will be eagerly at home in the mystery of life. Adroitness, expertness, readiness for any experience, will enlighten their activities even where they most miserably fail. They are all actors, ready to take any part, for they put themselves, and nothing else, into every part they play. Commonly their real success will depend on the familiarity of the moments into which they sink themselves; they will depend on convention more than others, because they have nothing else to depend on.

So with the poetry of Mr. Cummings we might be altogether contented and pleased, were he himself content with the measure of his actual performance. But no poetry is so pretentious. No poetry ever claimed to mean more; and in making this claim it cannot avoid submitting itself, disastrously, to the criticism of the intelligence. So soon as we take it seriously, trying to discover what it really says about human destiny and the terms of love and death, we see how little material there is in this poetry except the assurance, made with continuous gusto, that the material exists. We look at the poetry. Sometimes one word, in itself vague and cloudy, is made to take on the work of an entire philosophy—like flower. Sometimes words pile themselves up blindly, each defeating the purport of the others. No feeling is ever defined. No emotion betrays a structure. Experience is its own phantoms, and flows willy-nilly. With the reality of experience the reality of language is lost. No metaphor crosses the bridge of tautology, and every simile is unexpanded. All the "thought" is metonymy, yet the substance is never assigned; so in the end we have only the thrill of substance.

Such an art when it pretends to measure life is essentially vicarious; it is a substitute for something that never was—like a tin soldier, or Peter Pan. It has all the flourish of life and every sentimental sincerity. Taken for what it is, it is charming and even instructive. Taken solemnly, as it is meant to be, the distortion by which it exists is too much for it, and it seems a kind of baby-talk.

Examples of Wallace Stevens

[1 9 3 1]

The most striking if not the most important thing about Mr. Stevens' verse is its vocabulary—the collection of words, many of them uncommon in English poetry, which on a superficial reading seems characteristic of the poems. An air of preciousness bathes the mind of the casual reader when he finds such words as fubbed, girandoles, curlicues, catarrhs, gobbet, diaphanes, clopping, minuscule, pipping, pannicles, carked, ructive, rapey, cantilene, buffo, fiscs, phylactery, princox, and funest. And such phrases as "thrum with a proud douceur," or "A pool of pink, clippered with lilies scudding the bright chromes," hastily read, merely increase the feeling of preciousness. Hence Mr. Stevens has a bad reputation among those who dislike the finicky, and a high one, unfortunately, among those who value the ornamental sounds of words but who see no purpose in developing sound from sense.

Both classes of reader are wrong. Not a word listed above is used preciously; not one was chosen as an elegant substitute for a plain term; each, in its context, was a word definitely meant. The important thing about Mr. Stevens' vocabulary is not the apparent oddity of certain words, but the uses to which he puts those words with others. It is the way that Mr. Stevens combines kinds of words, unusual in a single context, to reveal the substance he had in mind, which is of real interest to the reader.

Good poets gain their excellence by writing an existing language *as if* it were their own invention; and as a rule success in the effect of originality is best secured by fidelity, in an extreme sense, to the individual words as they appear in the dictionary. If a poet knows precisely what his words represent, what he writes is much more likely to seem new and strange—and even difficult to understand—than if he uses his words ignorantly and at random. That is because when each word has definite character the combinations cannot avoid uniqueness. Even if a text is wholly quotation, the condition of quotation itself qualifies the text and makes it so far unique. Thus a quotation made from Marvell by Eliot has a force slightly different from what it had when Marvell wrote it. Though the combination of words is unique it is read, if the reader knows his words either by usage or dictionary, with a shock like that of recognition. The recognition is not limited, however, to what was already known in the words; there is a perception of something previously unknown, something new which is a result of the combination of the words, something which is literally an access of knowledge. Upon the poet's skill in combining words as much as upon his private feelings, depends the importance or the value of the knowledge.

In some notes on the language of E. E. Cummings I tried to show how that poet, by relying on his private feelings and using words as if their meanings were spontaneous with use, succeeded mainly in turning his words into empty shells. With very likely no better inspiration in the life around him, Mr. Stevens, by combining the insides of those words he found fit to his feelings, has turned his words into knowledge. Both Mr. Stevens and Cummings issue in ambiguity—as any good poet does; but the ambiguity of Cummings is that of the absence of known content, the ambiguity of a phantom which no words could give being; while Mr. Stevens' ambiguity is that of a substance so dense with being, that it resists paraphrase and can be truly perceived only in the form of words in which it was given. It is the difference between poetry which depends on the poet and poetry which depends on itself. Reading Cummings you either guess or supply the substance yourself. Reading Mr. Stevens you have only to know the meanings of the words and to submit to the conditions of the poem. There is a precision in such ambiguity all the more precise because it clings so closely to the stuff of the poem that separated it means nothing.

Take what would seem to be the least common word in the whole of *Harmonium*[1]—funest (page 74, line 6). The word means sad or calamitous or mournful and is derived from a French word meaning fatal, melancholy, baneful, and has to do with death and funerals. It comes ultimately from the Latin *funus* for funeral. Small dictionaries do not stock it. The poem in which it appears is called "Of the Manner of Addressing Clouds," which begins as follows:

> Gloomy grammarians in golden gowns,
> Meekly you keep the mortal rendezvous,
> Eliciting the still sustaining pomps
> Of speech which are like music so profound
> They seem an exaltation without sound.
> Funest philosophers and ponderers,
> Their evocations are the speech of clouds.
> So speech of your processionals returns
> In the casual evocations of your tread
> Across the stale, mysterious seasons. . . .

The sentence in which funest occurs is almost a parenthesis. It *seems* the statement of something thought of by the way, suggested by the clouds, which had better be said at once before it is forgotten. In such a casual, disarming way, resembling the way of understatement, Mr. Stevens often introduces the most important elements in his poems. The oddity of the word having led us to look it up we find that, once used, funest is better than any of its synonyms. It is the essence of the funeral in its sadness, not its sadness alone, that makes it the right word: the clouds are going to their death, as not only philosophers but less indoctrinated ponderers know; so what they say, what they evoke, in pondering, has that much in common with the clouds. Suddenly we realize that the effect of funest philosophers is due to the larger context of the lines preceding, and at the same time we become aware that the statement about their

---

[1] The references are to the new edition of *Harmonium*, New York: Alfred A. Knopf, 1931. This differs from the first edition in that three poems have been cut out and fourteen added.

[73

evocations is central to the poem and illuminates it. The word pomps, above, means ceremony and comes from a Greek word meaning procession, often, by association, a funeral, as in the phrase funeral pomps. So the pomps of the clouds suggests the funeral in funest.

The whole thing increases in ambiguity the more it is analyzed, but if the poem is read over after analysis, it will be seen that *in the poem* the language is perfectly precise. In its own words it is clear, and becomes vague in analysis only because the analysis is not the poem. We use analysis properly in order to discard it and return that much better equipped to the poem.

The use of such a word as funest suggests more abstract considerations, apart from the present instance. The question is whether or not and how much the poet is stretching his words when they are made to carry as much weight as funest carries above. Any use of a word stretches it slightly, because any use selects from among many meanings the right one, and then modifies that in the context. Beyond this necessary stretching, words cannot perhaps be stretched without coming to nullity—as the popular stretching of awful, grand, swell, has more or less nullified the original senses of those words. If Mr. Stevens stretches his words slightly, as a live poet should and must, it is in such a way as to make them seem more precisely themselves than ever. The context is so delicately illuminated, or adumbrated, that the word must be looked up, or at least thought carefully about, before the precision can be seen. This is the precision of the expert pun, and every word, to a degree, carries with it in any given sense the puns of all its senses.

But it may be a rule that only the common words of a language, words with several, even groups of meanings, can be stretched the small amount that is possible. The reader must have room for his research; and the more complex words are usually plays upon common words, and limited in their play. In the instance above the word funest is not so much itself stretched by its association with philosophers as the word philosophers—a common word with many senses—stretches funest. That is, because Mr. Stevens has used the word funest, it cannot easily be detached and used by others. The point is subtle. The meaning so doubles upon itself that it can be understood only in context. It is the context that is stretched by the insertion of the word *funest;* and it is that stretch, by its ambiguity, that adds to our knowledge.

A use of words almost directly contrary to that just discussed may be seen in a very different sort of poem—"The Ordinary Women" (page 13). I quote the first stanza to give the tone:

> Then from their poverty they rose.
> From dry catarrhs, and to guitars
> They flitted
> Through the palace walls.

Then skipping a stanza, we have this, for atmosphere:

> The lacquered loges huddled there
> Mumbled zay-zay and a-zay, a-zay.
> The moonlight
> Fubbed the girandoles.

The loges huddled probably because it was dark or because they didn't like the ordinary women, and mumbled perhaps because of the moonlight, perhaps because of the catarrhs, or even to keep key to the guitars. Moonlight, for Mr. Stevens, is mental, fictive, related to the imagination and meaning of things; naturally it fubbed the girandoles (which is equivalent to cheated the chandeliers, was stronger than the artificial light, if any) . . . Perhaps and probably but no doubt something else. I am at loss, and quite happy there, to know anything literally about this poem. Internally, inside its own words, I know it quite well by simple perusal. The charm of the rhymes is enough to carry it over any stile. The strange phrase, "Fubbed the girandoles," has another charm, like that of the rhyme, and as inexplicable: the approach of language, through the magic of elegance, to nonsense. That the phrase is not nonsense, that on inspection it retrieves itself to sense, is its inner virtue. Somewhere between the realms of ornamental sound and representative state-ment, the words pause and balance, dissolve and resolve. This is the mood of Euphues, and presents a poem with fine parts con-trolled internally by little surds of feeling that save both the poem and its parts from preciousness. The ambiguity of this sort of writing consists in the double importance of both sound and sense where neither has direct connection with the other but where neither can stand alone. It is as if Mr. Stevens wrote two poems at once with the real poem somewhere between, unwritten but vivid.

A poem which exemplifies not the approach merely but actual entrance into nonsense is "Disillusionment of Ten O'Clock" (page 88). This poem begins by saying that houses are haunted by white nightgowns, not nightgowns of various other colors, and ends with these lines:

> People are not going
> To dream of baboons and periwinkles.
> Only, here and there, an old sailor,
> Drunk and asleep in his boots,
> Catches tigers
> In red weather.

The language is simple and declarative. There is no doubt about the words or the separate statements. Every part of the poem makes literal sense. Yet the combination makes a nonsense, and a nonsense much more convincing than the separate sensible statements. The statement about catching tigers in red weather coming after the white nightgowns and baboons and periwinkles, has a persuasive force out of all relation to the sense of the words. Literally, there is nothing alarming in the statement, and nothing ambiguous, but by so putting the statement that it appears as nonsense, infinite possibilities are made terrifying and plain. The shock and virtue of nonsense is this: it compels us to scrutinize the words in such a way that we see the enormous ambiguity in the substance of every phrase, every image, every word. The simpler the words are the more impressive and certain is the ambiguity. Half our sleeping knowledge is in nonsense; and when put in a poem it wakes.

The edge between sense and nonsense is shadow thin, and in all our deepest convictions we hover in the shadow, uncertain whether we know what our words mean, nevertheless bound by the conviction to say them. I quote the second half of "The Death of a Soldier" (page 129):

> Death is absolute and without memorial,
> As in a season of autumn,
> When the wind stops,
> When the wind stops and, over the heavens,
> The clouds go, nevertheless,
> In their direction.

To gloss such a poem is almost impertinent, but I wish to observe that in the passage just quoted, which is the important half of the poem, there is an abstract statement, "Death is absolute and without memorial," followed by the notation of a natural phenomenon. The connection between the two is not a matter of course; it is syntactical, poetic, human. The point is, by combining the two, Mr. Stevens has given his abstract statement a concrete, sensual force; he has turned a conviction, an idea, into a feeling which did not exist, even in his own mind, until he had put it down in words. The feeling is not exactly in the words, it is because of them. As in the body sensations are definite but momentary, while feelings are ambiguous (with reference to sensations) but lasting; so in this poem the words are definite but instant, while the feelings they raise are ambiguous (with reference to the words) and have importance. Used in this way, words, like sensations, are blind facts which put together produce a feeling no part of which was in the data. We cannot say, abstractly, in words, any better what we know, yet the knowledge has become positive and the conviction behind it indestructible, because it has been put into words. That is one business of poetry, to use words to give quality and feeling to the precious abstract notions, and so doing to put them beyond words and beyond the sense of words.

A similar result from a different mode of the use of words may be noticed in such a poem as "The Emperor of Ice-Cream" (page 85):

> Call the roller of big cigars,
> The muscular one, and bid him whip
> In kitchen cups concupiscent curds.
> Let the wenches dawdle in such dress
> As they are used to wear, and let the boys

Bring flowers in last month's newspapers.
Let be be finale of seem.
The only emperor is the emperor of ice-cream.

Take from the dresser of deal,
Lacking the three glass knobs, that sheet
On which she embroidered fantails once
And spread it so as to cover her face.
If her horny feet protrude, they come
To show how cold she is, and dumb.
Let the lamp affix its beam.
The only emperor is the emperor of ice-cream.

The poem might be called Directions for a Funeral, with Two Epitaphs. We have a corpse laid out in the bedroom and we have people in the kitchen. The corpse is dead; then let the boys bring flowers in last month's (who would use today's?) newspapers. The corpse is dead; but let the wenches wear their everyday clothes—or is it the clothes they are used to wear at funerals? The conjunction of a muscular man whipping desirable desserts in the kitchen and the corpse protruding horny feet, gains its effect because of its oddity—not of fact, but of expression: the light frivolous words and rapid meters. Once made the conjunction is irretrievable and in its own measure exact. Two ideas or images about death—the living and the dead—have been associated, and are now permanently fused. If the mind is a rag-bag, pull out two rags and sew them together. If the materials were contradictory, the very contradiction, made permanent, becomes a kind of unison. By associating ambiguities found in nature in a poem we reach a clarity, a kind of transfiguration even, whereby we learn *what* the ambiguity was.

The point is, that the oddity of association would not have its effect without the couplets which conclude each stanza with the pungency of good epitaphs. Without the couplets the association would sink from wit to low humor or simple description. What, then, do the couplets mean? Either, or both, of two things. In the more obvious sense, "Let be be finale of seem," in the first stanza, means, take whatever seems to be, as really being; and in the second stanza, "Let the lamp affix its beam," means let it be plain that this woman is dead, that these things, impossibly ambiguous as they may be, are as they are. In this case, "The only emperor is the emperor of ice-cream," implies in both stanzas that the only power worth heeding is the power of the moment, of what is passing, of the flux.[2]

The less obvious sense of the couplets is more difficult to set down because, in all its difference, it rises out of the first sense, and while contradicting and supplanting, yet guarantees it. The connotation is, perhaps, that ice-cream and what it represents is the only power *heeded*, not the only power there is to heed. The irony recoils on itself: what seems *shall* finally be; the lamp *shall* affix its beam. The only emperor is the emperor of ice-cream. The king is dead; long live the king.

The virtue of the poem is that it discusses and settles these matters without mentioning them. The wit of the couplets does the work.

Allied to the method of this poem is the method of much of "Le Monocle de Mon Oncle." The light word is used with a more serious effect than the familiar, heavy words commonly chosen in poems about the nature of love. I take these lines from the first stanza (page 16):

> The sea of spuming thought foists up again
> The radiant bubble that she was. And then
> A deep up-pouring from some saltier well
> Within me, bursts its watery syllable.

The words foist and bubble are in origin and have remained in usage both light. One comes from a word meaning to palm false dice, and the other is derived by imitation from a gesture of the mouth. Whether the history of the words was present in Mr. Stevens' mind when he chose them is immaterial; the pristine flavor is still active by tradition and is what gives the rare taste to the lines quoted. By employing them in connection with a sea of spuming thought and the notion of radiance whatever vulgarity was in the two words is purged. They gain force while they lend their own

[2] Mr. Stevens wrote me that his daughter put a superlative value on ice-cream. Up daughters!

lightness to the context; and I think it is the lightness of these words that permits and conditions the second sentence in the quotation, by making the contrast between the foisted bubble and the bursting syllable possible.

Stanza IV of the same poem (pages 17–18) has a serious trope in which apples and skulls, love and death, are closely associated in subtle and vivid language. An apple, Mr. Stevens says, is as good as any skull to read because, like the skull, it finally rots away in the ground. The stanza ends with these lines:

> But it excels in this, that as the fruit
> Of love, it is a book too mad to read
> Before one merely reads to pass the time.

The light elegance and conversational tone give the stanza the cumulative force of understatement, and make it seem to carry a susurrus of irony between the lines. The word excels has a good deal to do with the success of the passage; superficially a syntactical word as much as anything else, actually, by its literal sense it saves the lines from possible triviality.

We have been considering poems where the light tone increases the gravity of the substance, and where an atmosphere of wit and elegance assures poignancy of meaning. It is only a step or so further to that use of language where tone and atmosphere are very nearly equivalent to substance and meaning themselves. "Sea Surface Full of Clouds" (page 132) has many lines and several images in its five sections which contribute by their own force to the sense of the poem, but it would be very difficult to attach special importance to any one of them. The burden of the poem is the color and tone of the whole. It is as near a tone-poem, in the musical sense, as language can come. The sense of single lines cannot profitably be abstracted from the context, and literal analysis does nothing but hinder understanding. We may say, if we like, that Mr. Stevens found himself in ecstasy—that he stood aside from himself emotionally—before the spectacle of endlessly varied appearances of California seas off Tehuantepec; and that he has tried to equal the complexity of what he saw in the technical intricacy of his poem. But that is all we can say. Neither the material of the poem nor what we get out of it is by nature susceptible of direct treatment in words. It might at first seem more a painter's subject than a poet's, because its interest is more obviously visual and formal than mental. Such an assumption would lead to apt criticism if Mr. Stevens had tried, in his words, to present a series of seascapes with a visual atmosphere to each picture. His intention was quite different and germane to poetry; he wanted to present the tone, in the mind, of five different aspects of the sea. The strictly visual form is in the background, merely indicated by the words; it is what the visual form gave off after it had been felt in the mind that concerned him. Only by the precise interweaving of association and suggestion, by the development of a delicate verbal pattern, could he secure the overtones that possessed him. A looser form would have captured nothing.

The choice of certain elements in the poem may seem arbitrary, but it is an arbitrariness without reference to their rightness and wrongness. That is, any choice would have been equally arbitrary, and, esthetically, equally right. In the second stanza of each section, for example, one is reminded of different kinds of chocolate and different shades of green, thus: rosy chocolate and paradisal green; chop-house chocolate and sham-like green; porcelain chocolate and uncertain green; musky chocolate and too-fluent green; Chinese chocolate and motley green. And each section gives us umbrellas variously gilt, sham, pied, frail, and large. The ocean is successively a machine which is perplexed, tense, tranced, dry, and obese. The ocean produces sea-blooms from the clouds, mortal massives of the blooms of water, silver petals of white blooms, figures of the clouds like blooms, and, finally, a wind of green blooms. These items, and many more, repeated and modified, at once impervious to and merging each in the other, make up the words of the poem. Directly they do nothing but rouse the small sensations and smaller feelings of atmosphere and tone. The poem itself, what it means, is somewhere in the background; we know it through the tone. The motley hue we see is crisped to "clearing opalescence."

> Then the sea
> And heaven rolled as one and from the two
> Came fresh transfigurings of freshest blue.

Here we have words used as a tone of feeling to secure the discursive evanescence of appearances; words bringing the senses into the mind which they created; the establishment of interior experience by the construction of its tone in words. In "Tattoo" (page 108), we have the opposite effect, where the mind is intensified in a simple visual image. The tone existed beforehand, so to speak, in the nature of the subject.

> The light is like a spider.
> It crawls over the water.
> It crawls over the edges of the snow.
> It crawls under your eyelids
> And spreads its webs there—
> Its two webs.
>
> The webs of your eyes
> Are fastened
> To the flesh and bones of you
> As to rafters or grass.
>
> There are filaments of your eyes
> On the surface of the water
> And in the edges of the snow.

The problem of language here hardly existed: the words make the simplest of statements, and the poet had only to avoid dramatizing what was already drama in itself, the sensation of the eyes in contact with what they looked at. By attempting *not* to set up a tone the tone of truth is secured for statements literally false. Fairy tales and Mother Goose use the same language. Because there is no point where the statements stop being true, they leap the gap unnoticed between literal truth and imaginative truth. It is worth observing that the strong sensual quality of the poem is defined without the use of a single sensual word; and it is that ambiguity between the words and their subject which makes the poem valuable.

There is nothing which has been said so far about Mr. Stevens' uses of language which might not have been said, with different examples, of any good poet equally varied and equally erudite[3]—by which I mean intensely careful of effects. We have been dealing with words primarily, and words are not limited either to an author or a subject. Hence they form unique data and are to be understood and commented on by themselves. You can hardly more compare two poets' use of a word than you can compare, profitably, trees to cyclones. Synonyms are accidental, superficial, and never genuine. Comparison begins to be possible at the level of more complicated tropes than may occur in single words.

Let us compare then, for the sake of distinguishing the kinds of import, certain tropes taken from Ezra Pound, T. S. Eliot, and Mr. Stevens.

From Mr. Pound—the first and third from the *Cantos* and the second from *Hugh Selwyn Mauberley*:

> In the gloom, the gold gathers the light against it.

> Tawn foreshores
> Washed in the cobalt of oblivion.

> A catalogue, his jewels of conversation.

From T. S. Eliot—one from "Prufrock," one from *The Waste Land*, and one from *Ash Wednesday*:

> I should have been a pair of ragged claws
> Scuttling across the floors of silent seas.

---

[3] See *Words and Idioms*, by Logan Pearsall Smith, Boston: Houghton Mifflin, 1926, page 121. "One of the great defects of our critical vocabulary is the lack of a neutral, non-derogatory name for these great artificers, these artists who derive their inspiration more from the formal than the emotional aspects of their art, and who are more interested in the masterly control of their material, than in the expression of their own feelings, or the prophetic aspects of their calling." Mr. Smith then suggests the use of the words erudite and erudition and gives as reason their derivation "from *erudire* (E 'out of,' and *rudis*, 'rude,' 'rough' or 'raw'), a verb meaning in classical Latin to bring out of the rough, to form by means of art, to polish, to instruct." Mr. Stevens is such an *erudite*; though he is often more, when he deals with emotional matters as if they were matters for *erudition*.

The awful daring of a moment's surrender
Which an age of prudence can never retract.

Struggling with the devil of the stairs who wears
The deceitful face of hope and of despair.

The unequaled versatility of Ezra Pound (Eliot in a dedication addresses him as *Il miglior fabbro*) prevents assurance that the three lines quoted from him are typical of all his work. At least they are characteristic of his later verse, and the kind of feeling they exhibit may be taken as Pound's own. Something like their effect may be expected in reading a good deal of his work.

The first thing to be noticed is that the first two tropes are visual images—not physical observation, but something to be seen in the mind's eye; and that as the images are so seen their meaning is exhausted. The third trope while not directly visual acts as if it were. What differentiates all three from physical observation is in each case the non-visual associations of a single word—*gathers*, which in the active voice has an air of intention; *oblivion*, which has the purely mental sense of forgetfulness; and, less obviously, *conversation*, in the third trope, which while it helps *jewels* to give the line a visual quality it does not literally possess, also acts to condense in the line a great many non-visual associations.

The lines quoted from T. S. Eliot are none of them in intention visual; they deal with a totally different realm of experience— the realm in which the mind dramatizes, at a given moment, its feelings toward a whole aspect of life. The emotion with which these lines charge the reader's mind is a quality of emotion which has so surmounted the senses as to require no longer the support of direct contact with them. Abstract words have reached the intensity of thought and feeling where the senses have been condensed into abstraction. The first distich is an impossible statement which in its context is terrifying. The language has sensual elements but as such they mean nothing: it is the act of abstract dramatization which counts. In the second and third distichs words such as *surrender* and *prudence, hope* and *despair*, assume, by their dramatization, a definite sensual force.

Both Eliot and Pound condense; their best verse is weighted—Pound's with sensual experience primarily, and Eliot's with beliefs. Where the mind's life is concerned the senses produce images, and beliefs produce dramatic cries. The condensation is important.

Mr. Stevens' tropes, in his best work and where he is most characteristic, are neither visual like Pound nor dramatic like Eliot. The scope and reach of his verse are no less but are different. His visual images never condense the matter of his poems; they either accent or elaborate it. His dramatic statements, likewise, tend rather to give another, perhaps more final, form to what has already been put in different language.

The best evidence of these differences is the fact that it is almost impossible to quote anything short of a stanza from Mr. Stevens without essential injustice to the meaning. His kind of condensation, too, is very different in character and degree from Eliot and Pound. Little details are left in the verse to show what it is he has condensed. And occasionally, in order to make the details fit into the poem, what has once been condensed is again elaborated. It is this habit of slight re-elaboration which gives the firm textural quality to the verse.

Another way of contrasting Mr. Stevens' kind of condensation with those of Eliot and Pound will emerge if we remember Mr. Stevens' *intentional* ambiguity. Any observation, as between the observer and what is observed, is the notation of an ambiguity. To Mr. Stevens the sky, "the basal slate," "the universal hue," which surrounds us and is always upon us is the great ambiguity. Mr. Stevens associates two or more such observations so as to accent their ambiguities. But what is ambiguous in the association is not the same as in the things associated; it is something new, and it has the air of something condensed. This is the quality that makes his poems grow, rise in the mind like a tide. The poems cannot be exhausted, because the words that make them, intentionally ambiguous at their crucial points, are themselves inexhaustible. Eliot obtains many of his effects by the sharpness of surprise, Pound his by visual definition; they tend to exhaust their words in the individual use, and they are successful because they know when to stop, they know when sharpness and definition lay most hold on their subjects, they know the maximal limit of their kinds of condensation. Mr. Stevens is just as precise in his kind; he brings ambiguity to the point of sharpness, of reality, without destroying, but rather preserving, clarified, the ambiguity. It is a difference in subject matter, and a difference in accent. Mr. Stevens makes you aware of how much is *already* condensed in any word.

The first stanza of "Sunday Morning" may be quoted (page 89). It should be remembered that the title is an integral part of the poem, directly affecting the meaning of many lines and generally controlling the atmosphere of the whole.

> Complacencies of the peignoir, and late
> Coffee and oranges in a sunny chair,
> And the green freedom of a cockatoo
> Upon a rug mingle to dissipate
> The holy hush of ancient sacrifice.
> She dreams a little, and she feels the dark
> Encroachment of that old catastrophe,
> As a calm darkens among water-lights.
> The pungent oranges and bright, green wings
> Seem things in some procession of the dead,
> Winding across wide water, without sound.
> The day is like wide water, without sound,
> Stilled for the passing of her dreaming feet
> Over the seas, to silent Palestine,
> Dominion of the blood and sepulchre.

A great deal of ground is covered in these fifteen lines, and the more the slow ease and conversational elegance of the verse are observed, the more wonder it seems that so much could have been indicated without strain. Visually, we have a woman enjoying her Sunday morning breakfast in a sunny room with a green rug. The image is secured, however, not as in Pound's image about the gold gathering the light against it, in directly visual terms, but by the almost casual combination of visual images with such phrases as *"complacencies of the peignoir,"* and *"the green freedom* of the cockatoo," where the italicized words are abstract in essence but rendered concrete in combination. More important, the purpose of the images is to show how they dissipate the "holy hush of ancient sacrifice," how the natural comfort of the body is aware but mostly unheeding that Sunday is the Lord's day and that it commemorates the crucifixion.

From her half-awareness she feels the more keenly the "old catastrophe" merging in the surroundings, subtly, but deeply, changing them as a "calm darkens among water-lights." The feeling is dark in her mind, darkens, changing the whole day. The oranges and the rug and the day all have the quality of "wide water, without sound," and all her thoughts, so loaded, turn on the crucifixion.

The transit of the body's feeling from attitude to attitude is managed in the medium of three water images. These images do not replace the "complacencies of the peignoir," nor change them; they act as a kind of junction between them and the Christian feeling traditionally proper to the day. By the time the stanza is over the water images have embodied both feelings. In their own way they make a condensation by appearing in company with and showing what was already condensed.

If this stanza is compared with the tropes quoted from Pound, the principal difference will perhaps seem that while Pound's lines define their own meaning and may stand alone, Mr. Stevens' various images are separately incomplete and, on the other hand, taken together, have a kind of completeness to which Pound's lines may not pretend: everything to which they refer is present. Pound's images exist without syntax, Mr. Stevens' depend on it. Pound's images are formally simple, Mr. Stevens' complex. The one contains a mystery, and the other, comparatively, expounds a mystery.

While it would be possible to find analogues to Eliot's tropes in the stanzas of "Sunday Morning," it will be more profitable to examine something more germane in spirit. Search is difficult and choice uncertain, for Mr. Stevens is not a dramatic poet. Instead of dramatizing his feelings, he takes as fatal the drama that he sees and puts it down either in its least dramatic, most meditative form, or makes of it a simple statement. Let us then frankly take as pure a meditation as may be found, "The Snow Man" (page 12), where, again, the title is integrally part of the poem:

[87

One must have a mind of winter
To regard the frost and the boughs
Of the pine-trees crusted with snow;

And have been cold a long time
To behold the junipers shagged with ice,
The spruces rough in the distant glitter

Of the January sun; and not to think
Of any misery in the sound of the wind,
In the sound of a few leaves,

Which is the sound of the land
Full of the same wind
That is blowing in the same bare place

For the listener, who listens in the snow,
And, nothing himself, beholds
Nothing that is not there and the nothing that is.

The last three lines are as near as Mr. Stevens comes to the peculiar dramatic emotion which characterizes the three tropes quoted from Eliot. Again, as in the passage compared to Pound's images, the effect of the last three lines depends entirely on what preceded them. The emotion is built up from chosen fragments and is then stated in its simplest form. The statement has the force of emotional language but it remains a statement—a modest declaration of circumstance. The abstract word *nothing*, three times repeated, is not in effect abstract at all; it is synonymous with the data about the winter landscape which went before. The part which is not synonymous is the emotion: the overtone of the word, and the burden of the poem. Eliot's lines,

> The awful daring of a moment's surrender
> Which an age of prudence can never retract,

like Pound's lines, for different reasons, stand apart and on their own feet. The two poets work in contrary modes. Eliot places a number of things side by side. The relation is seldom syntactical or logical, but is usually internal and sometimes, so far as the reader is concerned, fatal and accidental. He works in violent contrasts and produces as much by prestidigitation as possible. There was no reason in the rest of "Prufrock" why the lines about the pair of ragged claws should have appeared where they did and no reason, perhaps, why they should have appeared at all; but once they appeared they became for the reader irretrievable, complete in themselves, and completing the structure of the poem.

That is the method of a dramatic poet, who molds wholes out of parts themselves autonomous. Mr. Stevens, not a dramatic poet, seizes his wholes only in imagination; in his poems the parts are already connected. Eliot usually moves from point to point or between two termini. Mr. Stevens as a rule ends where he began; only when he is through, his beginning has become a chosen end. The differences may be exaggerated but in their essence is a true contrast.

If a digression may be permitted, I think it may be shown that the different types of obscurity found in the three poets are only different aspects of their modes of writing. In Pound's verse, aside from words in languages the reader does not know, most of the hard knots are tied round combinations of classical and historical references. A passage in one of the Cantos, for example, works up at the same time the adventures of a Provençal poet and the events in one of Ovid's *Metamorphoses*. If the reader is acquainted with the details of both stories, he can appreciate the criticism in Pound's combination. Otherwise he will remain confused: he will be impervious to the plain facts of the verse.

Eliot's poems furnish examples of a different kind of reference to and use of history and past literature. The reader must be familiar with the ideas and the beliefs and systems of feeling to which Eliot alludes or from which he borrows, rather than to the facts alone. Eliot does not restrict himself to criticism; he digests what he takes; but the reader must know what it is that has been digested before he can appreciate the result. The Holy Grail material in *The Waste Land* is an instance: like Tiresias, this material is a dramatic element in the poem.

Mr. Stevens' difficulties to the normal reader present themselves in the shape of seemingly impenetrable words or phrases which no wedge of knowledge brought from outside the body of Mr. Stevens' own poetry can help much to split. The wedge, if any, is in the words themselves, either in the instance alone or in relation to analogous instances in the same or other poems in the book. Two examples should suffice.

In "Sunday Morning," there is in the seventh stanza (page 93) a reference to the sun, to which men shall chant their devotion—

> Not as a god, but as a god might be,
> Naked among them, like a savage source.
> Their chant shall be a chant of paradise,
> Out of their blood, returning to the sky; . . .

Depending upon the reader this will or will not be obscure. But in any case, the full weight of the lines is not felt until the conviction of the poet that the sun is origin and ending for all life is shared by the reader. That is why the god might be naked among them. It takes only reading of the stanza, the poem, and other poems where the fertility of the sun is celebrated, to make the notion sure. The only bit of outside information that might help is the fact that in an earlier version this stanza concluded the poem. —In short, generally, you need only the dictionary and familiarity with the poem in question to clear up a good part of Mr. Stevens' obscurities.

The second example is taken from "The Man whose Pharynx was Bad" (page 128):

> Perhaps, if winter once could penetrate
> Through all its purples to the final slate.

Here, to obtain the full meaning, we have only to consult the sixth stanza of "Le Monocle de Mon Oncle" (page 18):

> If men at forty will be painting lakes
> The ephemeral blues must merge for them in one,
> The basic slate, the universal hue.
> There is a substance in us that prevails.

Mr. Stevens has a notion often intimated that the sky is the only permanent background for thought and knowledge; he would see things against the sky as a Christian would see them against the cross. The blue of the sky is the prevailing substance of the sky, and to Mr. Stevens it seems only necessary to look at the sky to share and be shared in its blueness.

If I have selected fairly types of obscurity from these poets, it should be clear that whereas the obscurities of Eliot and Pound are intrinsic difficulties of the poems, to which the reader must come well armed with specific sorts of external knowledge and belief, the obscurities of Mr. Stevens clarify themselves to the intelligence alone. Mode and value are different—not more or less valuable, but different. And all result from the concentrated language which is the medium of poetry. The three poets load their words with the maximum content; naturally, the poems remain obscure until the reader takes out what the poet puts in. What still remains will be the essential impenetrability of words, the bottomlessness of knowledge. To these the reader, like the poet, must submit.

Returning, this time without reference to Pound and Eliot, among the varieties of Mr. Stevens' tropes we find some worth notice which comparison will not help. In "Le Monocle de Mon Oncle," the ninth stanza (page 20), has nothing logically to do with the poem; it neither develops the subject nor limits it, but is rather a rhetorical interlude set in the poem's midst. Yet it is necessary to the poem, because its rhetoric, boldly announced as such, expresses the feeling of the poet toward his poem, and that feeling, once expressed, becomes incorporated in the poem.

> In verses wild with motion, full of din,
> Loudened by cries, by clashes, quick and sure
> As the deadly thought of men accomplishing
> Their curious fates in war, come, celebrate
> The faith of forty, ward of Cupido.
> Most venerable heart, the lustiest conceit
> Is not too lusty for your broadening.
> I quiz all sounds, all thoughts, all everything
> For the music and manner of the paladins

To make oblation fit. Where shall I find
Bravura adequate to this great hymn?

It is one of the advantages of a non-dramatic, meditative style, that pure rhetoric may be introduced into a poem without injuring its substance. The structure of the poem is, so to speak, a structure of loose ends, spliced only verbally, joined only by the sequence in which they appear. What might be fustian ornament in a dramatic poem, in a meditative poem casts a feeling far from fustian over the whole, and the slighter the relation of the rhetorical interlude to the substance of the whole, the more genuine is the feeling cast. The rhetoric does the same thing that the action does in a dramatic poem, or the events in a narrative poem; it produces an apparent medium in which the real substance may be borne.

Such rhetoric is not reserved to set interludes; it often occurs in lines not essentially rhetorical at all. Sometimes it gives life to a serious passage and cannot be separated without fatal injury to the poem. Then it is the trick without which the poem would fall flat entirely. Two poems occur where the rhetoric is the vital trope— "A High-Toned Old Christian Woman" (page 79), and "Bantams in Pine-Woods" (page 101), which I quote entire:

> Chieftain Iffucan of Azcan in caftan
> Of tan with henna hackles, halt!
>
> Damned universal cock, as if the sun
> Was blackamoor to bear your blazing tail.
>
> Fat! Fat! Fat! I am the personal.
> Your world is you. I am my world.
>
> You ten-foot poet among inchlings. Fat!
> Begone! An inchling bristles in these pines,
>
> Bristles, and points their Appalachian tangs,
> And fears not portly Azcan nor his hoos.

The first and last distichs are gauds of rhetoric; nevertheless they give not only the tone but the substance to the poem. If the reader is deceived by the rhetoric and believes the poem is no more than a verbal plaything, he ought not to read poetry except as a plaything. With a different object, Mr. Stevens' rhetoric is as ferociously comic as the rhetoric in Marlowe's *Jew of Malta*, and as serious. The ability to handle rhetoric so as to reach the same sort of intense condensation that is secured in bare, non-rhetorical language is very rare, and since what rhetoric can condense is very valuable it ought to receive the same degree of attention as any other use of language. Mr. Stevens' successful attempts in this direction are what make him technically most interesting. Simple language, dealing obviously with surds, draws emotion out of feelings; rhetorical language, dealing rather, or apparently, with inflections, employed with the same seriousness, creates a surface *equivalent* to an emotion by its approximately complete escape from the purely communicative function of language.[4]

We have seen in a number of examples that Mr. Stevens uses language in several different ways, either separately or in combination; and I have tried to imply that his success is due largely to his double adherence to words and experience as existing apart from his private sensibility. His great labor has been to allow the reality of what he felt personally to pass into the superior impersonal reality of words. Such a transformation amounts to an access of knowledge, as it raises to a condition where it may be rehearsed and understood in permanent form that body of emotional and sensational experience which in its natural condition makes life a torment and confusion.

With the technical data partly in hand, it ought now to be possible to fill out the picture, touch upon the knowledge itself, in Mr. Stevens' longest and most important poem, "The Comedian as the Letter C." Everywhere characteristic of Mr. Stevens' style and

---

[4]There is a point at which rhetorical language resumes its communicative function. In the second of "Six Significant Landscapes" (page 98), we have this image:

> A pool shines
> Like a bracelet
> Shaken at a dance,

which is a result of the startling associations induced by an ornamental, social, rhetorical style in dealing with nature. The image perhaps needs its context to assure its quality.

interests, it has the merit of difficulty—difficulty which when solved rewards the reader beyond his hopes of clarity.

Generally speaking the poem deals with the sensations and images, notions and emotions, ideas and meditations, sensual adventures and introspective journeyings of a protagonist called Crispin. More precisely, the poem expounds the shifting of a man's mind between sensual experience and its imaginative interpretation, the struggle, in that mind, of the imagination for sole supremacy and the final slump or ascent where the mind contents itself with interpreting plain and common things. In short, we have a meditation, with instances, of man's struggle with nature. The first line makes the theme explicit: "Nota: man is the intelligence of his soil, the sovereign ghost." Later, the theme is continued in reverse form: "His soil is man's intelligence." Later still, the soil is qualified as suzerain, which means sovereign over a semi-independent or internally autonomous state; and finally, at the end of the poem, the sovereignty is still further reduced when it turns out that the imagination can make nothing better of the world (here called a turnip), than the same insoluble lump it was in the beginning.

The poem is in six parts of about four pages each. A summary may replace pertinent discussion and at the same time preclude extraneous discussion. In Part I, called The World without Imagination, Crispin, who previously had cultivated a small garden with his intelligence, finds himself at sea, "a skinny sailor peering in the sea-glass." At first at loss and "washed away by magnitude," Crispin, "merest minuscule in the gales," at last finds the sea a vocable thing,

> But with a speech belched out of hoary darks
> Noway resembling his, a visible thing,
> And excepting negligible Triton, free
> From the unavoidable shadow of himself
> That elsewhere lay around him.

The sea "was no help before reality," only "one vast subjugating final tone," before which Crispin was made new. Concomitantly, with and because of his vision of the sea, "The drenching of stale lives no more fell down."

Part II is called Concerning the Thunder-Storms of Yucatan, and there, in Yucatan, Crispin, a man made vivid by the sea, found his apprehensions enlarged and felt the need to fill his senses. He sees and hears all there is before him, and writes fables for himself

> Of an aesthetic tough, diverse, untamed,
> Incredible to prudes, the mint of dirt,
> Green barbarism turning paradigm.

The sea had liberated his senses, and he discovers an earth like "A jostling festival of seeds grown fat, too juicily opulent," and a "new reality in parrot-squawks." His education is interrupted when a wind "more terrible than the revenge of music on bassoons," brings on a tropical thunder-storm. Crispin, "this connoisseur of elemental fate," identifies himself with the storm, finding himself free, which he was before, and "more than free, elate, intent, profound and studious" of a new self:

> the thunder, lapsing in its clap,
> Let down gigantic quavers of its voice,
> For Crispin to vociferate again.

With such freedom taken from the sea and such power found in the storm, Crispin is ready for the world of the imagination. Naturally, then, the third part of the poem, called Approaching Carolina, is a chapter in the book of moonlight, and Crispin "a faggot in the lunar fire." Moonlight is imagination, a reflection or interpretation of the sun, which is the source of life. It is also, curiously, this moonlight, North America, and specifically one of the Carolinas. And the Carolinas, to Crispin, seemed north; even the spring seemed arctic. He meditates on the poems he has denied himself because they gave less than "the relentless contact he desired." Perhaps the moon would establish the necessary liaison between himself and his environment. But perhaps not. It seemed

> Illusive, faint, more mist than moon, perverse,
> Wrong as a divagation to Peking. . . .

Moonlight was an evasion, or, if not,
A minor meeting, facile, delicate.

So he considers, and teeters back and forth, between the sun and
moon. For the moment he decides against the moon and imagination in favor of the sun and his senses. The senses, instanced by the
smell of things at the river wharf where his vessel docks, "round his
rude aesthetic out" and teach him "how much of what he saw he
never saw at all."

He gripped more closely the essential prose
As being, in a world so falsified,
The one integrity for him, the one
Discovery still possible to make,
To which all poems were incident, unless
That prose should wear a poem's guise at last.

In short, Crispin conceives that if the experience of the senses
is but well enough known, the knowledge takes the form of imagination after all. So we find as the first line of the fourth part, called
The Idea of a Colony, "Nota: his soil is man's intelligence," which
reverses the original statement that man is the intelligence of his
soil. With the new distinction illuminating his mind, Crispin plans
a colony, and asks himself whether the purpose of his pilgrimage is
not

to drive away
The shadow of his fellows from the skies,
And, from their stale intelligence released,
To make a new intelligence prevail?

The rest of the fourth part is a long series of synonymous tropes
stating instances of the new intelligence. In a torment of fastidious
thought, Crispin writes a prolegomenon for his colony. Everything
should be understood for what it is and should follow the urge of its
given character. The spirit of things should remain spirit and play
as it will.

> The man in Georgia waking among pines
> Should be pine-spokesman. The responsive man,
> Planting his pristine cores in Florida,
> Should prick thereof, not on the psaltery,
> But on the banjo's categorical gut.

And as for Crispin's attitude toward nature, "the melon should have apposite ritual" and the peach its incantation. These "commingled souvenirs and prophecies"—all images of freedom and the satisfaction of instinct—compose Crispin's idea of a colony. He banishes the masquerade of thought and expunges dreams; the ideal takes no form from these. Crispin will be content to "let the rabbit run, the cock declaim."

In Part V, which is A Nice Shady Home, Crispin dwells in the land, contented and a hermit, continuing his observations with diminished curiosity. His discovery that his colony has fallen short of his plan and that he is content to have it fall short, content to build a cabin,

> who once planned
> Loquacious columns by the ructive sea,

leads him to ask whether he should not become a philosopher instead of a colonizer.

> Should he lay by the personal and make
> Of his own fate an instance of all fate?

The question is rhetorical, but before it can answer itself, Crispin, sapped by the quotidian, sapped by the sun, has no energy for questions, and is content to realize, that for all the sun takes

> it gives a humped return
> Exchequering from piebald fiscs unkeyed.

Part VI, called And Daughters with Curls, explains the implications of the last quoted lines. The sun, and all the new intelligence which it enriched, mulcted the man Crispin, and in return gave him four daughters, four questioners and four sure answerers. He has been brought back to social nature, has gone to seed. The connoisseur of elemental fate has become himself an instance of all fate. He does not know whether the return was "Anabasis or slump, ascent or chute." His cabin—that is the existing symbol of his colony—seems now a phylactery, a sacred relic or amulet he might wear in memorial to his idea, in which his daughters shall grow up, bidders and biders for the ecstasies of the world, to repeat his pilgrimage, and come, no doubt, in their own cabins, to the same end.

Then Crispin invents his doctrine and clothes it in the fable about the turnip:

> The world, a turnip once so readily plucked,
> Sacked up and carried overseas, daubed out
> Of its ancient purple, pruned to the fertile main,
> And sown again by the stiffest realist,
> Came reproduced in purple, family font,
> The same insoluble lump. The fatalist
> Stepped in and dropped the chuckling down his craw,
> Without grace or grumble.

But suppose the anecdote was false, and Crispin a profitless philosopher,

> Glozing his life with after-shining flicks,
> Illuminating, from a fancy gorged
> By apparition, plain and common things,
> Sequestering the fluster from the year,
> Making gulped potions from obstreperous drops,
> And so distorting, proving what he proves
> Is nothing, what can all this matter since
> The relation comes, benignly, to its end.

> So may the relation of each man be clipped.

The legend or subject of the poem and the mythology it develops are hardly new nor are the instances, intellectually considered, very striking. But both the clear depth of conception and the extraordinary luxuriance of rhetoric and image in which it is expressed, should be at least suggested in the summary here furnished. Mr. Stevens had a poem with an abstract subject—man as an instance of fate, and a concrete experience—the sensual confusion in which the man is waylaid; and to combine them he had to devise a form suitable to his own peculiar talent. The simple statement—of which he is a master—could not be prolonged to meet the dimensions of his subject. To the dramatic style his talents were unsuitable, and if by chance he used it, it would prevent both the meditative mood and the accent of intellectual wit which he needed to make the subject his own. The form he used is as much his own and as adequate, as the form of *Paradise Lost* is Milton's or the form of *The Waste Land* is Eliot's. And as Milton's form filled the sensibility of one aspect of his age, Mr. Stevens' form fits part of the sensibility— a part which Eliot or Pound or Yeats do little to touch—of our own age.

I do not know a name for the form. It is largely the form of rhetoric, language used for its own sake, persuasively to the extreme. But it has, for rhetoric, an extraordinary content of concrete experience. Mr. Stevens is a genuine poet in that he attempts constantly to transform what is felt with the senses and what is thought in the mind—if we can still distinguish the two—into that realm of being, which we call poetry, where what is thought is felt and what is felt has the strict point of thought. And I call his mode of achieving that transformation rhetorical because it is not lyric or dramatic or epic, because it does not transcend its substance, but is a reflection upon a hard surface, a shining mirror of rhetoric.

In its nature depending so much on tone and atmosphere, accenting precise management of ambiguities, and dealing with the subtler inflections of simple feelings, the elements of the form cannot be tracked down and put in order. Perhaps the title of the whole poem, "The Comedian as the Letter C," is as good an example as any where several of the elements can be found together. The letter C is, of course, Crispin, and he is called a letter because he is small (he is referred to as "merest minuscule," which means small letter, in the first part of the poem) and because, though small, like a letter he stands for something—his colony, cabin, and children—as a comedian. He is a comedian because he deals finally with the quotidian (the old distinction of comedy and tragedy was between every-day and heroic subject matter), gorged with apparition, illuminating plain and common things. But what he deals with is not comic; the comedy, in that sense, is restricted to his perception and does not touch the things perceived or himself. The comedy is the accent, the play of the words. He is at various times a realist, a clown, a philosopher, a colonizer, a father, a faggot in the lunar fire, and so on. In sum, and any sum is hypothetical, he may be a comedian in both senses, but separately never. He is the hypothesis of comedy. He is a piece of rhetoric—a persona in words—exemplifying all these characters, and summing, or masking, in his persuasive style, the essential prose he read. He is the poem's guise that the prose wears at last.

Such is the title of the poem, and such is the poem itself. Mr. Stevens has created a surface, a texture, a rhetoric in which his feelings and thoughts are preserved in what amounts to a new sensibility. The contrast between his subjects—the apprehension of all the sensual aspects of nature as instances of fate—and the form in which the subjects are expressed is what makes his poetry valuable. Nature becomes nothing but words and to a poet words are everything.

New Thresholds, New Anatomies:

Notes on a Text of Hart Crane

[1 9 3 5]

I

It is a striking and disheartening fact that the three most ambitious poems of our time should all have failed in similar ways: in
composition, in independent objective existence, and in intelligibility of language. *The Waste Land*, the *Cantos*, and *The Bridge* all
fail to hang together structurally in the sense that "Prufrock," "Envoi,"
and "Praise for an Urn"—lesser works in every other respect—do
hang together. Each of the three poems requires of the reader that
he supply from outside the poem, and with the help of clues only,
the important, *controlling* part of what we may loosely call the
meaning. And each again deliberately presents passages, lines,
phrases, and single words which no amount of outside work can
illumine. The fact is striking because, aside from other considerations of magnitude, relevance, and scope, these are not the faults
we lay up typically against the great dead. The typical great poet is
profoundly rational, integrating, and, excepting minor accidents of
incapacity, a master of ultimate verbal clarity. Light, radiance, and
wholeness remain the attributes of serious art. And the fact is disheartening because no time could have greater need than our own
for rational art. No time certainly could surrender more than ours
does daily, with drums beating, to fanatic politics and despotically
construed emotions.

But let us desert the disheartening for the merely striking aspect, and handle the matter, as we can, within the realm of poetry, taking up other matters only tacitly and by implication. Let us say provisionally that in their more important works Eliot, Pound, and Crane lack the ultimate, if mythical, quality of aseity, that quality of completeness, of independence, so great that it seems underived and an effect of pure creation. The absence of aseity may be approached variously in a given poet; but every approach to be instructive, even to find the target at all, must employ a rational mode and the right weapon. These notes intend to examine certain characteristic passages of Hart Crane's poems as modes of language and to determine how and to what degree the effects intended were attained. The rationale is that of poetic language; the weapons are analysis and comparison. But there are other matters which must be taken up first before the language itself can be approached at all familiarly.

Almost everyone who has written on Crane has found in him a central defect, either of imagination or execution, or both. Long ago, in his Preface to *White Buildings*, Allen Tate complained that for all his talent Crane had not found a suitable theme. Later, in his admirable review of *The Bridge*, Yvor Winters brought and substantiated the charge (by demonstrating the exceptions) that even when he had found a theme Crane could not entirely digest it and at crucial points simply was unable to express it in objective form. These charges hold; and all that is here said is only in explication of them from a third point of view.

Waldo Frank, in his Introduction to the *Collected Poems*, acting more as an apologist than a critic, proffers two explanations of Crane's incompleteness as a poet, to neither of which can I assent, but of which I think both should be borne in mind. Mr. Frank believes that Crane will be understood and found whole when our culture has been restored from revolutionary collectivism to a predominant interest in the person; when the value of expressing the personal in the terms of the cosmic shall again seem supreme. This hypothesis would seem untenable unless it is construed as relevant to the present examination; when it runs immediately into the hands of the obvious but useful statement that Crane was interested in persons rather than the class struggle. Mr. Frank's other explanation is that Crane's poetry was based upon the mystical perception of the "organic continuity between the self and a seemingly chaotic world." Crane "was too virile to deny the experience of continuity; he let the world pour in; and since his nuclear self was not disciplined to detachment from his nerves and passions, he lived exacerbated in a constant swing between ecstasy and exhaustion." I confess I do not understand "organic continuity" in this context, and all my efforts to do so are defeated by the subsequent word "detachment." Nor can I see how this particular concept of continuity can be very useful without the addition and control of a thorough supernaturalism. The control for mystic psychology is theology, and what is thereby controlled is the idiosyncrasy of insight, not the technique of poetry.

What Mr. Frank says not-rationally can be usefully re-translated to that plane on which skilled readers ordinarily read good poetry; which is a rational plane; which is, on analysis, the plane of competent technical appreciation. Such a translation, while committing grave injustice on Mr. Frank, comes nearer doing justice to Crane. It restores and brings home the strictures of Tate and Winters, and it brings judgment comparatively back to the minute particulars (Blake's phrase) which are alone apprehensible. To compose the nuclear self and the seemingly chaotic world is to find a suitable theme, and the inability so to compose rises as much from immaturity and indiscipline of the major poetic uses of language as from personal immaturity and indiscipline. Baudelaire only rarely reached the point of self-discipline and Whitman never; but Baudelaire's language is both disciplined and mature, and Whitman's sometimes so. Les Fleurs du Mal are a profound poetic ordering of a life disorderly, distraught, and deracinated, a life excruciated, in the semantic sense of that word, to the extreme. And Whitman, on his side, by a very different use of language, gave torrential expression to the romantic disorder of life in flux, whereas his private sensibility seems either to have been suitably well-ordered or to have felt no need of order.

Whitman and Baudelaire are not chosen with reference to Crane by accident but because they are suggestively apposite. The suggestion may be made, not as blank truth but for the light there is in it, that Crane had the sensibility typical of Baudelaire and so misunderstood himself that he attempted to write *The Bridge* as if he had the sensibility typical of Whitman. Whitman characteristically let himself go in words, in any words and by all means the handiest, until his impulse was used up. Baudelaire no less characteristically caught himself up in his words, recording, ordering, and binding together the implications and tacit meanings of his impulse until in his best poems the words he used are, as I. A. Richards would say, inexhaustible objects of meditation. Baudelaire aimed at control, Whitman at release. It is for these reasons that the influence of Whitman is an impediment to the *practice* (to be distinguished from the reading) of poetry, and that the influence of Baudelaire is re-animation itself. (It may be noted that Baudelaire had at his back a well-articulated version of the Catholic Church to control the moral aspect of his meanings, where Whitman had merely an inarticulate pantheism.)

To apply this dichotomy to Crane is not difficult if it is done tentatively, without requiring that it be too fruitful, and without requiring that it be final at all. The clue of nexus is found, aside from the poems themselves, in certain prose statements. Letters are suspect and especially letters addressed to a patron, since the aim is less conviction by argument than the persuasive dramatization of an attitude. It is therefore necessary in the following extract from a letter to Otto Kahn that the reader accomplish a reduction in the magnitude of terms.

Of the section of *The Bridge* called "The Dance" Crane wrote: "Here one is on the pure mythical and smoky soil at last! Not only do I describe the conflict between the two races in this dance—I also became identified with the Indian and his world before it is over, which is the only method possible of ever really possessing the Indian and his world as a cultural factor." Etc. I suggest that, confronted with the tight, tense, intensely personal lyric quatrains of the verse itself, verse compact with the deliberately inarticulate interfusion of the senses, Crane's statement of intention has only an *ipse dixit* pertinence; that taken otherwise, taken as a living index of substance, it only multiplies the actual confusion of the verse and impoverishes its achieved scope. Taken seriously, it puts an impossible burden on the reader: the burden of reading two poems at once, the one that appears and the "real" poem which does not appear except by an act of faith. This would be reading by legerde-main, which at the moment of achievement must always collapse, self-obfuscated.

Again, in the same letter, Crane wrote that, "The range of *The Bridge* has been called colossal by more than one critic who has seen the ms., and though I have found the subject to be vaster than I had at first realized, I am still highly confident of its final articula-tion into a continuous and eloquent span. . . . *The Aeneid* was not written in two years—nor in four, and in more than one sense I feel justified in comparing the historical and cultural scope of *The Bridge* to that great work. It is at least a symphony with an epic theme, and a work of considerable profundity and inspiration."

The question is whether this was wishful thinking of the vague order commonest in revery, convinced and sincere statement of intention, or an effect of the profound duplicity—a deception in the very will of things—in Crane's fundamental attitudes toward his work; or whether Crane merely misunderstood the logical import of the words he used. I incline to the notion of duplicity, since it is beneath and sanctions the other notions as well; the very duplicity by which the talents of a Baudelaire appear to their possessor dis-guised and disfigured in the themes of a Whitman, the same fun-damental duplicity of human knowledge whereby an accustomed disorder seems the order most to be cherished, or whereby a religion which at its heart denies life enriches living. In the particular ref-erence, if I am right, it is possible to believe that Crane labored to perfect both the strategy and the tactics of language so as to animate and maneuver his perceptions—and then fought the wrong war and against an enemy that displayed, to his weapons, no vulnerable tar-get. He wrote in a language of which it was the virtue to accrete, modify, and interrelate moments of emotional vision—moments at which the sense of being gains its greatest access—moments at which, by the felt nature of knowledge, the revealed thing is its own mean-ing; and he attempted to apply his language, in his major effort, to a theme that required a sweeping, discrete, indicative, anecdotal language, a language in which, by force of movement, mere cata-loguing can replace and often surpass representation. He used the private lyric to write the cultural epic; used the mode of intensive contemplation, which secures ends, to present the mind's actions, which have no ends. The confusion of tool and purpose not only led him astray in conceiving his themes; it obscured at crucial moments the exact character of the work he was actually doing. At any rate we find most impenetrable and ineluctable, in certain places, the very matters he had the genius to see and the technique to clarify: the matters which are the substance of rare and valid emotion. The confusion, that is, led him to content himself at times with the mere cataloguing statement, enough for him because he knew the rest, of what required completely objective embodiment.

Another, if ancillary, method of enforcing the same suggestion (of radical confusion) is to observe the disparity between Crane's announced purpose and the masters he studied. Poets commonly profit most where they can borrow most, from the poets with whom by instinct, education, and accident of contact, they are most nearly unanimous. Thus poetic character is early predicted. In Crane's case, the nature of the influences to which he submitted himself remained similar from the beginning to the end and were the dominant ones of his generation. It was the influence of what we may call, with little exaggeration, the school of tortured sensibility—a school of which we perhaps first became aware in Baudelaire's misapprehension of Poe, and later, in the hardly less misapprehending resurrection of Donne. Crane benefited, and was deformed by, this influence both directly and by an assortment of indirection; but he never surmounted it. He read the modern French poets who are the result of Baudelaire, but he did not read Racine of whom Baudelaire was himself a product. He read Wallace Stevens, whose strength and serenity may in some sense be assigned to the combined influence of the French moderns and, say, Plato; but he did not, at least affectively, read Plato. He read Eliot, and through and in terms of him, the chosen Elizabethans—though more in Donne and Webster than in Jonson and Middleton; but he did not, so to speak, read the Christianity from which Eliot derives his ultimate strength, and by which he is presently transforming himself. I use the word *read* in a strong sense; there is textual evidence of reading throughout the poems. The last influence Crane exhibited is no different in character and in the use to which he put it than the earliest: the poem called "The Hurricane" derives immediately from the metric of Hopkins but not ultimately from Hopkins' integrating sensibility. Thus Crane fitted himself for the exploitation of the peculiar, the unique, the agonized and the tortured perception, and he developed language-patterns for the essentially incoherent aspects of experience: the aspects in which experience assaults rather than informs the sensibility. Yet, granting his sensibility, with his avowed epic purpose he had done better had he gone to school to Milton and Racine, and, in modern times, to Hardy and Bridges—or even Masefield—for narrative sweep.

Crane had, in short, the wrong masters for his chosen fulfillment, or he used some of the right masters in the wrong way: leeching upon them, as a poet must, but taking the wrong nourishment, taking from them not what was hardest and most substantial—what made them great poets—but taking rather what was easiest, taking what was peculiar and idiosyncratic. That is what kills so many of Crane's poems, what must have made them impervious, once they were discharged, even to himself. It is perhaps, too, what killed Crane the man—because in a profound sense, to those who use it, poetry is the only means of putting a tolerable order upon the emotions. Crane's predicament—that his means defeated his ends—was not unusual, but his case was extreme. In more normal form it is the predicament of immaturity. Crane's mind was slow and massive, a cumulus of substance; it had, to use a word of his own, the synergical quality, and with time it might have worked together, clarified, and become its own meaning. But he hastened the process and did not survive to maturity.

Certainly there is a hasty immaturity in the short essay on Modern Poetry, reprinted as an appendix to the *Collected Poems*, an immaturity both in the intellectual terms employed and in the stress with which the attitude they rehearse is held. Most of the paper tilts at windmills, and the lance is too heavy for the wielding hand. In less than five pages there is deployed more confused thinking than is to be found in all his poems put together. Poetry is not, as Crane says it is, an architectural art—or not without a good deal of qualification; it is a linear art, an art of succession, and the only art it resembles formally is plain song. Nor can Stravinsky and the cubists be compared, as Crane compares them, in the quality of their abstractions with the abstractions of mathematical physics: the aims are disparate; expression and theoretic manipulation can never exist on the same plane. Nor can psychological analyses, in literature, be distinguished in motive and quality from dramatic analyses. Again, and finally, the use of the term *psychosis* as a laudatory epithet for the substance of Whitman, represents to me the uttermost misconstruction of the nature of poetry: a psychosis is a mental derangement not due to an organic lesion or neurosis. A theory of neurosis (as, say, Aiken has held it in *Blue Voyage*) is more tenable scientifically; but neither it seems to me has other than a stultifying critical use. Yet, despite the confusion and positive irrationality of Crane's language the general tendency is sound, the aspiration sane. He wanted to write good poetry and his archetype was Dante; that is enough. But in his prose thinking he had the wrong words for his thoughts, as in his poetry he had often the wrong themes for his words.

I I

So far, if the points have been maintained at all, what I have written adds up to the suggestion that in reading Hart Crane we must make allowances for him—not historical allowances as we do for Shakespeare, religious allowances as for Dante and Milton, or philosophical as for Goethe and Lucretius—but fundamental allowances whereby we agree to supply or overlook what does not appear in the poems, and whereby we agree to forgive or guess blindly at those parts of the poems which are unintelligible. In this Crane is not an uncommon case, though the particular allowances may perhaps be unique. There are some poets where everything is allowed for the sake of isolated effects. Sedley is perhaps the supreme example in English; there is nothing in him but two lines, but these are famous and will always be worth saving. Waller is the more normal example, or King, where two or three poems are the whole gist. Crane has both poems and passages; and in fact there is hardly a poem of his which has not something in it, and a very definite something, worth saving.

The nature of that saving quality, for it saves him no less than ourselves, Crane has himself most clearly expressed in a stanza from the poem called "Wine Menagerie."

> New thresholds, new anatomies! Wine talons
> Build freedom up about me and distill
> This competence—to travel in a tear
> Sparkling alone, within another's will.

I hope to show that this stanza illustrates almost inexhaustibly, to minds at all aware, both the substance and the aspiration of Crane's poetry, the character and value of his perceptions, and his method of handling words to control them. If we accept the stanza as a sort of declaration of policy and apply it as our own provisional policy to the sum of his work, although we limit its scope we shall deepen and articulate our appreciation—a process, that of appreciation, which amounts not to wringing a few figs from thistles but to expressing the wine itself.

Paraphrase does not greatly help. We can, for the meat of it, no more be concerned with the prose sense of the words than Crane evidently was. Crane habitually re-created his words from within, developing meaning to the point of idiom; and that habit is the constant and indubitable sign of talent. The meanings themselves are the idioms and have a twist and life of their own. It is only by ourselves meditating on and *using* these idioms—it is only by emulation—that we can master them and accede to their life.

Analysis, however, does help, and in two directions. It will by itself increase our intimacy with the words as they appear; and it will as the nexus among comparisons disclose that standard of achievement, inherent in this special use of poetic language, by which alone the value of the work may be judged. (Analysis, in these uses, does not cut deep, it does not cut at all: it merely distinguishes particulars; and the particulars must be re-seen in their proper focus before the labor benefits.)

Moving in the first direction, toward intimacy, we can say that Crane employed an extreme mode of free association; that operation among words where it is the product rather than the addition that counts. There was, for example, no logical or emotional connection between thresholds and anatomies until Crane verbally juxtaposed them and tied them together with the cohesive of his meter. Yet, so associated, they modify and act upon each other mutually and produce a fresh meaning of which the parts cannot be segregated. Some latent, unsuspected part of the cumulus of meaning in each word has excited, so to speak, and affected a corresponding part in the other. It is the juxtaposition which is the agent of selection, and it is a combination of meter and the carried-over influence of the rest of the poem, plus the as yet undetermined expectations aroused, which is the agent of emphasis and identification. It should be noted that, so far as the poem is concerned, the words themselves contain and do not merely indicate the feelings which compose the meaning; the poet's job was to put the words together like bricks in a wall. In lesser poetry of the same order, and in poetry of different orders, words may only indicate or refer to or substitute for the feelings; then we have the poetry of vicarious statement, which takes the place of, often to the highest purpose, the actual complete presentation, such as we have here. Here there is nothing for the words to take the place of; they are their own life, and have an organic continuity, not with the poet's mind nor with the experience they represent, but with themselves. We see that thresholds open upon anatomies: upon things to be explored and understood and felt freshly as an adventure; and we see that the anatomies, what is to be explored, are known from a new vantage, and that the vantage is part of the anatomy. The separate meanings of the words fairly rush at each other; the right ones join and those irrelevant to the juncture are for the moment—the whole time of the poem—lost in limbo. Thus the association "New thresholds, new anatomies!" which at first inspection might seem specious or arbitrary (were we not used to reading poetry) not only does not produce a distortion but, the stress and strain being equal, turns out wholly natural and independently alive.

In the next phrase the association of the word "talons" with the context seems less significantly performed. So far as it refers back and expresses a seizing together, a clutching by a bird of prey, it is an excellent word well-chosen and spliced in. The further notion, suggested by the word "wine," of release, would also seem relevant. There is, too, an unidentifiable possibility—for Crane used words in very special senses indeed—of "talons" in the sense of cards left after the deal; and there is even, to push matters to the limit, a bare chance that some element of the etymon—ankle, heel—has been pressed into service. But the possibilities have among them none specially discriminated, and whichever you choose for use, the dead weight of the others must be provisionally carried along, which is what makes the phrase slightly fuzzy. And however you construe "wine talons" you cannot, without distorting what you have and allowing for the gap or lacuna of what you have not, make your construction fit either or both of the verbs which it governs. Talons neither build nor distill even when salvation by rhyme is in question. If Crane meant—as indeed he may have—that wines are distilled and become brandies or spirits, then he showed a poverty of technique in using the transitive instead of the intransitive form. Objection can be carried too far, when it renders itself nugatory. These remarks are meant as a kind of exploration; and if we now make the allowance for the unidentified distortion and supply with good will the lacuna in the very heart of the middle phrases, the rest of the stanza becomes as plain and vivid as poetry of this order need ever be. To complete the whole association, the reader need only remember that Crane probably had in mind, and made new use of, Blake's lines:

> For a Tear is an Intellectual Thing,
> And a Sigh is the Sword of an Angel King.

It is interesting to observe that Blake was talking against war and that his primary meaning was much the same as that expressed negatively in "Auguries of Innocence" by the following couplet:

> He who shall train the Horse to War
> Shall never pass the Polar Bar.

Crane ignored the primary meaning, and extracted and emphasized what was in Blake's image a latent or secondary meaning. Or possibly he combined—made a free association of—the intellectual tear with

> Every Tear from Every Eye
> Becomes a Babe in Eternity;

only substituting the more dramatic notion of will for intellect. What is important to note is that, whatever its origin, the meaning as Crane presents it is completely transformed and subjugated to the control of the "new thresholds, new anatomies!"

The stanza we have been considering is only arbitrarily separated from the whole poem—just as the poem itself ought to be read in the context of the whole *White Buildings* section. The point is, that for appreciation—and for denigration—all of Crane should be read thoroughly, at least once, with similar attention to detail. That is the way in which Crane worked. Later readings may be more liberated and more irresponsible—as some people read the Bible for what they call its poetry or a case history for its thrill; but they never get either the poetry or the thrill without a preliminary fundamental intimacy with the rational technique involved. Here it is a question of achieving some notion of a special poetic process. The principle of association which controls this stanza resembles the notion of wine as escape, release, father of insight and seed of metamorphosis, which controls the poem; and, in its turn, the notion of extralogical, intoxicated metamorphosis of the senses controls and innervates Crane's whole sensibility.

To illustrate the uniformity of approach, a few examples are presented, some that succeed and some that fail. In "Lachrymae Christi" consider the line

> Thy Nazarene and tinder eyes.

(Note, from the title, that we are here again concerned with tears as the vehicle-image of insight, and that, in the end, Christ is identified with Dionysus.) Nazarene, the epithet for Christ, is here used as an adjective of quality in conjunction with the noun tinder also used as an adjective; an arrangement which will seem baffling only to those who underestimate the seriousness with which Crane remodeled words. The first three lines of the poem read:

> Whitely, while benzine
> Rinsings from the moon
> Dissolve all but the windows of the mills.

Benzine is a fluid, cleansing and solvent, has a characteristic tang and smart to it, and is here associated with the light of the moon, which, through the word "rinsings," is itself modified by it. It is, I think, the carried-over influence of benzine which gives startling aptness to Nazarene. It is, if I am correct for any reader but myself, an example of suspended association, or telekinesis; and it is, too, an example of syllabic interpenetration or internal punning as habitually practiced in the later prose of Joyce. The influence of one word on the other reminds us that Christ the Saviour cleanses and solves and has, too, the quality of light. "Tinder" is a simpler instance of how Crane could at once isolate a word and bind it in, impregnating it with new meaning. Tinder is used to kindle fire, powder, and light; a word incipient and bristling with the action proper to its being. The association is completed when it is remembered that tinder is very nearly a homonym for tender and, *in this setting*, puns upon it.

   Immediately following, in the same poem, there is a parenthesis which I have not been able to penetrate with any certainty, though the possibilities are both fascinating and exciting. The important words in it do not possess the excluding, limiting power over themselves and their relations by which alone the precise, vital element in an ambiguity is secured. What Crane may have meant privately cannot be in question—his words may have represented for him a perfect tautology; we are concerned only with how the words act upon each other—or fail to act—so as to commit an appreciable meaning. I quote the first clause of the parenthesis.

> Let sphinxes from the ripe
> Borage of death have cleared my tongue
> Once and again . . .

It is syntax rather than grammar that is obscure. I take it that "let" is here a somewhat homemade adjective and that Crane is making a direct statement, so that the problem is to construe the right meanings of the right words in the right references; which will be an admirable exercise in exegesis, but an exercise only. The applicable senses of "let" are these: neglected or weary, permitted or prevented, hired, and let in the sense that blood is let. Sphinxes are inscrutable, have secrets, propound riddles to travelers and strangle those who cannot answer. "Borage" has at least three senses: something rough (sonantly suggestive of barrage and barrier), a blue-flowered, hairy-leaved plant, and a cordial made from the plant. The Shorter Oxford Dictionary quotes this jingle from Hooker: "I Borage always bring courage." One guess is that Crane meant something to the effect that if you meditate enough on death it has the same bracing and warming effect as drinking a cordial, so that the riddles of life (or death) are answered. But something very near the contrary may have been intended; or both. In any case a guess is ultimately worthless because, with the defective syntax, the words do not verify it. Crane had a profound feeling for the hearts of words, and how they beat and cohabited, but here they overtopped him; the meanings in the words themselves are superior to the use to which he put them. The operation of selective cross-pollination not only failed but was not even rightly attempted. The language remains in the condition of that which it was intended to express: in the flux of intoxicated sense; whereas the language of the other lines of this poem here examined—the language, not the sense—is disintoxicated and candid. The point is that the quality of Crane's success is also the quality of his failure, and the distinction is perhaps by the hair of accident.

In the part of The Bridge called "Virginia," and in scores of places elsewhere, there is a single vivid image, of no structural importance, but of great delight as ornament: it both fits the poem and has a startling separate beauty of its own, the phrase: "Peonies with pony manes." [1] The freshness has nothing to do with accurate observation, of which it is devoid, but has its source in the arbitrary

[1] Compare Marianne Moore's "the lion's ferocious chrysanthemum head."

character of the association: it is created observation. Another example is contained in

> Down Wall, from girder into street noon leaks,
> A rip-tooth of the sky's acetylene;

which is no more forced than many of Crashaw's best images. It is, of course, the pyramiding associations of the word acetylene that create the observation: representing as it does an intolerable quality of light and a torch for cutting metal, and so on.

Similarly, again and again, both in important and in ornamental phrases, there are effects only half secured, words which are not the right words but only the nearest words. E.g.: "What eats the pattern with *ubiquity*. . . . Take this *sheaf* of dust upon your tongue . . . Preparing *penguin* flexions of the arms . . . [A tugboat] with one *galvanic* blare . . . I heard the *hush of lava wrestling* your arms." Etc. Not that the italicized words are wrong but that they fall short of the control and precision of impact necessary to vitalize them permanently.

There remains to consider the second help of analysis (the first was to promote intimacy with particulars), namely, to disclose the standard of Crane's achievement in terms of what he actually accomplished; an effort which at once involves comparison of Crane with rendered possibilities in the same realm of language taken from other poets. For Crane was not alone; style, like knowledge, of which it is the expressive grace, is a product of collaboration; and his standard, whether consciously or not, was outside himself, in verse written in accord with his own bent: which the following, if looked at with the right eye, will exemplify.

> Sunt lacrimae rerum et mentem mortalia tangunt.—*Vergil.*

> Lo giorno se n'andava, e l'aer bruno
>   toglieva gli animai, che sono in terra,
>   dalle fatiche loro.—*Dante.*

> A brittle glory shineth in his face;
> As brittle as the glory is the face.—*Shakespeare.*

Adieu donc, chants du cuivre et soupirs de la flûte!
Plaisirs, ne tentez plus un coeur sombre et boudeur!
Le Printemps adorable a perdu son odeur!—*Baudelaire*.

But Love has pitched his mansion in
The place of excrement;
For nothing can be sole or whole
That has not been rent.—*Yeats*.

She dreams a little, and she feels the dark
Encroachment of that old catastrophe,
As a calm darkens among water-lights.—*Stevens*.

The relevant context is assumed to be present, as we have been assuming it all along with Crane. Every quotation, except that from Yeats which is recent, should be well known. They bring to mind at once, on one side, the sustaining, glory-breeding power of magnificent form joined to great intellect. Before that impact Crane's magnitude shrinks. On the other side, the side of the particulars, he shrinks no less. The significant words in each selection, and so in the lines themselves, will bear and require understanding to the limit of analysis and limitless meditation. Here, as in Crane, words are associated by the poetic process so as to produce a new and living, an idiomatic, meaning, differing from and surpassing the separate factors involved. The difference—which is where Crane falls short of his standard—is this. Crane's effects remain tricks which can only be resorted to arbitrarily. The effects in the other poets—secured by more craft rather than less—become, immediately they are understood, permanent idioms which enrich the resources of language for all who have the talent to use them. It is perhaps the difference between the immediate unbalance of the assaulted, intoxicated sensibility and the final, no less exciting, clarity of the sane, mirroring sensibility.

It is said that Crane's inchoate heart and distorted intellect only witness the disease of his generation; but I have cited two poets, if not of his generation still his contemporaries, who escaped the contagion. It is the stigma of the first order of poets (a class which includes many minor names and deletes some of the best known) that they master so much of life as they represent. In Crane the poet succumbed with the man.

What judgment flows from these strictures need not impede the appreciation of Crane's insight, observation, and intense, if confused, vision, but ought rather to help determine it. Merely because Crane is imperfect in his kind is no reason to give him up; there is no plethora of perfection, and the imperfect beauty, like life, retains its fascination. And there is about him, too—such were his gifts for the hearts of words, such the vitality of his intelligence—the distraught but exciting splendor of a great failure.

The Method of

Marianne Moore

[1 9 3 5]

In making a formal approach to Marianne Moore, that is in deliberately drawing back and standing aside from the flux and fabric of long reading to see where the flux flowed and how the fabric was made, what at once predominates is the need for special terms and special adjustments to meet the texture and pattern of her poems. So only can the substance be reconciled and brought home to the general body of poetry; so only, that is, can the substance be made available and availing. The facts are clear enough and many of them even obvious to a wakened attention; the problem is to name them with names that both discriminate her work and relate it—if only in parallel—to other work with which it is cognate. Time and wear are the usual agents of this operation, whereby mutual interpenetration is effected between the new and old—always to be re-discriminated for closer contact—and the new becomes formally merely another resource of the art. Here we may assist and provisionally anticipate a little the processes of time and wear. What we make is a fiction to school the urgency of reading; no more; for actually we must return to the verse itself in its own language and to that felt appreciation of it to which criticism affords only overt clues.

In making up our own fiction let us turn first to some of those with which Miss Moore herself supplies us; which we may do all the more readily and with less wariness because she is so plainly responsible and deliberate in her least use of language—being wary only not to push illustrations past intention, insight, and method, into the dark. Substance is the dark, otherwise to be known.[1] And this is itself the nub of the first illustration. I quote complete "The Past is the Present."[2]

> If external action is effete
>   and rhyme is outmoded,
>   I shall revert to you,
> Habakkuk, as on a recent occasion I was goaded
>   into doing by XY, who was speaking of unrhymed verse.
> This man said—I think that I repeat
>   his identical words:
>   'Hebrew poetry is
> prose with a sort of heightened consciousness.' Ecstasy affords
>   the occasion and expediency determines the form.

It is a delicate matter to say here only the guiding thing, both to avoid expatiation and to point the issue. I wish of course to enforce the last period, very possibly in a sense Miss Moore might not expect, yet in Miss Moore's terms too. A poem, so far as it is well-made for its own purpose, predicts much of which the author was not aware; as a saw cannot be designed for *all* its uses. Nor do the predictions emerge by deviling scripture, but rather by observation of the organic development of the words as they play upon each other. A poem is an idiom and surpasses the sum of its uses.[3]

---

[1] As Matthew Arnold distinguished between descriptions of nature written in "the Greek way" and those written in "the faithful way," and made his distinction fruitful, we might, without being too solemn about it, distinguish between the content of verse taken on a rational, conventional plane, and the content, itself non-rational and unique, which can be reached only *through* the rational form and conventional scaffold.

[2] Text of all quotations from *Selected Poems*, with an Introduction by T. S. Eliot, New York, The Macmillan Co., 1935. This differs from the earlier *Observations* (New York, The Dial Press, 1925) by the addition of eight poems and the omission of fourteen. Most of the reprinted poems have been revised slightly, one or two considerably, and one is entirely rewritten and much expanded.

[3] Put the other way round we can borrow, for what it is worth, a mathematician's definition of number and apply it to poetry. A poem is, we can say, like any number, "the class of all classes having the properties of a given class"; it is ready for all its uses, but is itself "only" the class to which the uses belong. The analogue should not be pushed, as its virtue is in its incongruity and as afterthought.

For ease of approach let us take the last and slightest fact first. In Miss Moore's work inverted commas are made to perform significantly and notably and with a fresh nicety which is part of her contribution to the language. Besides the normal uses to determine quotation or to indicate a special or ironic sense in the material enclosed or as a kind of minor italicization, they are used as boundaries for units of association which cannot be expressed by grammar and syntax. They are used sometimes to impale their contents for close examination, sometimes to take their contents as in a pair of tongs for gingerly or derisive inspection, sometimes to gain the isolation of superiority or vice versa—in short for all the values of setting matter off, whether in eulogy or denigration. As these are none of them arbitrary but are all extensions and refinements of the common uses, the reader will find himself carried along, as by rhyme, to full appreciation. Which brings us with undue emphasis to the inverted commas in this poem. In earlier versions the last three lines were enclosed; here the second sentence, which is crucial to the poem, stands free, and thus gains a strength of isolation without being any further from its context, becoming in fact nearer and having a more direct relation to the *whole* poem: so much so that the earlier pointing must seem to have been an oversight. Once part of what the man said, part of his identical words, it is now Miss Moore's or the poem's comment on what the man said and the conclusion of the poem. So read, we have in this sentence not only a parallel statement to the statement about Hebrew poetry but also a clue to the earlier lines. It is what the rest of the poem builds to and explains; and it in its turn builds back and explains and situates the rest of the poem. And it is the pointing, or at any rate the comparison of the two pointings, which makes this clear. If it were a mere exercise of Miss Moore's and our own in punctuation, then as it depended on nothing it would have nothing to articulate. But Miss Moore's practice and our appreciation are analogous in scope and importance to the score in music. By a refinement of this notion Mr. Eliot observes in his Introduction that "many of the poems are in exact, and sometimes complicated formal patterns, and move with the elegance of a minuet." It is more than that and the very meat of the music, and one need not tire of repeating it because it *ought* to be obvious. The pattern establishes, situates, and organizes material which without it would have no life, and as it enlivens it becomes inextricably a part of the material; it participates as well as sets off. The only difficulty in apprehending this lies in our habit of naming only the conventional or abstract aspects of the elements of the pattern, naming never their enactment.[4]

So far we exemplify generally that ecstasy affords the occasion and expediency determines the form. We perceive the occasion and seize the nearest peg to hang the form on, which happened to be the very slight peg of inverted commas. Working backward, we come on Hebrew poetry and Habakkuk, one of its more rhetorical practitioners. Hebrew poetry (not to say the Bible) is used throughout Miss Moore's work as a background ideal and example of poetic language, an ideal, however, not directly to be served but rather kept in mind for impetus, reference, and comparison. A good part of the poem "Novices" is eulogy of Hebrew poetry. Here, in this poem, we have Habakkuk, who has a special as well as a representative business. As a poet Habakkuk was less than the Psalmist or Solomon or Job; nor had he the pith of the Proverbs or the serenity of Ecclesiastes. His service here is in the fact that he was a prophet of the old school, a praiser of gone times, a man goaded, as Miss Moore is, into crying out against the spiritual insufficience and formal decay of the times. The goading was the occasion of his ecstasy; anathema and prayer his most expedient—his most satisfactory—form. Miss Moore is speaking of matters no less serious; she couples external action and rhyme; and for her the expedient form is a pattern of elegant balances and compact understatement. It is part of the virtue of her attack upon the formless in life and art that the attack should show the courtesy and aloofness of formal grace. There is successful irony, too, in resorting through masterly rhymes to Habakkuk, who had none, and who would no doubt have thought them jingling and effete. (The rhymes have also the practical function of binding the particles of the poem. The notions which compound the poem mutually modify each other, as Coleridge and Mr. Richards would prescribe, and reach an equivalence; and the medium

[4] Whether this is a defect of language or of thinking I leave to I. A. Richards who alone has the equipment (among critics) and the will to determine.

in which the modifications flow or circulate is emphasized and echoed in the rhymes.)

We note above that external action and rhyme are coupled, a juxtaposition which heightens the importance of each. If we conceive Habakkuk presiding upon it the import of the association should become clear. In the first line, "If external action is effete," the word *effete* is a good general pejorative, would have been suitable for Habakkuk in his capacity of goaded prophet. External action is the bodying forth of social life and when we call it effete we say the worst of it. Effete is a word much used of civilizations in decline— Roman, Byzantine, Persian—to represent that kind of sophistication which precedes the relapse into barbarism. What is effete may yet be bloody, stupid, and cruel, and its very refinements are of these. In the effete is the *flowering* of the vicious, a flowering essentially formless because without relation to the underlying substance. Thus, by Habakkuk, we find the morals implicit in the poem. Again, the poem may be taken declaratively (but only if it is tacitly held to include the implicit); if society and literature are in such shape that I cannot follow immediate traditions, well, I shall appeal to something still older. It is all the same. Ecstasy affords the occasion and expediency determines the form, whether I think of life or art.

I have, I think, laid out in terms of a lowered consciousness, a good deal of the material of this poem; but the reader need not think the poem has disappeared or its least fabric been injured. It is untouched. Analysis cannot touch but only translate for preliminary purposes the poem the return to which every sign demands. What we do is simply to set up clues which we can name and handle and exchange whereby we can make available all that territory of the poem which we cannot name or handle but only envisage. We emphasize the technique, as the artist did in fact, in order to come at the substance which the technique employed. Naturally, we do not emphasize all the aspects of the technique since that would involve discussion of more specific problems of language than there are words in the poem, and bring us, too, to all the problems of meaning which are *not* there.[5] We select, rather, those formal

[5]A perspective of just such a literally infinite labor is presented in I. A. Richards' *Mencius and the Mind,* which is fascinating but engulfing; as the opposite perspective is presented by

aspects which are most readily demonstrable: matters like rhyme and pattern and punctuation, which appear to control because they accompany a great deal else; and from these we reach necessarily, since the two cannot be detached except in the confusion of controversy, into the technical aspects, the conventional or general meanings of the words arranged by the form: as exemplified here by Habakkuk and the word effete. We show, by an analysis which always conveniently stops short, a selection of the ways in which the parts of a poem bear on each other; and we believe, by experience, that we thereby become familiar with what the various tensions produce: the poem itself. This belief is of an arbitrary or miraculous character, and cannot be defended except by customary use. It should perhaps rather be put that as the poet requires his technique (which is not his knowledge) before he can put his poem on paper, so the reader requires a thorough awareness of technique (which again is not *his* knowledge) before he can read the poem. However that may be—and the best we can do is a doubtful scaffold of terms—the point here is that all that can ever actually be brought into the discussion of a poem is its technical aspects. Which happens in all but the best poetry to be very near the whole of it. Here, in Miss Moore's poem, "The Past is the Present," we might provisionally risk the assertion that the last line is the surd of the "poetry" in it. The rest both leads up to it and is suffused by it. The rest is nothing without it; and it would itself remain only a dislocated aphorism, lacking poetry, without the rest. "Ecstasy affords the occasion and expediency determines the form."

As it happens the line is actually pertinent as a maxim for Miss Moore's uncollected poetics; its dichotomy is at the intellectual base of all her work; and if we examine next the poem called "Poetry" we shall find Miss Moore backing us up in carefully measured understatement neatly placed among expedient ornament. But let us put off examination of the poem as such, and consider first what there is in it that may be translated to intellectual terms. The poem

the same author (with C. K. Ogden) in various works on Basic English, which combines the discipline of ascetic poverty with the expansiveness of, in a few hundred words, verbal omniscience. But I quote from Miss Moore's "Picking and Choosing," with I hope no more solemnity than the text affords: "We are not daft about the meaning but this familiarity with wrong meanings puzzles one."

will outlast us and we shall come to it perhaps all the more sensitively for having libeled it; and it may indeed luckily turn out that our libel is the subject of the poem: that certainly will be the underlying set of argument. To translate is to cross a gap and the gap is always dark. Well then, whatever the injustice to the poem and to Miss Moore as an esthetician, the following notions may be abstracted from the text for purposes of discourse and amusement. Since these purposes are neither dramatic nor poetic the order in which the notions are here displayed is not that in which they appear in the poem.

Miss Moore's poem says, centrally, that we cannot have poetry until poets can be "literalists of the imagination." The phrase is made from one in W. B. Yeats's essay, "William Blake and the Imagination." The cogent passage in Yeats reads: "The limitation of his [Blake's] view was from the very intensity of his vision; he was a too literal realist of the imagination, as others are of nature; and because he believed that the figures seen by the mind's eye, when exalted by inspiration, were 'eternal essences,' symbols or divine essences, he hated every grace of style that might obscure their lineaments." Yeats first printed his essay in 1897; had he written it when he wrote his postscript, in 1924, when he, too, had come to hate the graces which obscure, he would, I think, have adopted Miss Moore's shorter and wholly eulogistic phrase and called Blake simply a "literalist of the imagination,"[6] and found some other words to explain Blake's excessively arbitrary symbols. At any rate, in Miss Moore's version, the phrase has a bearing on the poem's only other overt reference, which is to Tolstoy's exclusion of "business documents and school books" from the field of poetry. Here her phrase leads to a profound and infinitely spreading distinction. Poets who can present, as she says they must, "imaginary gardens with real toads in them," ought also to be able to present, and indeed will if their interest lies that way, real school books and documents. The whole flux of experience and interpretation is appropriate subject matter to an imagination *literal* enough to see the poetry in it; an

---

[6]My quotation is taken from the collected edition of Yeats's essays, New York, 1924, page 147; Miss Moore's reference, which I have not checked, was to the original *Ideas of Good and Evil*, printed some twenty years earlier by A. H. Bullen.

imagination, that is, as intent on the dramatic texture (on what is involved, is tacit, is immanent) of the quotidian, as the imagination of the painter is intent, in Velásquez, on the visual texture of lace. One is reminded here, too, of T. S. Eliot's dogma in reverse: "The spirit killeth; the letter giveth life"; and as with Eliot the result of his new trope is to refresh the original form by removing from it the *dead* part of its convention, so Miss Moore's object is to exalt the imagination at the expense of its conventional appearances. Her gardens are imaginary, which makes possible the reality of her toads. Your commonplace mind would have put the matter the other way round—with the good intention of the same thing—and would have achieved nothing but the sterile assertion of the imagination as a portmanteau of stereotypes: which is the most part of what we are used to see carried, by all sorts of porters, as poetic baggage.

It is against them, the porters and their baggage, that Miss Moore rails when she begins her poem on poetry with the remark: "I, too, dislike it: there are things that are important beyond all this fiddle." But in the fiddle, she discovers, there is a place for the genuine. Among the conventions of expression there is the possibility of vivid, particularized instances:

> Hands that can grasp, eyes
> that can dilate, hair that can rise
> if it must,

and so on. Such hands, hair, and eyes are, we well know, props and crises of poetastry, and are commonly given in unusable, abstract form, mere derivative gestures we can no longer feel; as indeed their actual experience may also be. They remain, however, exemplars of the raw material of poetry. If you take them literally and make them genuine in the garden of imagination, then, as the poem says, "you are interested in poetry." You have seen them in ecstasy, which is only to say beside themselves, torn from their demeaning context; and if you are able to give them a new form or to refresh them with an old form—whichever is more expedient—then you will have accomplished a poem.

Perhaps I stretch Miss Moore's intentions a little beyond the pale; but the process of her poem itself I do not think I have stretched at all—have merely, rather, presented one of the many possible descriptions by analogue of the poetic process she actually employs. The process, like any process of deliberate ecstasy, involves for the reader as well as the writer the whole complex of wakened sensibility, which, once awakened, must be both constrained and driven along, directed and freed, fed and tantalized, sustained by reason to the very point of seeing, in every rational datum—I quote from another poem, "Black Earth"—the "beautiful element of unreason under it." The quotidian, having been shown as genuine, must be shown no less as containing the strange, as saying more than appears, and, even more, as containing the print of much that cannot be said at all. Thus we find Miss Moore constantly presenting images the most explicit but of a kind containing inexhaustibly the inexplicable—whether in gesture or sentiment. She gives what we know and do not know; she gives in this poem, for example, "elephants pushing, a wild horse taking a roll, a tireless wolf under a tree," and also "the baseball fan, the statistician." We can say that such apposites are full of reminding, or that they make her poem husky with unexhausted detail, and we are on safe ground; but we have not said the important thing, we have not named the way in which we are illuminated, nor shown any sign at all that we are aware of the major operation performed—in this poem (elsewhere by other agents)—by such appositions. They are as they succeed the springboards—as when they fail they are the obliterating quicksands—of ecstasy. In their variety and their contrasts they force upon us two associated notions; first we are led to see the elephant, the horse, the wolf, the baseball fan, and the statistician, as a group or as two groups detached by their given idiosyncrasies from their practical contexts, we see them beside themselves, for themselves alone, like the lace in Velásquez or the water-lights in Monet; and secondly, I think, we come to be aware, whether consciously or not, that these animals and these men are themselves, in their special activities, obsessed, freed, and beside themselves. There is an exciting quality which the pushing elephant and the baseball fan have in common; and our excitement comes in feeling that quality, so integral to the apprehension of life, as it were beside and for itself, not in the elephant and the fan, but in terms of the apposition in the poem.

Such matters are not credibly argued and excess of statement perhaps only confuses import and exaggerates value. As it happens, which is why this poem is chosen rather than another, the reader can measure for himself exactly how valuable this quality is; he can read the "same" poem with the quality dominant and again with the quality hardly in evidence. On page 31 in *Observations* the poem appears in thirteen lines; in *Selected Poems* it has either twenty-nine or thirty, depending on how you count the third stanza. For myself, there is the difference between the poem and no poem at all, since the later version delivers—where the earlier only announces—the letter of imagination. But we may present the differences more concretely, by remarking that in the earlier poem half the ornament and all the point are lacking. What is now clearly the dominant emphasis—on poets as literalists of the imagination—which here germinates the poem and gives it career, is not even implied in the earlier version. The poem did not get that far, did not, indeed, become a poem at all. What is now a serious poem on the nature of esthetic reality remained then a half-shrewd, half-pointless conceit against the willfully obscure. But it is not, I think, this rise in level from the innocuous to the penetrating, due to any gain in the strength of Miss Moore's conception. The conception, the idea, now that we know what it is, may be as readily inferred in the earlier version as it is inescapably felt in the later, but it had not in the earlier version been articulated and composed, had no posture to speak of, had lacked both development and material to develop: an immature product. The imaginary garden was there but there were no real toads in it.

What we have been saying is that the earlier version shows a failure in the technique of making a thought, the very substantial failure to know when a thought is complete and when it merely adverts to itself and is literally insufficient. There is also—as perhaps there must always be in poetry that fails—an accompanying insufficience of verbal technique, in this instance an insufficience of pattern and music as compared to the later version. Not knowing, or for the moment not caring, what she had to do, Miss Moore had no way of choosing and no reason for using the tools of her trade. Miss Moore is to an extent a typographic poet, like Cummings or

Hopkins; she employs the effects of the appearance and arrangement of printed words as well as their effects sounding in the ear:
her words are in the end far more *printed* words than the words of
Yeats, for example, can ever be. And this is made clear by the earlier version which lacks the *printed* effect rather than by the later
version which exhibits it. When we have learned how, we often do
not notice what we appreciate but rather what is not there to *be*
appreciated.

But if we stop and are deliberate, by a stroke cut away our
intimacy with the poem, and regard it all round for its physiog-
nomy, an object with surfaces and signs, we see immediately that
the later version looks better on the page, has architecture which
springs and suggests deep interiors; we notice the rhymes and the
stanza where they are missing and how they multiply heavily, *both
to the ear and the eye*, in the last stanza; we notice how the phrasing
is marked, how it is shaded, and how, in the nexus of the first and
second stanzas, it is momentarily confused: we notice, in short, not
how the poem was made—an operation intractable to any description—but what about it, now that it is made, will strike and be felt
by the attentive examiner. Then turning back to the earlier version,
knowing that it has pretty much the same heart, gave as much occasion for ecstasy, we see indefeasibly why it runs unpersuasively through
the mind, and why the later, matured version most persuasively
invades us. It is no use saying that Miss Moore has herself matured—
as evidence the notion is inadmissible; the concept or idea or thought
of the poem is not difficult, new or intense, but its presentation, in
the later version, is all three. She found, as Yeats would say, the
image to call out the whole idea; that was one half. The other half
was finding how to dress out the image to its best advantage, so as
to arouse, direct, sustain, and consolidate attention.

That is not, or hardly at all, a question of Miss Moore's personal maturity; as may be shown, I think, if we consult two poems,
presumably more or less as early as the earlier version of "Poetry."
One is a poem which Miss Moore omits from her *Selected Poems*,
but which Mr. Eliot neatly reprints in his Introduction, called "The
Talisman." In the light of what we have been saying, Miss Moore
was right in omitting it (as she was mainly right in omitting thirteen

other poems); it lacks the fundamental cohesiveness of a thing made complete: with a great air of implying everything, it implies almost nothing. Yet Mr. Eliot was right in quoting it, and for the reasons given; it shows a mastery of heavy rhyme which produces its fatal atmosphere, and it shows that authoritative manner of speech-English which is one device to achieve persuasion. But the omission is more justifiable than the quotation; the substantial immaturity of the poem diseases the maturity of the form and makes it specious, like the brightness of fevered eyes.

The other poem, "Silence," which I quote, Miss Moore reprints verbatim except for the addition of a single letter to perfect the grammar and the omission of double quotes in the next to last line.

> My father used to say,
> 'Superior people never make long visits,
> have to be shown Longfellow's grave
> or the glass flowers at Harvard.
> Self-reliant like the cat—
> that takes its prey to privacy,
> the mouse's limp tail hanging like a shoelace from its mouth—
> they sometimes enjoy solitude,
> and can be robbed of speech
> by speech that has delighted them.
> The deepest feeling always shows itself in silence;
> not in silence, but restraint.'
> Nor was he insincere in saying, 'Make my house your inn.'
> Inns are not residences.

There was no reason for change, only for scruples maintained and minute scrutiny; for the poem reaches that limit of being—both in the life of what it is about and in that other, musical life which is the play of a special joining of words—which we call maturity. It is important to emphasize here what commonly we observe last, namely the magnitude or scope of the poem; otherwise the sense of its maturity is lost. The magnitude is small but universal within the universe of those who distinguish cultivated human relations, which leaves us all the room we need to grow while reading the poem; and which signifies, too, that we should only diminish the value and injure the genuineness of the poem if we held its magnitude greater, its reach further. Thus the reader must contribute his sense of its maturity to the poem before it can be situated, before, as Wallace Stevens says, we can "let be be finale of seem."

There is here the spirit of an old controversy which we need not re-enter, but which we ought to recognize in order to pass it by: the controversy about young men writing great poems and old men going to seed, about Wordsworth of the Lyrical Ballads and Wordsworth wordsworthian. It is a popular controversy in various senses of that adjective. A more pertinent phrasing of the seminal problem, by which we should escape the false controversy, is, I think, a phrasing in terms of the question of maturity; and the point is that there are various orders of maturity with complex mutually related conditions required to produce each. There are the broad and obvious classes of conditions which we list under the heads of technical competence and underlying import; but we do not, in actual poems, ever have import without competence or competence without import. Trouble rises from the confusion of import with intellectually demonstrable content, and technical competence with *mere* skill of execution. The music of words alone may lift common sentiment to great import, e.g., Take, O take those lips away; or at any rate we are faced with much great poetry which has only commonplace intellectual content and yet affects our fundamental convictions. Again—and I do not mean to leave the realm of poetry—we have, as an example of halfway house, such things as the best speeches in *The Way of the World*, where an effect like that of music and like that of thought, too, is had without full recourse to either, but rather through the perfection of the spoken word alone. And at the other end we have the great things in the great poets that do not *appear* to depend upon anything but their own barest bones. It is hard here to give an example beyond suspicion. There is Paolo's speech at the end of *Inferno* V, Blake's Time is the mercy of eternity, Shakespeare's Ripeness is all, perhaps the Epilogue to *The Poetaster*. The point is that a balance must be struck of complex conditions so that nothing is too much and nothing not enough; but most of all it must be remembered that the balance of conditions which produced maturity in one place will not necessarily produce it in another.

Nor is it just to judge the maturity of one poem by standards brought from another order of poetry; nor, lastly, does the maturity of a poem alone determine its magnitude. Drayton's "The Parting," the ballad "Waly Waly," and *Antony and Cleopatra*, are all, and equally, mature poetry. *Hamlet*, we say, has a sick place in it, and for us the first part of the first act of *King Lear* is puerile; but we do not judge *Hamlet* and *Lear* in terms of Drayton or the balladist, although we may, for certain purposes, apply to them the special perfection of *Antony*. Maturity is the touchstone of achievement, not of magnitude.

Returning to Miss Moore's "Silence," let us see if we can what balance it is she has struck to bring it to a maturity which makes the question of magnitude for the moment irrelevant. The outer aids and props familiar in her best verse are either absent or negligible. The poem has no imposed, repetitive pattern, no rhyme for emphasis or sound, it calls particularly neither upon the eye nor the ear; it ignores everywhere the advantage of referring the reader, for strength, to any but the simplest elements of overt form—the rudiment of continuous iambic syllabification, which prevails in all but one line. Only one phrase—that about the mouse's limp tail—is specifically characteristic of Miss Moore; all the rest of the phrasing represents cultivated contemporary idiom, heightened, as we see at first glance, because set apart.

Here is one of the secrets—perhaps we ought to say one of the dominant fixed tropes—of Miss Moore's verse; and it is here what she has relied upon almost altogether. She resorts, or rises like a fish, continually to the said thing, captures it, sets it apart, points and polishes it to bring out just the special quality she heard in it. Much of her verse has the peculiar, unassignable, indestructible authority of speech overheard—which often means so much precisely because we do not know what was its limiting, and dulling, context. The quality in her verse that carries over the infinite possibilities of the overheard, is the source and agent of much of her power to give a sense of invading reality; and it does a good deal to explain what Mr. Eliot, in his Introduction, calls her authoritativeness of manner—which is a different thing from a sense of reality.

It does not matter that Miss Moore frequently works the other way round, abstracting her phrase from a guidebook, an advertisement, or a biography; what matters is that whatever her sources she treats her material as if it were quoted, isolated speech, and uses it, not as it was written or said—which cannot be known—but for the purpose which, taken beside itself, seems in it paramount and most appropriate. In "Silence" she takes phrases from Miss A. M. Homans and from Prior's life of Edmund Burke, and combines them in such a way that they declare themselves more fully, because isolated, emphasized, and lit by the incongruous image of the cat and mouse, than either could have declared themselves in first context. The poet's labor in this respect is similar to that of a critical translation where, by selection, exclusion, and rearrangement a sense is emphasized which was found only on a lower level and diffusely in the original; only here there is no damage by infidelity but rather the reward of deep fidelity to what, as it turns out, was really there waiting for emphasis.

But besides the effect of heightened speech, Miss Moore relies also and as deeply upon the rhetorical device of understatement— by which she gains, as so many have before her, a compression of substance which amounts to the fact of form. Form is, after all, the way things are put, and it may be profitably though not finally argued that every device of saying is an element in the form of what is said, whether it be detachable and predictable like the stress of a syllable or inextricable and innate like the tone of a thought. Understatement is a misnomer in every successful instance, as it achieves exactly what it pretends not to do: the fullest possible order of statement consonant with the mode of language employed. In such classic examples as Shakespeare's "The rest is silence," or Wordsworth's "But oh, the difference to me!" who shall suggest that more could have been said another way? who rather will not believe that it is in phrases such as these that the radical failure of language (its inability ever explicitly to *say* what is in a full heart) is overcome? Never, surely, was there a poorer name for such a feat of imagination: what we call understatement is only secured when we have charged ordinary words with extraordinary content, content not naturally in words at all. But they must be the right words nonetheless. Did not Shakespeare and Wordsworth really state to the limit matters for which there are no large words, matters which must, to be apprehended at all, be invested in common words?

Such is the archetype, the seminal expectation of understatement, and Miss Moore's poem, on its special plane, subscribes to it. But we are here concerned more with its subordinate, its ancillary uses—with its composition with operative irony and with its use to avoid a *conventional form* while preserving the conventional intention in all freshness. These are the uses with which we are familiar in daily life—crassly in sarcasm and finely in shrewd or reasonable wit; and it is on the plane of daily life and what might be said there—only heightened and rounded off for inspection—that this poem is written. It is part of the understatement, in the sense here construed, that superior people should be compared not to the gods accredited to the great world but to the cat carrying a mouse into a corner. The advantage is double. By its very incongruity—its quaintness, if you will—the comparison forces into prominence the real nature of the following notion of chosen solitude. We cut away immediately all that does not belong to the business of the poem; and find ourselves possessed of a new point of view thrown up and "justified" by the contrast. By a proud irony, content barely to indicate itself, the conventional views of solitude and intimacy are both destroyed and re-animated. A similar effect is secured in the last two lines—perhaps most emphatically in the choice of the word *residences*, itself, in this context, an understatement for the emotional word *homes* that detonates far more than the word *homes* could have done.

Finally, it is perhaps worth noting that "Make my house your inn" is both an understatement and a different statement of Burke's intention. Burke did not have the glass flowers, nor cats proud with mice, preceding his invitation: "Throw yourself into a coach," said he. "Come down and make my house your inn." But Miss Moore heard the possibility and set it free with all it implied. That is the poem. As the reader agrees that it is successful without recourse to the traditional overt forms of the art, he ought perhaps to hold that its virtue rises from recourse to the mystery, the fount of implication, in the spoken word combined with a special use of understatement. It makes a sample of the paradigm in its purest order, but hardly its least complex. The ecstasy was of speech, the expediency the greatest economy of means—as it happened in this poem, understatement. Yet as it is genuine, the spirit of its imagination is seen through the letter of what the speech might say.

All this is meant to be accepted as a provisional statement of Miss Moore's practical esthetic—to denominate the ways her poems are made and to suggest the variety of purposes they serve. As it is acceptable, subject to modification and growth in any detail, it should be applicable elsewhere in her work, and if applied make intimacy easier. It may be profitable in that pursuit to examine lightly a selection of the more complex forms—both outward and inward—in which her work is bodied. Miss Moore is a poet bristling with notable facts—especially in the technical quarter—and it would be shameful in an essay at all pretentious not to make some indication of their seductiveness and their variety.

She is an expert in the visual field at compelling the incongruous association to deliver, almost startlingly to ejaculate, the congruous, completing image: e.g., in the poem about the pine tree called "The Monkey Puzzle,"—"It knows that if a nomad may have dignity, Gibraltar has had more"; "the lion's ferocious chrysanthemum head seeming kind in comparison"; and "This porcupine-quilled, complicated starkness." The same effect is seen with greater scope in the first stanza of "The Steeple-Jack."

> Dürer would have seen a reason for living
>   in a town like this, with eight stranded whales
> to look at; with the sweet sea air coming into your house
> on a fine day, from water etched
>   with waves as formal as the scales
> on a fish.

Here the incongruity works so well as perhaps to be imperceptible. The reader beholds the sea as it is for the poem, but also as it never was to a modern (or a sailor's) eye, with the strength and light of all he can remember of Dürer's water-etchings, formal and "right" as the scales on a fish. It is the same formal effect, the Dürer vision, that sets the continuing tone, as the moon sets the tide (with the sun's help), for the whole poem, bringing us in the end an emotion as clean, as ordered, as startling as the landscape which yields it.

> It could not be dangerous to be living
> in a town like this, of simple people,
> who have a steeple-jack placing danger signs by the church
> while he is gilding the solid
> pointed star, which on a steeple
> stands for hope.

In "The Hero," which is complementary to "The Steeple-Jack" and with it makes "Part of a Novel, Part of a Poem, Part of a Play,"[7] we have another type of association, on the intellectual plane, which *apparently* incongruous, is at heart surprising mainly because it is so exact. Some men, says Miss Moore, have been "lenient, looking upon a fellow creature's error with the feelings of a mother—a woman or a cat." The "cat" refines, selects and—removing the sentimental excess otherwise associated with "mother" in similar contexts—establishes the gesture and defines, in the apposition, the emotion. It is a similar recognition of identic themes in the apparently incongruous—though here the example is more normal to poetic usage—that leads to her defining statement about the Hero.

> He's not out
> seeing a sight but the rock
> crystal thing to see—the startling El Greco
> brimming with inner light—that
> covets nothing that it has let go.

What Mr. Eliot puts into his Introduction about Miss Moore's exploitation of some of the less common uses of rhyme—besides stress-rhyme, rhyme against the metric, internal auditory rhyme, light rhyme—should excite the reader who has been oblivious to

---

[7]Something a hasty reader might miss is that (page 2, bottom) the Steeple-Jack, so orderly in his peril, might be part of a novel, and that the frock-coated Negro (page 5, top) might, with his sense of mystery, be part of a play. The text is "part of a poem." Miss Moore's titles are often the most elusive parts of her poems.

pursuit and the reader who has been aware to perusal. Here let us merely re-enforce Mr. Eliot with an example or so, and half an addition to his categories.

In the stanza from "The Hero" just quoted there is the paradigm for a rhyme-sound refrain which the well-memoried ear can catch. The first and last two lines of this and every other stanza rhyme on the sound of long "o," some light and some heavy. It is a question whether devices of this order integrally affect the poem in which they occur. If they do affect it, it must be in a manner that can neither be named nor understood, suffusing the texture unascertainably. But such devices do not need to be justified as integrating forces. It is enough for appreciation that this example should set up, as it does, a parallel music to the strict music of the poem which cannot be removed from it once it is there any more than it can be surely brought into it. It is part of the poem's weather. The Provençal poets worked largely in this order of rhyme, and in our own day Wallace Stevens has experimented with it.

Although many of the poems are made on intricate schemes of paired and delayed rhymes—there being perhaps no poem entirely faithful to the simple quatrain, heroic, or couplet structure—I think of no poem which for its rhymes is so admirable and so alluring as "Nine Nectarines and Other Porcelain." Granting that the reader employs a more analytical pronunciation in certain instances, there is in the last distich of each stanza a rhyme half concealed and half overt. These as they are first noticed perhaps annoy and seem, like the sudden variations, trills, mordents and turns in a Bach fugue, to distract from the theme, and so, later, to the collected ear, seem all the more to enhance it, when the pleasure that may be taken in them for themselves is all the greater. More precisely, if there be any ears too dull, Miss Moore rhymes the penultimate syllable of one line with the ultimate syllable of the next. The effect is of course cumulative: but the cumulus is of delicacy not mass; it is cumulative, I mean, in that in certain stanzas there would be no rhyme did not the precedent pattern make it audible. If we did not have

> a bat is winging. It
> is a moonlight scene, bringing . . .

we should probably not hear

> and sets of Precious Things
> dare to be conspicuous.

What must be remembered is that anyone can arrange syllables, the thing is to arrange syllables at the same time you write a poem, and to arrange them as Miss Moore does, on four or five different planes at once. Here we emphasize mastery on the plane of rhyme. But this mastery, this intricacy, would be worthless did the poem happen to be trash.

Leaving the technical plane—at least in the ordinary sense of that term—there is another order of facts no less beguiling, the facts of what Miss Moore writes about—an order which has of course been touched on obliquely all along. What we say now must be really as oblique as before, no matter what the immediacy of approach; there is no meeting Miss Moore face to face in the forest of her poems and saying This is she, this is what she means and is: tautology is not the right snare for her or any part of her. The business of her poetry (which for us is herself) is to set things themselves delicately conceived in relations so fine and so accurate that their qualities, mutually stirred, will produce a new relation: an emotion. Her poems answer the question, What will happen in poetry, what emotion will transpire, when these things have been known or felt beside each other? The things are words and have qualities that may be called on apart from the qualities of the objects they name or connect. Keats's odes are composed on the same method, and Milton's *Lycidas*. But there are differences which must be mastered before the identity can be seen.

For Keats the nightingale was a touchstone and a liberating symbol; it let him pour himself forth and it gave him a free symbol under which to subsume his images and emotions; the nightingale was a good peg of metonymy, almost, when he was done, a good synecdoche. For his purposes, the fact that he had a nightingale to preside over his poem gave the poem a suffusing order; and in the end everything flows into the nightingale.

With Miss Moore, in such poems as "An Octopus," "England,"

"The Labours of Hercules," "The Monkeys," and "The Plumet Basilisk," there is less a freeing of emotions and images under the aegis of the title notion, than there is a deliberate delineation of specific poetic emotions with the title notion as a starting point or spur: a spur to develop, compare, entangle, and put beside the title notion a series of other notions, which may be seen partly for their own sakes in passing, but more for what the juxtapositions conspire to produce. Keats's emotions were expansive and general but given a definite symbolic form; Miss Moore's emotions are special and specific, producing something almost a contraction of the given material, and so are themselves their own symbols. The distinction is exaggerated, but once seized the reader can bring it down to earth. Put another way, it is comparatively easy to say what Keats's poem is about, or what it is about in different places: it is about death and love and nostalgia, and about them in ways which it is enough to mention to understand. It is not easy to say what one of Miss Moore's longer poems is about, either as a whole or in places. The difficulty is not because we do not know but precisely because we do know, far more perfectly and far more specifically than we know anything about Keats's poem. What it is about is what it does, and not at any one place but all along. The parts stir each other up (where Keats put stirring things in sequence) and the aura of agitation resulting, profound or light as it may be, is what it is about. Naturally, then, in attempting to explain one of these poems you find yourself reading it through several times, so as not to be lost in it and so that the parts will not only follow one another as they must, being words, but will also be beside one another as their purpose requires them to be. This perhaps is why Miss Moore could write of literature as a phase of life: "If one is afraid of it, the situation is irremediable; if one approaches it familiarly what one says of it is worthless."

It is a method not a formula; it can be emulated not imitated; for it is the consequence of a radical leaning, of more than a leaning an essential trope of the mind: the forward stress to proceed, at any point, to proceed from one thing to another, crossing all gaps regardless, but keeping them all in mind. The poem called "The Monkeys" (in earlier versions "My Apish Cousins") has monkeys in the first line only. We proceed at once to "zebras supreme in their

abnormality," and "elephants with their fog-coloured skin"; proceed, that is, with an abstract attribution and a beautifully inner-
vated visual image. But the monkeys were not there for nothing;
they signify the zoo and they establish an air for the poem that blows
through it taking up a burden, like seeds, as it passes. I cannot say
how the monkeys perform their function. But if it could be told it
would not help; no more than it helps to say that the poem is composed not only on a rhyme and a typographic but also on a rigidly
syllabic pattern. The first line of each stanza has fifteen syllables
and the second sixteen; the third lines have ten, and the last, with
which they balance, ten; and the fifth lines, except in the third
stanza with thirteen, have fifteen. The fact of syllabic pattern has a
kind of tacit interest, but we cannot say whether we can appreciate
it, because we do not know whether even the trained ear can catch
the weight of variations of this order. The monkeys are in a different
position, and even if we cannot say in blueprint words what it is,
we know that the interest is functional because we can report the
fact of its experience.

More could be said—and in description a poem merely difficult and complex enough to require deep and delicately adjusted
attention might seem a labyrinth; but let us rather move to a different poem, "An Octopus," and there select for emphasis a different
aspect of the same method. This is a poem, if you like, about the
Rocky Mountain Parks, Peaks, Fauna, and Flora; it is also about
the Greek mind and language, and a great deal else. It contains
material drawn from illustrated magazines, travel books, Cardinal
Newman, Trollope, Richard Baxter's *The Saint's Everlasting Rest*
(a book used in a dozen poems), W. D. Hyde's *Five Great Philosophies*, the Department of the Interior Rules and Regulations, and a
remark overheard at the circus. Composed in free rhythm, natural
cadence, and lines terminated by the criteria of conversational or
rhetorical sense, it has a resemblance in form and typical content to
certain of the Cantos of Ezra Pound; a resemblance strong enough
to suggest that Pound may have partly derived his method from Miss
Moore. The dates do not make derivation impossible, and the changes
in structure from the earlier to the later Cantos confirm the suggestion. The pity in that case is that Pound did not benefit more; for

there is a wide difference in the level and value of the effects secured. The elements in Pound's Cantos, especially the later ones, remain as I have argued elsewhere essentially disjunct because the substance of them is insufficiently present in the text; whereas in Miss Moore's poems of a similar order, and especially in "An Octopus," although themselves disjunct and even inviolate, coming from different countries of the mind, the substances are yet sufficiently present in the poem to compel conspiracy and co-operation. You cannot look in the words of a poem and see two objects really side by side without seeing a third thing, which will be specific and unique. The test, if reference can again be made to "Poetry," is in the genuineness of the presentation of the elements:[8] there must be real toads in the imaginary garden. Miss Moore has a habit of installing her esthetics in her poems as she goes along, and in "An Octopus" she pleads for neatness of finish and relentless accuracy, both in mountains and in literature; and the mountain has also, what literature ought to have and Miss Moore does have, a capacity for fact. These notions only refine the notion of the letter of the imagination. The point here is that the notions about the treatment of detail explain why Pound's later Cantos seem diffuse in character and intangible in import and why Miss Moore's poem has a unity that grows with intimacy.

There are more aspects of Miss Moore's method as there are other lights in which to see it, but enough has been touched on here to show what the method is like, that it is not only pervasive but integral to her work. It is integral to the degree that, with her sensibility being what it is, it imposes limits more profoundly than it liberates poetic energy. And here is one reason—for those who like reasons—for the astonishing fact that none of Miss Moore's poems attempt to be major poetry, why she is content with smallness in fact so long as it suggests the great by implication. Major themes are not susceptible of expression through a method of which it is the virtue to produce the idiosyncratic in the fine and strict sense of that word. Major themes, by definition of general and predominant interest, require for expression a method which produces

[8] Mr. Eliot in his Introduction and Mr. Kenneth Burke in a review agree in finding genuineness paramount in Miss Moore's work.

the general in terms not of the idiosyncratic but the specific, and require, too, a form which seems to *contain* even more than to *imply* the wholeness beneath. The first poem in the present collection, "Part of a Novel, Part of a Poem, Part of a Play," comes as near to major expression as her method makes possible; and it is notable that here both the method and the content are more nearly "normal" than we are used to find. Elsewhere, though the successful poems achieve their established purposes, her method and her sensibility, combined, transform her themes from the normal to the idiosyncratic plane. The poem "Marriage," an excellent poem, is never concerned with either love or lust, but with something else, perhaps no less valuable, but certainly, in a profound sense, less complete.

Method and sensibility ought never, in the consideration of a poet, to be kept long separate, since the one is but the agent of growth and the recording instrument of the other. It is impossible to ascertain the stress of sensibility within the individual and it is an injustice to make the attempt; but it is possible to make at least indications of the sensibility informing that objective thing a body of poetry. Our last observation, that there is in the poem "Marriage" no element of sex or lust, is one indication. There is no sex anywhere in her poetry. No poet has been so chaste; but it is not the chastity that rises from an awareness—healthy or morbid—of the flesh, it is a special chastity aside from the flesh—a purity by birth and from the void. There is thus, by parallel, no contact by disgust in her work, but rather the expression of a cultivated distaste; and this is indeed appropriate, for within the context of purity disgust would be out of order. Following the same train, it may be observed that of all the hundreds of quotations and references in her poems none is in itself stirring, although some are about stirring things; and in this she is the opposite of Eliot, who as a rule quotes the thing in itself stirring; and here again her practice is correct. Since her effects are obtained partly by understatement, partly by ornament, and certainly largely by special emphasis on the quiet and the quotidian, it is clear that to use the thing obviously stirring would be to import a sore thumb, and the "great" line would merely put the poem off its track. Lastly, in this train, and to begin another, although she refers eulogistically many times to the dazzling color, vivid strength, and torrential flow of Hebrew poetry, the tone of her references is quiet and conversational.

By another approach we reach the same conclusion, not yet named. Miss Moore writes about animals, large and small, with an intense detached intimacy others might use in writing of the entanglements of people. She writes about animals as if they were people minus the soilure of overweeningly human preoccupations, to find human qualities freed and uncommitted. Compare her animal poems with those of D. H. Lawrence. In Lawrence you feel you have touched the plasm; in Miss Moore you feel you have escaped and come on the idea. The other life is there, but it is round the corner, not so much taken for granted as obliviated, not allowed to transpire, or if so only in the light ease of conversation: as we talk about famine in the Orient in discounting words that know all the time that it *might* be met face to face. In Miss Moore life is remote (life as good *and* evil) and everything is done to keep it remote; it is reality removed, but it is nonetheless reality, because we *know* that it is removed. This is perhaps another way of putting Kenneth Burke's hypothesis: "if she were discussing the newest model of automobile, I think she could somehow contrive to suggest an antiquarian's interest." Let us say that everything she gives is minutely precise, immediately accurate to the witnessing eye, but that both the reality under her poems and the reality produced by them have a nostalgic quality, a hauntedness, that cannot be reached, and perhaps could not be borne, by these poems, if it were.

Yet remembering that as I think her poems are expedient forms for ecstasies apprehended, and remembering, too, both the tradition of romantic reticence she observes and the fastidious thirst for detail, how could her poems be otherwise, or more? Her sensibility—the deeper it is the more persuaded it cannot give itself away—predicted her poetic method; and the defect of her method, in its turn, only represents the idiosyncrasy of her sensibility: that it, like its subject matter, constitutes the perfection of standing aside.

It is provisionally worth noting that Miss Moore is not alone but characteristic in American literature. Poe, Hawthorne, Melville (in *Pierre*), Emily Dickinson, and Henry James, all—like Miss

Moore—shared an excessive sophistication of surfaces and a passionate predilection for the genuine—though Poe was perhaps not interested in too much of the genuine; and all contrived to present the conviction of reality best by making it, in most readers' eyes, remote.

The Later Poetry of W. B. Yeats
[1 9 3 6]

The later poetry of William Butler Yeats is certainly great enough in its kind, and varied enough within its kind, to warrant a special approach, deliberately not the only approach, and deliberately not a complete approach. A body of great poetry will awaken and exemplify different interests on different occasions, or even on the same occasions, as we may see in the contrasting and often contesting literatures about Dante and Shakespeare: even a relation to the poetry is not common to them all. I propose here to examine Yeats's later poetry with a special regard to his own approach to the making of it; and to explore a little what I conceive to be the dominant mode of his insight, the relations between it and the printed poems, and—a different thing—the relations between it and the readers of his poems.

The major facts I hope to illustrate are these: that Yeats has, if you accept his mode, a consistent extraordinary grasp of the reality of emotion, character, and aspiration; and that his chief resort and weapon for the grasping of that reality is magic; and that if we would make use of that reality for ourselves we must also make some use of the magic that inspirits it. What is important is that the nexus of reality and magic is not by paradox or sleight of hand, but is logical and represents, for Yeats in his poetry, a full use of intelligence. Magic performs for Yeats the same fructifying function that Christianity does for Eliot, or that ironic fatalism did for Thomas Hardy; it makes a connection between the poem and its subject matter and provides an adequate mechanics of meaning and value. If it happens that we discard more of Hardy than we do of Yeats and more of Yeats than we do of Eliot, it is not because Christianity provides better machinery for the movement of poetry than fatalism or magic, but simply because Eliot is a more cautious craftsman. Besides, Eliot's poetry has not even comparatively worn long enough to show what parts are permanent and what merely temporary. The point here is that fatalism, Christianity, and magic are none of them disciplines to which many minds can consciously appeal today, as Hardy, Eliot, and Yeats do, for emotional strength and moral authority. The supernatural is simply not part of our mental furniture, and when we meet it in our reading we say: Here is debris to be swept away. But if we sweep it away without first making sure what it is, we are likely to lose the poetry as well as the debris. It is the very purpose of a supernaturally derived discipline, as used in poetry, to set the substance of natural life apart, to give it a form, a meaning, and a value which cannot be evaded. What is excessive and unwarranted in the discipline we indeed ought to dismiss; but that can be determined only when what is integrating and illuminating is known first. The discipline will in the end turn out to have had only a secondary importance for the reader; but its effect will remain active even when he no longer considers it. That is because for the poet the discipline, far from seeming secondary, had an extraordinary structural, seminal, and substantial importance to the degree that without it he could hardly have written at all.

Poetry does not flow from thin air but requires always either a literal faith, an imaginative faith, or, as in Shakespeare, a mind full of many provisional faiths. The life we all live is not alone enough of a subject for the serious artist; it must be life with a leaning, life with a tendency to shape itself only in certain forms, to afford its most lucid revelations only in certain lights. If our final interest, either as poets or as readers, is in the reality declared when the forms have been removed and the lights taken away, yet we can never come to the reality at all without the first advantage of the form and lights. Without them we should *see* nothing but only glimpse something unstable. We glimpse the fleeting but do not see what it is that fleets.

So it was with Yeats; his early poems are fleeting, some of them beautiful and some that sicken, as you read them, to their own extinction. But as he acquired for himself a discipline, however unacceptable to the bulk of his readers, his poetry obtained an access to reality. So it is with most of our serious poets. It is almost the mark of the poet of genuine merit in our time—the poet who writes serious works with an intellectual aspect which are nonetheless poetry—that he performs his work in the light of an insight, a group of ideas, and a faith, with the discipline that flows from them, which taken together form a view of life most readers cannot share, and which, furthermore, most readers feel as repugnant, or sterile, or simply inconsequential.

All this is to say generally—and we shall say it particularly for Yeats later—that our culture is incomplete with regard to poetry; and the poet has to provide for himself in that quarter where authority and value are derived. It may be that no poet ever found a culture complete for his purpose; it was a welcome and arduous part of his business to make it so. Dante, we may say, completed for poetry the Christian culture of his time, which was itself the completion of centuries. But there was at hand for Dante, and as a rule in the great ages of poetry, a fundamental agreement or convention between the poet and his audience about the validity of the view of life of which the poet deepened the reality and spread the scope. There is no such agreement today. We find poets either using the small conventions of the individual life as if they were great conventions, or attempting to resurrect some great convention of the past, or, finally, attempting to discover the great convention that must lie, willy-nilly, hidden in the life about them. This is a labor, whichever form it takes, which leads as often to subterfuge, substitution, confusion, and failure, as to success; and it puts the abnormal burden upon the reader of determining what the beliefs of the poet are and how much to credit them before he can satisfy himself of the reality which those beliefs envisage. The alternative is to put poetry at a discount—which is what has happened.

This the poet cannot do who is aware of the possibilities of his trade: the possibilities of arresting, enacting, and committing to the language through his poems the expressed value of the life otherwise only lived or evaded. The poet so aware knows, in the phrasing of that prose-addict Henry James, both the sacred rage of writing and the muffled majesty of authorship; and knows, as Eliot knows, that once to have been visited by the muses is ever afterward to be haunted. These are qualities that once apprehended may not be discounted without complete surrender, when the poet is no more than a haunt haunted. Yeats has never put his poetry at a discount. But he has made it easy for his readers to do so—as Eliot has in his way—because the price he has paid for it, the expense he has himself been to in getting it on paper, have been a price most readers simply do not know how to pay and an expense, in time and labor and willingness to understand, beyond any initial notion of adequate reward.

The price is the price of a fundamental and deliberate surrender to magic as the ultimate mode for the apprehension of reality. The expense is the double expense of, on the one hand, implementing magic with a consistent symbolism, and on the other hand, the greatly multiplied expense of restoring, through the *craft* of poetry, both the reality and its symbols to that plane where alone their experience becomes actual—the place of the quickened senses and the concrete emotions. That is to say, the poet (and, as always, the reader) has to combine, to fuse inextricably into something like an organic unity the constructed or derived symbolism of his special insight with the symbolism animating the language itself. It is, on the poet's plane, the labor of bringing the representative forms of knowledge home to the experience which stirred them: the labor of keeping in mind *what* our knowledge is of: the labor of craft. With the poetry of Yeats this labor is, as I say, doubly hard, because the forms of knowledge, being magical, do not fit naturally with the forms of knowledge that ordinarily preoccupy us. But it is possible, and I hope to show it, that the difficulty is, in a sense, superficial and may be overcome with familiarity, and that the mode of magic itself, once familiar, will even seem rational for the purposes of poetry—although it will not thereby seem inevitable. Judged by its works in the representation of emotional reality—and that is all that can be asked in our context—magic and its burden of symbols may

be a major tool of the imagination. A tool has often a double function; it performs feats for which it was designed, and it is heuristic,
it discovers and performs new feats which could not have been
anticipated without it, which it indeed seems to instigate for itself
and in the most unlikely quarters. It is with magic as a tool in its
heuristic aspect—as an agent for discovery—that I wish here directly
to be concerned.

One of the finest, because one of the most appropriate to our
time and place, of all Yeats's poems, is his "The Second Coming."

> Turning and turning in the widening gyre
> The falcon cannot hear the falconer;
> Things fall apart; the centre cannot hold;
> Mere anarchy is loosed upon the world,
> The blood-dimmed tide is loosed, and everywhere
> The ceremony of innocence is drowned;
> The best lack all conviction, while the worst
> Are full of passionate intensity.
>
> Surely some revelation is at hand;
> Surely the Second Coming is at hand.
> The Second Coming! Hardly are those words out
> When a vast image out of *Spiritus Mundi*
> Troubles my sight: somewhere in sands of the desert
> A shape with lion body and the head of a man,
> A gaze blank and pitiless as the sun,
> Is moving its slow thighs, while all about it
> Reel shadows of the indignant desert birds.
> The darkness drops again; but now I know
> That twenty centuries of stony sleep
> Were vexed to nightmare by a rocking cradle,
> And what rough beast, its hour come round at last,
> Slouches towards Bethlehem to be born?

There is about it, to any slowed reading, the immediate conviction
of pertinent emotion; lines are stirring, separately and in their smaller
groups, and there is a sensible life in them that makes them seem
to combine in the form of an emotion. We may say at once then,
for what it is worth, that in writing his poem Yeats was able to

choose words which to an appreciable extent were the right ones to reveal or represent the emotion which was its purpose. The words deliver the meaning which was put into them by the craft with which they were arranged, and that meaning is their own, not to be segregated or given another arrangement without diminution. Ultimately, something of this sort is all that can be said of this or any poem, and when it is said, the poem is known to be good in its own terms or bad because not in its own terms. But the reader seldom reaches an ultimate position about a poem; most poems fail, through craft or conception, to reach an ultimate or absolute position: parts of the craft remain machinery and parts of the conception remain in limbo. Or, as in this poem, close inspection will show something questionable about it. It is true that it can be read as it is, isolated from the rest of Yeats's work and isolated from the intellectual material which it expresses, and a good deal gotten out of it, too, merely by submitting to it. That is because the words are mainly common, both in their emotional and intellectual senses; and if we do not know precisely what the familiar words drag after them into the poem, still we know vaguely what the weight of it feels like; and that seems enough to make a poem at one level of response. Yet if an attempt is made at a more complete response, if we wish to discover the precise emotion which the words mount up to, we come into trouble and uncertainty at once. There is an air of explicitness to each of the separate fragments of the poem. Is it, in this line or that, serious? Has it a reference?—or is it a rhetorical effect, a result only of the persuasive overtones of words?—or is it a combination, a mixture of reference and rhetoric?

Possibly the troubled attention will fasten first upon the italicized phrase in the twelfth line: *Spiritus Mundi*; and the question is whether the general, the readily available senses of the words are adequate to supply the specific sense wanted by the poem. Put another way, can the poet's own arbitrary meaning be made, merely by discovering it, to participate in and enrich what the "normal" meanings of the words in their limiting context provide? The critic can only supply the facts; the poem will in the end provide its own answer. Here there are certain facts that may be extracted from Yeats's prose writings which suggest something of what the words symbolize for him. In one of the notes to the limited edition of *Michael Robartes and the Dancer*, Yeats observes that his mind, like another's, has been from time to time obsessed by images which had no discoverable origin in his waking experience. Speculating as to their origin, he came to deny both the conscious and the unconscious memory as their probable seat, and finally invented a doctrine which traced the images to sources of supernatural character. I quote only that sentence which is relevant to the phrase in question: "Those [images] that come in sleep are (1) from the state immediately preceding our birth; (2) from the *Spiritus Mundi*—that is to say, from a general storehouse of images which have ceased to be a property of any personality or spirit." It apparently follows, for Yeats, that images so derived have both an absolute meaning of their own and an operative force in determining meaning and predicting events in this world. In another place (the Introduction to "The Resurrection" in *Wheels and Butterflies*) he describes the image used in this poem, which he had seen many times, "always at my left side just out of the range of sight, a brazen winged beast that I associated with laughing, ecstatic destruction." Ecstasy, it should be added, comes for Yeats just before death, and at death comes the moment of revelation, when the soul is shown its kindred dead and it is possible to see the future.

Here we come directly upon that central part of Yeats's magical beliefs which it is one purpose of this poem emotionally to represent: the belief in what is called variously *Magnus Annus*, The Great Year, The Platonic Year, and sometimes in a slightly different symbolism, The Great Wheel. This belief, with respect to the history of epochs, is associated with the precession of the equinoxes, which bring, roughly every two thousand years, a Great Year of death and rebirth, and this belief, with respect to individuals, seems to be associated with the phases of the moon; although individuals may be influenced by the equinoxes and there may be a lunar interpretation of history. These beliefs have a scaffold of geometrical figures, gyres, cones, circles, etc., by the application of which exact interpretation is secured. Thus, it is possible to predict, both in biography and history, and in time, both forward and backward, the character, climax, collapse, and rebirth in antithetical form of human types and cultures. There is a subordinate but helpful belief that signs, warnings, even direct messages, are always given, from *Spiritus Mundi* or elsewhere, which the poet and the philosopher have only to see and hear. As it happens, the Christian era, being nearly two thousand years old, is due for extinction and replacement, in short for the Second Coming, which this poem heralds. In his note to its first publication (in *Michael Robartes and the Dancer*) Yeats expresses his belief as follows:

At the present moment the life gyre is sweeping outward, unlike that before the birth of Christ which was narrowing, and has almost reached its greatest expansion. The revelation which approaches will however take its character from the contrary movement of the interior gyre. All our scientific, democratic, fact-accumulating, heterogeneous civilisation belongs to the outward gyre and prepares not the continuance of itself but the revelation as in a lightning flash, though in a flash that will not strike only in one place, and will for a time be constantly repeated, of the civilisation that must slowly take its place.

So much for a major gloss upon the poem. Yeats combined, in the best verse he could manage, the beliefs which obsessed him with the image which he took to be a specific illustration of the beliefs. Minor and buttressing glosses are possible for many of the single words and phrases in the poem, some flowing from private doctrine and some from Yeats's direct sense of the world about him, and some from both at once. For example: The "ceremony of innocence" represents for Yeats one of the qualities that made life valuable under the dying aristocratic social tradition; and the meaning of the phrase in the poem requires no magic for completion but only a reading of other poems. The "falcon and the falconer" in the second line has, besides its obvious symbolism, a doctrinal reference. A falcon is a hawk, and a hawk is symbolic of the active or intellectual mind; the falconer is perhaps the soul itself or its uniting principle. There is also the apposition which Yeats has made several times that "Wisdom is a butterfly/ And not a gloomy bird of prey." Whether the special symbolism has actually been incorporated in the poem, and in which form, or whether it is private debris merely, will take a generation of readers to decide. In the meantime it must be taken provisionally for whatever its ambiguity may seem to be worth. Literature is full of falcons, some that fly and some that lack immediacy and sit, archaic, on the poet's wrist; and it is not always illuminating to determine which is which. But when we come on such lines as

> The best lack all conviction, while the worst
> Are full of passionate intensity,

we stop short, first to realize the aptness of the statement to every plane of life in the world about us, and then to connect the lines with the remote body of the poem they illuminate. There is a dilemma of which the branches grow from one trunk but which cannot be solved; for these lines have, not two meanings, but two sources for the same meaning. There is the meaning that comes from the summary observation that this is how men are—and especially men of power—in the world we live in; it is knowledge that comes from knowledge of the "fury and the mire in human veins"; a meaning the contemplation of which has lately (April, 1934) led Yeats to offer himself to any government or party that, using force and marching men, will "promise not this or that measure but a discipline, a way of life." And there is in effect the same meaning, at least at the time the poem was written, which comes from a different source and should have, one would think, very different consequences in prospective party loyalties. Here the meaning has its source in the doctrines of the Great Year and the Phases of the Moon; whereby, to cut exegesis short, it is predicted as necessary that, at the time we have reached, the best minds, being subjective, should have lost all faith though desiring it, and the worst minds, being so nearly objective, have no need of faith and may be full of "passionate intensity" without the control of any faith or wisdom. Thus we have on the one side the mirror of observation and on the other side an imperative, magically derived, which come to the conclusion of form in identical words.

The question is, to repeat, whether the fact of this double control and source of meaning at a critical point defeats or strengthens the unity of the poem; and it is a question which forms itself again and again in the later poems, sometimes obviously but more often only by suggestion. If we take another poem on the same theme, written some years earlier, and before his wife's mediumship gave him the detail of his philosophy, we will find the question no easier to answer in its suggested than in its conspicuous form. There is an element in the poem called "The Magi" which we can feel the weight of but cannot altogether name, and of which we can only guess at the efficacy.

> Now as at all times I can see in the mind's eye,
> In their stiff, painted clothes, the pale unsatisfied ones
> Appear and disappear in the blue depths of the sky
> With all their ancient faces like rain-beaten stones,
> And all their helms of silver hovering side by side,
> And all their eyes still fixed, hoping to find once more,
> Being by Calvary's turbulence unsatisfied,
> The uncontrollable mystery on the bestial floor.

I mean the element which, were Yeats a Christian, we could accept as a species of Christian blasphemy or advanced heresy, but which since he is not a Christian we find it hard to accept at all: the element of emotional conviction springing from intellectual matters without rational source or structure. We ought to be able, for the poem's sake, to accept the conviction as an emotional possibility, much as we accept *Lear* or Dostoevski's *Idiot* as valid, because projected from represented experience. But Yeats's experience is not represented consistently on any one plane. He constantly indicates a supernatural validity for his images of which the authority cannot be reached. If we come nearer to accepting "The Magi" than "The Second Coming" it is partly because the familiar Christian paradigm is more clearly used, and, in the last two lines, what Yeats constructs upon it is given a more immediate emotional form, and partly because, *per contra*, there is less demand made upon arbitrary intellectual belief. There is, too, the matter of scope; if we reduce the scope of "The Second Coming" to that of "The Magi" we shall find it much easier to accept; but we shall have lost much of the poem.

We ought now to have enough material to name the two radical defects of magic as a tool for poetry. One defect, which we have just been illustrating, is that it has no available edifice of reason reared upon it conventionally independent of its inspiration. There is little that the uninspired reader can naturally refer to for authority outside the poem, and if he does make a natural reference he is likely to turn out to be at least partly wrong. The poet is thus in the opposite predicament; he is under the constant necessity of erecting his beliefs into doctrines at the same time that he represents their emotional or dramatic equivalents. He is, in fact, in much the same position that Dante would have been had he had to construct his Christian doctrine while he was composing *The Divine Comedy*: an impossible labor. The Christian supernaturalism, the Christian magic (no less magical than that of Yeats), had the great advantage for Dante, and imaginatively for ourselves, of centuries of reason and criticism and elaboration: it was within reason a consistent whole; and its supernatural element had grown so consistent with experience as to seem supremely *natural*—as indeed it may again. Christianity has an objective form, whatever the mysteries at its heart and its termini, in which all the phenomena of human life may find place and meaning. Magic is none of these things for any large fraction of contemporary society. Magic has a tradition, but it is secret, not public. It has not only central and terminal mysteries but has also peripheral mysteries, which require not only the priest to celebrate but also the adept to manipulate. Magic has never been made "natural." The practical knowledge and power which its beliefs lead to can neither be generally shared nor overtly rationalized. It is in fact held to be dangerous to reveal openly the details of magical experience: they may be revealed, if at all, only in arbitrary symbols and equivocal statements. Thus we find Yeats, in his early and innocuous essay on magic, believing his life to have been imperiled for revealing too much. Again, the spirits or voices through whom magical knowledge is gained are often themselves equivocal and are sometimes deliberately confusing. Yeats was told to remember, "We will deceive you if we can," and on another occasion was forbidden to record anything that was said, only to be scolded later because he had failed to record every word. In short, it is of the essence of magical faith that the supernatural cannot be brought into the natural world except through symbol. The distinction between natural and supernatural is held to be substantial instead of verbal. Hence magic may neither be criticized nor institutionalized; nor can it ever reach a full expression of its own intention. This is perhaps the justification of Stephen Spender's remark that there is more magic in Eliot's "The Hollow Men" than in any poem of Yeats; because of Eliot's Christianity, his magic has a rational base as well as a supernatural source: it is the magic of an orthodox, authoritative faith. The dogmas of magic, we may say, are all heresies which cannot be expounded except each on its own authority as a fragmentary insight; and its unity can be only the momentary unity of association. Put another way, magic is in one respect in the state of Byzantine Christianity, when miracles were quotidian and the universal frame of experience, when life itself was held to be supernatural and reason was mainly a kind of willful sophistication.

Neither Yeats nor ourselves dwell in Byzantium. At a certain level, though not at all levels, we conceive life, and even its nonrational features, in rational terms. Certainly there is a rational bias and a rational structure in the poetry we mainly agree to hold great— though the content may be what it will; and it is the irrational bias and the confused structure that we are mainly concerned to disavow, to apologize or allow for. It was just to provide himself with the equivalent of a rational religious insight and a predictable rational structure for the rational imagination that in his book, *A Vision* (published, in 1925, in a limited edition only, and then withdrawn), he attempted to convert his magical experience into a systematic philosophy. "I wished," he writes in the Dedication to that work, "for a system of thought that would leave my imagination free to create as it chose and yet make all that it created, or could create, part of the one history, and that the soul's." That is, Yeats hoped by systematizing it to escape from the burden of confusion and abstraction which his magical experience had imposed upon him. "I can now," he declares in this same Dedication, "if I have the energy, find the simplicity I have sought in vain. I need no longer write poems like 'The Phases of the Moon' nor 'Ego Dominus Tuus,' nor spend barren years, as I have done three or four times, striving with abstractions that substitute themselves for the play that I had planned."

"Having inherited," as he says in one of his poems, "a vigorous mind," he could not help seeing, once he had got it all down, that his system was something to disgorge if he could. Its truth as experience would be all the stronger if its abstractions could be expunged. But it could not be disgorged; its thirty-five years of growth was an intimate part of his own growth, and its abstractions were all of a piece with his most objective experience. And perhaps we, as readers, can see that better from outside than Yeats could from within. I suspect that no amount of will could have rid him of his magical conception of the soul; it was by magic that he knew the soul; and the conception had been too closely associated with his profound sense of his race and personal ancestry. He has never been able to retract his system, only to take up different attitudes toward it. He has alternated between granting his speculations only the validity of poetic myth and planning to announce a new deity. In his vacillation—there is a poem by that title—the rational defect remains, and the reader must deal with it sometimes as an intrusion, of indeterminate value, upon the poetry and sometimes as itself the subject of dramatic reverie or lyric statement. At least once he tried to force the issue home, and in a section of A Packet for Ezra Pound called "Introduction to the Great Wheel" he meets the issue by transforming it, for the moment, into wholly poetic terms. Because it reveals a fundamental honesty and clarity of purpose in the midst of confusion and uncertainty the section is quoted entire.

Some will ask if I believe all that this book contains, and I will not know how to answer. Does the word belief, as they will use it, belong to our age, can I think of the world as there and I here judging it? I will never think any thoughts but these, or some modification or extension of these; when I write prose or verse they must be somewhere present though it may not be in the words; they must affect my judgment of friends and events; but then there are many symbolisms and none exactly resembles mine. What Leopardi in Ezra Pound's translation calls that 'concord' wherein 'the arcane spirit of the whole mankind turns hardy pilot'—how much better it would be without that word 'hardy' which slackens speed and adds nothing—

persuades me that he has best imagined reality who has best imagined justice.

The rational defect, then, remains; the thought is not always in the words; and we must do with it as we can. There is another defect of Yeats's magical system which is especially apparent to the reader but which may not be apparent at all to Yeats. Magic promises precisely matters which it cannot perform—at least in poetry. It promises, as in "The Second Coming," exact prediction of events in the natural world; and it promises again and again, in different poems, exact revelations of the supernatural, and of this we have an example in what has to many seemed a great poem, "All Souls' Night," which had its first publication as an epilogue to A *Vision*. Near the beginning of the poem we have the explicit declaration: "I have a marvelous thing to say"; and near the end another: "I have mummy truths to tell." "Mummy truths" is an admirable phrase, suggestive as it is of the truths in which the dead are wrapped, ancient truths as old as Egypt perhaps, whence mummies commonly come, and truths, too, that may be unwound. But there, with the suggestion, the truths stop short; there is, for the reader, no unwinding, no revelation of the dead. What Yeats actually does is to summon into the poem various of his dead friends as "characters"—and this is the greatness, and only this, of the poem: the summary, excited, even exalted presentation of character. Perhaps the rhetoric is the marvel and the evasion the truth. We get an impact as from behind, from the speed and weight of the words, and are left with an ominous or terrified frame of mind, the revelation still to come. The revelation, the magic, was in Yeats's mind; hence the exaltation in his language; but it was not and could not be given in the words of the poem.

It may be that for Yeats there was a similar exaltation and a similar self-deceit in certain other poems, but as the promise of revelation was not made, the reader feels no failure of fulfillment. Such poems as "Easter, 1916," "In Memory of Major Robert Gregory," and "Upon a Dying Lady" may have buried in them a conviction of invocation and revelation; but if so it is no concern of ours: we are concerned only, as the case may be, with the dramatic

158]

presentations of the Irish patriots and poets, Yeats's personal friends, and Aubrey Beardsley's dying sister, and with, in addition, for minor pleasure, the technical means—the spare and delicate language, the lucid images, and quickening rhymes—whereby the characters are presented as intensely felt. There is no problem in such poems but the problem of reaching, through a gradual access of intimacy, full appreciation; here the magic and everything else are in the words. It is the same, for bare emotion apart from character, in such poems as "A Deep-Sworn Vow," where the words accumulate by the simplest means an intolerable excitement, where the words are, called as they may be from whatever source, in an ultimate sense their own meaning.

> Others because you did not keep
> That deep-sworn vow have been friends of mine;
> Yet always when I look death in the face,
> When I clamber to the heights of sleep,
> Or when I grow excited with wine,
> Suddenly I meet your face.

Possibly all poetry should be read as this poem is read, and no poetry greatly valued that cannot be so read. Such is one ideal toward which reading tends; but to apply it as a standard of judgment we should first have to assume for the poetic intelligence absolute autonomy and self-perfection for all its works. Actually, autonomy and self-perfection are relative and depend upon a series of agreements or conventions between the poet and his readers, which alter continually, as to what must be represented by the fundamental power of language (itself a relatively stable convention) and what, on the other hand, may be adequately represented by mere reference, sign, symbol, or blueprint indication. Poetry is so little autonomous from the technical point of view that the greater part of a given work must be conceived as the manipulation of conventions that the reader will, or will not, take for granted; these being crowned, or animated, emotionally transformed, by what the poet actually represents, original or not, through his mastery of poetic language. Success is provisional, seldom complete, and never permanently complete. The vitality or letter of a convention may perish although the form persists. *Romeo and Juliet* is less successful today than when produced because the conventions of honor, family authority, and blood-feud no longer animate and justify the action; and if the play survives it is partly because certain other conventions of human character do remain vital, but more because Shakespeare is the supreme master of representation through the reality of language alone. Similarly with Dante; with the cumulative disintegration, even for Catholics, of medieval Christianity as the ultimate convention of human life, the success of *The Divine Comedy* comes more and more to depend on the exhibition of character and the virtue of language alone—which may make it a greater, not a lesser poem. On the other hand, it often happens that a poet's ambition is such that, in order to get his work done at all, he must needs set up new conventions or radically modify old ones which fatally lack that benefit of form which can be conferred only by public recognition. The form which made his poems available was only gradually conferred upon the convention of evil in Baudelaire and, as we may see in translations with contrasting emphases, its limits are still subject to debate; in his case the more so because the life of his language depended more than usual on the viability of the convention.

Let us apply these notions, which ought so far to be commonplace, to the later work of Yeats, relating them especially to the predominant magical convention therein. When Yeats came of poetic age he found himself, as Blake had before him, and even Wordsworth but to a worse extent, in a society whose conventions extended neither intellectual nor moral authority to poetry; he found himself in a rational but deliberately incomplete, because progressive, society. The *emotion* of thought, for poetry, was gone, along with the emotion of religion and the emotion of race—the three sources and the three aims of the great poetry of the past. Tyndall and Huxley are the villains, Yeats records in his *Autobiographies*, as Blake recorded Newton; there were other causes, but no matter, these names may serve as symbols. And the dominant aesthetics of the time were as rootless in the realm of poetic import and authority as the dominant conventions. Art for Art's sake was the cry, the Ivory Tower the retreat, and Walter Pater's luminous languor and weak Platonism the exposition. One could say anything but it would mean nothing.

The poets and society both, for opposite reasons, expected the poet to produce either exotic and ornamental mysteries or lyrics of mood; the real world and its significance were reserved mainly to the newer sciences, though the novelists and the playwrights might poach if they could. For a time Yeats succumbed, as may be seen in his early work, even while he attempted to escape; and of his poetic generation he was the only one to survive and grow in stature. He came under the influence of the French Symbolists, who gave him the clue and the hint of an external structure but nothing much to put in it. He read, with a dictionary, Villiers de l'Isle-Adam's *Axel*, and so came to be included in Edmund Wilson's book *Axel's Castle*—although not, as Wilson himself shows, altogether correctly. For he began in the late 'nineties, as it were upon his own account, to quench his thirst for reality by creating authority and significance and reference in the three fields where they were lacking. He worked into his poetry the substance of Irish mythology and Irish politics and gave them a symbolism, and he developed his experiences with Theosophy and Rosicrucianism into a body of conventions adequate, for him, to animate the concrete poetry of the soul that he wished to write. He did not do these things separately; the mythology, the politics, and the magic are conceived, through the personalities that reflected them, with an increasing unity of apprehension. Thus more than any poet of our time he has restored to poetry the actual emotions of race and religion and what we call abstract thought. Whether we follow him in any particular or not, the general poetic energy which he liberated is ours to use if we can. If the edifice that he constructed seems personal, it is because he had largely to build it for himself, and that makes it difficult to understand in detail except in reference to the peculiar unity which comes from their mere association in his life and work. Some of the mythology and much of the politics, being dramatized and turned into emotion, are part of our common possessions. But where the emphasis has been magical, whether successfully or not, the poems have been misunderstood, ignored, and the actual emotion in them which is relevant to us all decried and underestimated, merely because the magical mode of thinking is foreign to our own and when known at all is largely associated with quackery and fraud.

We do not make that mistake—which is the mistake of unwillingness—with Dante or the later Eliot, because, although the substance of their modes of thinking is equally foreign and magical, it has the advantage of a rational superstructure that persists and which we can convert to our own modes if we will. Yeats lacks, as we have said, the historical advantage and with it much else; and the conclusion cannot be avoided that this lack prevents his poetry from reaching the first magnitude. But there are two remedies we may apply, which will make up, not for the defect of magnitude, but for the defect of structure. We can read the magical philosophy in his verse *as if* it were converted into the contemporary psychology with which its doctrines have so much in common. We find little difficulty in seeing Freud's preconscious as a fertile myth and none at all in the general myth of extroverted and introverted personality; and these may be compared with, respectively, Yeats's myth of *Spiritus Mundi* and the Phases of the Moon: the intention and the scope of the meaning are identical. So much for a secular conversion. The other readily available remedy is this: to accept Yeats's magic literally as a machinery of meaning, to search out the prose parallels and reconstruct the symbols he uses on their own terms in order to come on the emotional reality, if it is there, actually in the poems—when the machinery may be dispensed with. This method has the prime advantage over secular conversion of keeping judgment in poetic terms, with the corresponding disadvantage that it requires more time and patience, more "willing suspension of disbelief," and a stiffer intellectual exercise all around. But exegesis is to be preferred to conversion on still another ground, which may seem repellent: that magic, in the sense that we all experience it, is nearer the represented emotions that concern us in poetry than psychology, as a generalized science, can ever be. We are all, without conscience, magicians in the dark.

But even the poems of darkness are read in the light. I cannot, of course, make a sure prognosis; because in applying either remedy the reader is, really, doctoring himself as much as Yeats. Only this much is sure: that the reader will come to see the substantial unity of Yeats's work, that it is the same mind stirring behind the poems on Crazy Jane and the Bishop, on Cuchulain, on Swift, the political poems, the biographical and the doctrinal—a mind that sees the fury and the mire and the passion of the dawn as contrary aspects of the real world. It is to be expected that many poems will fail in part and some entirely, and if the chief, magic will not be the only cause of failure. The source of a vision puts limits upon its expression which the poet cannot well help overpassing. "The limitation of his view," Yeats wrote of Blake, "was from the very intensity of his vision; he was a too-literal realist of imagination, as others are of nature"; and the remark applies to himself. But there will be enough left to make the labor of culling worth all its patience and time. Before concluding, I propose to spur the reader, or inadvertently dismay him, by presenting briefly a few examples of the sort of reconstructive labor he will have to do and the sort of imaginative assent he may have to attempt in order to enter or dismiss the body of the poems.

As this is a mere essay in emphasis, let us bear the emphasis in, by repeating, on different poems, the sort of commentary laid out above on "The Second Coming" and "The Magi," using this time "Byzantium" and "Sailing to Byzantium." Byzantium is for Yeats, so to speak, the heaven of man's mind; there the mind or soul dwells in eternal or miraculous form; there all things are possible because all things are known to the soul. Byzantium has both a historical and an ideal form, and the historical is the exemplar, the dramatic witness, of the ideal. Byzantium represents both a dated epoch and a recurrent state of insight, when nature is magical, that is, at the beck of mind, and magic is natural—a practical rather than a theoretic art. If with these notions in mind we compare the two poems named we see that the first, called simply "Byzantium," is like certain cantos in the *Paradiso* the poetry of an intense and condensed declaration of doctrine; not emotion put into doctrine from outside, but doctrine presented as emotion. I quote the second stanza.

> Before me floats an image, man or shade,
> Shade more than man, more image than a shade;
> For Hades' bobbin bound in mummy-cloth
> May unwind the winding path;

A mouth that has no moisture and no breath
Breathless mouths may summon;
I hail the superhuman;
I call it death-in-life and life-in-death.

The second poem, "Sailing to Byzantium," rests upon the doctrine but is not a declaration of it. It is, rather, the doctrine in action, the doctrine actualized in a personal emotion resembling that of specific prayer. This is the emotion of the flesh where the other was the emotion of the bones. The distinction should not be too sharply drawn. It is not the bones of doctrine but the emotion of it that we should be aware of in reading the more dramatic poem: and the nearer they come to seeming two reflections of the same thing the better both poems will be. What must be avoided is a return to the poem of doctrine with a wrong estimation of its value gained by confusion of the two poems. Both poems are serious in their own kind, and the reality of each must be finally in its own words whatever clues the one supplies to the other. I quote the third stanza.

> O sages standing in God's holy fire
> As in the·gold mosaic of a wall,
> Come from the holy fire, perne in a gyre,
> And be the singing-masters of my soul.
> Consume my heart away; sick with desire
> And fastened to a dying animal
> It knows not what it is; and gather me
> Into the artifice of eternity.

We must not, for example, accept "perne in a gyre" in this poem merely because it is part of the doctrine upon which the poem rests. Its magical reference may be too explicit for the poem to digest. It may be merely part of the poem's intellectual machinery, something that will *become* a dead commonplace once its peculiarity has worn out. Its meaning, that is, may turn out not to participate in the emotion of the poem: which is an emotion of aspiration. Similarly a note of aspiration would have been injurious to the stanza quoted from "Byzantium" above.

Looking at other poems as examples, the whole problem of exegesis may be put another way; which consists in joining two facts and observing their product. There is the fact that again and again in Yeats's prose, both in that which accompanies the poems and that which is independent of them, poems and fragments of poems are introduced at strategic points, now to finish off or clinch an argument by giving it as proved, and again merely to balance argument with witness from another plane. A *Vision* is punctuated by five poems. And there is the complementary fact that, when one has read the various autobiographies, introductions, and doctrinal notes and essays, one continually finds echoes, phrases, and developments from the prose in the poems. We have, as Wallace Stevens says, the prose that wears the poem's guise at last; and we have, too, the poems turning backward, re-illuminating or justifying the prose from the material of which they sprang. We have, to import the dichotomy which T. S. Eliot made for his own work, the prose writings discovering and buttressing the ideal, and we have the poems which express as much as can be actualized—given as concrete emotion—of what the prose discovered or envisaged. The dichotomy is not so sharp in Yeats as in Eliot. Yeats cannot, such is the unity of his apprehension, divide his interests. There is one mind employing two approaches in the labor of representation. The prose approach lets in much that the poetic approach excludes: it lets in the questionable, the uncertain, the hypothetic, and sometimes the incredible. The poetic approach, using the same material, retains, when it is successful, only what is manifest, the emotion that can be made actual in a form of words that need only to be understood, not argued. If props of argument and vestiges of idealization remain, they must be felt as qualifying, not arguing, the emotion. It should only be remembered and repeated that the poet invariably requires more machinery to secure *his* effects—the machinery of his whole life and thought—than the reader requires to secure what he takes as the *poem's* effects; and that, as readers differ, the poet cannot calculate what is necessary to the poem and what is not. There is always the debris to be cut away.

In such a fine poem as "A Prayer for My Son," for example, Yeats cut away most of the debris himself, and it is perhaps an injury to judgment provisionally to restore it. Yet to this reader at least the poem seems to richen when it is known from what special circumstance the poem was freed. As it stands we can accept the symbols which it conspicuously contains—the strong ghost, the devilish things, and the holy writings—as drawn from the general stock of literary conventions available to express the evil predicament in which children and all innocent beings obviously find themselves. Taken so, it is a poem of natural piety. But for Yeats the conventions were not merely literary but were practical expressions of the actual terms of the predicament, and his poem is a prayer of dread and supernatural piety. The experience which led to the poem is recounted in A *Packet for Ezra Pound*. When his son was still an infant Yeats was told through the mediumship of his wife that the Frustrators or evil spirits would henceforth "attack my health and that of my children, and one afternoon, knowing from the smell of burnt feathers that one of my children would be ill within three hours, I felt before I could recover self-control the mediaeval helpless horror of witchcraft." The child *was* ill. It is from this experience that the poem seems to have sprung, and the poem preserves all that was actual behind the private magical conventions Yeats used for himself. The point is that the reader has a richer poem if he can substitute the manipulative force of Yeats's specific conventions for the general literary conventions. Belief or imaginative assent is no more difficult for either set. It is the emotion that counts.

That is one extreme to which the poems run—the extreme convention of personal thought. Another extreme is that exemplified in "A Prayer for My Daughter," where the animating conventions *are* literary and the piety *is* natural, and in the consideration of which it would be misleading to introduce the magical convention as more than a foil. As a foil it is nevertheless present; his magical philosophy, all the struggle and warfare of the intellect, is precisely what Yeats in this poem *puts out of mind*, in order to imagine his daughter living in innocence and beauty, custom and ceremony.

A third extreme is that found in the sonnet "Leda and the Swan," where there is an extraordinary sensual immediacy—the

words meet and move like speaking lips—and a profound combination of the generally available or literary symbol and the hidden,
magical symbol of the intellectual, philosophical, impersonal order.
Certain longer poems and groups of poems, especially the series
called "A Woman Young and Old," exhibit the extreme of combination as well or better; but I want the text on the page.

> A sudden blow: the great wings beating still
> Above the staggering girl, her thighs caressed
> By the dark webs, her nape caught in his bill,
> He holds her helpless breast upon his breast.
>
> How can those terrified vague fingers push
> The feathered glory from her loosening thighs?
> And how can body, laid in that white rush,
> But feel the strange heart beating where it lies?
>
> A shudder in the loins engenders there
> The broken wall, the burning roof and tower
> And Agamemnon dead.
>   Being so caught up,
> So mastered by the brute blood of the air,
> Did she put on his knowledge with his power
> Before the indifferent beak could let her drop?

It should be observed that in recent years new images, some
from the life of Swift, and some from the Greek mythology, have
been spreading through Yeats's poems; and of Greek images he has
used especially those of Oedipus and Leda, of Homer and Sopho-
cles. But they are not used as we think the Greeks used them, nor
as mere drama, but deliberately, after the magical tradition, both to
represent and hide the myths Yeats has come on in his own mind.
Thus "Leda and the Swan" can be read on at least three distinct
levels of significance, none of which interferes with the others: the
levels of dramatic fiction, of condensed insight into Greek mythology, and a third level of fiction and insight combined, as we said,
to represent and hide a magical insight. This third level is our present concern. At this level the poem presents an interfusion among

the normal terms of the poem two of Yeats's fundamental magical doctrines in emotional form. The doctrines are put by Yeats in the following form in his essay on magic: "That the borders of our mind are ever shifting, and that many minds can flow into one another, as it were, and create or reveal a single mind, a single energy. . . . That this great mind can be evoked by symbols." Copulation is the obvious nexus for spiritual as well as physical seed. There is also present I think some sense of Yeats's doctrine of Annunciation and the Great Year, the Annunciation, in this case, that produced Greek culture. It is a neat question for the reader, so far as this poem is concerned, whether the poetic emotion springs from the doctrine and seizes the myth for a safe home and hiding, or whether the doctrine is correlative to the emotion of the myth. In neither case does the magic matter as such; it has become poetry, and of extreme excellence in its order. To repeat the interrogatory formula with which we began the commentary on "The Second Coming," is the magical material in these poems incorporated in them by something like organic reference or is its presence merely rhetorical? The reader will answer one way or the other, as, to his rational imagination, to all the imaginative understanding he can bring to bear, it either seems to clutter the emotion and deaden the reality, or seems rather, as I believe, to heighten the emotional reality and thereby extend its reference to what we call the real world. Once the decision is made, the magic no longer exists; we have the poetry.

Other approaches to Yeats's poetry would have produced different emphases, and this approach, which has emphasized little but the magical structure of Yeats's poetic emotions, has made that emphasis with an ulterior purpose: to show that magic may be a feature of a rational imagination. This approach should be combined with others, or should have others combined with it, for perspective and reduction. No feature of a body of poetry can be as important as it seems in discussion. Above all, then, this approach through the magical emphasis should be combined with the approach of plain reading—which is long reading and hard reading—plain reading of the words, that they may sink in and do as much of their own work as they can. One more thing: When we call man a rational animal we mean that reason is his great myth. Reason is plastic and takes to any form provided. The rational imagination in poetry, as elsewhere, can absorb magic as a provisional method of evocative and heuristic thinking, but it cannot be based upon it. In poetry, and largely elsewhere, imagination is based upon the reality of words and the emotion of their joining. Yeats's magic, then, like every other feature of his experience, is rational as it reaches words; otherwise it is his privation, and ours, because it was the rational defect of our society that drove him to it.

Emily Dickinson:

Notes on Prejudice and Fact

[1 9 3 7]

The disarray of Emily Dickinson's poems is the great obvious fact about them as they multiply from volume to volume—I will not say from edition to edition, for they have never been edited—just as a kind of repetitious fragmentariness is the characterizing fact of her sensibility. No poet of anything like her accomplishment has ever imposed on the reader such varied and continuous critical labor; and on few poets beyond the first bloat of reputation has so little work been done. Few poets have benefited generally, and suffered specifically, from such a handsome or fulsome set of prejudices, which, as they are expressed, seem to remove the need for any actual reading at all.

The barriers to critical labor are well known, and some of them are insuperable. No text will be certain so long as the vaults at Amherst remain closed. Without benefit of comparative scholarship it is impossible to determine whether a given item is a finished poem, an early version of a poem, a note for a poem, a part of a poem, or a prose exclamation. Worse, it is impossible to know whether what appear to be crotchets in the poems as printed are correctly copied. The poet's handwriting was obscure, loose, and run-over; hence it is plain that unskilled copyists cannot be relied on in matters of punctuation, line structure, and the terminal letters of words. It is plainer still, if suspicion be in case, that many examples of merely irritating bad grammar—mistakes that merely hinder the reader—may well represent systematic bad guessing by the copyist. Perhaps it is not plain, but it is plausible, to imagine that a full and open view of the manuscripts would show the poet far less fragmentary and repetitious than the published work makes her seem. Most poets have a desk full of beginnings, a barrel of fragments and anything up to an attic full of notes. The manner of notation, if it were known, might make a beginning at the establishment of a canon. With the obvious fragments cut out, or put in an appendix, a clean, self-characterizing, responsive, and responding body of poetry, with limits and a fate and a quaking sensibility, might then be made to show itself.

Then is not now. This essay cannot enact a prophecy. This disarray of fragments, this mob of verses, this din of many motions, cannot be made to show itself in its own best order—as the strong parade we hoped it really was. This essay proposes, in lieu of adumbrating a complete criticism, first to examine a set of prejudices which are available as approaches to Emily Dickinson, and then to count—and perhaps account for—a few staring facts: obvious, animating, defacing facts about the verses as they now appear. If the essay has a good eye for the constitution of poetic facts, the affair of counting will be adventurous, a part of the great adventure of sensibility which consists, one sometimes thinks, in an arduous fealty to facts. If the fealty is sound, perhaps the vestiges of a complete criticism will be there too, or at least a bias, a prejudice, in that direction.

For it takes a strong and active prejudice to see facts at all, as any revolutionist will tell you. And just as the body must have a strong prejudice, which is its wisdom, about the nature of time in order to wake up exactly *before* the alarm goes off—an affair of counting, if ever—so the sensibility must have a pretty firm anterior conviction about the nature of poetry in order to wake up to a given body of poetry at all. We suddenly realize that we have, or have *not*—which in a very neat way comes to the same thing—counted some of these facts before. We know where we are in terms of where we thought we were, at home, lost, or shaking: which is when the alarm goes off. To depend on prejudice for the nature of time or poetry may seem a little willful and adventitiously mysterious. But it is a method that allows for mistakes, and in the present condition of Emily Dickinson's poetry, it is imperative to allow for continuous error, both in the facts and in their counting—in the prejudices by which we get at them.

Most prejudices are frivolous to the real interests concerned, which is why they are so often made to appear as facts instead of mere keys to facts. That Emily Dickinson is a great poet, "with the possible exception of Sappho, the greatest woman poet of all time," or the author of poetry "perhaps the finest by a woman in the English language," or that in one of the volumes of her verse "there are no dregs, no single drop can be spared,"—these are variations upon an essentially frivolous prejudice. Only the last variation is dangerous, because by asserting perfection it makes the poet an idol and removes her from the possibility of experience. On the whole, statements of this order are seldom taken seriously, but are felt as polite salutations and farewells. The trouble is that it is hard to persuade oneself to read work toward which one has accomplished gestures so polite. If not a drop can be spared, let us not risk spilling any; let us say, rather, here is great poetry—we know what *that* is like! A chalice, a lily, a sea-change. Old memories are mulled. We have the equivalent of emotion. And equivalents, like substitutes, though not so good as what you asked for, are often, for sensibilities never exercised enough to have been starved, a full meal.

It would be unfair, though, to leave the prejudice of Emily Dickinson's magnitude so naked. Politeness may conceal a legitimate wish that dare not put itself in bald speech. I am convinced that Conrad Aiken, in referring to Emily Dickinson's poetry as "perhaps the finest by a woman in the English language," had the legitimate wish to condition the reader with a very good fundamental prejudice—which we shall come to—about Emily Dickinson to the effect that there was something exciting or vital or amusing in her work. It is a kind of flag-waving; it reminds you of what you ought to be able to feel. Most readers of poetry are flag-wavers, and in order to get them to be more, you have to begin by waving a flag. I cannot imagine Mr. Aiken, or any other reader, addressing a Dickinson poem as "perhaps the finest by a woman in the English language." That is only how he addresses other people, hoping that they will thus be prejudiced into responding to the poem as he actually does, in terms of the words and the motions of the words which make it up: which are the terms (not the thing itself) of magnitude. I too would like to begin and end with the idea that in some such sense Emily Dickinson is sometimes a great poet.

There is a more dangerous but no less frivolous type of prejudice in the following sentence. "Her revolt was absolute; she abandoned rhyme altogether when she chose, and even assonance, writing in meter alone, like a Greek." There is a Spanish proverb that if God does not bless you with children, the devil will send you nieces. As a literary critic, if not as a niece, Mme. Bianchi, who is responsible for the sentence quoted, is thoroughly diabolic; as idolaters are by rule. The idea is to make you feel that the slips and roughnesses, the truncated lines, false rhymes, the inconsistencies of every description which mar the majority of Emily Dickinson's poems are examples of a revolutionary master-craftsman. Only the idol is served here; no greater disservice could be done to the poetry the reader reads than to believe with however great sincerity that its blemishes have any closer relation than contrast to its beauty. Emily Dickinson never knew anything about the craft of verse well enough to exemplify it, let alone revolt from it. If, where you are autonomous as in the *practice* of verse, you revolt first, you only revolve in a vacuum; and you will end as Emily Dickinson did in many of her failures by producing chaotic verses which have no bearing on the proper chaos of their subject—the life where precisely, as Emily Dickinson well enough knew, you are not autonomous but utterly dependent and interlocked.

As for Mme. Bianchi's specific terms: if the ear and arithmetic of this essay are right, Emily Dickinson did not abandon rhyme so much as she failed to get that far—her lines strike *as if* they intended to end in rhyme; and her assonances seem frequently incomplete substitutes for rhyme, and not assonances at all. She did not write in meter alone; her meters were most often exiguous or overrun proximations of common English meter—or again they met the pattern of meter in syllabification miter-perfect without meeting the enlivening movement of meter. And as for writing like a Greek it would be more nearly correct, metrically, to say that she wrote like an Italian with recurring pairs of stressed syllables. I do not refer here to the successful meters in Emily Dickinson, but only to the variously deficient meters.

But Mme. Bianchi is not half so dangerous in idealizing her aunt's technical inadequacy as absolute, as Ludwig Lewisohn is in magnifying her intellectual and mystical force—a composition of magnitudes not commonly come by outside Dante. "She can be," says Mr. Lewisohn, "of a compactness of expression and fullness of meaning not less than Goethean in Goethe's epigrammatic mood. . . . She can soar like the intense mystical poets of the seventeenth century." This is the method of instilling prejudice by means of the unexpanded comparison. We are assumed to have the American poet in front of us and to know what she is; then our knowledge of her is heightened by a comparison with Goethe's epigrams, which are probably not in front of us except by reputation. As we think, we suddenly realize that the cognate qualities in Emily Dickinson are not with us either. They are precisely as far off as Goethe. Mr. Lewisohn has compared abstracted qualities for a concrete effect: the effect, I take it, of vivid moral insight; but he has not *made* the comparison. He has not shown us what it is in either poet that he is talking about. If he expanded and did show us, he might prove right; I do not at the moment say he is wrong—although I suspect an intolerable identification: the target of insight for the two poets could hardly have been the same. What I want to emphasize is merely this: Mr. Lewisohn is actually only saying that Emily Dickinson's poetry possesses moral insight. What he pretends to do is to put her insight on the level of the supreme type of moral insight—by mentioning Goethe's name. He would have done better to distinguish the *difference* between the achieved qualities in the epigrams of the two poets—the difference between insight as wisdom, say, and insight as vision.

Mr. Lewisohn's other comparison, with the intense mystical poets of the seventeenth century, is equally unexpanded and equally misleading. He does not say which poets nor in what respects; and what we actually get out of his comparison is the idea that Emily Dickinson was intensely mystical in an exciting and inexpensive way. The spread of such a prejudice may multiply readers, but it fosters bad reading. Poetic mysticism, as the term is loosely used, is a kind of virus that gets about through the medium of the printed page, and its chief effect is to provide a matchless substitute for the discipline of attention in incapable minds. By making ultimate apprehension of God—or matter—free in words, it relieves the poet of the necessity to make his words first apprehend the *manifestation*—what is actually felt—in this world; and it relieves the reader of the obligation to apprehend anything at all when everything may always be apprehended at once. To exercise this sort of prejudice on a really interesting poet is to carry politeness too far—and far beyond, as it happens, Emily Dickinson's poems' own idea of their operative reach and willed intention. I quote, as facts worth counting in this connection, the following lines and phrases: they illuminate Mr. Lewisohn's prejudice by reducing it to the actual scope of the poems.

> The missing All prevented me
> From missing minor things . . .

> Almost we wish the end
> Were further off—too great it seems
> So near the Whole to stand . . .

> Was the Pine at my window a "Fellow"
> Of the Royal Infinity?
> Apprehensions are God's introductions
> Extended inscrutably.

These lines are, I think, characteristic of the general "mystical" attitude in the poems. It is not mysticism itself. It is an attitude composed partly of the English Hymnal, partly of instinctive protestant transcendentalism, partly of instinctively apprehended Puritan theology, and partly of human sensibility bred with experience to the point of insight. There is besides an element of composition at work, which is the most important of all the distinguishable elements, and which makes the lines quoted, at least in their contexts, into poetry.

Admittedly this language is as loose as Mr. Lewisohn's, and as open to reduction; but I, too, am dealing with initial prejudice. My prejudice is that Emily Dickinson is a mid-nineteenth century New England Christian poet. Christianity moved her, and experience moved through her poems upon the machinery of Christianity, which is a machinery for the worship of God in all his works, and, among other things, for the redemption, which is to say the completion, of the soul. Christianity in action, especially in poetry, often looks to the outsider like an exercise in mysticism; and that is perhaps the mistake Mr. Lewisohn makes—just as so many have made a similar mistake about Gerard Manley Hopkins, or, for that matter, about Herbert and Vaughan. All these poets approached the mystery of God which is unity, but they approached it in human terms; they did what every Christian must; but they never seized or lost themselves in the unity of God as St. Francis and St. Theresa seemed to do—or as the great cathedrals and the great Church music, to the lay imagination, indubitably did. Put another way, there is nothing in the poems of Hopkins or Emily Dickinson which passes the willing understanding; if their poems sometimes confront the supersensible—and they mostly do not—it is always on the plane of the rational imagination, never in the incomprehensible terms of the mystical act. The mystery is there, but like the mystery of physical death the relation of the poetry to it is heuristic—an affair of discovery of which the very excitement, promise, and terror are that it never takes place, yet may, indeed momently, must.

Those who persist in calling this relationship mystical underestimate the scope of rational imagination working in language and in the face of mystery. That scope is exhausted only in the instance; the mystery is never exhausted merely by being expressed; and the mystery, as a fact, is always the same. When Shakespeare, who never troubled directly about God, mastered the emotion of jealousy in *Othello*, he was precisely as rational or precisely as "mystical" in his approach to mystery—and the same mystery, the mystery of the actual—as Emily Dickinson was in her deliberate approach to God in terms of nature and death. What differs is the machinery, or sometimes the formula, of approach.

Here we come on a different type of prejudice, in its own way as general and as beyond the point if taken too solemnly as those we have been discussing, but with an air of specificity about it which is disarming. This is the prejudice about the poet in relation to his time, where the poet is taken as a fatal event in cultural history. The time produced the poet, we say, and the poet crowned the time— crowned it with its own meaning. If we go far enough on this line, the time, or the age, tends to disappear in the meaning—as for many of us early Greece disappears in Homer; which is only a way of bringing the time up to date, of telescoping all the co-ordinates rashly into the one image of meaning. Mr. Allen Tate has in an admirable essay (in his *Reactionary Essays*) performed this labor upon Emily Dickinson, with the further labor that when he has got his image all made he proceeds to sort out its component parts. It is hard to separate what Mr. Tate found in Emily Dickinson as traces or inklings from what he brought with him on his own account; which is all in his favor if you like what he says, as I do, and if the combination illuminates and enlivens Emily Dickinson, as I believe it does. Mr. Tate as a critic has the kind of rightness that goes with insight, and not at all the kind of wrongness that goes with sincerity—which is perhaps how we should characterize Mr. Lewisohn.

At any rate, Mr. Tate builds up a pretty good historical prejudice and makes it available in the guise of insight. Emily Dickinson came, he says, exactly at the dying crisis of Puritan New England culture—not at the moment of death, but at the moment—it was years long—when the matrix began to be felt as broken. Spiritual meaning and psychic stability were no longer the unconscious look and deep gesture worn and rehearsed life-long; they required the agony of doubt and the trial of deliberate expression in specifically, willfully objective form. Faith was sophisticated, freed, and terrified—but still lived; imagination had suddenly to do all the work of embodying faith formerly done by habit, and to embody it with the old machinery so far as it could be used. There was no other machinery available. Thus the burden of poetry was put upon the New England version of the Christian sensibility.

It is arguable that Greek tragedy came at the analogous moment in Athenian history, when the gods were seen as imaginative instead of magical myths. The advantage for the poet is in both instances double and pays in poetry for the burden. There is the advantage of the existing machinery of meaning in the specific culture, which is still able to carry any weight and which is universally understood; and there is the advantage of a new and personal plasticity in the meanings themselves. Faith, in the agonized hands of the individual, becomes an imaginative experiment of which all the elements are open to new and even blasphemous combinations, and which is subject to the addition of new insights. It is no longer enough to repeat prayers and to rehearse Mass or its protestant equivalent; indeed the institutional part of culture is the first to show itself as dead; faith becomes to the secularized imagination of Emily Dickinson "the Experiment of our Lord!"—which it could never have seemed, on the same foundation, half a century earlier. The great advantage for a poet to come at a time of disintegrating culture is, then, to sum up, just this: the actuality of what we are and what we believe is suddenly seen to be nearly meaningless as habit, and must, to be adequately known, be translated to the terms and modes of the imagination. Nothing can be taken for granted but the machinery, which is there, all available, and which indeed cannot help being taken for granted. These are the conditions of belief—though not the only conditions—which may produce great poetry: the conditions of spiritual necessity and mechanical freedom. It is worth adding, for proportion, that the opposite conditions—spiritual freedom (a unity of belief and discipline) and mechanical necessity—produced such a great poet as Dante; and, again, it is quite possible that Shakespeare may have been produced at the nexus of quite a different set of conditions which had more to do with the state of language than with the state of belief. Here we are concerned with the occurrence of Emily Dickinson at the precise time when it became plain that Puritan Christianity was no longer the vital force in New England culture and before any other force had recognizably relieved the slack. If we are inclined to see a causal connection it is only as a more vivid and dramatic way of seeing the association it may really and only have been.

Now I do not want to let it appear that Mr. Tate would assent to my treatment of his idea; he has his own treatment, which is certainly not so highfalutin as mine; and besides, I am not sure how far I can assent to my own remarks without a feeling that I am merely succumbing to the temptation of a bright idea, which like the idea of chance explains less and less the more you look into it. Let us take the idea provisionally, and more provisionally for me than for Mr. Tate. So taken, it indicates a source, and with the source a tragic strength, for the fund and flow of Emily Dickinson's meaning. As the Massachusetts theocracy failed, became, say, more humane and individualized, its profoundly dramatic nature—all that it had left—became sharper and plainer, until in the imagination of Hawthorne and Melville and Emily Dickinson it took in, or implied, pretty near the whole of human experience. Then it died. It fed the imagination; then it died; and at the same time that particular form of the New England imagination reached its small surfeit and died too.

In the last sentence lies buried, but not in the least dead, the fundamental prejudice we have been looking for all the time: the prejudice contained in the idea of imagination being fed and dying, or for that matter living or doing anything whatever—that is to say, a prejudice about the nature of poetry itself as the chief mode of imagination. Poetry is composed of words and whenever we put anything into poetry—such as meaning or music; whenever poetry is affected by anything—such as the pattern of a culture or the structure of a stanza; whenever anything at all happens in poetry it happens in the medium of words. It is also near enough the truth to say that whenever we take anything out of poetry, either to use it or to see just what it is, we have to take it out in the words—and then put it right back before it gets lost or useless. The greatness of Emily Dickinson is not—to review our select list of prejudices—going to be found in anybody's idea of greatness, or of Goethe, or intensity, or mysticism, or historical fatality. It is going to be found in the words she used and in the way she put them together; which we will observe, if we bother to discriminate our observations, as a series of facts about words. What is behind the words or beyond them, we cannot know as facts, as any discussion amply demonstrates. Our knowledge of implication and inkling, quite as much as our knowledge of bald sound and singing sense, will be governed solely by what we can recognize, and perhaps by a good deal that we cannot recognize, of the poetic relations of the words—that is to say, by what they make of each other. This rule, or this prejudice, applies, which is why it is mentioned at all, exactly as strongly to our method of determining the influence of a culture or a church or a philosophy, alive, dead, or dying, upon the body of Emily Dickinson's poetry. We will see what the influence did to the words, and more important, what the words did to the influence.

So far as poetry goes, then, the influence of intellectual or other abstracted considerations can be measured only as it affects the choice and arrangement of words—as it richens or impoverishes the texture of the imaginative vehicle of the poetry. The puritan theory of renunciation, for example, will be not at all the same thing in a hortatory tract, no matter how eloquent and just, as in a poem of Emily Dickinson, which might well have drawn from the tract, however loose or fragmentary the poem may be. Imagination, if it works at all, works at the level of actualized experience. Here is the example, pat to the purpose, and to other purposes as well.

> Renunciation
> Is a piercing virtue,
> The letting go
> A presence for an expectation—
> Not now.

There is no forensic here, nor eloquence, nor justness; it is a bare statement amounting to vision—vision being a kind of observation of the ideal. It has nothing to do with wisdom, there is no thinking in it; and there is no ordinary observation in it—in the sense that there is no relation between an observer and a thing observed. The lines do not prove themselves, or anything else; they make a statement. Yet it is not a naive statement—it is not directly itself—however much it may seem to be. It rises rather out of a whole way of life—the protestant, puritan way, felt suddenly at what can be called nothing less than a supremely sophisticated level. The feeling is in the sophistication. As a religious or philosophical statement it is probably vain and tragic and an example of self-arrogation; certainly it is without humility. Perhaps I am not competent to judge, being in a worse predicament than the poet, but it is possible to say that this is the sort of thing that happens to a religious notion when one's awareness of it becomes personal and without authority, when one is driven to imagine—in words or otherwise—the situation actually felt.

We do not examine these lines with a view to calling them great poetry but in order to present a series of facts as to how they derive their being and to afford a clue to the facts about a whole species of Dickinson poems—those that deal with the renunciation of love, the death of the beloved, and the heavenly reward. The machinery of meaning remains roughly the same throughout the group; what differs is the degree or amount of experience actualized in the verse. The machinery and the experience are perhaps insep-arable, or at any rate are in their varying proportions equally nec-essary to the production of the kind of poetry Emily Dickinson wrote. When the balance is lost, when the fusion is not made, or when resort is had to feeling alone or to machinery insufficiently felt, something less than good poetry appears. We have either a poem without mooring or a poem without buoyancy.

Let us provisionally inquire what it is in the words that makes poetry of the statement about renunciation. Let us treat the machin-ery, not as what we may or may not know it to be intellectually, but as an example of words in operation; and let us look at the image— what is imagined—as the emergent fact of the words in operation, indeed, as the operation itself. That is how our best reading takes poetry in its stride; here we arrest the stride or make slow motion of it. The words are all simple words, parts of our stock vocabulary. Only one, *renunciation*, belongs to a special department of experi-ence or contains in itself the focus of a particular attitude, a depart-ment and an attitude we condition ourselves to keep mostly in abeyance. We know what renunciation is; we know it turns up as heroism or hypocrisy or sentimentality; and we do as little as possi-ble about it. Only one word, *piercing*, is directly physical; some-thing that if it happens cannot be ignored but always shocks us into reaction. It is the shock of this word that transforms the phrase from a mere grammatical tautology into a metaphorical tautology which establishes as well as asserts identity. Some function of the word *pierce* precipitates a living intrinsic relation between renunciation and virtue; it is what makes the phrase incandesce. The two adjectives in the last line of the following quatrain exhibit a similar incandescent function.

> Rehearsal to ourselves
> Of a withdrawn delight
> Affords a bliss like murder,
> Omnipotent, acute.

It is the adjectives that transform the verbal and mutually irrelevant association of delight and murder into a self-completing metaphor. But, to return to our other quotation, the word *pierce* enlivens not only the first phrase but the whole statement about renunciation; it is the stress or shock of it that is carried forward into and makes specific the general notion—physical but vague—of letting go; and letting go, in its turn, perhaps by its participial form, works back upon the first phrase. The piercing quality of renunciation is precisely, but not altogether, that it is a continuing process, takes time, it may be infinite time, before the renounced presence transpires in expectation in the "Not now." It is—if we may provisionally risk saying so—the physical elements in the word *pierce* and the participial phrase *letting go* that, by acting upon them, make the other words available to feeling, and it is the word *renunciation* that, so enlightened, focuses the feeling as actuality. That operation is almost enough to make the statement poetry; we have only pseudo-names for whatever else it is that it takes. There is no advantage here of meter or rhyme. There is instead the speech-tone of authority, a directness in the manner of the words which has nothing to do with their meaning, and the speech-quality of speed, an inner speed of the syllables like the inner velocity of an atom, which has nothing directly to do with the outward relations of the words. These qualities are characteristic of verse that is felt as actual; at least we say that these qualities exist in verse that exacts the sense of precise feeling in the reader. Perhaps it is simpler to say that there is an excitement in the language beyond the excitement of any meaning we can communicate through any medium different from that of the poem itself: the excitement of being. It is gained, that excitement, by the exercise of the fundamental technique of language as a mode of finding objective form for even the most abstract feelings. A further, and I hope not absurd, simplification is to say that the poet whose work showed these qualities had an aptitude for language; and if that is so, then all we have been saying merely illustrates how much that is complicated and beyond conscious control the word *aptitude* may sometimes simplify.

So be it. Emily Dickinson had an aptitude for language, and in the passage we have examined she needed nothing else to induce her verses to reach their appropriate objective level; for the aptitude included every necessary mechanical relation both to her age and to the general craft of verse. Although the same aptitude persists superficially through the rest of the poem, the persistence is only superficial and not substantial. The rest of the poem is not transformed, as the quoted stanza was, into something felt as actual in which the parts work upon themselves mutually. We can say either that the aptitude was not carried far enough *per se*—the poet did not pay enough attention to the words; or we can say that the conceiving imagination was not strong enough to carry the material through; or we can say that the poet was not sufficiently master of the compositional devices of external form—form as the organizing agent— to give the work crisis and consistency. The first statement is true anyway; the second is probably true; and the third is true in relation to the other two. Perhaps the three statements are merely different emphases of the same idea: the idea we took up a little while ago of the imagination being insufficiently fed into the words of the poem. Either the machinery of the poem was inadequate to objectify its purpose, or the motive of the poem, as it emerged, was inadequate to activate the machinery. The alternatives are not mutually exclusive; a combined view is possible. It is at least plausible to consider that if there is a state of culture which produces or precipitates a body of poetry, then there may also be a state of language—a general level of poetic habit—which is necessary to give that body of poetry relative perfection, and that, further, if there is failure in one quarter, no matter which, it is a likely sign of failure in the other, if not at the same point then round the nearest corner. The trouble is that the condition of language at a given time is just as hard to determine as the condition of a culture. We guess at something wrong or swear that everything was right, and are not sure which case produced the better poetry.

We can say, amiably enough, that the verse-language of mid-nineteenth century America was relatively nerveless, unsupple, flat in pattern, had very little absorptive power and showed no self-luxuriating power whatever. The mounting vitality that shows itself as formal experiment and the matured vitality that shows itself as the masterly penetration of accepted form (say Kyd followed by the mature Shakespeare) were equally absent. The great estate of poetry as an available condition of language lay flat in a kind of desiccated hibernation, and the clue to resurrection was unknown. It is not for nothing that our poets never mastered form in language. Poe and Longfellow accepted the desiccation, contributing a personal music which perhaps redeemed but never transfigured their talents. Whitman and Emily Dickinson, with more genius, or as we have been saying with more favorable cultural situations, were unable to accept the desiccation and drove forward on the élan of their natural aptitudes for language, resorting regardless to whatever props, scaffolds, obsessive symbols, or intellectual mechanisms came to hand, but neither of them ever finding satisfactory form—and neither, apparently, ever consciously missing it. The great bulk of the verse of each appears to have been written on the sustaining pretense that everything was always possible. To see boundless good on the horizon, to see it without the limiting discipline of the conviction of evil, is in poetry as in politics the great stultifier of action.

Hence the great, repetitious wastes in both poets. With no criterion of achievement without there could be no criterion of completion within. Success was by accident, by the mere momentum of sensibility. Failure was by rule, although the rule was unknown, and often doubtless thought of in the shameless guise of simple self-expression. The practice of craft came to little more than so many exercises in self-expression. Thus something over two-thirds of Emily Dickinson's nine hundred odd printed poems are exercises, and no more, some in the direction of poetry, and some not. The object is usually in view, though some of the poems are but exercises in pursuit of an unknown object, but the means of attainment are variously absent, used in error, or ill-chosen. The only weapon constantly in use is, to repeat once more, the natural aptitude for language; and it is hardly surprising to find that that weapon, used alone and against great odds, should occasionally produce an air of frantic strain instead of strength, of conspicuous oddity instead of indubitable rightness.

Let us take for a first example a reasonably serious poem on one of the dominant Dickinson themes, the obituary theme of the great dead—a theme to which Hawthorne and Henry James were equally addicted—and determine if we can where its failure lies.

> More life went out, when He went,
> Than ordinary breath,
> Lit with a finer phosphor
> Requiring in the quench
>
> A power of renownéd cold—
> The climate of the grave
> A temperature just adequate
> So anthracite to live.
>
> For some an ampler zero,
> A frost more needle keen
> Is necessary to reduce
> The Ethiop within.
>
> Others extinguish easier—
> A gnat's minutest fan
> Sufficient to obliterate
> A tract of citizen.

The first thing to notice—a thing characteristic of exercises—is that the order or plot of the elements of the poem is not that of a complete poem; the movement of the parts is downward and toward a disintegration of the effect wanted. A good poem so constitutes its parts as at once to contain them and to deliver or release by the psychological force of their sequence the full effect only when the poem is done. Here the last quatrain is obviously wrongly placed; it comes like an afterthought, put in to explain why the third stanza was good. It should have preceded the third stanza, and perhaps with the third stanza—both of course in revised form—might have come at the very beginning, or perhaps in suspension between the first and second stanzas. Such suggestions throw the poem into disorder; actually the disorder is already there. It is not the mere arrangement of stanzas that is at fault; the units in disorder are deeper in the material, perhaps in the compositional elements of the conception, perhaps in the executive elements of the image-words used to afford circulation to the poem, perhaps elsewhere in the devices not used but wanted. The point for emphasis is that it is hard to believe that a conscientious poet could have failed to see that no amount of correction and polish could raise this exercise to the condition of a mature poem. The material is all there—the inspiration and the language; what it requires is a thorough revision—a re-seeing calculated to compose in objective form the immediacy and singleness of effect which the poet no doubt herself felt.

Perhaps we may say—though the poem is not near so bad an example as many—that the uncomposed disorder is accepted by the poet because the poem was itself written automatically. To the sensitive hand and expectant ear words will arrange themselves, however gotten hold of, and seem to breed by mere contact. The brood is the meaning we catch up to. Is not this really automatic writing *tout court?* Most of the Dickinson poems seem to have been initially as near automatic writing as may be. The bulk remained automatic, subject to correction and multiplication of detail. Others, which reach intrinsic being, have been patterned, inscaped, injected one way or another with the élan or elixir of the poet's dominant attitudes. The poem presently examined remains too much in the automatic choir; the élan is there, which is why we examine it at all, but without the additional advantage of craft it fails to carry everything before it.

The second stanza of the poem is either an example of automatic writing unrelieved, or is an example of bad editing, or both. Its only meaning is in the frantic strain toward meaning—a strain so frantic that all responsibility toward the shapes and primary significance of words was ignored. "A temperature just adequate/So anthracite to live" even if it were intelligible, which it is not, would be beyond bearing awkward to read. It is not bad grammar alone that works ill; words sometimes make their own grammar good on the principle of ineluctable association—when the association forces the words into meaning. Here we have fiat meaning. The word *anthracite* is the crux of the trouble. Anthracite is coal, is hard, is black, gives heat, and has a rushing crisp sound; it has a connection with carbuncle and with a fly-borne disease of which one symptom resembles a carbuncle; it is stratified in the earth, is formed of organic matter as a consequence of enormous pressure through geologic time; etc., etc. One or several of these senses may contribute to the poem; but because the context does not denominate it, it does not appear which. My own guess is that Emily Dickinson wanted the effect of something hard and cold and perhaps black and took *anthracite* off the edge of her vocabulary largely because she liked the sound. This is another way of saying that *anthracite* is an irresponsible product of her aptitude for language.

The word *phosphor* in the third line of the first stanza is a responsible example of the same aptitude. It is moreover a habitual symbol word rather than a sudden flight; it is part of her regular machinery for concentrating meaning in a partly willful, partly natural symbol. Phosphor or phosphorus—in various forms of the word— is used by Emily Dickinson at least twelve times to represent, from the like characteristic of the metal, the self-illumining and perhaps self-consuming quality of the soul. The "renownéd cold," "ampler zero," and "frost more needle keen," are also habitual images used to represent the coming or transition of death as effected seasonably in nature and, by analogue, in man. Examples of these or associated words so used run to the hundreds. The "gnat" in the fourth stanza with his "minutest fan" (of cold air?) is another example of a portmanteau image always ready to use to turn on the microcosmic view. In the word *Ethiop* in the third stanza we have a mixture of a similar general term—this time drawn from the outside and unknown world—and a special significance released and warranted by the poem. Ethiops live in tropical Africa; and we have here a kind of synecdoche which makes the Ethiop himself so full of heat that it would take great cold to quench it. That the contrary would be the case does not affect the actuality of the image, but makes it more intriguing and gives it an odd, accidental character. The misconception does, however, bring out the flavor of a wrong image along with the shadow of the right one; and it is a question whether the flavor will not last longer in the memory than the shadow. Another nice question is involved in the effect of the *order* of the verbs used to represent the point of death: *quench, reduce, extinguish, obliterate.* The question is, are not these verbs pretty nearly interchangeable? Would not any other verb of destructive action do just as well? In short, is there any word in this poem which either fits or contributes to the association at all exactly? I think not—with the single exception of "phosphor."

The burden of these observations on words will I hope have made itself plain; it is exactly the burden of the observations on the form of the whole poem. The poem is an exercise whichever way you take it: an approach to the organization of its material but by no means a complete organization. It is almost a rehearsal—a doing over of something not done—and a variation of stock intellectual elements in an effort to accomplish an adventure in feeling. The reader can determine for himself—if he can swallow both the anthracite and the gnat—how concrete and actual the adventure was made.

Perhaps determination will be assisted by a few considerations on Emily Dickinson's vocabulary as a whole and how it splits up under inspection into different parts which are employed for different functions, and which operate *from*, as it were, different levels of sensibility. It is not a large vocabulary compared to Whitman's, nor rich like Melville's, nor perspicuous like Henry James's, nor robust like Mark Twain's. Nor is it a homogeneous vocabulary; its unity is specious for the instance rather than organic for the whole of her work. Its constant elements are mostly found, like most of the poems, in arrangements, not in compositions. The pattern of association is kaleidoscopic and extraneous far more frequently than it is crystalline and inwardly compelled. What it is, is a small, rigidly compartmented vocabulary of general and conventional groups of terms, plus a moderately capacious vocabulary of homely, acute, directly felt words from which the whole actualizing strength of her verse is drawn. The extraordinary thing is how much of the general and conventional vocabulary got activated by the homely word. In the

[189

fragment about renunciation, "piercing" and "letting go" are examples. The depressing thing is how much of the conventional vocabulary was not activated by the homely word but distracted by the homely word strained odd.

Let us list a few of the conventional types that turn up most often and most conspicuously. The most conspicuous of all is the vocabulary of romance royalty, fairy-tale kings, queens and courts, and the general language of chivalry. Emily Dickinson was as fond as Shakespeare of words like *imperial, sovereign, dominion,* and the whole collection of terms for rank and degree. Probably she got them more from Scott and the Bible and the Hymnal than from Shakespeare. There is none of Shakespeare's specific and motivating sense of kings and princes as the focus of society, and none of his rhetoric of power; there is nothing tragic in Emily Dickinson's royal vocabulary. On the other hand, there is a great deal of vague and general assumption that royalty is a good thing and that escape into the goodness of it is available to everyone: like the colorful escape into romance and fairy-tale. Besides this general assumption, and more important, there is continuous resort to the trope of heavenly coronation for the individual and a continuous ascription of imperial titles and a chivalric, almost heraldic, code to God and the angels, to flowers and bees. This vocabulary, taken as a whole, provides a mixed formula which rehearsed like a ritual or just a verbal exercise sometimes discovers a poem and sometimes does not. I extract one stanza as example.

> He put the belt around my life,—
> I heard the buckle snap,
> And turned away, imperial,
> My lifetime folding up
> Deliberate as a duke would do
> A kingdom's title-deed,—
> Henceforth a dedicated sort,
> A member of the cloud.

Other vocabularies include words taken from sewing and the kinds of cloth used in women's clothes—*stitch, seam, needle, dimity, serge, silk, satin, brocade,* etc.; legal words—*tenant, rent, liti-*

gant, title, etc.; the names of jewels—*diamond, ruby, pearl, opal, amethyst, beryl*, and *amber*; words taken from the Civil War—*bayonet*, various images of musket and cannon fire, and of the soldier's heroism; words taken from sea-borne commerce—*port, harbor*, various kinds of ships and the parts of ships; the names of distant places—especially of mountains and volcanoes; and, not to exhaust but merely to stop the list, words taken from the transcendental theology of her time. It should be noted that only the first, second, and possibly the last of these groups named or activated anything she found in her daily life; but they had, like the vocabulary of royalty, everything to do with the stretching of her daily fancy, and they made a constant provision, a constant rough filling and occupation, for what did actually concern her—her prevision of death and her insight into the spiritual life. This is another way of saying that in what is quantitatively the great part of her work Emily Dickinson did not put the life of meaning into her words; she leaned on the formulas of words in the hope that the formulas would fully express what she felt privately—sometimes the emotion of escape and sometimes the conviction of assent—in her own self-centered experience. This is partly the mode of prayer, partly the mode of nonce-popular romance (which must always be repeated), and partly the mode of the pathetic fallacy applied to form—the fiat mode of expression which asserts that the need is equivalent to the object, that if you need words to mean something then they will necessarily mean it. But it is not except by accident the mode of the rational or actualizing imagination. The extraordinary thing in Emily Dickinson is, to repeat, that fragmentary accidents occur so often, and the terrible thing is that they need not have been accidents at all. The net result may be put as a loss of consistent or sustained magnitude equal to the impulse. We have a verse in great body that is part terror, part vision, part insight and observation, which must yet mostly be construed as a kind of *vers de société* of the soul—not in form or finish but in achievement.

This is to say that control was superficial—in the use, not the hearts, of words. We saw an example in the word *anthracite* a little above. Let us present two more examples and stop. We have the word *plush* in different poems as follows. "One would as soon assault a plush or violate a star . . . Time's consummate plush . . . A dog's belated feet like intermittent plush . . . We step like plush, we stand like snow . . . Sentences of plush." The word is on the verge of bursting with wrong meaning, and on account of the bursting, the stress with which the poet employed it, we are all prepared to accept it, and indeed do accept it, when suddenly we realize the wrongness, that "plush" was not what was meant at all, but was a substitute for it. The word has been distorted but not transformed on the page; which is to say it is not in substantial control. Yet it is impossible not to believe that to Emily Dickinson's ear it meant what it said and what could not otherwise be said.

The use of the word *purple* is another example of a word's getting out of control through the poet's failure to maintain an objective feeling of responsibility toward language. We have, in different poems, a "purple host" meaning "soldiers"; "purple territories," associated with salvation in terms of "Pizarro's shores"; "purple" meaning "dawn"; a "purple finger" probably meaning "shadow"; a purple raveling of cloud at sunset; ships of purple on seas of daffodil; the sun quenching in purple; a purple brook; purple traffic; a peacock's purple train; purple none can avoid—meaning death; no suitable purple to put on the hills; a purple tar wrecked in peace; the purple well of eternity; the purple or royal state of a corpse; the Purple of Ages; a sowing of purple seed which is inexplicable; the purple of the summer; the purple wheel of faith; day's petticoat of purple; etc., etc. Taken cumulatively, this is neither a distortion nor a transformation of sense; it is very near an obliteration of everything but a favorite sound, meaning something desirable, universal, distant, and immediate. I choose the word as an example not because it is particularly bad—it is not; it is relatively harmless—but because it is typical and happens to be easy to follow in unexpanded quotation. It is thoroughly representative of Emily Dickinson's habit of so employing certain favorite words that their discriminated meanings tend to melt into the single sentiment of self-expression. We can feel the sentiment but we have lost the meaning. The willing reader can see for himself the analogous process taking place—with slightly different final flavors—in word after word: for example in the words *dateless, pattern, compass, circumference, ecstasy, immor-*

tality, white, ruby, crescent, peninsula, and *spice.* The meanings
become the conventions of meanings, the asserted agreement that
meaning is there. That is the end toward which Emily Dickinson
worked, willy-nilly, in her words. If you can accept the assertion for
the sake of the knack—not the craft—with which it is made you will
be able to read much more of her work than if you insist on actual
work done.

But there were, to repeat and to conclude, three saving accidents at work in the body of Emily Dickinson's work sufficient to
redeem in fact a good many poems to the state of their original
intention. There was the accident of cultural crisis, the skeptical
faith and desperately experimental mood, which both released and
drove the poet's sensibility to express the crisis personally. There was
the accident that the poet had so great an aptitude for language that
it could seldom be completely lost in the conventional formulas
toward which her meditating mind ran. And there was the third
accident that the merest self-expression, or the merest statement of
recognition or discrimination or vision, may sometimes also be, by
the rule of unanimity and a common tongue, its best objective
expression.

When two or more of the accidents occur simultaneously a
poem or a fragment of a poem may be contrived. Sometimes the
thing is done directly—with the compactness which Mr. Lewisohn
compared to that of Goethe, but which had better be called the
compactness of that which is unexpanded and depends for context
entirely upon its free implications.

> Presentiment is that long shadow on the lawn
> Indicative that suns go down;
> The notice to the startled grass
> That darkness is about to pass.

If the reader compares this poem with Marvell's "To His Coy Mistress," he will see what can be gotten out of the same theme when
fully expanded. The difference is of magnitude; the magnitude
depends on craft; the Dickinson poem stops, Marvell's is completed.
What happens when the poem does not stop may be shown in the
following example of technical and moral confusion.

I got so I could hear his name
Without—
Tremendous gain!—
That stop-sensation in my soul,
And thunder in the room.

I got so I could walk across
That angle in the floor
Where he turned—so—and I turned how—
And all our sinew tore.

I got so I could stir the box
In which his letters grew—
Without that forcing in my breath
As staples driven through.

Could dimly recollect a Grace—
I think they called it "God,"
Renowned to ease extremity
When formula had failed—

And shape my hands petition's way—
Tho' ignorant of word
That Ordination utters—
My business with the cloud.

If any Power behind it be
Not subject to despair,
To care in some remoter way
For so minute affair
As misery—
Itself too vast for interrupting more,
Supremer than—
Superior to—

Nothing is more remarkable than the variety of inconsistency this effort displays. The first three stanzas are at one level of sensibility and of language and are as good verse as Emily Dickinson ever wrote. The next two stanzas are on a different and fatigued level of sensibility, are bad verse and flat language, and have only a serial connection with the first three. The last stanza, if it is a stanza, is on a still different level of sensibility and not on a recognizable level of language at all: the level of desperate inarticulateness to which no complete response can be articulated in return. One knows from the strength of the first three stanzas what might have been meant to come after and one feels like writing the poem oneself—the basest of all critical temptations. We feel that Emily Dickinson let herself go. The accidents that provided her ability here made a contrivance which was not a poem but a private mixture of first-rate verse, bad verse, and something that is not verse at all. Yet—and this is the point—this contrivance represents in epitome the whole of her work; and whatever judgment you bring upon the epitome you will, I think, be compelled to bring upon the whole.

No judgment is so persuasive as when it is disguised as a state-ment of facts. I think it is a fact that the failure and success of Emily Dickinson's poetry were uniformly accidental largely because of the private and eccentric nature of her relation to the business of poetry. She was neither a professional poet nor an amateur; she was a pri-vate poet who wrote indefatigably as some women cook or knit. Her gift for words and the cultural predicament of her time drove her to poetry instead of antimacassars. Neither her personal education nor the habit of her society as she knew it ever gave her the least inkling that poetry is a rational and objective art and most so when the theme is self-expression. She came, as Mr. Tate says, at the right time for one kind of poetry: the poetry of sophisticated, eccentric vision. That is what makes her good—in a few poems and many passages representatively great. But she never undertook the great profession of controlling the means of objective expression. That is why the bulk of her verse is not representative but mere fragmentary indicative notation. The pity of it is that the document her whole work makes shows nothing so much as that she had the themes, the insight, the observation, and the capacity for honesty, which had she only known how—or only known why—would have made the major instead of the minor fraction of her verse genuine poetry. But her dying society had no tradition by which to teach her the one lesson she did not know by instinct.

Unappeasable and Peregrine:
Behavior and the Four Quartets
[1 9 5 1]

I

It is the actual behavior of things that willy-nilly gets into poetry, and what poetry does to behavior is to give it some sort of order, good for the time, or the life, of the poem. What behavior does in this relation to order is to give the sense, the pressure toward incarnation, of reality greater than can be apprehended. Poetry is something we do to the actual experience of this relation between behavior and order; it is something we do to these partial incarnations. So it is with Eliot's *Four Quartets*; a poem dense with behavior and brimming with order.

The problem is always two-ended in making notes about a live poem: how to begin far enough in to catch on to the momentum of the poem, and how to stop soon enough to let it go on. What is the right point in reading to say, here is the midst of things in motion (what is meant by *in medias res*), and what is the appropriate point to say, now the poem goes of itself? The first point is where the words and the action of the poem seem to be at work on each other in such a way that they *together* look out upon you. The second point is reached perhaps when the composed order of word and action begins to decompose. The order of poetry is achieved between two disorders, the disorder in which feelings and thoughts are found in behavior, and the second disorder in which the order of the poem (what the poem has done to the feelings and thoughts by joining them in an action of the mind) is lost or seems exorbitant. The adventure of poetry is in taking the risk that what has been found in behavior may be lost if it is cared for too much.

Eliot's poetry is full of phrases which exemplify this condition and this risk. In "Gerontion" there are the phrases:

> I have lost my passion: why should I need to keep it
> Since what is kept must be adulterated?

In *Ash Wednesday* there is:

> Terminate torment
> Of love unsatisfied '
> The greater torment
> Of love satisfied

In the *Four Quartets* there is the imperative: "Old men ought to be explorers," which being interpreted means, the mind should cry out upon what it finds, for that is the burden of the word "explore," if you will look in the dictionary; and that is the burden of this poem, if you will look into its words. And does Eliot not say it himself, at the beginning of the final passage of the poem?

> We shall not cease from exploration
> And the end of all our exploring
> Will be to arrive where we started
> And know the place for the first time.

To explore is to search into the unknown, known step by step, behavior by behavior, "Through the unknown, remembered gate," and there to cry out upon what is recognized and also to weep. Exploration is the agony of prophecy as the action of the mind upon behavior. The passage goes on to resume, image by image, the order the poem has made, an order now at the point both of disintegration as a human order and of consummation into a divine order. There the poem stops, and there it also goes on.

How did it begin? In the childhood of the poet, where there were the gifts of all later imagination. The poet's labor is re-accession, not to the childhood (which ran free, till brooked) but to the gifts. One's own childhood is where the past experience of the race appears as pure behavior and pure authority. Each season of growth, unless the child die, a new ring of green wood toughens into heart wood. But in the beginning there is the green heart: ever irrecoverable except at the center which never disappears, what we know through the voices of the children in the apple tree.

But there is nothing innocent, in the trivial senses of the word, about this child, this *anima semplicetta*; there is nothing innocent in the quality of its experience. On the contrary it is naive, native, the moving image of the whole burden of experience we want to explore. There is no innocence about it, unless there is a kind of innocence to the authority of experience itself—unless there is innocence in unprotectedness from both good and evil. The child is very near reality, and is in this sense the child in the man, which the man both builds over and seeks to recover, as in this poem the poet seeks to recover the hidden laughter of children among the leaves of the garden.

There is here a relation not only to the image of the simple soul issuing from the hand of him who loves her in *Purgatorio* XVI but perhaps, as Helen Gardner says, also a relation to Kipling's "They": the children in which are " 'what might have been and what has been,' appearing to those who have lost their children in the house of a blind woman who has never borne a child." *Vere tu es Deus absconditus.* The mind of the poet and the mind of the reader reach after texts to help in the exploration: reach after analogies, after paths, arrests, traps, betrayals, reversals, and, above all, reach after reminders; for there is today no strict interpretation in these matters, no substitute for either experience or for the full mimesis of experience.

The mind uses what it must. I would suppose that in the voices of these children which reverberate through the *Four Quartets* lie more than echoes of Grimm's tales of *The Juniper Tree* and of *The Singing Bone.* They were present in *Ash Wednesday* and they are present here. In *The Juniper Tree* a woman kills her stepson and by a trick puts the crime upon her own daughter. Of the flesh was made black puddings which the father ate. Of the bones the little girl made a bundle in a silk handkerchief and sat down weeping tears of blood under a juniper tree. "After she had lain down there, she suddenly felt light-hearted and did not cry any more. Then the juniper tree began to stir itself, and the branches parted asunder, and moved together again, just as if some one were rejoicing and clapping his hands. At the same time a mist seemed to arise from the tree, and in the center of this mist it burned like a fire, and a beautiful bird flew out of the tree singing magnificently, and he flew high up in the air, and when he was gone, the juniper tree was just as it had been before, and the handkerchief with the bones was no longer there. Marlinchen, however, was as gay and happy as if her brother were still alive. And she went merrily into the house, and sat down to dinner and ate." Meanwhile the bird proceeds through the world, getting a chain from a goldsmith, red shoes from a shoe-maker, and from a miller a millstone: each in exchange for the identical song:

> My mother she killed me,
> My father he ate me,
> My sister, little Marlinchen,
> Gathered together all my bones,
> Tied them in a silken handkerchief,
> Laid them together beneath the juniper tree,
> Kywitt, kywitt, what a beautiful bird am I!

Then the bird returns to the father's house and sings to all three. Marlinchen laughs and weeps, the mother chatters her teeth and dreads and is on fire, the father goes out to see what bird is singing. The father is given the gold chain; Marlinchen, joyous and danc-ing, the red shoes; " 'Well,' said the woman, and sprang to her feet and her hair stood up like flames of fire, 'I feel as if the world were coming to an end. I, too, will go out and see if my heart feels lighter.' " At that the bird drops the millstone on her head.

In this tale the woman, in Eliot's language, could not bear very much reality; the man did not know reality when he saw it; and the little girl was herself reality in the form of behavior. It is not so very different in the tale of *The Singing Bone*. There is a wild boar, a great terror to the king's lands, and the king offers his daughter to whoso kills it. Two brothers go into the forest from opposite sides, the elder proud, crafty, shrewd; the younger innocent, simple, kind-hearted. The younger is given a spear for purity and goodness and with it kills the boar. The elder brother, who could not kill the boar, kills the younger brother and marries the king's daughter. Years later a shepherd found a snow-white bone in the sand of the stream where the body had been thrown and made out of it a mouthpiece for his horn. "Of its own accord" the bone "began to sing":

> Ah, friend, thou blowest upon my bone!
> Long have I lain beside the water;
> My brother slew me for the boar,
> And took for his wife the King's young daughter.

The wicked brother "was sewn up in a sack and drowned. But the bones of the murdered man were laid to rest in a beautiful tomb in the churchyard."

It is images like these that loom through the surface of Eliot's poems. Both the tales are magic formula; are neither sentimental nor didactic; they are precisely means for reaching into behavior under morals and sentiment. Every child knows this; only a mature poetic mind seems to know how to deal with it, or to remember it, or be reminded of it, or put it together.

There is a more abstract way of putting the significance of the presence of these tales in Eliot's poems. As a part of the composition they are a constant reminder of the presence of the barbaric, of other and partial creations within our own creation. Their presence makes a criticism of the Mediterranean tradition, whether in "complete" religion, or in "complete" reason, or in terms of our long heritage of Latin rhetoric as the instrument of interpretation. It seems worse than useless, it is mutilating, to think of this sort of composition as if it were rational allegory, but it would be fatal to our understanding to forget the presence of the old rhetorical allegory. There is, rather, a mutually related transformation of two modes of the mind.

There is a text in Eliot's prose *(Notes Towards the Definition of Culture)* which is specially apt to this aspect of all his poetry:

The reflection that what we believe is not merely what we formulate and subscribe to, but that behavior is also belief, and that even the most conscious and developed of us live also at the level on which belief and behavior cannot be distinguished, is one that may, once we allow our imagination to play upon it, be very disconcerting. It gives an importance to our most trivial pursuits, to the occupation of our every minute, which we cannot contemplate long without the horror of nightmare.

Let us say that the presence of the fairy tales in the deserted garden, the earthly paradise unused, in the first part of the first Quartet, gives the effect of belief merging in behavior. The rhymed and formal verses which begin the second part of the same Quartet give the different but related effect of behavior rising into belief, as it were altering the experience of belief if not the belief itself.

> Garlic and sapphires in the mud
> Clot the bedded axle-tree.
> The trilling wire in the blood
> Sings below inveterate scars
> And reconciles forgotten wars.
> The dance along the artery
> The circulation of the lymph
> Are figured in the drift of stars
> Ascend to summer in the tree
> We move above the moving tree
> In light upon the figured leaf
> And hear upon the sodden floor
> Below, the boarhound and the boar
> Pursue their pattern as before
> But reconciled among the stars.

Note that the axle tree does not move, that inveterate means confirmed by age and hence ineradicable. Note, too, that it is a *drift* of stars: drift is a deep dominance from a force outside knowledge—it is occult knowledge showing—and contrary or across other forces; like a current, like a tide; like what the current brings—strange movements in calm, the debris, the flotsam, in a drift of order. And again, note the two uses of "reconcile," one for something that happens in the blood under scars, the other for something that happens above among the stars. "Reconciled" is the burden word in this passage. It has to do with the means of submission to greater force— to harmony—to wisdom—to unity. It is the means of drawing together again, in a superior drift, which is also, and at the same time, the drift of the fortune which we still tell in the stars.

Let us look at the two aspects of drift together. It is the drift from Mallarmé (in the first line) through the body to Fortuna, Scientia, Man's Will, and the Reason of the Stars (for the stars are our best double image of that which is ordained and that which we can make or reach) to the boarhound and the boar—no doubt in a tapestry, a weaving in beauty together—as well as upon a sodden floor. We see at once the innocent and the native working together; how they work, and with what beside them, the drift of the stars, and with what above or beyond them, what is reconciled among the stars. It is *so*. It is so that we understand the garlic and the sapphires in the mud. We see what the words mean: what is incarnated in them—though it is a partial incarnation: partial ecstasy and partial horror, and it may be we do not grasp what is not incarnated.

I I

Here certainly the order of poetry has done something to the apprehension of behavior. The three old modes of the mind—the poetic, rhetorical, dialectical—are here at work synergically in a polarity of the intellectual and the sensual: upon the still point of the turning world and the pressure of behavior into consciousness. It would seem a maxim if not a rule for this sort of poetry, that the more the behavior presses in the more order must be found to take care of it. As Coleridge says, in poetry you have more than usual emotion and more than usual order; and as he does not say, the orders you use are no more yours to come by than is the emotion or the behavior you find. It is in you—in the poet, in the reader— that the old orders and the old emotions become more than usual. Let us now turn to some of the old orders, which Eliot has made unusual, and then return, if we can, to old behavior.

Let decorum be a name for the possession of a good supply of old orders through which we cope with or understand our experience. Ages with a highly developed decorum find verse a relatively easy medium. Recent ages have clearly a low decorum and have run toward prose. This is not a trivial consideration: it has to do with the possibility of getting work done, and it tends to set the level at which the work gets done; also it affects the ease of the reader's access to what has got done. The circumstance of decorum in which Eliot writes led him to declare in Sweden some years ago, that we live in an incredible public world and an intolerable private world. In a public world of low decorum we get many intolerable private worlds; and all the more intolerable to a man like Eliot who preserves in himself the "inveterate scars," the living sore points, of what he takes once to have been a credible public world; the man who, believing, lives in a world which does not believe what he believes, though to him it shows the privation of that belief. Such a man may well feel that he has a one-man job of making a decorum in which the experience of belief can be restored along with the experience of unbelief. His subject may well be rather more the effort than the accomplishment because he will try to sack the whole citadel of old orders whether he has dramatic (or mimetic) need of them or not. But if we remember his burden, as readers we can carry our share of it the more easily.

Eliot took up his burden early and has never been able quite to balance the load. His most important early essay was on "Tradition and the Individual Talent," in which the continuous modifiable whole of all literature was maintained as simultaneously existing. In the 'twenties he made the serious statement that the spirit killeth, the letter giveth life, and a little later, with regard to his conversion, he said he was not one of those who swallow the dogma for the sake of the emotion but put up with the emotion for the sake of the dogma. Again, he remarked that whereas intellectual belief was easily come by, emotional belief was the pursuit of a lifetime. These are the remarks of a man in anguish over the privation of decorum not that of his own time, yet intensely alive in his time. Unwilling to accept as sufficient the commitments visible in his society, yet himself committed to that society, he attempts to express its predicament in terms of the Christian tradition which ought to enlighten it. This is not, for many minds, a tenable position; and to many it seems to have forced Eliot back upon an ancestral utopia. That may be so—though Eliot might say, rather, that he had been forced not back but forward.

What is important is that Eliot has been forced, as none of the religious poetry of other Christian ages has been forced, to make present in his poetry not only Christian dogma and Christian emotion, but also the underlying permanent conditions, stresses, forces with which that dogma and that emotion are meant to cope. That is to say, Eliot as poet is compelled to present the aesthetic, the actual experience *of and under* Christianity at the same time that he uses his faith to understand, or express, that experience. This is the source of the power and influence and also of the weakness of his poetry.

There is no wonder in that. This is the burden which Arnold, better understood than he understood himself, imposed on poetry: not to replace religion but to give the actual experience of it *in its conditions.* It was under this kind of poetic impulse (not then directed toward religion) that Eliot *discovered* (which is why he had neither time nor need to *develop*) the notion that the emotion or feeling in the poetic situation to be expressed needed an objective correlative in the poem or play. It is only a further movement of this impulse that led him to his early argument about the poet as mere catalyst, the mere precipitator of a reaction between order and behavior, and the still further notion that intensity of poetic process was the sign of poetic maturity. It is this, now, in the Quartets, that leads him to say the poetry does not matter. It can be suggested, as a consequence of these observations, that Christian belief—any belief—is susceptible of the state where, if aesthetic experience is not the only possible experience, it is the experience most capable of authority. I do not say that Eliot believes any such thing—assuredly he does not—but in his poetry he is compelled to act as though he did: he has to take up that burden also.

It is for these and similar reasons that though we know what the poetry does as excitement and though we possess the excitement, it is not easy to say what it is about. It gives us the raw force of what it is about, plus something more, but we are not sure of the plus. So, also, though these poems move us, and in a direction among directions, we cannot say whether they have or do not have composition. Only by a decorum we do not possess could they come to have full composition: that is, a decorum with the realm of the ideal felt everywhere in apposition to the real and experienced in the realm of the actual. Meanwhile we rest on so much composition as may be secured by a combination of external form and so much of the traditional decorum as can be made to apply. If this is not enough, it is still a great deal; for it is by this combination that we *know* that we live in an incredible public world and an intolerable private world.

From his version of this knowledge Eliot proceeds in his search for the reality, and makes a kind of excess or aesthetic actuality by resort to what techniques of the mind he can find for making manifestations or epiphanies or incarnations of the real into the actual. We may say that these Quartets, having the *dogma* of the real, are an exemplary vade mecum for Eliot's pilgrimage toward the *emotion* of reality; or we can put it the other way round, that in these poems the actual is the riddle of the real, where the riddle is not so much for solution as for redemption. We begin, then, where pilgrimages should begin, with what we have, in intellect, on the edge of faith—the edge of what we have and the edge of what we have not.

We have a great deal in the intellect, in our citadel of old orders, and in various stages of development and disrepair, all in one way or another reflecting Eliot's one-man job of making a decorum. When listed out they seem more than any poem could stand, but that is because we tend to underestimate the unusual capacity for order that belongs to poetic imagination and because we ignore the tremendous pressure of behavior, or emotion, to fit into a proper order or orders. Here are five fourfold sequences as they apply to the four Quartets.

I. The immediate apprehension of timeless reality. The sickness of the soul when it comes short of timeless reality. The conditions of the soul: the river and the sea of life. The sin of the soul: in pride and humility.

II. The formal garden: the imposition of pattern: human actuality. Pattern as cycle in history: non-human actuality. Metaphorical patterns of the absolute actual: that is, of Annunciation. Metaphorical patterns of rebirth: the meaning of history.

III. The Rose-garden of any place: the present: the chance visit. The Ancestry of the dead: history: where one comes from. The ancestry of the forces showing only in nature: where one grows up; sempiternity. The ancestry and the inheritance by will and contemplation: where one thinks of self: enternity.

IV. The cycle of the elements. Air: the breath of life. Earth: decay and renewal. Water: what is in course and what is in permanence. Fire: of purgation and of love; of consumption and of consummation.

V. The Christian Cycle. Innocence in the garden. The Life of History. The Annunciation. The Incarnation and Crucifixion. Pentecost.

Also running through the poem there are at least three dramatic struggles: with time as the struggle with the pattern of the four elements; the struggle of the Fortune Teller and the Saint; and the struggle with language. All of these are part of the struggle to get at reality. Also, there are at least nine ideas or general notions implicated in this struggle. There is the idea of death in life and life in death: death as the condition of rebirth. The idea of the steps of Humility. The idea of getting at central reality by negative mysticism. The idea of music as the absolute condition of contemplation. The idea of the dance as the absolute condition of action. The idea of the still point: the intersection of time and the timeless. The idea of the sea, over and above any relation to the river. The idea of up and down, and how they are the same. The idea of beginning and end. The idea that the human enterprise is necessarily renewable.

Besides all this, the reminder is offered that each Quartet has in its parts the following five elements. I. A statement and counterstatement of the theme as predicament, given in terms of a scene or a landscape. II. A formal lyric: a birth by forms: with comment and conditions of further statement. III. Movement and action at the level of actual life. IV. A short lyric: an equivalent movement in the medium of music and the dance. V. Resumption and resolution (with consideration of the poet's job in his struggle with language) at the maximum level of statement—the level where the poetry does not matter.

It was looking forward to this sort of conspectus of orders that it was said above that, in a way, Eliot's effort to find his subject *is* his subject. To find the means of poetry is a step toward finding the subject, for the poetry will be its actual form. If you have the poetry the object may be found that corresponds to the subject.

Reflecting on this conspectus can we not sum up as follows? This is Court poetry without the operative aid of a court; religious poetry without the operative aid of a church; classical poetry without the effective presence of the classics. The presence and aid are all putative. They are there, like orthodoxy in Eliot's phrase, whether anybody knows it or not. This is religious, royalist, classical poetry written for a secular world which has not yet either shown its shape or declared its commitments—without which it cannot have a decorum of its own.

Let us now still further close our summary, at that point where the order is merged in the behavior. "Burnt Norton" is actual innocence and immediate experience. "East Coker" is actual experience and direct history. "Dry Salvages" is the conditions in nature in which innocence and experience take place: epiphanies of the reality which they engage. "Little Gidding" is the epiphany of the reality—that other, fatal reality—in *human* nature: the river and the sea within, as other and the same as the river and the sea without.

Again, "Dry Salvages" deals with the actual experience of pride and humility without doctrine, and without the ability to cope with them. "Little Gidding" deals with the experience of pride and humility under doctrine or dogma, but in the condition where they are forced into the actual. At this point we see that this man of necessary institutions would restore the ground upon which institutions are built: the ground of our beseeching. That is his actual experience of his institutions, and that is why they are live to him. There is the ground swell of the sea in "Dry Salvages," the ground of our beseeching in "Little Gidding." Both swells are from afar, both from mystery, both from reality. The ground swell is reality manifest in time. The ground of our beseeching is the reality manifest in timeless moments. The ground swell is all that is irredeemable. The ground of our beseeching is the hope of redemption; but there is a pattern of timeless moments which we cannot apprehend except in the ground swell.

I I I

It is in this aspect of apprehension that our behavior becomes belief. Apprehension is in the backward look, the backward half-look, into the primitive mystery where things are themselves, what they always were, like the rock in the "Dry Salvages," which is also the Trois Sauvages, and lastly a rock worn by the sea off Cape Ann. This is the outside, ending in the calamitous annunciation. It is not much different (only wholly different) within: as we say that the time of death is every moment. It is only the difference between menace and caress.

The menace and caress of wave that breaks on water; for does not a menace caress? does not a caress menace? It is the difference between the annunciation that becomes death and the Annunciation that becomes Incarnation. In the one life and the one mind and the one prayer ("the hardly, barely prayable prayer") that perceives both, we apprehend in actuality "the impossible union of spheres of existence."

So the order of the poem, for the moment it lasts, fuses the levels of belief and behavior. It would seem that in our institutions we have no means of coping (until the moment of death) with the "daemonic, chthonic powers," except the means of liberation from them. In the things that go toward death, we are driven. In the things that go toward new life, the things within us move us. There are many annunciations but only one Annunciation of Incarnation, "Costing not less than everything."

In this poem—which like other efforts at major poetry is a kind of provisional institution—it is often not possible to tell which annunciation into the actual is being dealt with. That is because of Eliot's own honesty; he cannot himself always tell. Nobody can tell honestly what is lost of the real when it gets into the actual. Meaning withers and is replaced by—either a fresh bloom, or a straw-flower from an older harvest; replaced by a need, or by an error. Thus (in "Little Gidding") the need to forgive both good and bad;

and thus the shame at motives late revealed. Nobody can tell a miracle, at sight, from a hallucination; though the one purifies and the other betrays the actual experience. The fuller the faith, the more difficult the task of honesty.

Is not this why in the Dante-like section of "Little Gidding," the "compound ghost both intimate and unidentifiable," is made to represent this final predicament of full faith: that there may be, always (though I do not myself believe it), *another* path, *another* pattern of timeless moments: not an anarchy, not a damnation, but another pattern, another revelation. Does not the great sin of human pride, within the forms of Eliot's belief, consist in *putting* God (one's own grasp, or loss, of reality) into first place? One should *find* reality; one cannot create it. Thus "The unknown, remembered gate," and thus "Taking any route." It is not in experience (as in "East Coker") but in prayer (as in "Little Gidding")—it is in the taking of things together, and in beseeching, that there is the sense of having found: "With the drawing of this Love and the voice of this Calling"—where drawing is attraction, and calling is summons.

But Eliot, being a believer, envisaging full faith, having the dogma of vital purpose, ends with the great idiosyncratic assertion—but only at the end. The emotion of the actual lasts up to the end. But the emotion can be *only* actual. It is the idiosyncrasy of Christian reality to be ineffable: a mystery which we do not so much experience as partake of. It is what suffers in us; and perhaps what it suffers, is, in part, the blows of other reality to which belief has not reached. So the poetic imagination sometimes compels us to think. It is eminently natural that, since reality is a mystery, man's institutions, and especially those institutions which are poems, as they cluster about that mystery, must again and again be made to feel the pressure of the real into the actual, lest the institutions lose their grasp of ideal aspiration and become mere formulae. We only *know* the real by what happens to it and to us; which is a true paradox. Man dwells in the actual, between the real and the real.

If this is true for Eliot, then his poem would seem to tell us, with examples, that man's ideals ought to be nourished by the cumulus of manifestations of the real into the actual (and of the actual into the real; for it is a reversible relation), and that these manifestations are enacted by Annunciation and Incarnation—the ideal of the fire to come; and also by Resurrection and the Immanence (or Descent) of the Holy Ghost.

But if this were all, then his poem would be only a set of doctrines out of dogmas, of verses made out of the traditional orders of the mind, put to work manipulating what images came to hand. Luckily there is more, as there is always more in poetry. Poetry by its use of language makes something—is always a *poiesis*—out of the doctrines in exact but unpredictable relation to the orders employed upon it. Poetry is more than usual emotion *and* more than usual order, and this double condition is the very condition of the language of poetry. Our language, as we understand it, purify it, keep it alive, is the great exemplary cumulus of our knowledge of the actual. Language is our memory, which we can partially master, of approximate intrusions of the real into the actual, just as it is also the body of our structures of the actual as it aspires into the real. To use Kenneth Burke's language, for the one, language is *symbolic* action, as for the other it is symbolic *action*. That is why Eliot's poem says of right language, *that it is the complete consort dancing together.* That is also why the poem says the poetry does not matter; the poetry is the way to get into language as a living resource. That is why this poem is a poetry of pattern and recurrence and modified repetition. That kind of poetry will drag more into being, as it is more nearly the condition of the actual, than that terribly deprived deformity of language known as polemic. Here the poetry is the "objective correlative" to the poem's *own* ineffable actual experience. The point is, the poem is not as near full response as the language the poem uses. All poems are imperfect. One cannot say of one's own calling, what one can say of what it aims at.

IV

Let us now think of the conditions of language where order and behavior work upon each other, but not forgetting the conditions of the mind using the language.

We must be still and still moving
Into another intensity
For a further union, a deeper communion
Through the dark cold and the empty desolation,
The wave cry, the wind cry, the vast waters
Of the petrel and the porpoise. In my end is my beginning.

In these lines, from the end of "East Coker," is an example of everything that needs still to be said. The mind is in a circle and it proceeds by analogy; and the mind needs to know nothing it does not
already know except the life in the words that it has not yet apprehended. The petrel is a bird of storm and its name is a diminutive
of Peter who walked upon the waters. The porpoise is that creature
not a fish of the most beautiful of all motion either in emerging
from water or submerging and the motion is single: this porpoise
who bore the souls of the dead to Hades and who even now precedes
us on our ocean voyages. Thus, as well as analogy and circle we
have images which are their own meanings.

In this Pilgrimage—by invocation, prayer, and ritual; all, like
rhythm, means of prolonging the contemplation of the moment—
in this Pilgrimage toward the emotion of reality (which is also the
vision of reality, the meaning of reality) the movement is circular
and the medium is allegory. These we will explore, then end on
image.

The circle is because things lead into themselves, because
experience leads into itself, or back to itself, or to the moment when
it confronts itself; and because also the things of experience meet
each other at different stages of development or relationship.

The analogy is because the things of experience do not pass out
of themselves but into different phases of themselves, and not always
at different times, but sometimes together and sometimes dispa-
rately, sometimes converging and concentrating, sometimes diverg-
ing and dissipating; and because it is by analogy alone, or almost
alone, that words record the drift and shift, the sequence and the
leap, from phase to phase, which seem the substance of our experience, moving us where we are moved: in our imitation of which
is our one act of creation, our one means of expressing something
more than was *already* in ourselves.

The circle is the serpent swallowing his own tail; but it is the serpent where no point is anywhere nearer the mouth than the tail. It is also, this circle, the up and the down, the end and the beginning, the sea and the river, the rock and the Incarnation.

The analogy is the correspondence of the members of the circle. It is the congruence, proportion, ratio, equivalence, correlation, but never the identity, of the members. It is in analogy that the action of the mind moves from one to the other, keeping both present: and does this in plurality as well as in duality. It is when we keep analogy in mind, that we see how it is that Eliot's correspondences move both ways, each requiring the other for its own elucidation; each working a little incongruously (with something left over and something left out) on the other; each imitating the other, or as we say, representing or enacting the other. It is the habit of analogy that keeps the circle *in* motion, *in* the actual, *in* a critical state. It keeps the circle from being finished; keeps it inclusive rather than exclusive; keeps it from self-satisfaction. The habit of analogy is the great reminder of what we would like to forget and what we must remember: that no revelation expressed or understood in human terms is total or complete, however we may believe it total beyond our terms of expression and understanding. It is by analogy that we create approximations of the experience we have not had: faith as the substance of things hoped for, and, as it were equally, the substance of things dreaded.

I suspect that this is kin to what Eliot meant by saying that the advantage for the poet was to see beneath both beauty and ugliness (the One and the other than One, order and chaos), to see the boredom, the horror, and the glory. Certainly, at any rate, in the *Four Quartets* it is analogies of these three that in beauty and ugliness we are brought to see. Again, in an older phrase, it is in the context of habitual analogy that we take upon us the mystery of things and become God's spies. Lear himself is a multiple analogy—both in pattern and in image—of the boredom, the horror, and the glory; and the ripeness (which is all) is the ripeness of each phase as it drifts, or crosses the gap, into the other place.

It is because Eliot's mind is both circular and dramatic that it has had to resort so much to analogy; and it is because his mind, as sensibility, is a great onion of analogy that he has had to resort to so many patterns and frames of experience. If you think of the Mediterranean catholic mind, it is one thing, which is not the same as the northern mind, catholic or not. The northern catholic mind would seem to require (since it contains so much more material which has not been incorporated into the Graeco-Christian rationale) a greater recourse to analogy to explain, or express, its own content to itself. This is only a suspicion, and only thrown out. But in any case, the Christian mind is never the whole mind, though the whole mind may aspire to be Christian, and it is one way of construing the Christian poet's task to make something—to make as much as he can—of the struggle of the whole mind to enact that aspiration. That is one way of accounting for what Eliot is up to in these poems. He has to discover what it is in that mind which struggles, and he has to find ways—analogies—by which he can keep his discoveries present. He has to keep present all those creations other than Christian, all those conditions of life other than human, which affect his sensibility and press into his behavior. As a poet, he must know and deal with, what as a Christian he perhaps has only to know and transcend, all that knowledge and experience which is not Christian and which is so much greater in quantity than the Christian. It would seem that in our stage of history, all the phases of the relations between behavior and belief have become live and urgent issues in the action of the mind to a degree that they have not been since the twelfth or thirteenth century. There was a deadness of the mind after Dante that destroyed more than did the Black Death of 1348.

If this sort of consideration is pertinent at all it is more pertinent to the avowedly Christian mind than another: he will see the predicament in greater extremity, and the more especially if, like Eliot, he has also an anti-clerical cast of mind. The war between emotion and belief, and the impurity of that war, will press him hardly. He will be forced to much deliberate and individual creation and re-creation of both image and pattern. He will be forced to attempt what he cannot do, and what, though he knows he cannot do it, he must nevertheless attempt if only because he sees that it is there to do. He must make what he does *stand for* what he cannot do, but he must never permit it (though it will happen, as the inevitable abuse of powers) to substitute for what he cannot do. These considerations seem to me to explain partially the fragmentary interrupted character of Eliot's composition from "Gerontion" onward, to explain the materials that get into his poems and the ineffable tensions between them, and also to explain the over-arching dramatic gestures of analogy by which he unites them. These considerations perhaps also explain the force of the poetry: why it is so much of ourselves we find struggling there—a special case of ourselves, as James would say—and as much so whether we are with or are without the special version of belief we take to be his belief. We are engaged in the same war, with different tokens, and the same substance unknown. We "are the music while the music lasts," and while the music lasts we make the same pilgrimage toward reality.

Let us look at some examples, in none of which do I wish to distinguish the circular from the analogic aspects. The distinction would be merely analytic, and the two aspects are much better taken in single perception.

In "East Coker" the first line is the motto of Mary Queen of Scots: but in reversed order; and the last half of the last line is the same motto but in its original order. We move from In my beginning is my end, to In my end is my beginning. I take it that this motto is in analogy to the references to Heraclitus and St. John of the Cross in its first use, and that in the second use it is joined with the analogy of earth and sea, and with

> The wave cry, the wind cry, the vast waters
> Of the petrel and the porpoise. In my end is my beginning.

Here are two chains-of-being in human history (social and Christian) drawn together and put into relation with the history which is not human in such a way that all three are united in a single perception. This perception jumps the gap into the last iteration of the initial phrase: In my end is my beginning. This is analogy reaching up to the condition of the medieval anagoge: actually reaching the modern equivalent for it.

Eliot is quite aware of the distinction between the medieval and the modern analogy—and he makes us quite aware of it in at least two instances in "East Coker," both in the second section. One is in the word "grimpen" which is without meaning in itself, but is a place name, that is to say a word meaning itself entirely, taken from the Great Grimpen Mire in *The Hound of the Baskervilles*. Eliot's line, "On the edge of a grimpen, where is no secure foothold," is inserted in a reference to the deceits made by the patterns imposed by knowledge derived from experience, and has to do with the knowledge so to speak which *is* experience: the grimpen in short, the thing itself with its *own* pattern, new every moment, and perhaps with ultimate deceits, all that must be sought for and shunned, on the way to knowledge beyond experience. That is one instance. The other is in the formal song which begins the second section of "East Coker," together with the verses immediately following in comment on the song. It is a song of the disturbance of things out of season, with flowers of all seasons in bloom at once, and with stars belonging to July and November in constellated wars: it is the condition when the world goes into the dark and into the fire "which burns before the icecap reigns." The flowers are of the senses, the stars are of astronomy and astrology both. The footwork is neat, the meaning is derivable (as any large dictionary will show), and the first seven lines have an analogous relation with the remainder of the song, but the analogy is not vital. That is almost why it is there; for the poem goes on:

> That was a way of putting it—not very satisfactory:
> A periphrastic study in a worn-out poetical fashion,
> Leaving one still with the intolerable wrestle
> With words and meanings. The poetry does not matter.

The poetry does not matter, but what does matter must be put in poetry to keep it in place. *That* historical skill has become periphrastic. The language of the stars is no longer a mature language, in the sense that it no longer works, except through the dictionary, and has only the fascination of a dead game, no matter what the astrologers think; it plays something, but we no longer know what. Yet it

contributes to, and is in analogy with, the two lines which end this
section of "East Coker," two lines with a space between them:

> The houses are all gone under the sea.

> The dancers are all gone under the hill.

This section deals with the humiliation *and* the humility that go
with the struggle for faith

> On the edge of a grimpen, where is no secure foothold,
> And menaced by monsters, fancy lights,
> Risking enchantment.

And it leads by right into the Dark of the next section, at first a
Miltonic dark (O dark dark dark. They all go into the dark) and then
the darkness of God of St. John of the Cross. The dark of moonlight
becomes the dark of the stars. In the very failure of the equivalence
lies the strength of these analogies: the failure is part of the experience of "the intolerable wrestle with words and meanings."

It all comes back to the relation and the struggle between belief
and behavior: and this is all the more clearly seen if we move from
"East Coker" to the "Dry Salvages," from the history of man to the
life of the individual, from human history to the history of the conditions in which humans live: to the river within and the sea all
about us: to the gods and to God: to the many annunciations and
the one Annunciation: to the sea and the Virgin: and also to the
half-guessed, half-understood life which is somehow—not in our
old skills of interpretation, not in what we have understood either
in our experience or our revelation—which is somehow one Incarnation. There, by the fiat of incarnation, by the images of ultimate
behavior actually in the poem,

> The hint half guessed, the gift half understood, is Incarnation.
> Here the impossible union
> Of spheres of existence is actual,
> Here the past and the future

Are conquered, and reconciled. . . .
We, content at the last
If our temporal reversion nourish
(Not too far from the yew-tree)
The life of significant soil.

Not too far from the yew-tree. Sir Thomas Browne says the yew is "an emblem of Resurrection from its perpetual verdure." In our temporal reversion. Reversion is residue, is going back; in law is the returning of an estate to the grantor or his heirs. Hence the significant soil.

It is these lines, this fiat, at the end of the last part of "Dry Salvages," that establishes the relations, perfects the analogy, back through the other parts to the great sestina of the sea which is in the second part, and the double invocation of the river and the sea in the first part. Thus we understand that the "ragged rock in the restless waters," no matter what else it is, "is what it always was." And thus, also, we understand:

The salt is on the briar rose,
The fog is in the fir trees.

"East Coker" was incarnation in history, and purgation in darkness. "Dry Salvages" is Incarnation in Nature, and, through the Virgin, through the hint *and* the gift, in significant soil. The annunciations—the troubling messages—become the Annunciation, and are included by it.

These, then, are examples of analogies within their circles, and if we think of them together certain questions raise themselves about the relation of the patterns of the analogies to the images which are their elements. Which is the primary element of the correspondence: all the borrowed frames or the found images? The hollyhocks or the stars, the petrel and the porpoise or the ragged rock which is what it always was. There is the question of patterns and that which requires us to find patterns; the question of images (reaches, drifts, in perception) and that which requires us to find images. Perhaps there is a reversible relation; either the images or the patterns renew and change and come to zero, to the fecund still

point of the turning world. There is a pattern in the pressing images—
if only we could find it. There are images in the pattern—if only
we could feel them.

V

With that effort to find and feel, the remainder of these notes
is concerned. That is, we shall deal with poetic composition by the
attractive force of images which are neither circular nor analogical,
images which are set in the center and draw things to them, compelling the things to declare their own meaning, transforming the
things into enclosed tautologies. It is in part five of each quartet that
such images are conspicuously found. In "Burnt Norton" there is
the form or pattern of the Chinese jar.

> Only by the form, the pattern,
> Can words or music reach
> The stillness, as a Chinese jar still
> Moves perpetually in its stillness.

In "East Coker" there is this:

> Not the intense moment
> Isolated, with no before or after,
> But a lifetime burning in every moment
> And not the lifetime of one man only
> But of old stones that cannot be deciphered.

In "Dry Salvages," there is this:

> For most of us, there is only the unattended
> Moment, the moment in and out of time,
> The distraction fit, lost in a shaft of sunlight,
> The wild thyme unseen, or the winter lightning
> Or the waterfall, or music heard so deeply
> That it is not heard at all, but you are the music
> While the music lasts.

In "Little Gidding," there is this:

Every phrase and every sentence is an end and a beginning,
Every poem an epitaph. And any action
Is a step to the block, to the fire, down the sea's throat
Or to an illegible stone: and that is where we start.

And again in "Little Gidding," there is this:

> The voice of the hidden waterfall
> And the children in the apple-tree
> Not known, because not looked for
> But heard, half-heard, in the stillness
> Between two waves of the sea.

And this, in its turn, works back upon the following lines in "Dry Salvages," but is also an image for its own sake:

> The sea howl
> And the sea yelp, are different voices
> Often together heard; the whine in the rigging,
> The menace and caress of wave that breaks on water.

All but the last of these images have to do with the poet meditating his job of *poiesis*, meditating as if making an aesthetic: unearthing, discovering, exploring, beseeching a skill which, when he has it, will do the work over which *otherwise* he has no control. This is the skill of inspiration, of invoking the muses by ritual, in short the skill of incantation. It is the skill of skills, the mystery of the craft. It is how you get through the mere skills of poetry (what may be learned and rehearsed) into the skill of language itself (whatever *reality* is there) without losing the mere skill of poetry. It is then that you find that the poetry no longer matters; it matters, but *no longer*.

All of us, some of the time, seem to believe that it is by images like these (in their sequences, relations, triangulations) that Eliot composes his poems. At any rate, we believe that Eliot wants such images to act like compositors—as magic agents of composition. Beliefs of this kind are representatives of a deeper, troubled belief (the stage of belief when it is troubled and exasperated by unbelief—the movement of the exasperated spirit from wrong to wrong), the belief that the mind is not up to the task of responding to what confronts it; the belief that the mind must somehow incorporate into the response part of what confronts it; the belief that there is a failure of rational imagination when it ought least to be expected— at the very center of interest, the identification of the subject (or object) of response. I would say that this troubled belief is a part, but only a part, of Eliot's experience. It is one of the persisting conditions of experience, and a condition which has a relation to the conditions of our experience of poetry and language, what we do with language and what language does itself, what we create in language and what language creates in us. But it is not central; it cannot be ignored. It must not be destroyed. It is certainly a corrective. It interrupts and modulates the rhythm of our footfalls, and sometimes seems the substance of the rhythm itself—but only seems. I would suppose then that these images (these closed tautologies) are present as symbolic reminders of the uneven rhythm of the rational imagination; that they operate—where they come—as a very high-level ad libbing habit of the rational poetic imagination; and that they furnish a consciously incomplete additional symbolic form of one persisting pattern of experience: one among many ways of composition: the way from the point of view of which Eliot spoke when he called poetry a mug's game.

It is true that for most of us most of the time any operation belonging to the full intelligence is a mug's game; and for all of us there is the precipice, either just behind us or just ahead of us.

Possibly this mug should be kept in mind whenever inspiration of the muses or ritual are under consideration, for all of these objects are counterparts in the mug's game of the mind. But, with this caution, I prefer to think of these images as primarily concerned with wooing the muse; that wooing which is the steady passion of the poet; and one of the reasons for this preference is that although each of these images seems independent, tautological, and generative, each is also appropriate—or keyed to—the general frame of rational imagination in which it occurs. The Chinese bowl belongs to the children in the apple-tree, to the formal garden. The lifetime of old stones that cannot be deciphered belongs to history and the conditions of human life in history. The music heard so deeply that you are the music while the music lasts, belongs both to the river within us, to the sea that is all about us, and to the vast waters of the petrel and the porpoise, as these are annunciated. And every poem is an epitaph belongs to the birth in death, to the death and birth which are *both* perennial and permanent, to the one and the One. It seems to me that seen as *so* keyed, seen as *thus* appropriate, these images become indeed agents of composition.

That is to say they are seen as themselves analogies which by enlightening each other are themselves enlightened, but which never enlighten themselves. The analogies are always pretty much undeclared, they do not say what they are about. They are ungoverned: they do not come *directly* under the head or the power of anything, but only by association. They are incomplete: they always require their parallels, and they always represent more than they state. To understand this, two sets of words from Shelley's "Defense of Poetry" seem useful. Words, says Shelley, "unveil the permanent analogies of things by images which participate in the life of truth." Here the word "participate" is the moving term. Again, Shelley remarks that misery, terror, despair itself, in poetry, create "approximations to the highest good." Here it is the word "approximations" that we want to keep in mind. Shelley seems to have hit on something which if it did not describe his own poetry, yet could not have been more expressly written to describe the poetry of Eliot; as, in another way, at a much fuller extension of his terms, it describes that of Dante.

In Dante the extension is to all the modes of the mind. In Eliot the reduction is to the images or small metaphors as they work and build on one another. In Dante there are many languages of the mind conspicuously and consciously at work. In Eliot, though there are other modes working, a predominance of the work is done in the language of the words themselves. We deal largely with what has got into the language *as* words, relatively little with what the words call on. In Eliot the authority is more direct, more limited, and with greater gaps. We are left with what the words will bear and with reminders of what the language will not bear. There is a radical difference in the *magnitude* of the authority of language as poetry in the two poets, which I believe has something to do with the *magnitude* of *achieved* mind confronted with life. This is not to condemn Eliot but to describe him, and in a sense, since he is writing our poetry, to describe ourselves. It seems, looking back, that with Dante the great rebellious troubles of unbelief fed and strengthened his belief, but that with Eliot there is a struggle between belief and unbelief in which each devours the other, except at the moment of desperation. Eliot has passed through the stages of Montaigne, St. John of the Cross, Pascal, Baudelaire, Mallarmé, and Valéry. It is a destructive process. In St. Francis our little sisters the flowers were left as well as our little sister Death. In Dante the Love still moved the sun and the other stars; and there is everywhere the continuous declaration of indestructible human identity. In Eliot there is the choice of pyre or pyre, of consumption or consummation, in either case a destruction. It would seem that the purgation destroys that which was to have been purged, and that refinement is into nothingness.

At least this is the sort of judgment into which we should be pushed by the "doctrine" of the poem, if we had to accept the doctrine by itself and without benefit of the images of permanent analogy to which it clings and with which it corrects itself. It is the sort of doctrine to which the unimpeded mind of our day turns as if by instinct—and to which the unimpeded part of all minds is drawn, tempted, called. The impediments, what holds us back, brings us up, concentrates us, are in poetry in the images. The impediments are to the point, and *Every poem an epitaph*, from "Little Gidding," is an excellent example; it is beside the doctrine, illuminates the doctrine, redeems the doctrine.

An epitaph is a funeral oration, a commendatory inscription; it gets rid of the dead, understands the dead, rejoins the dead, and also takes off from the dead. Every poem is an epitaph; but an epitaph is a poem, precisely because it has a life of its own which modifies the life of what died, and because it thereby instigates the renewal of the life which never died. It gets us back to the reality from which we started and thereby forward to the reality in which we shall end. It is thus, in Shelley's phrase, that even our despair is an approximation of the highest good; and in Eliot's mood we have only our despair with which to make an approximation. Thus: "we shall not cease from exploration."

And so on, there is image after image that could be tackled with similar results. Let us, to conclude, take rather a single line from the second part of "Little Gidding," which both has a special interest and generalizes the whole poem: "To the spirit unappeased and peregrine." For the most part Eliot's metaphors of analogy restore us to the underblows or the cellarage of the primitive in our souls and mind and behavior. But in the Dante-like section from which this line is taken it is everywhere the power of statement—the power of the rational imagination at the point of maximum control of the irrational and primitive in behavior—that is at stake. It is a mirror of the mind more like Shakespeare than like Dante. There is a terrible *disinterestedness* here quite different from the terrible *interestedness* of Dante. It is as if Eliot had to write "like Dante," which happens to be in singularly pure traditional blank verse, in order to feel "like Shakespeare." It is as if he had to do this in order to get at his full compound ghost of poet and man. The dark dove with the flickering tongue has gone, the disfigured street remains in the waning dusk and breaking day. The whole job of man's world is to be done over again and the whole role of man in his world is to be re-created. Yet it is all the same, all perennial and all permanent and all unique. "The words sufficed to compel the recognition they preceded."

> the passage now presents no hindrance
> To the spirit unappeased and peregrine
> Between two worlds become much like each other.

Here is the American expatriate; the uprooted man in a given place; the alien making a home; man the alien on earth; man as the wanderer becoming the pilgrim; and the pilgrim returning with the last and fatal power of knowing that what was the pilgrim in him is only the mature and unappeasable state of the first incentive. All this is immediately present in the word "peregrine," and it is also gradually present with the aid of a little knowledge, and it is also finally present as something that reveals itself as you let the content of the word work into its surroundings and as you invite what surrounds it to join naturally to the word itself.

In the Republic and the Empire, *Peregrini* were, in Rome, citizens of any state other than Rome, with an implied membership in a definite community. So says the Oxford Classical Dictionary. The Shorter Oxford Dictionary says of "Peregrine": one from foreign parts, an alien, a wanderer; and goes on to say that in astrology (that ironic refuge of Eliot as of Donne and of Dante) a peregrine is a planet situated in a part of the zodiac where it has none of its essential dignity. In Italian the meanings are similar, and the notion of pilgrim is a late development.—Have we not an expatriate looking for a *patria*—an American turned Anglican—a perpetual peregrine at Rome? To clinch it, let us look to Dante (*Purgatorio* XIII, 94–96):

> *O frate mio, ciascuna è cittadina*
> *d'una vera città; ma tu vuoi dire*
> *che vivesse in Italia peregrina.*

> O my brother, each is citizen
> of a true City; but you would say
> one that lived in Italy peregrine.

I do not know how much nearer home we need to come, but if we think of Arnold's Grande Chartreuse poem, surely we are as close to the quick of the peregrine's home as we are likely to come. There looking at the old monastery Arnold felt himself hung between two worlds, one dead and the other powerless to be born. I do not think this is too much to pack into a word, but it is no wonder that it should take the attribute unappeasable, for it is the demands of the peregrine, whether outsider or pilgrim, that cannot be met. I will add that the peregrine is also a hawk or falcon found the world over but never at home: always a migrant but everywhere met; and, wherever found, courageous and swift.

T W O

The Expense of Greatness:
Three Emphases on
Henry Adams
[1 9 3 6]

Where your small man is a knoll to be smoothed away, Henry Adams is a mountain to be mined on all flanks for pure samples of human imagination without loss of size or value. That is the double test of greatness, that it show an attractive force, massive and inexhaustible, and a disseminative force which is the inexhaustible spring or constant declaration of value. As we elucidate our reaction to the two forces we measure the greatness.

In Adams the attractive force is in the immediate relevance that his life and works have for our own. The problems he posed of human energy and human society are felt at once to be special and emphatic articulations of our own problems. The disseminative, central force, which we find objectified in his works, may be felt and seen as the incandescence of the open, enquiring, sensitive, and skeptical intelligence, restless but attentive, saltatory but serial, provisional in every position yet fixed upon a theme: the theme of thought or imagination conceived as the form of human energy. We feel the incandescence in the human values and aspirations that were fused by it, from time to time, in persuasive form; and the cumulus of his life and works makes a focus, different as differently felt, whereby the particular values actually rendered shine concentrated as it were in their own best light. We make the man focus upon himself, make him achieve—as he never could for himself in the flux and flexion of life—his own most persuasive form. To make such a focus is the labor and the use of critical appreciation.

The approaches to such a labor are varied and must be constantly renewed and often revised. No single approach is omniscient or even sufficient. Here, in this essay, I want to take Henry Adams in a single perspective and submit it to three related emphases. I want to regard him as he often chose to regard himself, as a representative example of education: but education pushed to the point of failure as contrasted with ordinary education which stops at the formula of success.

The perspective is worth a preliminary emphasis of its own. It was as failure both in perspective and lesson by lesson that Adams himself saw his education. Success is not the propitious term for education unless the lesson wanted is futile. Education has no term and if arrested at all is only arrested by impassable failure. Surely the dominant emotion of an education, when its inherent possibilities are compared with those it achieved, must strike the honest heart as the emotion of failure. The failure is not of knowledge or of feeling. It is the failure of the ability to react correctly or even intelligently to more than an abbreviated version of knowledge and feeling: failure in the radical sense that we cannot consciously react to more than a minor fraction of the life we yet deeply know and endure and die. It is the failure the mind comes to ultimately and all along when it is compelled to measure its knowledge in terms of its ignorance.

Most failures we have the tact to ignore or give a kinder name. That is because we know by instinct at what a heavy discount to put most proffered examples of failure. There was no effort of imagination in them and only private agony, where for great failure we want the utmost unrelenting imagination and the impersonal agony of knowledge searching the haven of objective form. Most failures come too easily, take too little stock of the life and forces around them: like the ordinary failure in marriage, or business, or dying; and so too much resemble the ordinary success—too solemn and scant and zestless for realization. A genuine failure comes hard and slow, and, as in a tragedy, is only fully realized at the end. A man's success is in society, precarious and fatal; his failure is both in spite and because of society—as he witnesses its radical imperfection and is himself produced by it, its ultimate expression. Thus in a great man we often find inextricably combined the success which was his alone, though posthumously recognized, with the failure which as we feel it is also our own in prospect.

Let us take for our first emphasis Adams as a failure in society. If we assume that an education means the acquisition of skills and the mastery of tools designed for intelligent reaction in a given context, it will appear that Adams's failure in American political society after the Civil War was a failure in education. Society was bound for quick success and cared only for enough intelligence to go on with. It cared nothing for political mastery, and commonly refused to admit it had a purpose beyond the aggregation of force in the form of wealth. The effect on Adams as a young man was immediate but took time to recognize. If *vis inertiae* was enough for society, any education was too much; and an Adams—with the finest education of his times—was clearly useless. The question was perhaps not initially of Adams's failure but of society's inability to make use of him: its inability to furnish a free field for intelligent political action. Washington was full of wasted talent—of able young men desperately anxious to be of use—as it is now; but no one knows what talent might accomplish, then or now, because talent has never been given a chance without being at the same moment brutally hamstrung.

The discovery—that he was to be wasted whether he was any good or not—was all the bitterer to Henry Adams because he had three generations of conspicuous ability and conspicuous failure behind him. Every Adams had ended as a failure after a lifetime of effort—marked by occasional and transitory success—to handle political power intelligently. Their intelligence they had kept; none had ever succumbed to the criminal satisfaction of power on its lowest terms—whether power for interest, or, worst of all, power for its own sake: the absolute corruption, as it seems to a scrupulous mind, of giving in; but all equally had failed at the height of their abilities. If times had changed for Henry it was for the worse. Where his ancestors found in a combination of scruple and temper an effective termination of useful public careers, Henry found his scruple alone enough to preclude a public career altogether. Scruple is sometimes only a name for snobbery, stiffness, or even an inner coldness—all, forms of disability; but in an Adams scruple was the mark of ability itself, and its limit, as it made intelligence acute, responsible, and infinitely resourceful, but a little purblind to the advantage of indirection. An Adams could meet an issue, accept facts, and demonstrate a policy, but he could never gamble with a public matter. Jefferson's epitaph for John applied to them all: as disinterested as his maker. If the odds grew heavy against an Adams he resorted to an access of will—or, if you choose to call it, a wall of stubbornness, which is merely will grown hysterical. But acts of will or stubbornness are merely the last resorts of minds compelled to act scrupulously against the unintelligent or the unintelligible.

Thus it is that many great men, if seen as examples of intellectual biography, seem either sports or parasites upon the society that produced them. They were compelled to act against or outside it; and our sense of radical connection and expressive identity is only reestablished in the examples of their works aside from their lives. Certainly something of the sort is true, with different emphases, of Whitman, Mark Twain, Henry James, Melville, and in our own day of Hart Crane and George Santayana. They stand out too much from their native society: all outsiders from the life they expressed and upon which they fed. If all knew the ignominy of applause, applause from the wrong people, for the wrong thing, or for something not performed at all, it only accented their own sense of eccentricity and loneliness. That is how Adams stood out, but without much applause ignominious or otherwise, eccentric and lonely; but within him, as within the others in their degrees, was an intelligence whose actions were direct, naked, and at their best terrifyingly sane.

If, as I think, it was the scruple of his mind that made Adams an outsider and that at the same time gave precise value to his eccentricity, then the scruple should be defined both for itself and in terms of Adams. It is what I have been deviously leading up to: as it represents the single heroic and admirable quality of the modern and skeptical mind as such; and a quality not called for by the occasion but crowning it, even when disastrously.

Scruple, generally speaking, is the agent of integrity, what keeps action honest on the level of affairs, or on the level of imagination when actuality or truth is the object. The etymology of the word refreshes the meaning I emphasize, where we have the Latin *scrupulus*, a small sharp stone, a stone in one's shoe, an uneasiness, difficulty, small trouble, or doubt. Scruples differ with the type of mind and education. Most men either get rid of them or show pride in their calluses. In either case the process of thought is made easy and reaction insensitive; you give in, you are practically carried along, but you get nowhere except where you are taken, and you know nothing at all of what you have been through, or of its meaning.

Specifically, with Henry Adams, scruple of thinking and thence of action was the whole point of his education for public life. Men without scruples either victimized power or succumbed to it; and if you had the wrong scruples you succumbed, like Grant, without knowing it. Political education was meant to supply the right scruples at the start, to teach sensitiveness to new ones as they came up, and to ingrain a habit of feeling for them if not apparent. It is scruples that compel attention to detail and subordinate the detail to an end. When excess, whether of scruples or the lack of them, atrophies the mind, it is because either an impossible end or no end was in view. In science the adjudication of scruples is called method and taken for granted; but the whole test of the democratic process is whether or not the seat of power attracts the scrupulous intelligence and gives it rein. Here we may conceive Henry Adams as a provisional focus for that test.

In a sense no test is possible. Adams never held office. He only made himself embarrassingly available in the near background of Grant's Washington. Power was what he wanted, but on his own terms: the terms of his training. Perhaps he offered too much; perhaps his offers seemed too much like demands; at any rate he got nothing. But if we take him as a type—whether of 1868 or 1932— we can see that he was in the predicament of all young men whose abilities seem to lie in public life but who refuse waste motion. Society has no use for them as they are, and the concessions it requires are fatal to self-respect and taste, and lead either to futility, the treason of submission, or an aching combination of the two.

[233

Both Adams and society saw politics was a game, but the difference in their angles of vision made their views irreconcilable. Adams saw the game as played impersonally with, as ultimate stake, the responsible control of social energy. Since ultimate value was never sure, every move ought to be made with the maximum intelligence and subject to every criticism your experience provided. If you stuck scrupulously to your intelligence you had the chance to come out right in the end under any scruples, democratic or not. You had a chance to put your society in control of itself at the center of its being. That was Adams's idea of the game, the idea of any honest young man.

Society played differently. The stake was immediate power, the values were those of personal interest. Thus the actual stake—control of social energy—was left for the ventures of interests irresponsible to the government meant to control them. Society in its political aspect cared more for chaos than unity; and the democratic process was an unconfessed failure, obliviously committing itself to social anarchy. Yet the failure remained unconfessed; the society lived and gathered energy; it was omnivorous, rash, and stupid; it threatened to become uncontrollably leviathan; it seemed occasionally on the point of committing suicide in the full flush of life. Always it had been saved, so far, by its vitality, its prodigious capacity for successive ruination, or by the discovery of a new and available source of power.

There was the young man's predicament. Should he assume that society was no field for intelligence and that its own momentum was sufficient to its needs? Should he rather enter the field, outwardly playing society's version of the game, while inwardly playing his own as best he could? Or should he work on society from the outside, accepting his final defeat at the start, and express the society rather than attempt to control it?

The first choice is the hardest; taken mostly by weak minds, it resembles more the dullness of indifference than disconsolate impartiality. Most men of ability, fortunately, make the second choice; it is they that make the administration of society possible and intermittently tolerable. Individually, most of them disappear, either lose office or succumb to it; but the class is constantly replenished from the bottom. A few survive the struggle in their own identity, and these are the ideals the young men hope to cap. J. Q. Adams was one of these, Gallatin and Schurz are clearly two more, as Senators Walsh and Norris make two examples for our own day. Men like Cleveland and Theodore Roosevelt are partial survivals. Adams thought his friend John Hay not only survived but succeeded in establishing a sound foreign policy; history is a harsher judge than friendship. As a general thing promise in politics not only dies early but is resurrected in the corruption of party or unwitting interest, which is what happened to Adams's friend Lodge. For the most part Adams's reiterated sentiment remains apt: "A friend in power is a friend lost." Small men might pass unnoticed to honorable graves but the great were lost.

Henry Adams lacked the dimensions suitable to a small man in public life and lacked the coarseness of will and ability to dissimulate to seize the larger opportunity, had it offered. Hence he made gradually the third choice, and brought the pressure of all the education he could muster upon society from the outside. It took him seven to ten years to make the choice complete. The first form of pressure he exerted was that of practical political journalism, of which the principal remaining results are the essays on "The New York Gold Conspiracy," "The Session, 1869–1870," and the essay on American financial policy called "The Legal-Tender Act." The second form of pressure was also practical, and combined the teaching of history at Harvard with the editorship of *The North American Review*. Already, however, the emphasis of his mind was becoming imaginative and speculative. Seven years in Cambridge taught him the impossibility of affecting society to any practical extent through the quarterly press, or through any press at all. Two of his essays were made campaign documents by the Democrats—their import reduced to the level of vituperative rhetoric—and then forgotten; so that by the test of the widest publication possible their practical effect was nil. There remained a third form of pressure not so much indirect as remote, and that was pressure by the imaginative expression, through history and fiction and philosophy, of social character and direction; and the aim was to seize the meaning of human energy by defining its forms and to achieve, thus, if it was possible, a sense of unity both for oneself and one's society.

Expression is a form of education, and the form that was to occupy the rest of Adams's life, the subject of our second emphasis. Put another way, society had failed to attract Adams to its center, and Adams undertook to see whether or not he could express a center for it. Unity or chaos became the alternative lesson of every effort. Here we have gone over or climbed up to a second level of failure, which is the failure of the human mind, pushed to one of its limits, to solve the problem of the meaning, the use, or the value of its own energy: in short the failure to find God or unity. What differentiates Adams's mind from other minds engaged in the same effort is his own intense and progressive recognition of his failure; and that recognition springs from the same overload of scruples that made him eccentric to the society that produced him. What he did not recognize was the ironical consolation that the form his work took as a whole was itself as near the actual representative of unity as the individual mind can come; which is what we have now to show.

Henry Adams's mind acquired, as his work stretched out, a singular unity of conception and a striking definiteness of form. It was the idiosyncrasy of his genius to posit unity in multiplicity, and by exploring different aspects of the multiplicity to give the effect, known to be false or specious but felt as true, of apprehending the unity. In reading *The Life of Albert Gallatin*, so successfully is the effect of Gallatin's career composed, we have to think twice before realizing that it is meant to show one aspect in the story of the failure of the democratic process to unite American society. Published in 1879, when Adams was forty-one, it so well struck the theme of Adams's whole career that it can be bracketed with Adams's own autobiography and be called "The Education of Albert Gallatin."

As important here, striking his theme gave Adams his first mature prose. The previous essays had been comparatively metallic, brittle, and rhetorical, and carried a tone of intermittent assertiveness rather than of cumulative authority. It was the subject perhaps that matured the style: Gallatin was the best in character, ability, and attainment that American history had to offer. At any rate, the biography of John Randolph, which came in 1882 and portrayed the worst waste in ability and personal disintegration in American history, showed a reversion to the earlier immature style. If Adams was, as Hay said, half angel and half porcupine, then it was altogether the porcupine that got into this book. The tragedy of Randolph was personal eccentricity, his constant resorts hysteria and violence, and Adams brought those elements over into his own style. Later, in his History, Adams repaired his injustice and treated him with charity of understanding, as an energetic sample of his times.

Meanwhile and just afterwards, in 1880 and 1884, Adams published his two novels, *Democracy* and *Esther*. These suffer about equally from Adams's incompetence as a novelist, and the reader can take them best as brilliant documentary evidence of Adams's insights and preoccupations. To intrude the standards of the art of fiction would be to obviate the burden the books actually carry. *Democracy* exhibits a political society full of corruption, irresponsible ambition, and stupidity, against the foil of a woman's taste and intelligence. So brilliant and light is Adams's execution, it is hard to decide which vice is worst of the three.

Madeleine Lee, Adams's foil, is struck a heavy blow in the face by her first and only presidential reception. She stands fascinated and aghast at the endless wooden procession. "What a horrid warning to ambition! And in all that crowd there was no one beside herself who felt the mockery of this exhibition. To all the others this task was a regular part of the President's duty, and there was nothing ridiculous about it." It was Adams, not Mrs. Lee, who felt the full force of the blow. He remembered what he had seen at Devonshire House a few years back when Madame de Castiglione, the famous beauty of the Second Empire, entered.

How beautiful she may have been, or indeed what sort of beauty she was, Adams never knew, because the company, consisting of the most refined and aristocratic society in the world, instantly formed a lane, and stood in ranks to stare at her, while those behind mounted on chairs to look over their neighbors' heads; so that the lady walked through the polite mob, stared completely out of countenance, and fled the house.

[237

In *Democracy*, Mrs. Lee received a second blow, which we may obscurely feel as a consequence of the first, when, after his corruption is discovered to her and she taxes him with it, her suitor, Secretary of the Treasury Ratcliffe, defends himself by minimizing his offense, passing it off as commonplace, and asks her to purify American politics through marriage to him and with his aid.

The audacity of the man would have seemed sublime if she had felt sure that he knew the difference between good and evil, between a lie and the truth; but the more she saw of him, the surer she was that his courage was mere moral paralysis, and that he talked about virtue and vice as a man who is color-blind talks about red and green; he did not see them as she saw them; if left to choose for himself he would have nothing to guide him.

Which blow was the harder to bear? Was corruption, like stupidity, only an atrophied form of intelligence? Given the system and the society, did not the practice of politics necessarily produce one form or the other?

Adams himself did not feel the full force of the second blow until twenty years later when Theodore Roosevelt inherited office from McKinley. Secretary Ratcliffe in *Democracy* was the archetype of all he hated and Roosevelt represented an approximation of a good deal he admired. Ratcliffe was about the worst you got and Roosevelt was the best you could expect. But the lesson the two men taught about the disease of power was much the same, however they taught it on different levels. At heart Roosevelt, as a type, was more source of despair than Ratcliffe.

Power is poison. Its effects on Presidents had always been tragic, chiefly as an almost insane excitement at first, and a worse reaction afterwards; but also because no mind is so well balanced as to bear the strain of seizing unlimited force without habit or knowledge of it; and finding it disputed with him by hungry packs of wolves and hounds whose lives depend on snatching the carrion. Roosevelt enjoyed a singularly direct nature and honest intent, but he lived naturally in restless agitation that would have worn out most tempers in a month, and his first year of Presidency showed chronic excitement that made a friend tremble. The effect of unlimited power on limited mind is worth noting in Presidents because it must represent the same process in society, and the power of self-control must have limit somewhere in face of the control of the infinite.

"Here," Adams goes on, "education seemed to see its first and last lesson." Certainly it is part of the lesson of the second Roosevelt as well as of the first; and certainly it is a lesson that in one form or another can be drawn not only from Presidents, but from every concentration of power in single hands. Power is greater than the hands that hold it and compels action beyond any tolerable volition. No wonder men make a game of it, as they make mathematics of time and space, since it is only as converted into a game that the experience of fatal struggles is commonly found tolerable.

But the lesson had other forms, as the energy it attempted to express took other forms than the political. There is the well of character, the abyss of science, and the aspiring form of religion, all expressions of human energy, and a wakened and scrupulous mind was compelled to respond to them all. Experience is only separated into its elements in the *tour de force* of expression, and as in *Democracy* Adams separated the bottom level of political experience, in *Esther* he separated the highest level of religious experience he could find in America and measured it against the response of a woman's intelligence. The question asked and the lesson to be learned were simple and fundamental and desperate. Assuming the Christian insight in its highest contemporary form, could the Church supply a sense of unity, of ultimate relation with God or the sum of energy, to which intelligence could respond? If the Church couldn't—and the Church had no other motive for being—nothing else could, and the soul was left on its own and homeless. Or so it seemed to Adams; hence the desperateness of the question; and hence the disproportionate importance relative to its achievement that Adams himself assigned to the book. Writing to John Hay from Japan in 1886, he suggests that it was written in his heart's blood, and again to Elizabeth Cameron from Papeete five years later, he says: "I care more for one chapter, or any dozen pages of 'Esther' than for the whole history, including maps and indexes." The nine-volume history represented the predicament of the society he had abandoned, and

Esther represented his own predicament in relation to that God or unity the hope of which he could never in his heart altogether abandon. Like Spinoza, Adams was god-intoxicated, like Pascal godridden. His heart's hope was his soul's despair.

That the responding intelligence in *Esther* as in *Democracy* should have been a woman's, only reflects a major bias of Adams's imagination. Women, for Adams, had instinct and emotion and could move from the promptings of the one to the actualities of the other without becoming lost or distraught in the midway bog of logic and fact. Impulse proceeded immediately to form without loss of character or movement. More than that, women had taste; taste was what held things together, showing each at its best, and making each contribute to a single effect. Thus the argument of a woman's taste dissipated every objection of logic, and at its highest moments made illogicality itself part of its natural charm. Taste was the only form of energy sure enough of itself—as all non-human energies may be—to afford beauty; elsewhere the rashest extravagance.

Thus Adams tried everywhere to answer great questions in terms of a woman's taste and intelligence. Who else but Esther Dudley could form the center of the book she named? Only the strength of her instinct could accept the Church if it showed itself alive, and only the courage of her taste could reject it if it proved dead or a shell. That she might be confused in instinct and unconscious of her taste, only made the drama more vivid and its outcome more desperate. The problem was hers, but an artist could help her solve it, and perhaps a scientist, too, if he felt the struggle as an artist feels it. So Wharton, the artist, puts the question to her and answers it. "It all comes to this: is religion a struggle or a joy? To me it is a terrible battle, to be won or lost." The object of the battle is Nirvana or paradise. "It is eternal life, which, my poet says, consists in seeing God." The poet is Petrarch, and his words: *Siccome eterna vita è veder dio.* Strong, the scientist, for his part tells her: "There is no science that does not begin by requiring you to believe the incredible. I tell you the solemn truth that the doctrine of the Trinity is not so difficult to accept for a working proposition as any one of the axioms of physics." Between them—between art as it aspires to religion and science that springs from the same occult source—Esther might have been able to accept religion as that great form of poetry which is the aspiration of instinct and informs the whole of taste; but the Church itself, in the person of the Reverend Mr. Hazard, her lover, failed her both in persuasiveness and light. Power in politics and pride in the Church were much alike.

The strain of standing in a pulpit is great. No human being ever yet constructed was strong enough to offer himself long as a light to humanity without showing the effect on his constitution. Buddhist saints stand for years silent, on one leg, or with arms raised above their heads, but the limbs shrivel, and the mind shrivels with the limbs.

There is a kind of corruption in the best as well as the worst exemplars of each—which I suppose the Church would admit sooner than the state; a corruption in each case that makes for the self-falsifying effort of fanaticism. Hazard in his last argument appeals neither to instinct, intelligence, nor taste; he appeals to Esther's personal desperation and fear and so shows the ruination of emptiness within him. Esther can only answer him from the depth of revolted taste. "Why must the church always appeal to my weakness and never to my strength! I ask for spiritual life and you send me back to my flesh and blood as though I were a tigress you were sending back to her cubs." Although she loves him, the inadequacy of his church to its own purpose compels her to dismiss him, but neither for science nor for art, but for despair. That is the blood in which the book was written.

As *Democracy* foreshadowed the major theme of the *Education*, the theme of *Esther* is given deeper expression throughout *Mont-Saint-Michel*, and, as well, in at least one place in the *Education*. *Esther* is a representation of the failure in fact of American society to find God in religion. As he grew older, especially after the tragic death of his wife, and felt more and more that society had abandoned him, Adams grew more preoccupied with the ultimate failure of imagination itself, as illustrated in every faculty of the mind, than with the mere indicative failure of fact. Not facts which could be met but their meanings which could not be escaped were his meat. The meaning of *Esther* is intensified and made an object of inexhaustible meditation in the meanings Adams found in the monument Saint-Gaudens made for his wife in Rock Creek Cemetery. Part of the meaning lay in its meaninglessness to most of those who saw it, and part in the horror of the clergy who saw in it their defeat instead of their salvation. In a letter, Adams gave the monument the same motto he had embedded in *Esther: Siccome eterna vita è veder dio;* you could, in a gravestone, if you had the will, see what life needed but never provided. In the *Education* Adams suggests that the monument mirrors to the beholder whatever faith he has.

In *Mont-Saint-Michel and Chartres* the problem of *Esther* is made at once more universal and more personal. There Adams made an imaginative mirror of his own effort toward faith in terms of the highest point of faith—that is, of effective unity—the world had ever seen: the Christianity of the great cathedrals and the great intellectual architecture of the schools. The Virgin dominated the cathedrals as a matter of course; and Saint Thomas dominated the schools by an effort of will; but without the Virgin the schools would merely have paltered, as the cathedrals would never have been built. The Virgin was pure energy and pure taste, as her spires and roses were pure aspiration. Adams's book is the story of her tragedy; not that she was destroyed or even denied, but that men no longer knew and loved her, so lost their aspiration with the benefit of her taste, and no longer felt any unity whatsoever. The Virgin herself is still there, "but looking down from a deserted heaven, into an empty church, on a dead faith." She no longer gave orders or answered questions, and without her the orders and answers of Saint Thomas were useless; and similarly, for Adams, the orders and answers of all later authorities.

Thus the education that led Adams to the Virgin was the greatest failure of all; the highest form of unity was, in effect, for the modern man, only the most impossible to recapture. Where Esther had very simply repulsed the church because it appealed only to her weakness, Adams was in the worse ail of having no strength with which to seize it when it called for all the strength there was: he had no faith, but only the need of it. The Virgin's orders were the best ever given; obeyed, they made life contribute to great art and shine in it; but he had nothing with which to accept her administration. Her answers to his problems were final; she was herself the cumulus and unity of energy, and she removed, by absorbing, all the contradictions of experience; but seven centuries of time had made life too complicated for the old answers to fit. The same energy would need a new form to give the same meaning.

The failure of education was the failure of the unity which it grasped; the pupil was left with a terrible and weary apprehension of ignorance. Thinking of the Virgin and of the Dynamo as equally inexplicable concentrations of energy, Adams was led into the last phase of his education in the application of the mechanical theory of the inevitable change of all energy from higher to lower forms. What he wrote may be found in the later chapters of the *Education*, and in his two essays "A Letter to Teachers" and "The Rule of Phase Applied to History." It was, I think, the theory of a desperate, weary mind, still scrupulous in desperation and passionately eager in weariness, in its last effort to feel—this time in nature herself—the mystery in energy that keeps things going. It was the religious mind applying to physics on exactly the same terms and with exactly the same honest piety that it applied to the Virgin.

The nexus between the two was shown in the need for either in that fundamental condition of the mind known as ennui; and Adams quotes Pascal, the great scrupulous mind of the seventeenth century.

"I have often said that all the troubles of man come from his not knowing how to sit still." Mere restlessness forces action. "So passes the whole of life. We combat obstacles in order to get repose, and, when got, the repose is insupportable; for we think either of the troubles we have, or of those that threaten us; and even if we felt safe on every side, *ennui* would of its own accord spring up from the depths of the heart where it is rooted by nature, and would fill the mind with its venom."

Nature was full of ennui too, from star to atom. What drove it? What made energy change form in *this* direction and not that? Adams tried to find the answer in the second law of thermodynamics—the law that assumes the degradation of energy; the law which sees infinite energy becoming infinitely unavailable; and he tried hard to *feel* that law as accounting for change in human society. The attempt only put his ignorance on a new basis. As analogues, the laws of physics only made the human predicament less soluble because less tangible. You might learn a direction, but physics prevented you from feeling what moved.

Reason, in science, as Adams had discovered earlier in *Esther*, deserted you rather sooner than in religion; and the need of faith was more critical. Had Adams had the advantage of the development of the quantum theory from the thermal field to the whole field of physics, had he known that all change was to come to seem discontinuous and that nature was to reveal a new and profoundly irrational face, he would have given up his last effort before he began it. A *discontinuous* multiplicity cannot be transformed into unity except by emotional vision. Adams had earlier said it himself. "Unity is vision; it must have been part of the process of learning to see. The older the mind, the older its complexities, and the further it looks, the more it sees, until even the stars resolve themselves into multiples; yet the child will always see but one." In 1915 Adams wrote to Henry Osborn Taylor that "Faith not Reason goes beyond" the failure of knowledge, and added that he felt himself "in near peril of turning Christian, and rolling in the mud in an agony of human mortification." But he had not the faith; only the apprehension of its need which made him struggle toward it all his life.

Failure is the appropriate end to the type of mind of which Adams is a pre-eminent example: the type which attempts through imagination to find the meaning or source of unity aside from the experience which it unites. Some artists can be content with experience as it comes, content to express it in the best form at hand. Adams gives LaFarge as an instance. "His thought ran as a stream runs through grass, hidden perhaps but always there; and one felt often uncertain in what direction it flowed, for even a contradiction was to him only a shade of difference, a complementary color, about which no intelligent artist would dispute." Shakespeare is another instance. In such artists failure is incidental, a part of the experience expressed. But Adams, by attempting to justify experience and so to pass beyond it had like Milton and Dante to push his mind to the limit of reason and his feelings to the limit of faith. Failure, far from incidental, is integral to that attempt, and becomes apparent just so soon as reason falters and becomes abstract, or faith fails and pretends to be absolute. Aside from the question of magnitude, one difference between Adams and his prototypes is, to repeat once more, just this: that his scrupulous sophistication made him emphatically aware of his own failure; and this awareness is the great drive of his work.

Here is our third emphasis. The failure of Adams in society—or society's failure to use Adams—was perhaps self-evident when stated. The singular unity of Adams's subsequent efforts to express the unity he felt has, I hope, been indicated. There remains the question of Adams's special value in the light of his avowed failure. The value is double.

The greatness of the mind of Adams himself is in the imaginative reach of the effort to solve the problem of the meaning, the use, or the value of its own energy. The greatness is in the effort itself, in variety of response deliberately made to every possible level of experience. It is in the acceptance, with all piety, of ignorance as the humbled form of knowledge; in the pursuit of divers shapes of knowledge—the scientific, the religious, the political, the social and trivial—to the point where they add to ignorance, when the best response is silence itself. That is the greatness of Adams as a type of mind. As it is a condition of life to die, it is a condition of thought, in the end, to fail. Death is the expense of life and failure is the expense of greatness.

If there is a paradox here, or an irony hard to digest, it is not in the life experienced or the failure won, but in the forms through which they are conceived, in the very duplicity of language itself, in the necessarily equivocal character, earned by long use, of every significant word. Thought asks too much and words tell too much; because to ask anything is to ask everything, and to say anything is to ask more. It is the radical defect of thought that it leaves us discontented with what we actually feel—with what we know and do not know—as we know sunlight and surfeit and terror, all at once perhaps, and yet know nothing of them. Thought requires of us that we make a form of our knowledge which is personal, declarative, and abstract at the same time that we construe it as impersonal, expressive, and concrete. It is this knowledge that leads to the conviction of ignorance—to the positive ignorance which is the final form of contradictory knowledge; but it is the triumph of failure that in the process it snares all that can be snared of what we know.

The true paradox is that in securing its own ends thought cannot help defeating itself at every crisis. To think straight you must overshoot your mark. Orthodoxy of the human mind—the energy of society in its highest stable form—is only maintained through the absorption into it of a series of heresies; and the great heresy, surely, is the gospel of unity, whether it is asserted as a prime mover, as God, or, as in art, as the mere imposed unity of specious form. In adopting it for his own, Adams knew it for a heresy. Again and again he describes unifying conceptions as working principles; without them no work could be done; with them, even at the expense of final failure, every value could be provisionally ascertained. That is the value of Adams for us: the double value of his scrupulous attitude toward his unifying notions and of the human aspirations he was able to express under them. To feel that value as education is a profound deliverance: the same deliverance Adams felt in the Gothic Cathedral. "The delight of its aspiration is flung up to the sky. The pathos of its self-distrust and anguish of doubt is buried in the earth as its last secret." The principles asserted are nothing, though desperate and necessary; the values expressed because of the principles are everything. For Adams, as for everyone, the principle of unity carried to failure showed the most value by the way, and the value was worth the expense.

THREE

The Critical Prefaces of
Henry James
[1 9 3 4]

I

The Prefaces of Henry James were composed at the height of
his age as a kind of epitaph or series of inscriptions for the major
monument of his life, the sumptuous, plum-colored, expensive New
York edition of his works. The labor was a torment, a care, and a
delight, as his letters and the Prefaces themselves amply show. The
thinking and the writing were hard and full and critical to the point
of exasperation; the purpose was high, the reference wide, and the
terms of discourse had to be conceived and defined as successive
need for them arose. He had to elucidate and to appropriate for the
critical intellect the substance and principle of his career as an artist,
and he had to do this—such was the idiosyncrasy of his mind—
specifically, example following lucid example, and with a consistency of part with part that amounted almost to the consistency of a
mathematical equation, so that, as in the *Poetics*, if his premises
were accepted his conclusions must be taken as inevitable.

Criticism has never been more ambitious, nor more useful.
There has never been a body of work so eminently suited to criticism as the fiction of Henry James, and there has certainly never
been an author who saw the need and had the ability to criticize
specifically and at length his own work. He was avid of his opportunity and both proud and modest as to what he did with it. "These
notes," he wrote in the preface to *Roderick Hudson*, "represent, over

a considerable course, the continuity of an artist's endeavour, the growth of his whole operative consciousness and, best of all, perhaps, their own tendency to multiply, with the implication, thereby, of a memory much enriched." Thus his strict modesty; he wrote to Grace Norton (5 March 1907) in a higher tone. "The prefaces, as I say, are difficult to do—but I have found them of a jolly interest; and though I am not going to let you read one of the fictions themselves over I shall expect you to read all the said Introductions." To W. D. Howells he wrote (17 August 1908) with very near his full pride. "They are, in general, a sort of plea for Criticism, for Discrimination, for Appreciation on other than infantile lines—as against the so almost universal Anglo-Saxon absence of these things; which tends so, in our general trade, it seems to me, to break the heart. . . . They ought, collected together, none the less, to form a sort of comprehensive manual or *vade mecum* for aspirants in our arduous profession. Still, it will be long before I shall want to collect them together for that purpose and furnish *them* with a final Preface."

In short, James felt that his Prefaces represented or demonstrated an artist's consciousness and the character of his work in some detail, made an essay in general criticism which had an interest and a being aside from any connection with his own work, and that finally, they added up to a fairly exhaustive reference book on the technical aspects of the art of fiction. His judgment was correct and all a commentator can do is to indicate by example and a little analysis, by a kind of provisional reasoned index, how the contents of his essay may be made more available. We have, that is, to perform an act of criticism in the sense that James himself understood it. "To criticise," he wrote in the Preface to *What Maisie Knew*, "is to appreciate, to appropriate, to take intellectual possession, to establish in fine a relation with the criticised thing and make it one's own."

What we have here to appropriate is the most sustained and I think the most eloquent and original piece of literary criticism in existence. (The only comparable pieces, not in merit of course but in kind, are by the same author, "The Art of Fiction," written as a young man and printed in *Partial Portraits*, and "The Novel in 'The Ring and the Book,' " written in 1912 and published in *Notes on Novelists*; the first of which the reader should consult as an example of general criticism with a prevailing ironic tone, and the second as an example of what the same critical attitude as that responsible for the Prefaces could do on work not James's own.) Naturally, then, our own act of appropriation will have its difficulties, and we shall probably find as James found again and again, that the things most difficult to master will be the best. At least we shall require the maximum of strained attention, and the faculty of retaining detail will be pushed to its limit. And these conditions will not apply from the difficulty of what James has to say—which is indeed lucid—but because of the convoluted compression of his style and because of the positive unfamiliarity of his terms as he uses them. No one else has written specifically on his subject.

Before proceeding to exhibition and analysis, however, it may be useful to point out what kind of thing, as a type by itself, a James Preface is, and what kind of exercise the reader may expect a sample to go through. The key fact is simple. A Preface is the story of a story, or in those volumes which collect a group of shorter tales the story of a group of stories cognate in theme or treatment. The Prefaces collocate, juxtapose, and separate the different kinds of stories. They also, by cross reference and development from one Preface to another, inform the whole series with a unity of being. By "the story of a story" James meant a narrative of the accessory facts and considerations which went with its writing; the how, the why, the what, when, and where which brought it to birth and which are not evident in the story itself, but which have a fascination and a meaning in themselves to enhance the reader's knowledge. "The private history of any sincere work," he felt, "looms large with its own completeness."

But the "story of a story" is not simple in the telling; it has many aspects that must be examined in turn, many developments that must be pursued, before its center in life is revealed as captured. "The art of representation bristles with questions the very terms of which are difficult to apply and appreciate." Only the main features can be named simply. There is the feature of autobiography, as a rule held to a minimum: an account of the Paris hotel, the Venetian palace, the English cottage, in which the tale in question was written. Aside from that, there is often a statement of the anecdote and the circumstances in which it was told, from which James drew the germ of his story. There is the feature of the germ in incubation, and the story of how it took root and grew, invariably developing into something quite different from its immediate promise. Then there is an account—frequently the most interesting feature—of how the author built up his theme as a consistent piece of dramatization. Usually there are two aspects to this feature, differently discussed in different Prefaces—the aspect of the theme in relation to itself as a balanced and consistent whole, the flesh upon the articulated plot; and the aspect of the theme in relation to society, which is the moral and evaluating aspect. Varying from Preface to Preface as the need commands, there is the further feature of technical exposition, in terms of which everything else is for the moment subsumed. That is, the things which a literary artist does in order to make of his material an organic whole—the devices he consciously uses to achieve a rounded form—are rendered available for discussion, and for understanding, by definition and exemplification.

These are the principal separate features which compose the face of a Preface. There are also certain emphases brought to bear throughout the Prefaces, which give them above all the savor of definite character. Again and again, for example, a novel or story will raise the problem of securing a compositional center, a presiding intelligence, or of applying the method of indirect approach. Again and again James emphasizes the necessity of being amusing, dramatic, interesting. And besides these, almost any notation, technical, thematic, or moral, brings James eloquently back to the expressive relation between art and life, raises him to an intense personal plea for the difficulty and delight of maintaining that relation, or wrings from him a declaration of the supreme labor of intelligence that art lays upon the artist. For James it is the pride of achievement, for the reader who absorbs that pride it is the enthusiasm of understanding and the proud possibility of emulation.

None of this, not the furthest eloquence nor the most detached precept, but flows from the specific observation and the particular example. When he speaks of abjuring the "platitude of statement," he is not making a phrase but summarizing, for the particular occasion, the argument which runs throughout the Prefaces, that in art what is merely stated is not presented, what is not presented is not vivid, what is not vivid is not represented, and what is not represented is not art. Or when, referring to the method by which a subject most completely expresses itself, he writes the following sentence, James is not indulging in self-flattery. "The careful ascertainment of how it shall do so, and the art of guiding it with consequent authority—since this sense of 'authority' is for the master-builder the treasure of treasures, or at least the joy of joys—renews in the modern alchemist something like the old dream of the secret of life." It is not indulgence of any description; it is the recognition in moral language of the artist's privileged experience in the use of his tools—in this instance his use of them in solving the technical problems of *The Spoils of Poynton*. James unfailingly, unflaggingly reveals for his most general precept its specific living source. He knew that only by constantly retaining the specific in the field of discussion could he ever establish or maintain the principles by which he wrote. That is his unique virtue as a critic, that the specific object is always in hand; as it was analogously his genius as a novelist that what he wrote about was always present in somebody's specific knowledge of it. In neither capacity did he ever succumb to the "platitude of statement."

It is this factor of material felt and rendered specifically that differentiates James from such writers as Joyce and Proust. All three have exerted great technical influence on succeeding writers, as masters ought. The difference is that writers who follow Joyce or Proust tend to absorb their subjects, their social attitudes, and their personal styles and accomplish competent derivative work in so doing, while the followers of James absorb something of a technical mastery good for any subject, any attitude, any style. It is the difference between absorbing the object of a sensibility and acquiring something comparable to the sensibility itself. The point may perhaps be enforced paradoxically: the mere imitators of the subject matter of Proust are readable as documents, but the mere imitators of James are not readable at all. It is not that James is more or less great than his compeers—the question is not before us—but that he consciously and articulately exhibited a greater technical mastery of the

[253

tools of his trade. It is a matter of sacrifice. Proust made no sacrifice but wrote always as loosely as possible and triumphed in spite of himself. Joyce made only such sacrifices as suited his private need—as readers of these Prefaces will amply observe—and triumphed by a series of extraordinary *tours de force*. James made consistently every sacrifice for intelligibility and form; and, when the fashions of interest have made their full period, it will be seen I think that his triumph is none the less for that.

There remains—once more before proceeding with the actual content of the Prefaces—a single observation that must be made, and it flows from the remarks above about the character of James's influence. James had in his style and perhaps in the life which it reflected an idiosyncrasy so powerful, so overweening, that to many it seemed a stultifying vice, or at least an inexcusable heresy. He is difficult to read in his later works—among which the Prefaces are included—and his subjects, or rather the way in which he develops them, are occasionally difficult to co-ordinate with the reader's own experience. He enjoyed an excess of intelligence and he suffered, both in life and art, from an excessive effort to communicate it, to represent it in all its fullness. His style grew elaborate in the degree that he rendered shades and refinements of meaning and feeling not usually rendered at all. Likewise the characters which he created to dramatize his feelings have sometimes a quality of intelligence which enables them to experience matters which are unknown and seem almost perverse to the average reader. James recognized his difficulty, at least as to his characters. He defended his "super-subtle fry" in one way or another a dozen times, on the ground that if they did not exist they ought to, because they represented, if only by an imaginative irony, what life was capable of at its finest. His intention and all his labor was to represent dramatically intelligence at its most difficult, its most lucid, its most beautiful point. This is the sum of his idiosyncrasy; and the reader had better make sure he knows what it is before he rejects it. The act of rejection will deprive him of all knowledge of it. And this precept applies even more firmly to the criticisms he made of his work—to the effort he made to reappropriate it intellectually—than to the direct apprehension of the work itself.

I I

Now to resume the theme of this essay, to "remount," as James says of himself many times, "the stream of composition." What is that but to make an *ex post facto* dissection, not that we may embalm the itemized mortal remains, but that we may intellectually understand the movement of parts and the relation between them in the living body we appreciate. Such dissection is imaginative, an act of the eye and mind alone, and but articulates our knowledge without once scratching the flesh of its object. Only if the life itself was a mockery, a masquerade of pasted surfaces, will we come away with our knowledge dying; if the life was honest and our attention great enough, even if we do not find the heart itself at least we shall be deeply exhilarated, having heard its slightly irregular beat.

Let us first exhibit the principal objects which an imaginative examination is able to separate, attaching to each a summary of context and definition. Thus we shall have equipped ourselves with a kind of eclectic index or provisional glossary, and so be better able to find our way about, and be better prepared to seize for closer examination a selection of those parts of some single Preface which reveal themselves as deeply animating. And none of this effort will have any object except to make the substance of all eighteen Prefaces more easily available.

There is a natural division between major subjects which are discussed at length either in individual essays or from volume to volume, and minor notes which sometimes appear once and are done, and are sometimes recurrent, turning up again and again in slightly different form as the specific matter in hand requires. But it is not always easy to see under which heading an entry belongs. In the following scheme the disposition is approximate and occasionally dual, and in any case an immediate subject of the reader's revision.

To begin with, let us list those major themes which have no definite locus but inhabit all the Prefaces more or less without favor. This is the shortest and for the most part the most general of the divisions, and therefore the least easily susceptible of definition in summary form.

The Relation of Art and the Artist. The Relation of Art and Life. Art, Life, and the Ideal. Art and Morals. Art as Salvation for its Characters. These five connected subjects, one or more of them, are constantly arrived at, either parenthetically or as the definite terminus of the most diverse discussions. The sequence in which I have put them ought to indicate something of the attitude James brings to bear on them. Art was serious, he believed, and required of the artist every ounce of his care. The subject of art was life, or more particularly someone's apprehension of the experience of it, and in striving truly to represent it art removed the waste and muddlement and bewilderment in which it is lived and gave it a lucid, intelligible form. By insisting on intelligence and lucidity something like an ideal vision was secured; not an ideal in the air but an ideal in the informed imagination, an ideal, in fact, actually of life, limited only by the depth of the artist's sensibility of it. Thus art was the viable representation of moral value; in the degree that the report was intelligent and intense the morals were sound. This attitude naturally led him on either of two courses in his choice of central characters. He chose either someone with a spark of intelligence in him to make him worth saving from the damnation and waste of a disorderly life, or he chose to tell the story of some specially eminent person in whom the saving grace of full intelligence is assumed and exhibited. It is with the misfortunes and triumphs of such persons, in terms of the different kinds of experience of which he was master, that James's fiction almost exclusively deals.

It is this fact of an anterior interest that largely determines what he has to say about *The Finding of Subjects* and *The Growth of Subjects*. Subjects never came ready-made or complete, but always from hints, notes, the merest suggestion. Often a single fact reported at the dinner table was enough for James to seize on and plant in the warm bed of his imagination. If his interlocutor, knowing him to be a novelist, insisted on continuing, James closed his ears. He never wanted all the facts, which might stupefy him, but only enough to go on with, hardly enough to seem a fact at all. If out of politeness he had to listen, he paid no recording attention; what he then heard was only "clumsy Life at her stupid work" of waste and mud-dlement. Taking his single precious germ he meditated upon it, let it develop, scrutinized and encouraged, compressed and pared the developments until he had found the method by which he could dramatize it, give it a central intelligence whose fortune would be his theme, and shape it in a novel or a story as a consistent and self-sufficient organism. James either gives or regrets that he cannot give both the original *donnée* and an account of how it grew to be a dramatic subject for almost every item in the New York edition.

Art and Difficulty. Of a course, a man with such a view of his art and choosing so great a personal responsibility for his theme would push his rendering to the most difficult terms possible. So alone would he be able to represent the maximum value of his theme. Being a craftsman and delighting in his craft, he knew also both the sheer moral delight of solving a technical difficulty or securing a complicated effect, and the simple, amply attested fact that the difficulties of submitting one's material to a rigidly con-ceived form were often the only method of representing the material in the strength of its own light. The experience of these difficulties being constantly present to James as he went about his work, he constantly points specific instances for the readers of his Prefaces.

Looseness. Looseness of any description, whether of concep-tion or of execution, he hated contemptuously. In both respects he found English fiction "a paradise of loose ends," but more espe-cially in the respect of execution. His own themes, being complex in reference and development, could only reach the lucidity of the apprehensible, the intelligibility of the represented state, if they were closed in a tight form. Any looseness or laziness would defeat his purpose and let half his intention escape. A selection of the kinds of looseness against which he complains will be given among the minor notes.

The Plea for Attention and Appreciation. The one faculty James felt that the artist may require of his audience is that of close atten-tion or deliberate appreciation; for it is by this faculty alone that the audience participates in the work of art. As he missed the signs of it so he bewailed the loss; upon its continuous exertion depended the very existence of what he wrote. One burden of the Prefaces was to prove how much the reader would see if only he paid attention and how much he missed by following the usual stupid routine of skipping and halting and letting slide. Without attention, without intense appreciation an art of the intelligent life was impossible and without intelligence, for James, art was nothing.

The Necessity for Amusement. James was willing to do his part to arouse attention, and he labored a good deal to find out exactly what that part was. One aspect of it was to be as amusing as possible, and this he insisted on at every opportunity. To be amusing, to be interesting; without that nothing of his subject could possibly transpire in the reader's mind. In some of his books half the use of certain characters was to amuse the reader. Henrietta Stackpole, for example, in *The Portrait of a Lady*, serves mainly to capture the reader's attention by amusing him as a "character." Thus what might otherwise have been an example of wasteful overtreatment actually serves the prime purpose of carrying the reader along, distracting and freshening him from time to time.

The Indirect Approach and *The Dramatic Scene*. These devices James used throughout his work as those most calculated to command, direct, and limit or frame the reader's attention; and they are employed in various combinations or admixtures the nature of which almost every Preface comments on. These devices are not, as their names might suggest, opposed; nor could their use in equal parts cancel each other. They are, in the novel, two ends of one stick, and no one can say where either end begins. The characterizing aspect of the Indirect Approach is this: the existence of a definite created sensibility interposed between the reader and the felt experience which is the subject of the fiction. James never put his reader in direct contact with his subjects; he believed it was impossible to do so, because his subject really was not what happened but what someone felt about what happened, and this could be directly known only through an intermediate intelligence. The Dramatic Scene was the principal device James used to objectify the Indirect Approach and give it self-limiting form. Depending on the degree of limitation necessary to make the material objective and visible all round, his use of the Scene resembled that in the stage-play. The complexities of possible choice are endless and some of them are handled below.

The Plea for a Fine Central Intelligence. But the novel was not a play however dramatic it might be, and among the distinctions between the two forms was the possibility, which belonged to the novel alone, of setting up a fine central intelligence in terms of which everything in it might be unified and upon which everything might be made to depend. No other art could do this; no other art could dramatize the individual at his finest; and James worked this possibility for all it was worth. It was the very substance upon which the directed attention, the cultivated appreciation, might be concentrated. And this central intelligence served a dual purpose, with many modifications and exchanges among the branches. It made a compositional center for art such as life never saw. If it could be created at all, then it presided over everything else, and would compel the story to be nothing but the story of what that intelligence felt about what happened. This compositional strength, in its turn, only increased the value and meaning of the intelligence *as* intelligence, and vice versa. The plea for the use of such an intelligence both as an end and as a means is constant throughout the Prefaces—as the proudest end and as the most difficult means. Some of the specific problems which its use poses are discussed in the Prefaces to the novels where they apply. Here it is enough to repeat once more— and not for the last time—that the fine intelligence, either as agent or as the object of action or as both, is at the heart of James's work.

So much for the major themes which pervade and condition and unite the whole context of the Prefaces. It is the intention of this essay now to list some of the more important subjects discussed in their own right, indicating where they may be found and briefly what turn the discussions take. The Roman numerals immediately following the heading refer to the volume numbers in the New York edition.[1] The occasional small Roman numerals refer to pages within a preface.

[1] For possible convenience in reference I append the numbers and titles of those volumes which contain Prefaces. I Roderick Hudson; II The American; III The Portrait of a Lady; V The Princess Casamassima; VII The Tragic Muse; IX The Awkward Age; X The Spoils of

The International Theme (XII, XIV, XVIII). The discussion of the International Theme in these three volumes has its greatest value in strict reference to James's own work; it was one of the three themes peculiarly his. It deals, however, with such specific questions as the opposition of manners as a motive in drama, the necessity of opposing positive elements of character, and the use of naive or innocent characters as the subjects of drama; these are of perennial interest. There is also a discussion under this head of the difference between major and minor themes. In X (p. xix), speaking of "A London Life," there is a discussion of the use of this theme for secondary rather than primary purposes.

The Literary Life as a Theme (XV) and *The Artist as a Theme* (VII). The long sections of these two Prefaces dealing with these themes form a single essay. XV offers the artist enamored of perfection, his relation to his art, to his audience, and himself. VII presents the artist in relation to society and to himself. In both sections the possibilities and the actualities are worked out with specific reference to the characters in the novels and the tales. The discussion is of practical importance to any writer. Of particular interest is the demonstration in VII that the successful artist as such cannot be a hero in fiction, because he is immersed in his work, while the amateur or the failure remains a person and may have a heroic downfall. The thematic discussion in XVI properly belongs under this head, especially pp. vii–ix.

The Use of the Eminent or Great (VII, XII, XV, XVI) and *The Use of Historical Characters* (XII, XV). The separation of these two subjects is artificial, as for James they were two aspects of one problem. Being concerned with the tragedies of the high intelligence and the drama of the socially and intellectually great (much as the old tragedies dealt death to kings and heroes) he argues for using the *type* of the historical and contemporary figure. The *type* of the great gives the artist freedom; the *actual* examples condition him without advantage. If he used in one story or another Shelley, Coleridge,

Poynton; XI What Maisie Knew; XII The Aspern Papers; XIII The Reverberator; XIV Lady Barbarina; XV The Lesson of the Master; XVI The Author of Beltraffio; XVII The Altar of the Dead; XVIII Daisy Miller; XIX The Wings of the Dove; XXI The Ambassadors; XXIII The Golden Bowl.

Browning, and (I think) Oscar Wilde, he took them only as types and so far transformed them that they appear as pure fictions. The real argument is this: the novelist is concerned with types and only with the eminent case among the types, and the great man is in a way only the most eminent case of the average type, and is certainly the type that the novelist can do most with. To the charge that his "great" people were such as could never exist, James responded that the world would be better if they did. In short, the novelist's most lucid representation may be only his most ironic gesture.

The Dead as a Theme (XVII). Five pages (v–ix) of this Preface present "the permanent appeal to the free intelligence of some image of the lost dead" and describe how this appeal may be worked out in fiction. "The sense of the state of the dead," James felt, "is but part of the sense of the state of living."

On Wonder, Ghosts, and the Supernatural (XII, XVII) and *How to Produce Evil* (XII). These again make two aspects of one theme and the rules for securing one pretty much resemble those for securing the other. They are shown best "by showing almost exclusively the way they are felt, by recognising as their main interest some impression strongly made by them and intensely received." That was why Psychical Research Society Ghosts were unreal; there was no one to apprehend them. The objectively rendered prodigy always ran thin. Thickness is in the human consciousness that records and amplifies. And there is also always necessary, for the reader to feel the ghost, the history of somebody's *normal* relation to it. Thus James felt that the climax of Poe's *Pym* was a failure because there the horrific was without connections. In both Prefaces the ghost story is put as the modern equivalent of the fairy story; and the one must be as economical of its means as the other. The problem of rendering evil in "The Turn of the Screw" (XII) was slightly different; it had to be represented, like the ghosts who performed it, in the consciousness of it by normal persons, but it could not be described. The particular act when rendered always fell short of being evil, so that the problem seemed rather to make the character *capable* of anything. "Only make the reader's general vision of evil intense enough, I said to myself—and that is already a charming job—and his own experience, his own sympathy (with the children) and horror (of their false friends) will supply him quite sufficiently with all the particulars. Make him *think* the evil, make him think it for himself, and you are released from weak specifications" (XII, xxi).

On the Use of Wonder to Animate a Theme (XI). This is the faculty of wonder on a normal plane and corresponds to freshness, intelligent innocence, and curiosity in the face of life; a faculty which when represented in a character almost of itself alone makes that character live. It is a faculty upon which every novelist depends, both in his books to make them vivid, and in his readers where it is the faculty that drives them to read. It is to be distinguished from the wonder discussed in the paragraph next above.

Romanticism and Reality (II). Seven pages in this Preface (xiv–xx) attempt to answer the question: Why is one picture of life called romantic and another real? After setting aside several answers as false or misleading, James gives his own. "The only *general* attribute of projected romance that I can see, the only one that fits all its cases, is the fact of the kind of experience with which it deals— experience liberated, so to speak; experience disengaged, disembodied, disencumbered, exempt from the conditions that we usually know to attach to it, and if we wish so to put the matter, drag upon it, and operating in a medium which relieves it, in a particular interest, of the inconvenience of a *related*, a measurable state, a state subject to all our vulgar communities." Then James applies his answer to his own novel *(The American)*. "The experience here represented is the disconnected and uncontrolled experience— uncontrolled by our general sense of 'the way things happen'—which romance alone more or less successfully palms off on us." Since the reader knows "the way things happen," he must be tactfully drugged for the duration of the novel; and that is part of the art of fiction.

The Time Question (I, xii–xvi). Although the efforts dependent on the superior effect of an adequate lapse of time were consciously important to James, the lapse of time itself was only once discussed by him in the Prefaces, and there to explain or criticize the failure to secure it. Roderick Hudson, he said, falls to pieces too quickly. Even though he is special and eminent, still he must not live, change and disintegrate too rapidly; he loses verisimilitude by so doing. His great capacity for ruin is projected on too small a field. He should have had more adventures and digested more experience before we can properly believe that he has reached his end. But James was able to put the whole matter succinctly. "To give all the sense without all the substance or all the surface, and so to summarise or foreshorten, so to make values both rich and sharp, that the mere procession of items and profiles is not only, for the occasion, superseded, but is, for essential quality, almost 'compromised'— such a case of delicacy proposes itself at every turn to the painter of life who wishes both to treat his chosen subject and to confine his necessary picture." Composition and arrangement must give the *effect* of the lapse of time. For this purpose elimination was hardly a good enough device. The construction of a dramatic center, as a rule in someone's consciousness, was much better, for the reason that this device, being acted upon in time, gave in parallel the positive effect of action, and thus of lapsing time.

Geographical Representation (I, ix–xi). These three pages deal with the question: to what extent should a named place be rendered on its own account? In *Roderick Hudson* James named Northampton, Mass. This, he said, he ought not to have done, since all he required was a humane community which was yet incapable of providing for "art." For this purpose a mere indication would have been sufficient. His general answer to the question was that a place should be named if the novelist wanted to make it an effective part of the story, as Balzac did in his studies of the ville de province.

The Commanding Center as a Principle of Composition (I, II, VII, X, XI, XIX, XXI, XXIII). This is allied with the discussion of the use of a Central Intelligence above and with the three notes immediately below. It is a major consideration in each of the Prefaces numbered and is to be met with *passim* elsewhere. The whole question is bound up with James's exceeding conviction that the art of fiction is an organic form, and that it can neither be looked at all round nor will it be able to move on its own account unless it has a solidly posed center. Commanding centers are of various descriptions. In I it is in Rowland Mallet's consciousness of Roderick. In II it is in the image of Newman. In VII it is in the combination of relations between three characters. In X it is in a houseful of beautiful furniture. In XI it is the "ironic" center of a child's consciousness against or illuminated by which the situations gather meaning. In XIX it is in the title *(The Wings of the Dove)*, that is, in the influence of Milly Theale, who is seen by various people from the outside. In XXI it is wholly in Strether's consciousness. In XXIII it is, so to speak, half in the Prince, half in the Princess, and half in the motion with which the act is performed.

The Proportion of Intelligence and Bewilderment (V). Upon the correct proportion depends the verisimilitude of a given character. Omniscience would be incredible; the novelist must not make his "characters too interpretative of the muddle of fate, or in other words too divinely, too priggishly clever." Without bewilderment, as without intelligence, there would be no story to tell. "Experience, as I see it, is our apprehension and our measure of what happens to us as social creatures—any intelligent report of which has to be based on that apprehension." Bewilderment is the subject and someone's intelligent feeling of it the story. The right mixture will depend on the *quality* of the bewilderment, whether it is the vague or the critical. The vague fool is necessary, but the *leading* interest is always in the intensifying, critical consciousness.

The Necessity of Fools (V, X, XI), and *The Use of Muddlement* (XI, XIX). These subjects are evidently related to that of Intelligence and Bewilderment. In themselves nothing, fools are the very agents of action. They represent the stupid force of life and are the cause of trouble to the intelligent consciousness. The general truth for the spectator of life was this: (X, xv)—"The fixed constituents of almost any reproducible action are the fools who minister, at a particular crisis, to the intensity of the free spirit engaged with them." Muddlement is the condition of life which fools promote. "The effort really to see and really to represent is no idle business in face of the *constant* force that makes for muddlement. The great thing is indeed that the muddled state too is one of the very sharpest of the realities, that it also has colour and form and character, has often in fact a broad and rich comicality, many of the signs and values of the appreciable" (XI, xiii).

Intelligence as a Receptive Lucidity (XI, XXI). The first of this pair of Prefaces almost wholly and the second largely deals with the methods of conditioning a sensibility so as to make a subject. In XI James shows how the sensibility of a child, intelligent as it may be, can influence and shape and make lucid people and situations outside as well as within its understanding. She, Maisie, is the presiding receptive intelligence, the sole sensibility, in the book, and is furthermore the sole agent, by her mere existence, determining and changing the moral worth of the other characters. In XXI Strether is outlined as the example of the adult sensibility fulfilling similar functions, with the additional grace of greatly extended understanding.

The Dramatic Scene (III, VII, IX, XI, XIX, XXI, and *passim*). We have already spoken under the same heading of James's general theory of the dramatic scene. It is too much of the whole substance of the technical discussion in many of the Prefaces to make more than a mere outline of its terms here possible. In III, xxii and XIX, xxiii, there is developed the figure of windows opening on a scene. The eye is the artist, the scene the subject, and the window the limiting form. From each selected window the scene is differently observed. In VII is discussed the theory of alternating scenes in terms of a center (p. xv). In IX which is the most purely scenic of all the books, the use of the alternating scene is developed still further. At the end of XI there is a bitter postscript declaring the scenic character of the form. In XXI there is intermittent discussion of how to use the single consciousness to promote scenes, and a comparison with the general scenic method in XIX. It is principally to IX that the reader must resort for a sustained specific discussion of the Scene in fiction and its relation to the Scene in drama, and to XIX, of which pp. xii–xxiii deal with the scenic structure of that book, where the distinction is made between Scenes and Pictures and it is shown how one partakes of the other, and where it is insisted on that the maximum value is obtained when both weights are felt. Subordinate to this there is, in the same reference, a description of the various reflectors (characters) used to illuminate the subject in terms of the scene.

On Revision (I, XXIII). The Notes on Revision in these Prefaces are mainly of interest with reference to what James actually did in revising his earlier works. He revised, as a rule, only in the sense that he re-envisaged the substance more accurately and more representatively. Revision was responsible re-seeing.

On Illustrations in Fiction (XXIII). This is perhaps the most amusing note in all the Prefaces, and it is impossible to make out whether James did or did not like the frontispieces with which his collected volumes were adorned. He was insistent that no illustration to a book of his should have any direct bearing upon it. The danger was real. "Anything that relieves responsible prose of the duty of being, while placed before us, good enough, interesting enough, and, if the question be of picture, pictorial enough, above all *in itself*, does it the worst services, and may well inspire in the lover of literature certain lively questions as to the future of that institution."

The Nouvelle as a Form (XV, XVI, XVIII). The nouvelle—the long-short story or the short novel—was perhaps James's favorite form, and the form least likely of appreciation in the Anglo-Saxon reading world, to which it seemed neither one thing nor the other. To James it was a small reflector capable of illuminating or mirroring a great deal of material. To the artist who practiced in it the difficulties of its economy were a constant seduction and an exalted delight.

On Rendering Material by its Appearances Alone (V). James had the problem of rendering a character whose whole life centered in the London underworld of socialism, anarchism, and conspiracy, matters of which he personally knew nothing. But, he decided, his wanted effect and value were "precisely those of our not knowing, of society's not knowing, but only guessing and suspecting and trying to ignore, what 'goes on' irreconcilably, subversively, beneath the vast smug surface." Hints and notes and observed appearances were always enough. The real wisdom was this:—that "if you haven't, for fiction, the root of the matter in you, haven't the sense of life and the penetrating imagination, you are a fool in the very presence of the revealed and the assured; but that if you *are* so armed you are not really helpless, not without your resource, even before mysteries abysmal."

And that is a good tone upon which to close our rehearsal of the major subjects James examines in his Prefaces. Other readers and other critics (the two need not be quite the same) might well have found other matters for emphasis; and so too they may reprehend the selection of Minor Notes which follow.

On Development and Continuity (I). Developments are the condition of interest, since the subject is always the related state of figures and things. Hence developments are ridden by the principle of continuity. Actually, relations never end, but the artist must make them appear to do so. Felicity of form and composition depend on knowing to what point a development is *indispensable*.

On Antithesis of Characters (I.) The illustration is the antithesis of Mary and Christina in this book. James observes that antitheses rarely come off and that it may pass for a triumph, if taking them together, one of them is strong (p. xix).

On the Emergence of Characters (X, xiii). James's view may be summarized in quotation. "A character is interesting as it comes out, and by the process and duration of that emergence; just as a procession is effective by the way it unrolls, turning to a mere mob if it all passes at once."

On Misplaced Middles (VII, XIX). Misplaced Middles are the result of excessive foresight. As the art of the drama is of preparations, that of the novel is only less so. The first half of a fiction is the stage or theater of the second half, so that too much may be expended on the first. Then the problem is consummately to mask the fault and "confer on the false quantity the brave appearance of the true." James indicates how the middles of VII and XIX were misplaced, and although he believed the fault great, thought that he had in both cases passed it off by craft and dissimulation.

On Improvisation (XII, xvi). Nothing was so easy as improvisation, and it usually ran away with the story, e.g., in *The Arabian Nights*. "The thing was to aim at absolute singleness, clearness and roundness, and yet to depend on an imagination working freely, working (call it) with extravagance; by which law it wouldn't be thinkable except as free and wouldn't be amusing except as controlled."

The Anecdote (XIII, vi). "The anecdote consists, ever, of something that has oddly happened to some one, and the first of its duties is to point directly to the person whom it so distinguishes."

The Anecdote and the Development (XV, ix, XVI, v). In the first of these references James observes that whereas the anecdote may come from any source, specifically complicated states must come from the author's own mind. In the second he says that *The Middle Years* is an example of imposed form (he had an order for a short story) and the struggle was to keep compression rich and accretions compressed; to keep the form that of the concise anecdote, whereas the subject would seem one comparatively demanding developments. James solved the problem by working from the outward edge in rather than from the center outward; and this was law for the small form. At the end of this Preface, there is a phrase about chemical reductions and compressions making the short story resemble a sonnet.

On Operative Irony (XV, ix). James defended his "super-subtle fry" on the ground that they were ironic, and he found the strength of applied irony "in the sincerities, the lucidities, the utilities that stand behind it." If these characters and these stories were not a campaign for something better than the world offered then they were worthless. "But this is exactly what we mean by operative irony. It implies and projects the possible other case, the case rich and edifying where the actuality is pretentious and vain."

On Foreshortening (VII, XV, XVII, XVIII). This is really a major subject, but the discussions James made of it were never extensive, seldom over two lines at a time. I append samples. In VII, xii, he speaks of foreshortening not by adding or omitting items but by figuring synthetically, by exquisite chemical adjustments. In XVII, xxv, the nouvelle *Julia Bride* is considered as a foreshortened novel to the extreme. In XVIII, xv, after defining once again the art of representation and insisting on the excision of the irrelevant, James names Foreshortening as a deep principle and an invaluable device. It conduced, he said, "to the only compactness that has a charm, to the only spareness that has a force, to the only simplicity that has a grace—those, in each order, that produce the *rich* effect."

On Narrative in the First Person (XXI, xvii–xix). James bore a little heavily against this most familiar of all narrative methods. Whether his general charge will hold is perhaps irrelevant; it holds perfectly with reference to the kinds of fiction he himself wrote, and the injury to unity and composition which he specifies may well be observed in Proust's long novel where every dodge is unavailingly resorted to in the attempt to get round the freedom of the method. The double privilege (in the first person), said James, of being at once subject and object sweeps away difficulties at the expense of discrimination. It prevents the possibility of a center and prevents real directness of contact. Its best effect, perhaps, is that which in another connection James called the mere "platitude of statement."

On Ficelles (XXI, xx). Taking the French theatrical term, James so labeled those characters who belong less to the subject than to the treatment of it. The invention and disposition of *ficelles* is one of the difficulties swept away by the first-person narrative.

On Characters as Disponibles (III, vii–viii). Here again James adapted a French word, taking it this time from Turgenev. *Disponibles* are the active or passive persons who solicit the author's imagination, appearing as subject to the chances and complications of existence and requiring of the author that he find for them their right relations and build their right fate.

The rule of space forbids extending even so scant a selection from so rich a possible index. But let me add a round dozen with page references alone. On Dialogue (IX, xiii); Against Dialect (XVIII, xvi); On Authority (XVIII, xviii); On Confusion of Forms (IX, xvii); On Overtreatment (III, xxi; IX, xxii); On Writing of the Essence and of the Form (III, xvii); On Making Compromises Conformities (XIX, xii); On the Coercive Charm of Form (IX, xvii); On Major Themes in Modern Drama (IX, xviii); On Sickness as a Theme (XIX, vi); On Reviving Characters (V, xviii); On Fiction Read Aloud (XXIII, xxiv); and so on.

The reader may possibly have observed that we have nowhere illustrated the relation which James again and again made eloquently plain between the value or morality of his art and the form in which it appears. It is not easy to select from a multiplicity of choice, and it is impossible, when the matter emerges in a style already so compact, to condense. I should like to quote four sentences from the middle and end of a paragraph in the Preface to *The Portrait of a Lady* (III, x–xi).

There is, I think, no more nutritive or suggestive truth in this connexion than that of the perfect dependence of the "moral" sense of a work of art on the amount of felt life concerned in producing it. The question comes back thus, obviously, to the kind and degree of the artist's prime sensibility, which is the soil out of which his subject springs. The quality and capacity of that soil, its capacity to "grow" with due freshness and straightness any vision of life, represents, strongly or weakly, the projected morality. . . . Here we get exactly the high price of the novel as a literary form—its power not only, while preserving that form with closeness, to range through all the differences of the individual relation to its general subject-matter, all the varieties of outlook on life, of disposition to reflect and project, created by conditions that are never the same from man to man (or, as far as that goes, from woman to woman), but positively to appear more true to its character in proportion as it strains, or tends to burst, with a latent extravagance, its mould.

These sentences represent, I think, the genius and intention of James the novelist, and ought to explain the serious and critical devotion with which he made of his Prefaces a *vade mecum*—both for himself as the solace of achievement, and for others as a guide and exemplification. We have, by what is really no more than an arbitrary exertion or interest, exhibited a rough scheme of the principal contents; there remain the Prefaces themselves.

III

Although the Prefaces to *The Wings of the Dove* or *The Awkward Age* are more explicitly technical in reference, although that to *What Maisie Knew* more firmly develops the intricacies of a theme, and although that to *The Tragic Muse* is perhaps in every respect the most useful of all the Prefaces, I think it may be better to fasten our single attention on the Preface to *The Ambassadors*. This was the book of which James wrote most endearingly. It had in his opinion the finest and most intelligent of all his themes, and he thought it the most perfectly rendered of his books. Furthermore in its success it constituted a work thoroughly characteristic of its author and of no one else. There is a contagion and a beautiful desolation before a great triumph of the human mind—before any approach to perfection—which we had best face for what there is in them.

This preface divides itself about equally between the outline of the story as a story, how it grew in James's mind from the seed of a dropped word (pp. v–xiv), and a discussion of the form in which the book was executed with specific examination of the method of presentation through the single consciousness of its hero Lambert Strether (pp. xv–xxiii). If we can expose the substance of these two discussions we shall have been in the process as intimate as it is possible to be with the operation of an artist's mind. In imitating his thought, step by step and image by image, we shall in the end be able to appropriate in a single act of imagination all he has to say.

The situation involved in *The Ambassadors*, James tells us, "is gathered up betimes, that is in the second chapter of Book Fifth, . . . planted or 'sunk,' stiffly or saliently, in the centre of the current." Never had he written a story where the seed had grown into so large a plant and yet remained as an independent particle, that is in a single quotable passage. Its intention had been firm throughout.

This independent seed is found in Strether's outburst in Gloriani's Paris garden to little Bilham. "The idea of the tale resides indeed in the very fact that an hour of such unprecedented ease should have been felt by him *as* a crisis." Strether feels that he has missed his life, that he made in his youth a grave mistake about the possibilities of life, and he exhorts Bilham not to repeat his mistake. "Live all you can. Live, live!" And he has the terrible question within him: "*Would* there yet perhaps be time for reparation?" At any rate he sees what he had missed and knows the injury done his character. The story is the demonstration of that vision as it came about, of the vision in process.

The original germ had been the repetition by a friend of words addressed him by a man of distinction similar in burden to those addressed by Strether to little Bilham. This struck James as a theme of great possibilities. Although any theme or subject is absolute once the novelist has accepted it, there are degrees of merit among which he may first choose. "Even among the supremely good—since with such alone is it one's theory of one's honour to be concerned—there is an ideal *beauty* of goodness the invoked action of which is to raise the artistic faith to a maximum. Then, truly, one's theme may be said to shine."

And the theme of *The Ambassadors* shone so for James that it resembled "a monotony of fine weather," in this respect differing much from *The Wings of the Dove*, which gave him continual trouble. "I rejoiced," James said, "in the promise of a hero so mature, who would give me thereby the more to bite into—since it's only into thickened motive and accumulated character, I think, that the painter of life bites more than a little." By maturity James meant character and imagination. But imagination must not be the *predominant* quality in him; for the theme in hand, the *comparatively* imaginative man would do. The predominant imagination could wait for another book, until James should be willing to pay for the privilege of presenting it. (See also on this point the discussion of Intelligence and Bewilderment above.)

There was no question, nevertheless, that *The Ambassadors* had a major theme. There was the "supplement of situation logically involved" in Strether's delivering himself to Bilham. And James proceeds to describe the novelist's thrill in finding the situation involved by a conceived character. Once the situations are rightly found the story "assumes the authenticity of concrete existence"; the labor is to find them.

"Art deals with what we see, it must first contribute full-handed that ingredient; it plucks its material, otherwise expressed, in the garden of life—which material elsewhere grown is stale and uneatable." The subject once found, complete with its situations, must then be submitted to a process. There is the subject, which is the story of one's hero, and there is the story of the story itself which is the story of the process of telling.

Still dealing with the story of his hero, James describes how he accounted for Strether, how he found what led up to his outburst in the garden. Where has he come from and why? What is he doing in Paris? To answer these questions was to possess Strether. But the answers must follow the principle of probability. Obviously, by his outburst, he was a man in a false position. What false position? The most probable would be the right one. Granting that he was American, he would probably come from New England. If that were the case, James immediately knew a great deal about him, and had to sift and sort. He would, presumably, have come to Paris with a definite view of life which Paris at once assaulted; and the situation would arise in the interplay or conflict resulting. . . . There was also the energy of the story itself, which once under way, was irresistible, to help its author along. In the end the story seems to know of itself what it's about; and its impudence is always there—"there, so to speak, for grace, and effect, and *allure.*"

These steps taken in finding his story gave it a functional assurance. "*The* false position, for our belated man of the world—belated because he had endeavoured so long to escape being one, and now at last had really to face his doom—the false position for him, I say, was obviously to have presented himself at the gate of that boundless menagerie primed with a moral scheme which was yet framed to break down on any approach to vivid facts; that is to any at all liberal appreciation of them." His note was to be of discrimination and his drama was to "become, under stress, the drama of discrimination."

There follows the question, apparently the only one that troubled James in the whole composition of this book, of whether he should have used Paris as the scene of Strether's outburst and subsequent conversion. Paris had a trivial and vulgar association as the obvious place to be tempted in. The revolution performed by Strether was to have nothing to do with that *bêtise.* He was to be thrown forward rather "upon his lifelong trick of intense reflexion," with Paris a minor matter symbolizing the world other than the town of Woolet, Mass., from which he came. Paris was merely the *likely* place for such a drama, and thus saved James much labor of preparation.

Now turning from the story of his hero to the story of his story, James begins by referring to the fact that it appeared in twelve installments in the *North American Review,* and describes the pleasure he took in making the recurrent breaks and resumptions of serial publication a small compositional law in itself. The book as

we have it is in twelve parts. He passes immediately to the considerations which led him to employ only one center and to keep it
entirely in Strether's consciousness. It was Strether's adventure and
the only way to make it rigorously his was to have it seen only
through his eyes. There were other characters with situations of
their own and bearing on Strether. "But Strether's sense of these
things, and Strether's only, should avail me for showing them; I
should know them only through his more or less groping knowledge
of them, since his very gropings would figure among his most interesting motions." This rigor of representation would give him both
unity and intensity. The difficulties, too, which the rigor imposed,
made the best, because the hardest, determinants of effects. Once
he adopted his method he had to be consistent; hence arose his
difficulties. For example, there was the problem of making Mrs.
Newsome (whose son Strether had come to Paris to save), actually
in Woolet, Mass., "no less intensely than circuitously present"; that
is, to make her influence press on Strether whenever there was need
for it. The advantage of presenting her through Strether was that
only Strether's feeling of her counted for the story. Any other method
would not only have failed but would have led to positive irrelevance. Hence, "One's work should have composition, because
composition alone is positive beauty."

Next James considers what would have happened to his story
had he endowed Strether with the privilege of the first person.
"Variety, and many other queer matters as well, might have been
smuggled in by the back door." But these could not have been
intensely represented as Strether's experience, but would have been
his only on his own say-so. "Strether, on the other hand, encaged
and provided for as *The Ambassadors* encages and provides, has to
keep in view proprieties much stiffer and more salutary than our
straight and credulous gape are likely to bring home to him, has
exhibitional conditions to meet, in a word, that forbid the terrible
fluidity of self-revelation."

Nevertheless, in order to represent Strether James had to resort
to confidants for him, namely Maria Gostrey and Waymarsh, *ficelles*
to aid the treatment. It is thanks to the use of these *ficelles* that James
was able to construct the book in a series of alternating scenes and

274]

thus give it an objective air. Indispensable facts, both of the present and of the past, are presented dramatically—so the reader can *see* them—only through their use. But it is necessary, for the *ficelles* to succeed in their function, that their character should be artfully dissimulated. For example, Maria Gostrey's connection with the subject is made to carry itself as a real one.

Analogous to the use of *ficelles*, James refers to the final scene in the book as an "artful expedient for mere consistency of form." It gives or adds nothing on its own account but only expresses "as vividly as possible certain things quite other than itself and that are of the already fixed and appointed measure."

Although the general structure of the book is scenic and the specific center is in Strether's consciousness of the scenes, James was delighted to note that he had dissimulated throughout the book many exquisite treacheries to those principles. He gives as examples Strether's first encounter with Chad Newsome, and Mamie Pocock's hour of suspense in the hotel salon. These are insisted on as instances of the representational which, "for the charm of opposition and of renewal," are other than scenic. In short, James mixed his effects without injuring the consistency of his form. "From the equal play of such oppositions the book gathers an intensity that fairly adds to the dramatic." James was willing to argue that this was so "for the sake of the moral involved; which is not that the particular production before us exhausts the interesting questions that it raises, but that the Novel remains still, under the right persuasion, the most independent, most elastic, most prodigious of literary forms."

It is this last sentiment that our analysis of this Preface is meant to exemplify; and it is—such is the sustained ability of James's mind to rehearse the specific in the light of the general—an exemplification which might be repeated in terms of almost any one of these Prefaces.

I V

There is, in any day of agonized doubt and exaggerated certainty as to the relation of the artist to society, an unusual attractive force in the image of a man whose doubts are conscientious and whose certainties are all serene. Henry James scrupled relentlessly as to the minor aspects of his art but of its major purpose and essential character his knowledge was calm, full, and ordered. One answer to almost every relevant question will be found, given always in specific terms and flowing from illustrative example, somewhere among his Prefaces; and if the answer he gives is not the only one, nor to some minds necessarily the right one, it has yet the paramount merit that it results from a thoroughly consistent, informed mind operating at its greatest stretch. Since what he gives is always specifically rendered he will even help you disagree with him by clarifying the subject of argument.

He wanted the truth about the important aspects of life as it was experienced, and he wanted to represent that truth with the greatest possible lucidity, beauty, and fineness, not abstractly or in mere statement, but vividly, imposing on it the form of the imagination, the acutest relevant sensibility, which felt it. Life itself—the subject of art—was formless and likely to be a waste, with its situations leading to endless bewilderment; while art, the imaginative representation of life, selected, formed, made lucid and intelligent, gave value and meaning to, the contrasts and oppositions and processions of the society that confronted the artist. The emphases were on intelligence—James was avowedly the novelist of the free spirit, the liberated intelligence—on feeling, and on form.

The subject might be what it would and the feeling of it what it could. When it was once found and known, it should be worked for all it was worth. If it was felt intensely and intelligently enough it would reach, almost of itself, toward adequate form, a prescribed shape and size and density. Then everything must be sacrificed to the exigence of that form, it must never be loose or overflowing but always tight and contained. There was the "coercive charm" of Form, so conceived, which would achieve, dramatize or enact, the moral intent of the theme by making it finely intelligible, better than anything else.

So it is that thinking of the difficulty of representing Isabel Archer in *The Portrait of a Lady* as a "mere young thing" who was yet increasingly intelligent, James was able to write these sentences. "Now to see deep difficulty braved is at any time, for the really addicted artist, to feel almost even as a pang, the beautiful incentive, and to feel it verily in such sort as to wish the danger intensified. The difficulty most worth tackling can only be for him, in these conditions, the greatest the case permits of." It is because such sentiments rose out of him like prayers that for James art was enough.

Henry James

[1 9 4 8]

I

On the level of the ideal—on the level of art—American fiction achieved in the novels and short stories of Henry James a kind of reality different from both the literal record of a Howells and the philosophical naturalism of a Zola. This reality was his response to the human predicament of his generation, which James felt with unusual acuteness because of the virtual formlessness of his education—the predicament of the sensitive mind during what may be called the interregnum between the effective dominance of the old Christian-classical ideal through old European institutions and the rise to rule of the succeeding ideal, whatever history comes to call it. To express that predicament in fiction no education could have been more fitting than his, for it excluded him from assenting to the energies of social expansion, of technology, of the deterministic sciences, and of modern finance and business. Unconscious assent to these forces, over and above any rebellion against their moral values, caused most active minds in his day to conceal the fact of interregnum. James's mind reacted only to the shadows of those forces as revealed in human emotion and in social behavior and convention. With his abiding sense of the indestructible life, he expressed the decay and sterility of a society pretending to live on conventions and institutions but lacking the force of underlying convictions. He described what he saw, and he created what lay under what he saw.

They tell a story of Henry James which cannot be verified as to fact, but one which is so true and just in spirit that we may take it as the scriptural text for this chapter. Once, in the nineties, while James was staying in an English country house, the only child of a neighbor died of a sudden illness; and although James had quarreled with the neighbor and they had not been on speaking terms he announced to his host that he would attend the funeral of the little boy. His host argued that, in the small church in the small village, it would be conspicuously unseemly for him to go—the bereaved parents could only take it as an affront; but James was obstinate. When he returned, his host asked him how on earth he could have brought himself to go, and to sit, as he had, in the pew directly behind the mourners. James brushed all argument aside and, with that intensity in his eyes which made his face seem naked, stated firmly: "Where emotion is, there am I!"

All his life long, and in all but his slightest work, James struggled to use the conventions of society, and to abuse them when necessary, to bring himself directly upon the emotion that lay under the conventions, coiling and recoiling, ready to break through. So to bring himself, and so to see, was for him action in life and creation in art. "Where emotion is, there am I!" If he could find the emotion he could for himself realize life, and if he could create the reality of the emotion in his art, in terms of actual characters and situations, he could make his art—in James Joyce's phrase at the end of A *Portrait of the Artist As a Young Man*—the uncreated conscience of his race. The story of that struggle to realize life as emotion and to create it as art is the abiding story of Henry James, as near as we can come to the Figure in his Carpet.

With the events of his life we have here little to do except see how their conditions, both those imposed upon him and those which he imposed upon himself, led him to an increasing devotion to that struggle, and to the final decision at full maturity that in the very passion of pleading for full life in others, for him life had to be sacrificed to art. As he sometimes put it, his own life had to disappear into his art just to the degree that he was a successful artist.

The conditions imposed upon him were freedom of sensibility and conscience and the emotional insecurity that is apt to accompany that freedom. His was a minimum financial security and the curious need to prove one's own value that in responsive natures sometimes goes with that security. His also was so wide a variety of social and educational exposures, which had in common only their informality, that he was left the most social man in the world but without a society or an institution that could exact his allegiance. His, further, was an accidental injury by a slip or a fall in early manhood which seems to have left him with the sense of a physical uprootedness and isolation that only aggravated, as it fed upon, his emotional isolation. Like Abélard who, after his injury, raised the first chapel to the Holy Ghost, James made a sacred rage of his art as the only spirit he could fully serve.

II

Henry James was born in New York City, April 15, 1843, the second son of Henry James, Sr.—a peripatetic philosopher and dissenting theologian of considerable means, a friend of Emerson and Carlyle, and a great believer in a universal but wholly informal society. It was he who on his deathbed directed that the only words spoken at his funeral should be: "Here lies a man, who has thought all his life that the ceremonies attending both marriage and death were all damned nonsense." To his sons William and Henry he gave a kind of infant baptism after his own heart by taking them abroad before they could speak and dipping them generously in the font of Europe: a rite which was to mark them both with particular strength and weakness for life. After Europe in 1843 and 1844, the family alternated between Albany and New York. The children were sent to at least three schools before 1855, when in June they went to Europe for a three-year educational experiment at Geneva, London, Paris, and Boulogne. The year 1858–1859 was passed at Newport, Rhode Island; 1859–1860, at Geneva and Bonn. Thus the boys learned languages and manners and fragments of many systems of formal education; but more important were the incalculable effects of years of exposure to the sights and sounds and tones of "other" worlds than that in which by birth they might have been expected to grow up. Part of their father's intention was to give them, by keeping them safe from any particular soil, the richest and most varied human soil to grow in. When he had given them as much of Europe as possible, he removed them to what was at that time the least American of all towns, and for two years they lived again at Newport. There they came under the influence of a young man who was to become the least American of all American painters, John La Farge. Then, in 1862, Henry James made his one attempt at formal education, in the Harvard Law School, a venture which seems to have had no effect on him at all. It was at this time that he sustained his injury and was kept out of the Civil War, the great historical action of his time.

The young James then turned to literature, at first uncertainly and as a "possible" occupation but within four or five years firmly and fully as a profession. His earliest story appeared in the *Atlantic Monthly* in 1865, when he was twenty-two, and he published stories, sketches, and critical reviews frequently thereafter in that magazine, in the *Nation*, and elsewhere. In the fiction and sketches the writing was easy to the point of facility, romantic in tone except where it was humorous, and distinguished chiefly by its competence; in the criticism, it was high-toned and even captious. It showed the influences of Dickens and Hawthorne, Washington Irving and perhaps a little Balzac, in short the dominant literary influences of his time. The American scene, as characterized by Boston and New York, kept him alive but did not provoke reaction or experiment in his writing.

In 1869 he went abroad again, this time to literary as well as social Europe, and for ten or twelve years paid visits to America rather than to Europe. Abroad he alternated between London and Paris, London and Italy. London was to live in, Paris was to learn in, Italy to love; America had become chiefly something for his literary and social sensibility to react on. London gave him the support of an institutionalized society which made for security and position. Italy gave him color and form and warmth, and the ideal satisfaction of all his romantic nostalgia for those qualities. But Paris gave him his profession; for there he met Turgenev, whom he called the "beautiful genius," and Flaubert, whom he found vulgar in person but perfect in writing. It was in Paris that he learned that the novel was an art and that art was the mastering, all-exacting profession that alone made life tolerable by making it intelligible. He learned also that the art of literature, like the art of painting or of music, was an international art, however locally rooted it might have to be in inspiration, and for himself he made the decision that his inspiration might well be as international as the art. It was a decision for which his education had prepared him, just as was his decision to live in London but to keep up his American and French connections. Perhaps it was the very informality of his education that made him grasp for safety at the formalism of English society and the form of the French novel of Flaubert and the Russian novel of Turgenev who was himself a result of the French influence. Formalism and form were for him the means of understanding the formlesssness which was life itself; but he never confused the two, though he sometimes made the mistake of refusing to see the life, either in America or in the novels of "disorderly" writers like Dostoevski and Zola, if the form was not within the habit of his perception.

The effect of these years of discipleship and decision was triple. They transformed James from one more American writer working at his trade to an addicted artist working to perfect the form of his chosen art. They gave him his three themes: the international theme, the theme of the artist in conflict with society, and the theme of the pilgrim in search of society. And through his work, the form of the novel in England and America was developed to a new maturity and variety and responsibility. In 1881, with the publication of *The Portrait of a Lady*, the European novel as a form became part of the resources of the English language, and James himself a great novelist, for in that novel his three major themes were for the first time combined in a single objective form.

These years ended the first long period in James's literary life with a high climax, at the same time that they ended the actually international aspect of his personal life. Perhaps his father's death in 1882 helped diminish his sense of personal American connection. Perhaps his loss of popularity after *The Portrait of a Lady*, which was the last book to sell really well in his own lifetime, forced him into the more private reality of his English connection. Perhaps he had merely finally made up his mind. At any rate, he remained in England without visiting America until 1904 (when he made the tour which is recorded in part in *The American Scene*), and in the nineties he established himself in the nearest he ever had to a real home, at Lamb House, Rye, in Sussex.

The "middle period," from 1882 to 1897, when he published *The Spoils of Poynton*, was one of experimentation, refinement of medium, exacerbation of sensibility, and extreme sophistication of perception. Nothing written during that period reached the stature of *The Portrait of a Lady*; much of it was water in sand that only rearranged the grains, though much of it was exquisitely molded. It was then that he earned his reputation for finickiness, difficulty beyond the necessities, unreality, and remoteness. His disappointment was so great that, during the latter part of this period, he succumbed to the temptation to write deliberately "popular," deliberately "well made" plays, none of which did well, and one of which, at its London performance, brought him the humiliation of personal hisses when he appeared on the stage at the call for author. Yet he had finally mastered the art that was to make it possible for him to write, in the third period, from 1897 to 1904, first-rate novels and tales, among them the series of three great novels, *The Ambassadors*, *The Wings of the Dove*, and *The Golden Bowl*. Perhaps his failure in his one effort at treason to his high calling when he turned to drama, and the personal humiliation of that failure, jolted him back with new strength by reaction to his old conception of the novel; perhaps he had merely needed the long time of experiment for secret incubation; in any case, preparation was necessary for maturity of technique and, more important, for maturity of sensibility.

The fourth period began with a visit to America in 1904 and 1905 and might well have prepared him, had he lived longer or had the First World War not intervened, for the still greater art of which we can see the signs in the volume of stories called *The Finer Grain*, collected in 1910. These years were spent in the revision of his novels and tales for the New York Edition, in the volume on *The American Scene* (1907), and in the writing of several volumes of memoirs. After 1910 two experimental novels were begun but never finished, *The Ivory Tower* and *The Sense of the Past*. War and sickness prevented their completion and they were published as he left them after his death in the winter of 1916. At his life's end he had a number of friends but none close, many acquaintances but none important to him, and considerable influence on the younger writers of his time, though nothing commensurate to the influence he was later to exert when the luxury of his sensibility and the rigors of his form became increasingly necessary to a larger number of readers and writers. Howells, Bennett, Wells, Ford Madox Ford, Conrad, and Edith Wharton gained by his example, and the last three avowedly made use of his method—Conrad notably in *Chance* and *Under Western Eyes*, Ford in *The Good Soldier* and his remarkable tetralogy about the war, of which the first volume was *Some Do Not*, and Mrs. Wharton in all but her early work. Of the later generation, Virginia Woolf and Dorothy Richardson would have been impossible without him, as less directly Faulkner and Hemingway and Graham Greene would also have been impossible without the maturity to which he had brought their craft. But essentially he died, as he had lived, lonely both in art and in life, a very special case indeed.

I I I

Yet he is no more special than Swift or Donne or Proust. He is merely one of those writers in whom succeeding ages find differing values and to whom each age assigns a different rank; nor is it likely that within a particular age he will ever escape violently opposed opinions as to the character of what he wrote. He is thus a perpetual anomaly. How he came to be so, why he must remain so and for what literary good and ill, it is the purpose of this chapter to inquire. For in the stresses and oppositions and active conflicts that make him anomalous, we see what he stood for and we measure the varying stature of what he did.

He stood for that universal human society which is held to underlie any and all existing forms of society; and what he did was to attempt to express the supremacy of universal society over the very narrow existing society he fed on for material. What he stood for was deep in him, a shaping part of his nature; but for what he did he was ill equipped with the conventional kind of sensibility, though excellently equipped with the passion—the suffering readiness and tenacity—of extraordinary sensibility. He was therefore driven to excesses of substitution and renunciation and refinement (in experience and morals and style) beyond warrant of any other successful author's use. Yet in these very excesses lay the virtue of his fundamental insight. Given the broad poverty and intense riches of his known world, it was his insight that forced upon him his excesses. He had to go out of the world to judge the world.

That necessity, the privations which caused it, and its consequent excesses were almost family traits. They show in William as well as in Henry, and pretty much combine in their father. Each of the three suffered in youth a central damage from an experience of the immanence of overwhelming evil and its menace to the self, a damage which was never repaired and never forgotten, so that life always remained perilous. But each was able to balance his experience of evil by an experience of something like religious conversion. None of these conversions except that of the father were on Christian terms; none left its subject attached permanently to any particular form of religion or to any particular form of society. Each of them was left rather with the sense of access to the very center of society itself. William James gives an account of his own conversion anonymously in *The Varieties of Religious Experience*; Henry gives his, in adumbration, in the story called "The Jolly Corner," and in a manuscript note of a New Year's visitation of his Genius which Lubbock prints in his edition of James's *Letters*. But the version which the elder Henry James gives will do for all three. The last book he himself published, *Society the Redeemed Form of Man*, suggests the works of his two sons as well. There the old man, thirty years after the event, said that in his own religious conversion he had been "lifted by a sudden miracle into felt harmony with universal man, and filled to the brim with the sentiment of indestructible life." Such experiences left all three with what the younger Henry was to call in his old age that "obstinate finality" which had made him an artist in spite of all privations.

If the nature of those privations remained always vague, like an obscure and spreading hurt, and if the experience of conversion was always vague, a force from outside that compelled him to go on beyond and in spite of the hurt, nevertheless the result in Henry James's written works is as clear as need be. There is everywhere in it the presence of a deep, almost instinctive, incentive to create the indestructible life which, to his vision, must lie at the heart of the actual life that has been hurt. He began at once to cultivate what his father had planted in him, the habit of response across any barrier—the more barrier the more response. His peculiar education had given him the straight look, acute ear, keen touch, and receptive mind. In his writing life, that mind received so much and reacted so constantly that it became itself a primary and trustworthy sense. This is the hallmark of the homemade mind, and it serves pretty well for home affairs, but in the affairs of the wide world it drives its victims partly to makeshift and partly to reliance upon naked humanity. To the elder James, such a mind was enough, because he never had any real intent to do more than goad and gad the society he lived in. To William James it was not enough, but he was partly able to make up his losses by the systematic study of physiology and philosophy. To Henry James it was not enough either, and he was driven all his life long, without ever acknowledging it, to make substitutes pass for the real thing. It was perhaps that necessity that made him an artist. At any rate the eloquence and passion with which he made the substitutes, rather than the act of substitution, pass for the actual, were what gave his writing stature a kind of contingent or inner reality. Not until war came in 1914 did he see that the true forces of society had all the time been leading to a final treachery to the values its conventions could no longer defend. He had seen it in his art, but not in his life. His immediate response was to throw himself into the war and to become a British subject. The British gave him the Order of Merit; but his response had been lifelong and was already recorded time after time in book after book.

There, in his "International" books, he set the two kinds of society he knew against each other for balance and contrast and mutual criticism. There are two kinds of society which demand writing like this of James: the society of Europe where the vital impulse has so far run out that all its meanings are expressed by the deliberate play of conventions and their refinements; and, second, the society of America where the original convictions and driving impulse have not yet matured in conventions adequate to express them on high levels. James belonged by birth and primary exposure to the second (New York and New England so far as he could deal with them by instinct), and he had a vision—alternately ideal and critical, alternately discouraged and disillusioned—of the first in the Europe of France and Italy and particularly England. Each gave him the means of dealing with the other; each kept the other from seeming the only society on earth; and together they gave him, at his best, great formality and passionate substance.

The International Theme, in short, was what his education had led to. It was the machinery at hand, and in the lack of anything else it had to provide momentum for everything else. Unlike most writers of his time, but a precursor of many who came to maturity after the First World War, he was barred from the help of religion and history, and a perverse critic might say barred even from the help of literature. He could not use religion because he knew nothing of the Christian Church, hardly even so much of its language as remains alive in the speech of those outside it. He did not know what had happened either to the institutions or the practice of religion; he had only the core of religion within him, and it got into his work only by indirection. He could not have written, like his brother, *The Varieties of Religious Experience*, because he was so obstinately a central form, beneath all varieties, of the religious experience itself. He was an example of what happens to a religious man when institutional religion is taken away. What happen to Maggie Verver in *The Golden Bowl*, to Milly Theale in *The Wings of the Dove*, to Isabel Archer in *The Portrait of a Lady*, to George Stransom in "The Altar of the Dead," are examples of religious experience outside a creed, just as what happens to John Marcher in "The Beast in the Jungle" is an example of the privation of religious experience, and just, too, as what happens to the governess in "The Turn of the Screw" is an example of what happens when positive evil inverts religious experience. James would have been wholly unable to relate any of these affairs in formal Christian terms; where for once, in "The Altar of the Dead," he tried to invoke the experience of the Catholic Church, he saved his story to actuality only by the eloquence of his hero's emotion.

As with religion, so with history, only the other way around. If religion was in James an inner primal piety, history was a felt objective residue. He took his history in a single jump from the living man to the ancestral Adam. He was contemporary to an extreme. He took his tradition almost entirely on its face value; yet because he knew so much must have been behind that face, he actually felt more continuity, more unity, than had ever been really there. In that feeling lay the intensity of his sense of history. He lacked historical imagination because his mind lacked historical content; he had never been inside any history but his own; but he had the sense of history because he saw all around him in Europe how he himself came at its end, and all around him in America how he came at its beginning. He felt in himself, so far as history went, the power to represent the flash between the two eternities.

The strangest privation in James, and one that troubled him even less than the others—though it has caused much trouble for many readers—was the privation of his relation to the whole body of literature. He was, as Santayana ironically said of himself, "an ignorant man, almost a poet." It was because he knew so little great literature in quantity that to many he seemed excessively literary in manner; there were not enough professional barriers between himself and the printed page to prevent his mere unredeemed idiosyncrasy from now and then taking over. He knew well enough the things read around the house as a boy—Dickens and Scott and Hawthorne; he knew even better his chosen masters, Balzac and Turgenev and Flaubert; but it is not an exaggeration to say that he had no organized command of any of the possible general traditions of literature a writer living in his time might have taken up. There is very little evidence of reading in his letters, except for the books of his friends; and when his brother complained that he ought to read more, he answered that he had no time. His critical writing, even when it was not frank book reviewing, was almost entirely contemporary, of narrow range and narrower sympathies; it is worth reading chiefly as an illumination of his own mind and writing.

Only when he tackled the technical problems—by the very narrowness of his solutions of which, in his own work, he so greatly stretched the scope and responsibilities of the novel as a form—was he critically at home and master in his house.

He was indeed virtually an ignorant man, actually a poet; but he had, besides that sense of the human which he shared with his father and brother, only the two natural weapons of a direct eye and an expert knowledge of surfaces. He had thus everywhere to depend more on his method than—in Plato's sense—on his madness. Only by resources of method which he had often to develop and sometimes to invent could he get his poetry into the objective form of novel or tale; for example, put another way, his use of dialogue is an example of development from illustration to substance; his use of an active consciousness interposed between the story and the reader, as in *The Ambassadors*, is almost an invention. He had to find means to get around the problems which trouble most novelists—as war and lust, love and God, troubled Tolstoy—in order to get at the problems that troubled him. Between him and the world he knew he had to interpose the story of the story, the passion of the passion, the problem of the problem; otherwise he could not aesthetically possess the story, the passion, the problem.

So central were morals to James, even though he was a dissenter to the forms in which morals are abused, that there was not ever quite enough for him in any part of the world either to fall back on or to go forward with. It was so in his own mind; his convictions never matured as ideas, but as images or metaphors, as aesthetic creations, always to be created afresh. As he never went backward into the full Christian tradition, but tapped his sense of what underlay it, so he never went back into the whole force of love, only into so much of it as could be conceived morally. It is for reasons such as these that, though he aimed always at the full picture, the full drama, James had to resort successively to the lesser forms of the allegory, the fable, the ghost story, and at the end, where he was nearest his target, to a kind of cross between the drama and the fairy story; for this is the journey James made between "A Passionate Pilgrim" and "The Madonna of the Future," through "The Turn of the Screw" and *The Sacred Fount*, to *The Golden Bowl* and "The

Bench of Desolation," where the last two are almost pure Cinderella and Ugly Duckling dramatized and made haunting for every reader who can see himself in their terms. This is the reverse of what happens in novels wholly dramatized. Whereas great drama seems to rest on the driving power of myth, the thing deeply believed and subject to change and criticism only in externals, the fairy tale seems to rest on an insight anxious to prove itself ideal and therefore dependent on externals for access to essentials. In the fairy tale the skeleton is on the outside, sometimes so much so that there is nothing else, while in the drama the skeleton is always fleshed. This is what Edith Wharton meant when she asked James why he left out of his novels all the fringes of what really happened to his people; to which James answered that he didn't know that he had. James leaves the reader relatively everything to put in; all his density and richness develop in the details of his chosen skeleton. The big things are all fairy tale, with that threat of sudden dark illumination at the edge of which the fairy tale, even more than the fable or the ghost story, so often hovers. The bones that articulate the skeleton can be named. Candor, innocence, aloneness, the pure intelligence on one side, and mendacity, unspecified corruption, crowdedness, and a kind of cunning rapacity on the other are given at equally high value; but are given always at a point where each is about to break down, in the contest with actual life, either into renunciation (which to James as to Emily Dickinson was a "piercing" virtue) or into some deep and ambiguous kind of capitulation of good to evil and evil to good—as in the end of *The Wings of the Dove* or of *The Golden Bowl*, where the capitulations are mutual, affirmative, abysmal, shifting. At that point of capitulation, the dramatized fairy tale becomes the instrument and substance—form united with content—of revelation and judgment. This was the prodigy James made of the novel.

I V

If this account of privations and defects is any way correct, James's accomplishment in the art of fiction was certainly a prodigy. No writer in the England or America of his time surpassed him, whether with or relatively without his defects, and his peers—Stevenson and Hardy and Moore and Meredith, Mark Twain and Melville and Howells—played in different fields. He had the extraordinary luck to come on a whole baggage of themes and conventions and situations in the same process by which he himself lived, and the luck, too, that made them suited to replenish each other in his chosen forms of the fable and the fairy story; he had had the luck to find a garden which he could cultivate, and did. He deliberately undertook, and invoked for himself, the profession, the role, the vocation of what he called "that obstinate finality" of the artist. As a profession, art gave occupation to his habit of omnivorous curiosity and to his knowledge of surfaces, and it made the sacrifice of other forms of life acceptable for the sake of good practice. As a role, it gave him both an inner independence and the protection of an outer identity no matter what sacrifices and failures might come his way. As a vocation, it overrode or made negative all sacrifices and failures whatever with the conviction of purpose, and so put him in unassailable relation with that universal man and that indestructible life which he felt under any society, no matter what any society in existence might think of his feelings about it. Art was his pride of energy. So much so that the profession and role of artist—both for themselves and as foils and ideal contrasts to other professions and roles—provided the major obsession for his fictions, as did the obsession of the International Theme, of which it was only another, and equivalent, version.

Where the International Theme showed the American against the European, whether as pilgrim or victim, the theme of the artist showed the writer or painter or actress against the world. The underlying theme which he used perhaps first in *Daisy Miller* (1879), but first clearly in *Washington Square* (1881), and at the last made his chief overt theme, was that of the innocent, loyal, candid spirit at the mercy of the world but reacting to it with high intelligence and spiritual strength, precisely with the artist's perception of what for good and ill it actually was. These stories of young American girls smirched or driven out of society by the cruel stupidity of its conventions alternated with stories of artists who were also smirched or driven out. In James's imagination the two themes became identical. Perhaps this is again a sign of the interregnum in the thinking of modern man: that the artist should suddenly come to have exorbitant value as subject matter—should seem a hero or a traitor to his proper heroic role—and should seem so to the artist himself and not merely to his biographer. In this James is not alone; he is followed by Mann and Proust and Gide and Pirandello and Joyce, to all of whom the artist became the type of hero most precious; but James was first and most copious and most intransigent in moralizing the desperate straits through which the artist pursued his role— sometimes as if he had chosen it, as in "The Figure in the Carpet" (1896), sometimes as if he had been condemned to it, as in "The Lesson of the Master" (1892), and sometimes, as in "The Middle Years" (1893) as if he had accepted it.

In all these stories the fate of the artist is somehow the test of society. As a consequence he finds his own value so high that he cannot assent to society as it is, but has a great craving to assent to it as it ought to have been, for he knows that his very being declares, or is prevented from declaring, its possibilities. The degree of self-consciousness in these tales is equal to this conscious sense of self-value, and it is hard to say which overcomes the other. In "The Figure in the Carpet," the author Hugh Vereker has a secret pattern to his work that, when he dies, no amount of fanatic frenetic work can reveal. In "The Middle Years," on the contrary, the dying author leaves such a sure consciousness of his essential value that his disciple, a young doctor, gives up the certainty of a fortune to remain in the presence of the master to whom in his disciple's "young voice" is "the ring of a marriage bell." To them both, without "the madness of art," which both share, life is frustration. In "The Lesson of the Master," the Master urges the disciple to give up everything, marriage, money, children, social position—all the things to which the Master has himself succumbed—for the sake of his art. The artist is not a man, declares the Master, but a disfranchised monk, and the rarity of his art must be his only passion. To this teaching the disciple is true; he makes his retreat, and writes; but when he returns he finds that the Master, having become a widower, has married his girl, "partly" to make sure that the disciple sticks to his art, and has himself given up writing. James ends his fable with the remark that the disciple felt himself dedicated by nature to intellectual, not personal, passion. One hardly knows whether society or the artist is worse flayed in this brilliant story; but one knows certainly that the moral of the fable, and of that final remark, lies in the representation of the artist's life as the fullest possible human profession.

James thus raised his profession to a vocation—a calling from beyond himself by a familiar within himself—which, as he followed it, was a virtually continuous conversion, for strength, for identity, for piety to life, of his whole being. Who will say that it was not an invoked obsessive device, a ruse to transform life otherwise intolerable? But who will say, in the conditions of his life, that he had an alternative? To him the sense of his vocation was a predominant part of his sense of the animating truth, as anyone can see who reads his own invocation to his own genius, quoted by Lubbock in his edition of James's *Letters*. Unlike his friend Henry Adams, who thought that if anything he sat too much in the center of the whole world, James knew himself actually at the periphery, and had therefore to make himself a center in invoked reality. As an individual he felt himself to be so many *disjecta membra poetae*. But by raising his profession to a vocation, he celebrated, like priest and prophet at once, a rite in his own chapel of the true church. He became thus the individual who knew best how little individual he truly was, and was therefore able to overcome the dead weight of all those who merely thought themselves individuals because they wielded power and direction and routine to society by the accident of rank or privilege or money. The difference lay in the presence of the sense of vocation; and the only profession James could by nature see as vocation was that of artist; and he saw the artist as alternately cheated and blest in his vocation regardless of his immense task.

But he went further; the sense of vocation is primary in most of his fiction. He made a dramatic tansposition of the artist's sense of vocation and he saw it as motivating rare and precious conduct everywhere. James habitually envisaged people as either with vocation in an extreme devoted sense—Isabel Archer in *The Portrait of a Lady* no less than Miriam Rooth in *The Tragic Muse* or Fleda Vetch in *The Spoils of Poynton* or Lambert Strether in *The Ambassadors*—or as without vocation, as in the foils to the characters just named, and more or less brutally against those who had it. He did not deal with the much greater numbers of people who are merely occupied as confused human animals. That is the difference between a writer like James and writers like his masters, Balzac and Flaubert. Hence perhaps his failure to understand the degree of remove at which the conventions of society actually work out (at some distance from where any of us are sitting) and how much of human energy other than the animal is merely manipulated rather than absorbed by the conventions. His novels have no ordinary people, except as barriers to the extraordinary; his people feel either the passion of the passion, or they feel nothing.

As an instance of the extremity to which James carried his transposition, one might take that great and beautiful tale "The Altar of the Dead" in which the hero devotes his life to the cultivation of the memory of his loved dead and is led finally, at the moment of his own death, to celebrate also the memory of the one dead man he hated, who seems suddenly to have been equal in need and just obligation to all the rest. But perhaps an example more sharply drawn may be exhibited in the bare bones of "Maud-Evelyn." Here a young man named Marmaduke, after being as he mistakenly thinks half jilted, goes off to Switzerland where he falls in with an elderly American couple named Dedrick. The Dedricks had some years since lost their daughter Maud-Evelyn, and now, to salvage their loss, take up the new young man in the role of imaginary son-in-law. The young man so far falls in with the fantasy that the role becomes as good as the thing itself, and he proceeds to realize it, stage by stage, for all it is worth; that is, as a vocation. Thus he passes through courtship, wedding, married life, into widowerhood and mourning till finally the Dedricks—whose fantasy he had authorized in the transformation of his own nature—die at peace. Shortly afterwards he himself dies, leaving, as his one gesture toward his erstwhile life, all his money to the girl to whom he had been originally engaged. Perhaps the theme is like Proust's, that the past, brooded on, grows and grows. What the old couple wanted was to get from the past what they would have wanted of the future. They made a temple of death in order to profane it, to stretch its precincts to cover the living world. To the young man—otherwise, by James's assertion, empty of clear intent—it was a chance to seize on the offered backward pattern with the intensity of vocation, in full belief that he might make out of it a true self. Thus, in this story, obsession with the dead reaches hallucination and hallucination reaches the new reality of art.

V

$\mathbf{F}$urther than this James never went, though in "The Friends of the Friends" he went as far, for he was eager to perfect his mastery of substance as well as of form. In that story an ordinary ghost is made into something monstrously human, and presides over one of those deep abortions of the human spirit which are yet, in their catastrophe, but "a response to an irresistible call": that is, are acts performed in the assumption of vocation. Had he gone further James would not have been so much unreadable—as this last example nearly is—as silly. He was content with his handful of dark fables of unassayable devotion, because they complemented and hinted at the filling out of such clear dramatic fables as *Washington Square* (1881) and *The Tragic Muse* (1890). The first of these is a light piece, done on the side, to show the opposite case to that of *The Portrait of a Lady*, which was published the same year. Catherine Sloper is the only one of James's heroines who is all round dull and plain, the only one whose intelligence is not equal to her innocence. Without intelligence, she is unable either to reject or to assent to her gradual exile from society at the hands of an egocentric father and a casually mercenary lover; she merely sticks it out. Her story is not there, and neither are the stories of her father and her lover. If anything carries the book along it is the atmosphere suggested in the title, neither of which—atmosphere nor title—have anything except accidentally to do with the theme of the book; which is that human decency, even when unaware of its grounds and its ends, can, if it is taken as a vocation, come cleanly through any soiling assault. It would have taken the passion of a Flaubert for working the riches of ordinary and inarticulate things to have made excellence out of this Madame Bovary in reverse; and perhaps James was trying to do so; but he did not have that skill, and his book remained in the deep sense only an intention.

Miriam Rooth in *The Tragic Muse,* on the other hand, has at least a real struggle because she has the weapons of beauty and intelligence and a vocation as an artist to fight with. She makes the center (together with the bright figure of the aesthete Gabriel Nash a little off center for fun) of a brilliant account, in large scale, of the perpetual struggle between the artist of any sort and society of any sort. But there is more gaiety, more business of the great world and the studio without the concrete representation of the underlying perception of and reaction to it, than a novel can stand and still ring true. James himself thought it moved too fast, and certainly the values asserted are far ahead of the values rendered. As a result, the validity, whether for triumph or assault, of Miriam Rooth's or Nick Dormer's vocation is not so much proved as it is by its own self-insistence impugned. In short, it is very much the same sort of relative failure, but at the opposite extreme, as *Washington Square.* But it is often in his relative failures that an artist's drive is most clearly defined; if only because in his purest successes there is the sense of the self-born, self-driven, and self-complete and these qualities escape definition.

What we can see in these novels which relatively fail, and indeed in a full ten of the nineteen novels which he published in his lifetime (as in perhaps a greater proportion of his hundred-odd shorter pieces) is that James's work constitutes a great single anarchic rebellion against society—against the laws of society—in the combined names of decency, innocence, candor, good will, and the passionate heroism of true vocation. His work as a body is the dramatized or pictured exhibition, at those chosen points most familiar to him in his own society, of the revolt implied in the title of his father's book, *Society the Redeemed Form of Man.* Both Jameses were basic dissenters to all except the society that was not yet; and in both cases the rebellion or dissent was merely eccentric or extravagant in life and manners, but central and poetic in work and insight. That is why in these tales of people who renounce or ignore so much of life which to other eyes would have been precious and even necessary to living, the last legitimate cry is still: Live, live all you can! James was compelled to accomplish his rebellion of the ideal through the very conventions he meant to re-create; they were the given medium in which the underlying reality and the invoked ideal could meet and, in dramatic actuality, merge; conventions were what he knew.

The importance of this is worth any amount of reemphasis; for James is only an exaggerated instance of the normal author, and his works are only a special case of what always goes on in the relations between an artist and a society whose values have become chiefly secular without having quite lost the need or the memory of values divinely ordered. His case is representative of literature in America, whenever it has been ambitious, to a degree greater than we care to say; in their necessary addiction to external conventions, Hemingway and Dos Passos, for example, are no less representative than James. But, granting the addiction, we are here concerned with what the conventions were and what happened to them in James's imagination.

With the *haut monde* and the *beau monde*, somewhat of Italy and France, and particularly of England, together with their high Bohemias—to none of which did he actually belong—James had the expert familiarity of the observer. He knew the dinner table and drawing room, the country house and tea table, the library and smoking room, the city square and the estate park, the spas and hotels and promenades, and all the means and times and ceremonies for moving from one to another. They were the straps the people he knew swung on, and with which they held against the lurches which proved that their society was a going concern. Similarly, he knew how they got married, or jilted, or cheated; and he knew beautifully how they made cads and swindlers and lackeys of themselves almost as often as they made berths for themselves. To all this he turned first as to the form of a living society. Then he saw, rather, that this was but the mechanical arrangement of a society, that it was but the reflected tradition of values which the society might not otherwise possess and which indeed it often possessed only to soil and sully—though it could not destroy them. Those who ought to have embodied the truth of tradition in living conventions were in fact those who most demeaned it. He saw through the people, but what he saw was still the convention: the ultimate decency between human beings that could be created or ruined, equally, only by convention.

Thus James knew expertly what people's superficial obsessions were. If he did not know what their ordinary day-to-day preoccupations were, nor what, in consequence, they were likely to do, he did know the basic preoccupations of all people without regard to country or manners: he knew at what point of value men or women wanted, regardless, to live or die and what barriers they could put between themselves and affirmation. Hence, he had, as a writer, to combine his two knowledges and jump the ignorance that lay between. Like a child, also a moralist, he had to use fables as the means of the jump.

Sometimes, of course, James tried to make his fables carry more than they could bear. We have touched on two examples in "The Figure in the Carpet" and "Maud-Evelyn." "The Great Good Place" is another, in which the heavenly world is seen as resembling an unusually comfortable club. But *What Maisie Knew* (1897) and *The Awkward Age* (1899) are better and fuller examples still, for in each a major use of social convention was attempted, and in each the failure was virtually, but not actually, saved by the bounty of the author's sensibility and the fertility of his technical invention. In the first the question is asked, what will happen to a little girl exposed to the breakdown of marriage in a succession of increasingly shabby divorces and liaisons? James was able to give so much through the innocence of his beautiful little girl's exposed consciousness that his story constantly both winces and cries out because the conventions through which Maisie is compelled to see her situation prevent the rest of the story, the whole story, the true story, from being told. In *The Awkward Age* the primary question is, what will happen to the publicly exposed relations of a set of people when the daughter of the house comes of social age and first takes part in those public relations? It is sometimes said that the relative failure of this book comes about because James restricted his presentation of his answer to a masterly use of scene and dialogue. But that argument would reduce Congreve to the stature of Wilde. The true cause of failure would seem to lie in the inability of all the characters in the book,

[299

including its presumably fresh and plastic young heroine, to bring into the conventions to which they restrict themselves the actual emotions and stresses that the conventions are meant to control, but of which they were never, in a living society, meant to be the equivalent.

In short, neither the domestic economy of social conventions nor the vocation of the artist was ever enough to bring out in James a mastery of substance equal to his mastery of form. What he seems to have needed was either an enlargement of the theme of the artist into terms of ordinary life, an enlargement of the social conventions into the International Theme, or a combination, in the press of one composition, of the artist and the international and the ordinary. At any rate, within these three fields lie his great successes, in which are to be included some fifteen or twenty tales as well as six or seven novels. The International Theme in its simplest form is the felt contrast of Europe and America. But it is a very different thing from the internal American contrast between New England and Virginia, and it resembles the contrast between the Old East and the New West only to the limited degree that, during James's lifetime, the Old East had digested and reversed its contrast with Europe. For the prime purpose of the contrast to James was that it furnished him with a reversible dualism which created as well as adjudicated values. It was not just a question of American girls marrying European men and of European women never, or seldom, marrying American men, though that question suggested many others having to do with the relative values of the maternal and the paternal in the conventional great world. Nor was it only the question of why American men went to Europe for culture, except in the secondary question of whether or not they could apply what they got in Europe to the American scene. It was these and much more. It was a dualism of right and wrong, of white and black, home or exile; and like any true dualism, before it becomes lost in an institution, its terms were reversible, without impairment of their reality. Reversed, right and wrong became fresh and stale, white and black became decent and corrupt, home or exile became integrity or destruction. With these reversals in mind, the questions at the heart of the International Theme can be put afresh. What happens to Americans in Europe?

What does Europe do to them? bring out of them? give them, by threatening its loss, to struggle for? And, on the contrary, what happens to Europeans under impact of Americans? What new source do they find to make up for the loss which the exposure has laid bare? And so on.

In the beginning the American is conceived as having in him a dead or unborn place, and is, in moral perception if not in moral nature, gray or black; the European, in contrast, is conceived as alive with inherited life as well as his own and is all gold and pearls in moral perception, however black he may be in moral nature. Thus the gain of the European adventure ought, for the American, to be greater than the loss risked: James never quite rid himself of this speculative frame of mind and could supply, at the peak of his writing life, in the novel he cared most for, *The Ambassadors* (1903), an example in which one American gains every possible strength for his own moral nature through immersion in European moral perception. But he became increasingly forced to draw from his chosen examples the opposite conclusion, and in so doing he was only carrying one great step further the conclusion drawn in his best early work. In *The American* (1877) and in *The Portrait of a Lady* (1881) Newman and Isabel Archer are victimized by Europe; Europe is the disillusion for Newman, and for Isabel the evil and treachery, which overcame them; if they are left intact they are also left shrunk; their strength was in the strength to renounce. But in *The Wings of the Dove* (1902) and in *The Golden Bowl* (1904), the two American girls, Milly Theale and Maggie Verver, although victimized by Europe, triumph over it, and convert the Europeans who victimized them, by the positive strength of character and perceptive ability which their experience of treachery only brings out. Neither Milly's death nor Maggie's re-creation of her adulterous marriage is an act of renunciation or disillusion; they are deliberate acts of life fully realized and fully consented to, done because it is necessary to keep intact the conviction that life has values greater than any renunciation can give up or any treachery soil. By these means, in the figure of the American girl, candor, innocence, and loyalty become characteristic though not exclusive American virtues which redress the deep damage done by a blackened Europe. Thus James dramatized a reversal of the values in his International Theme so full as to make of the American's necessary journey to Europe a pilgrimage reversed. It was as if in his writing life he had made a series of withdrawals into a waste in which he assumed there must be an oasis, only to find himself strengthened, on each return, to meet the high values which had all along flourished at home.

It might be said that James had taken for his text the verse from the Sermon on the Mount, "For where your treasure is, there will your heart be also," and used it alternately, first just as it is and then with a reversal of the two nouns, so that a man might expect to find his treasure where and when he had discovered his heart. If we ask by what means he had come to be able to do this, an answer which is at least possible suggests itself: by merging the dynamic dualism of his International Theme with the static, if tragic, insight of the theme of the artist in stories of people extraordinary only for their unusual awareness of life and their unusual liberty to maintain their awareness. Putting it more strongly, if less certainly, James by combining his obsessive themes managed to equip his central insight into the indestructible life of man with a genuinely contingent body of morals and living tradition, regardless of the privation of his life, his education, and his times; and further, in so far as he was able to do this, he found released for use the inexhaustible wealth of felt life in quantities and qualities capable of receiving, and filling out durably, the stamp of form.

The stamp of form was itself a prodigy of accomplishment—and we shall come to it directly—but first it ought to be reemphasized how difficult it was for a writer like James to get hold of life in a way amenable to that stamp. Having no adequate tradition to fall back on for morals (values) or ethics (decision or judgment), James had to make the intelligence do for both, had to make it do as the equivalent of order and law in operation; and, not finding enough of intelligence in the world, he had to create it, and in creating it, had to put it in conflict with facts and stupidities it could not face without choice. For to James the height of intelligence was choice; intelligence was taste in action, and the utmost choice taste could make was the choice to live or die. It was by taste that James got hold of, valued, and judged the life to which his intelligence reacted.

If this is so, it explains why his readers divide into such hostile camps of repulsion and attraction. Those who are repelled think the result, in the face of actual life, drivel; those who are attracted seem to find that taste and intelligence operate through his various themes and combinations of themes to drag into being a kind of ultimate human decency which expresses all the values a given soul can stand.

To those who recognize that decency in his work, James was full of the terrible basic ambition—but stripped of its ordinary ordeals—to create characters who meet the conditions of society so as to choose to live or choose to die. Thus his characters take on the heroism and the abnegation, as alternative and equivalent roles, of the artist and of the man or woman who ought to have been an artist in life itself. Isabel Archer in *The Portrait of a Lady*, Milly Theale in *The Wings of the Dove*, Maggie Verver in *The Golden Bowl*, and Lambert Strether in *The Ambassadors* are all clear examples of human decency operating through taste and intelligence to confront life heroically and with success. One is divided between thinking that the force of this decency is a transformation of the force of sex, and that it is a new kind of vocation in morals; in either case specially designed for the novelist to represent in the figures of ideally normal human beings; for such, in the four great novels named, he has created his three American girls and his one American man.

V I

But the explanation of how James harmonized his substance and his art had better be put on a little lower plane. Just twice in his life was James able to lift his work to major stature, once at the age of thirty-eight in *The Portrait of a Lady* and once again for a five-year period beginning at the age of fifty-eight, when he produced beside the other three great novels just spoken of, two characteristic projections of the artist's faith, *The Sacred Fount* (1901) and *The American Scene* (1907). The first set up the conscience of the artist to act as the conscience of people who did not have enough for themselves; the second demonstrated the record of that conscience

[303

in action during his American visit—the first in over twenty years—
of 1904. The period before the *Portrait* was no doubt the normal
period of the growth and formation of his own character as a writer;
the novels of that time could almost as well have been written by
someone else, for they were carried forward by a combination of the
existing institution of literature and the élan of first impressions.
Then, suddenly, in his seventh novel, James added to the institution a momentum or élan which was his own; the character and
fate of Isabel Archer were greater than both the social and the novelistic conventions through which she was exhibited. James had
combined his themes for the first time, and for the first time told a
story that demanded of him his full powers. Not until he again
combined his themes, in *The Ambassadors* (1903), did he again
reach full power. It is further notable that the best of the novels that
came in between, *The Spoils of Poynton* (1897), is really only an
elongated tale or *nouvelle*, like "The Turn of the Screw" or "The
Altar of the Dead," and that it lacked the American or International
Theme. Its story remains a melodramatic fable and never reaches
the state of dramatized fairy tale in which the novels of full power
are so strangely happy. Otherwise, aside from *The Awkward Age*,
What Maisie Knew, and *The Tragic Muse*, which have already been
discussed, there are two experiments in a genre of which James
never became a master, *The Bostonians* and *The Princess Casamassima* (both dated 1886).

On their faces both Balzacian novels as modified by the general current of French naturalism, they were actually inhibited from
becoming naturalistic by certain elements in James's own character
as a writer, and so were partially transformed into something else.
Each of these novels plunged him into centers of human conduct
and motivation and obsession—into conditions of behavior—of which
he was only superficially aware. In *The Bostonians* he made his
center the infatuation of a grown woman for a young girl, with its
havoc in each of them, and its final destruction by a violently conventional "rescue." In *The Princess Casamassima*, the center is the
equally disastrous infatuation of the Princess for the little book-
binder's clerk, Hyacinth Robinson, against a general background of
conspiratorial, underground, bomb-throwing revolution, ending in

the violence of Hyacinth's suicide in the shabbiest, blackest room in London. Being fascinated by such subjects, James tried to make what he could see stand for what he could not; and if his attempt had been on a lesser scale—on something not the scale of a naturalistic novel—he might well have succeeded.

What did happen to his attempt in these two books suggests a general conclusion about all his work: his repeated argument that the artist should be released from the burden of things as they were ordinarily understood to happen, probably came from his ignorance of ordinary things in general. It also suggests a rudimentary principle for the art of fiction; that if you want the surface to stand for the whole you must put in enough specifications to make sure it is the surface of the thing wanted and not merely the surface of the writer's mind. In shorter forms this certainty may be provided by intensity of form or perception, but the full-length novel requires extensiveness of form and perception, and extensiveness requires knowledge and specification all around. Then James's argument against naturalistic detail would be sound; economy of strong specification would persuade the reader to put in, out of his own stock of perception, all else that was required. Then, too, the further argument would have been sounder still, that most of what we know deeply comes to us without ever fitting the specifications we had prepared for it. If we deliberately free ourselves of all specifications except those that lay us open to experience, who knows what of the vast unspecified actual will not press in?

It is this last question that must have lurked under James's practice, and this inviting risk he must often have felt he was taking. In *The Bostonians* and *The Princess Casamassima* he made a misjudgment of what detail he could do without and of what he needed, as a carpenter says of his tools, to do with. It is not that he left out the details that clutter but that he omitted to put in those that would lay his readers, and in effect the novels themselves, open to respond to the pressure of the actual—the special shabby underground menacing actual that presses inchoate at the threshold of the stories without ever getting in; so that the novels have a strangely transformed air of protecting themselves from what they are really about.

In the four great novels this is not so. There the unspecified actual does press in as the general menace of folly, inadequacy, or sheer immanent evil. Whatever it is, it ruins loyalty, prevents love, sullies innocence. It is the morass in which some part of every human being is in a nameless mortal combat, and which is felt as the dumb part of despair, the horror at the nether end of boredom, or the futility no bigger than a man's hand in any perspective of effort looked at; it is the menace of life itself. To measure, to represent, to reenact the force of that menace is one extreme of the moral feat of art; as the other extreme is to reenact the equally nameless good that combats it. To reenact both in full measure required of James his combined sense of the reversible dualism of Europe and America, the heroism of the artist's vocation, and the two focused in an otherwise ordinary set of characters. In the shorter pieces, intensity of form and relatively limited perception are enough to give the sense of the menacing, altering force without need of any further articulation. It is its intensity that gives the sense of the jungle to "The Beast in the Jungle," of the corner to "The Jolly Corner," of the screw to "The Turn of the Screw," of the dead to "The Altar of the Dead," and of desolation to "The Bench of Desolation." Each of these tales, if you asked for articulation, would fall flat, but when inarticulated, each shows an indestructible habit of growth into at least the hallucination of actual experience.

The one occasion on which James at all successfully tried for full articulation by direct means was in that testamentary novel *The Sacred Fount*. There the nameless narrator records the passage of the force of life through half a dozen people, with himself as the medium whereby they become conscious of the exchange, and, gradually, conscious of the nature of the force exchanged. He is their conscience and their creator because he is their intelligence; he makes them see what they are. In the end they reject his intelligence, and the reader is left with the ambiguous sense either that the author is crazy and had merely invented his perceptions or that he was right but his creations had now taken over the life with which he had endowed them, with a quite human insistence on mutilating and battening on each other as they themselves chose. The halves of the ambiguity shade into each other interminably in that indestructible association of the moral life in which evil is ignorance but actual, and good is knowledge created real.

Such success as *The Sacred Fount* has is by tour de force; but it is the essential tour de force of James's sensibility; it is the represented hallucination of what, as artist and as man, he wanted to do for life; it is the poetic equivalent, the symbol and example, of what, on his own shaking ground, he wanted to stand for. If he could not say what it was, that is because it was so deeply himself that he could only show it in action, like a man in love or deadly fear. But read with good will and with a sense of the title kept turning in the mind, *The Sacred Fount* becomes the clue to the nature of the intent and to the quality of the achieved substance of the novels and tales, and then in turn becomes clear itself. If there is a secret in Henry James and if there is a way in which we can assent to that secret, both may be found in *The Sacred Fount*. It is the secret of why he was obsessed with the story of the story, the sense of the sense, the passion of the passion. He wanted, in all the areas of life he could reach, to be the story, the sense, the passion not just of the life itself but of the conscience he could create for it. So deep and hidden were the springs of conviction within him, and at the same time so sure the credit he gave to his actual perception, that he could not help believing what he created to be the conscience of truth as well as the reality of art. The being was one with the seeming.

V I I

In such a life work, making so little call on the ordinary means whereby we symbolize the struggle for our relations with God, society, and ourselves, it was necessary for James to make extraordinary demands upon the formal resources of the institution of literature. His essential subject matter compelled him to transform not only the English novel but also the French and Russian novel from something relatively loose and miraculous to something relatively tight and predictable. Neither *The Sacred Fount* nor *The Golden Bowl* could have been written within anything resembling the form of *Madame Bovary* or *Vanity Fair*. His own view of what magnificence his transformation amounted to may be found in the critical prefaces he wrote for the collected edition of his novels and tales. Perhaps the best sense of it is contained in the single phrase: "the coercive charm of form," and perhaps its best aspiration is found at the end of the preface to *The Ambassadors*: "The Novel remains still, under the right persuasion, the most independent, most elastic, most prodigious of literary forms." For, in James's argument, form coerced true freedom upon the novel; form freed the novel for independent prodigies which, without the force of that form, it could not undertake. For his own work, that is what his rules of form did. He developed out of the resources of the old novel, and by invention of new resources, what we now call the James novel.

Since other novelists have used and misused the James novel and since by contagion it has modified the actual practice of many novelists who never read James at all, we had better try to say what the James novel is. It is consistent to its established variety of skeleton forms; it is faithful to its established method of reporting; and it insists on its chosen center of attraction. To do these things it first of all gets rid of the omniscient author; the author is never allowed to intrude directly or in his own person; the story is always some created person's sense of it, or that of some group of persons, so that we see or feel the coercive restriction of someone's conscious experience of the story as the medium through which we ourselves feel it. Secondly, the James novel uses device after device, not merely to invite the reader's ordinary attention, but to command his extraordinary attention. For example, the dialogue in all the later work is as close in structure and in mutual relationships, and as magnetic upon the reader's mind, as an essay in mathematical logic. The scenes between persons are dramatized as substance, not as ornament; true action is in speech and gesture; and thus the dialogue creates a new form of attention, in which we always sail close-hauled or trembling on the tack. As the command to attend is obeyed, the reader learns a new game which, as it seems to partake of actual experience, he can take for truth; and which, as it shows a texture of sustained awareness never experienced in life, he knows to be art. To gain that effect, to make art truth, is the whole object of James's addiction to the forms of fiction; it was the only avenue to truth he could recognize.

Hence he was compelled to be tight, close, firm, restrictive, and extraordinarily conscious in the process of his art; and had to pretend to be so, like any believer, when he was not, because to an unexampled degree he was unconscious of all the other machineries of the mind and of many of the forces to which the mind reacts. He could not think otherwise, as he grew older and lonelier, than that only the most restrictive possible form could stamp his vision of life as recognizable truth and transform the fine conscience of his imagination into recognizable art. That he wrote both novels and tales only less than the very greatest, and that he added permanently to the scope and resources of his art in the process of doing so, was for him only the achieved act of his nature, the "obstinate finality," as he called it, of what he was—an artist. For us, the finality is equally obstinate, but it is also, as he thought the novel was, independent, elastic, prodigious; a version, not the vision, of life; a language, which, as we learn its beauty for his purposes, we can adapt and develop for our own—especially when we are in those moods he has himself created in us—those moods when taste is intelligence, intelligence is conscience, and the eloquence of conscience is heroic truth. Then he is the special case of our own point of view: he is one version of the story of our story, the sense of our sense, the passion of our passion—to be satisfied nowhere else.

James seems to inspire intoxication either of taste or disgust. But these opposite reactions come to the same thing. Born in 1843, designed by his father to be a perceptive luxury in a society whose chief claims to luxury lay along singularly imperceptive lines and whose institutions during his lifetime grew predominantly deterministic, he took to himself the further luxury of expression as a profession. So long as he expressed chiefly, or at any rate superficially, what was taken for granted, he had a fair share of popularity: he was taken as a smart if somewhat overrefined young man. As his expression came under control and exhibited deeper perceptions, he lost most of his small audience. As the quality of his work not only enriched but became characteristic and informed with passionate taste, his work was positively disliked and regarded as a luxury no one could afford.

This was about 1890. Exiled and alienated as well as dispatriated, he was stung to a new and powerful reaction by his failure with the well made play. He became again a novelist, and in this second life, beginning in 1896, more than any other writer, he was ever consciously himself; it was his self that had grown, and was more fully and formally a luxury of expression than ever, so that fewer and fewer could afford to read him. At the same time, he had become an institution, by no means ignored but not in much resort. There were always those who read him, some as a cult and as a means of escape, others because he added to the stature of their own perception. He visited America, after twenty years, not as a triumph but as a venture in discovery. Then he revised and collected his work, deepening his tone and making a cumulus of his weight, and began a new career, partly in the form of memoirs, partly in what promised to be a new form of fiction of which the only finished examples are the stories in *The Finer Grain* (1910) where he began to show a remote intimacy, through the poetry of his language, with the preoccupations of ordinary men and women. That same year—1910—his brother William, then in England, fell ill and he went with him to help him die in America. On his return to England, his own health weakened and he finished nothing but memoirs and short essays in the remaining five years of his life.

But he was more an institution than ever. On his seventieth birthday he was presented by three hundred friends with his portrait by Sargent. In July, 1915, he became a British subject; in the following New Year Honours, he was awarded the Order of Merit; and in February, 1916, he died, still a luxury of perception and expression. Gradually that luxury has become an institution of increasing resort for those who require to find upon what assumptions, in a society like ours, unconscious of any unity and uncertain even of direction, the basic human convictions can yet grow—whether for life or for the judgment of life in art.

Crime and Punishment:
Murder in Your Own Room
[*1 9 4 3*]

Crime and Punishment has upon most readers an impact as immediate and obvious and full as the news of murder next door; one *almost* participates in the crime, and the trivial details become obsessively important. It has besides a secondary impact, by which, as one feels it, one discovers that one has been permanently involved in the nature of the crime: one has somehow contributed to the clarification of the true residual nature of crime in general through having contributed to the enactment of this crime in particular. It is the feeling of this impact that leads us to say our powers of attention have been exhausted. But there is a third and gradual impact, which comes not only at the end but almost from the beginning to the end, creating in us new and inexhaustible powers of attention. This is the impact of what Dostoevski meant by punishment. The three impacts are united by the art of the novelist, and they are felt simultaneously. It is only that we are not aware at the time of the triple significance, and must, when it does transpire, rebuild it analytically. Thus we may come to estimate what it is that we know— what it is that has been clarified in the history of Raskolnikov which we had known all along in ourselves without being aware of it: we estimate our own guilt.

A crime is above all an act against the institutions of human law, custom, or religion; and there is a sense in which any act may be understood as criminal, for if the institution cannot be found against which it is committed, then it may be called an anarchic act—against some institution that has not yet come to exist, but which will exist because of the crime. This notion comes from putting Rousseau's dusty vision in reverse. If, as Rousseau thought for one inspired moment, the evils of living come mostly from human institutions, it is as likely true, though not as inspired, that our institutions arise out of the evil that we do. It is Laforgue who has said it best, and without any but poetic logic to blister his cry:

> Allez, sterile ritournelles!
> La Vie est vraie et criminelle!

This cry of Laforgue represents the lyric sense that must inhabit every criminal who truly imagines his crime, if only for a flash, *before* he commits it to act. What the criminal imagines afterwards is another thing and we shall come to it. Here it is the crime only that has been imagined, and the promise of liberation in the cry within.

So it is with Raskolnikov. If we feel his case in terms of the Laforgue lines we can understand both the motivation of his crime and the external logic of most of his conduct afterwards. It is the story of *Crime and Punishment* at the level of its immediate impact. We are very near it; it is the murder that only by some saving accident we did not ourselves commit—as we did not make a million, win a race, or conquer Europe, all the things it is still not impossible to do, and which, because we have not done them, may yet tempt us to murder. Between temptation and deed there is no distance at all in symbolic meaning. With that symbolic strength in mind, the story of Raskolnikov becomes not only possible but probable, and, as we attend it, not only probable but proved. Let us look and see.

How easy it is to believe that this young, handsome, proud, and sensitive boy might be drawn *first of all* to the possibility of murder as the way out of an intolerable situation. It is the situation of poverty, debt, starvation, shabbiness, sickness, loneliness; for Raskolnikov has reached such a stage of privation that even thought has become a luxury—a kind of luxurious hallucinated hysteria; an extremity in which only the rashest dream seems a normal activity. It is the situation of the sponge, too, for Raskolnikov has come to depend on his mother and sister for help they cannot afford to give, for help they can give only by prostituting themselves in marriage and servile relationships. The sponge who is aware that he is a sponge is in an awkward situation; the pride of his awareness deprives him of the use of the exactions he makes; and that is how it is with Raskolnikov, as he lies in his attic committing symbolic murder. He deceives himself, proudly, that he has conceived murder to symbolize his mother's and sister's freedom as well as his own. He lends his dark motive the external color of a good deed, and then identifies the color with the motive, and forgets what the murder, dark within him, really is. But to starve and be a sponge, that is not all Raskolnikov has to put up with in his pride; he is in the situation, too, of the proud man of intellect who has as yet done nothing and who is afraid that there will be nothing for him to do unless he invents it. Not only can he do nothing for his poverty or for his family, he is in the terrible position of being unable to do anything for himself. Such is his pride, that one of the ordinary things men do will be enough; and such is his pride, too, that none of the things ordinary people—his mother, his sister, his forgotten friends—can do for him are tolerable to him; he is the man for whom no one can do anything. Deeper still, he is that part of all men which cannot be touched, but which must create an image of itself in some extraordinary deed, some act against ordinary people and against the ordinary part of himself. The extraordinary wells within him and inundates the ordinary self with its fever. And in that fever, which never leaves him while we know him, the possibility of murder becomes the necessity of murder.

What is fully imagined as necessary has goodness and freedom at the very heart of its horror, a sentiment which may be interpreted in different ways, having to do either with the tearing down of order or with the envelopment of disorder, or, finally, with the balancing of several disorders so as to form an order. At the level of immediate impact, Raskolnikov's story is concerned with the tearing down of order; that is the melodrama which carries us along and exhausts our attention. What Dostoevski does to that story, the immense clarification of secret life and intimate impulse which he brings to it, composes the secondary impact of the story, and brings us to the second stage where the disorder brought about in the first stage is enveloped by the created personality of Raskolnikov. Actually, the two processes go on at once, in the sense that no matter how far into the second stage Dostoevski leads us, the first stage is never left behind, but is rather always present, a frame of action and image, to carry the significance of the second stage. This is to say that Dostoevski never fails of the primary task of the novelist: if his story seems for the moment to have been left behind, it is only that in reality it has got ahead of us, and when we catch up we see how much has been done without our noticing it. The story of the Crime is blended with the clarification of the Punishment; the actor creates the role which expresses the nature and significance of his deed; Raskolnikov, in the end, becomes the product of his crime, but still depends on it to command our attention.

That is how Dostoevski envelops the disorder consequent upon Raskolnikov's attempt at the destruction of order. With the third possibility, whereby the imagination not only envelops disorder—our substantial chaos—in a created personality, but proceeds to balance the sense of several disorders—the tensions of chaos—against each other so as to form a new order; with this possibility Dostoevski has little to do. It is not that he was necessarily unequal to the task, but that the nature, source, and direction of his insights did not lead him to undertake it. His view of necessity was simpler, and his sense of possibility more simplified, than the task would require; his vision was that of the primitive Christian, and that vision was so powerful within him that it blinded him to everything else. To him the edge of the abyss of sin was the horizon of salvation by faith, and suffering was the condition of vision. Sin was the Crime, and the suffering created by faith was the Punishment.

If we push the operation of this insight one step further, it becomes evident that the act of life itself is the Crime, and that to submit, by faith, to the suffering of life at the expense of the act is to achieve salvation—or, if you like a less theological phrase, it is to achieve integration or wholeness of personality. It is only dramatically true that the greater the sin the greater the salvation, and it is only arbitrarily true that any one act is sinful more than another act or than all acts. The crime of Raskolnikov, and its punishment in created suffering, could have been as great if he had never stirred from his room, if only the novelist's imagination could have conceived them. But the imagination requires images, as vision requires fables and thought requires formulas, before conceptions can be realized; which is to say that the faculties of men are not equal to their needs except by the intervention of symbols which they discover rather than create, and which they discover best of all in stories of violence, or of the sense of violence, or of the promise of violence.

So we watch, with the immediate attention which discovers meaning, the process of Raskolnikov trying to make a hero—a complete man—of himself by committing a foul and frivolous murder. Any animal might strike another down without need when the odor of blood is thick, and it means nothing. But we are shown how much this murder of an old and malevolent pawnbroker, ripe for death, as Raskolnikov says, ripe as a louse, is not meaningless but huge with meaning. The meaning begins with the stench of Petersburg, the stench of the detailed plans, the stench of pothouses, the pervading sense of the filthy possibilities of the human heart, and the glittering eyes of the victim peering through the slit of the door. The meaning grows more meaningful, irretrievably meaningful, when in the second chapter we are exposed to Marmeladov in the stinking tavern and hear his confession of drunken humiliation and of what it has brought upon Katerina his wife in the way of sickness and shame and anger and hairpulling, and brought upon his daughter too, in her glad submissive acceptance of the humiliation of prostitution. It is impossible to *say* how this adds to the richness of Raskolnikov's motive, but like the general images of stench and violence and drunkenness, it is impossible not to *know*, and very precisely, how much it does add. Let us say that it exposes Raskolnikov, and through him the reader, to a kind of dead-level human degradation in terms of images which revolt him as he assents to them.

At any rate they fit him—for the purposes of the story—they fit him to see as further degradation the events which his mother's letter reports to him. Before he opens the letter we see his cluttered mind in his sleazy room trying to work around the idea of a "fortune all at once"; and in the letter he reads how indeed that is precisely what Douania his sister is about to get by selling herself to Luzhin. Douania has permitted herself or has been driven to do just the practical, ordinary thing which Raskolnikov, the extraordinary man, is unable to do, and which—as it is being done for *him*—is the more intolerably humiliating to him. Her marriage is like the prostitution of Sonia. Thinking of it, Hamlet-like, the idea of the murder redis-covers itself most naturally in his mind, and he finds that he had *felt beforehand* that it would come back; it has begun to acquire a kind of reality quite independent of him except that it requires to be completed.

Your ordinary novelist might well have now proceeded to the completion of the deed, but Dostoevski saw deeper into the nature of the deed and knew that it required further preparation, so that it might be as ripe as the victim. Raskolnikov goes out for a breath of air and to escape the pressure of his dilemma. But there is no escape, except from one level of intensity to a deeper level. Walking on the boulevard the double pressure of Sonia and of Douania springs upon him in the shape of the drunken young girl, with the torn dress, and indecorous posture, evidently just seduced and then discarded, who is being pursued by the plump gentleman. In his shabby and dishevelled pride, and with his uprooted and irresolute mind he first attempts to save the girl and then gives it up as a bad job; he revolts against his revulsion, reminding himself of the percentage theory of vice whereby "a certain number" are bound to go that way, and resolves forthwith to go see Razumihin, that simpleton of a man who takes things as they are. But again he changes his mind; he cannot see Razumihin till after "It." The image of the debauched girl has set the murder to pursuing him still more closely. He con-trives for himself, as he thinks, an escape in the green islands of the Neva, where there is no stench, no drunkenness, no human filth. The human filth is stronger. He first buys himself a glass of vodka, and then walks out exhausted, turning aside on the way home, and falls asleep in the bushes, where a dream assaults him with a fresh image of the little sorrel horse beaten to death because it cannot pull all humanity. In the dream he rushes to kiss the bleeding face of the horse as it dies, and at that moment wakes. The moment of waking is the nearest he comes to renouncing his crime before committing it, and it is the nearest, too, that he comes to realizing its nature before the event. "It was as though an abscess that had been forming for a month past in his heart had suddenly broken. Freedom, freedom! He was free from that spell, that sorcery, that obsession!" He had reached the point which Shakespeare, in his own play of Crime and Punishment, *Measure for Measure*, calls the point where the two prayers cross, where, in the human heart, good and evil are created in the one gesture.

It was coincidence, you will remember, that decided the event. Raskolnikov happened to hear, on his way home, that the old pawnbroker would be left alone at seven the following evening, and he heard it at precisely the moment that he had given up the idea of the murder, when he had, in fact, begun again to use his reason and will. But the other thing had grown in him like a disease, and feeding on the coincidence, was able to destroy his will and reason, that is to say his sense of propriety in the social order. It may be observed, for those who carp at the use of coincidence as belittling the probabilities, that on the contrary the use of coincidence in art, like the sense of it in life, heightens the sense of inevitability; for coincidence is the artist's way of representing those forces in us not ourselves. Coincidence, properly dealt with, creates our sense of that other self within us whom we neither can ever quite escape nor quite meet up with.

In this case it is the perfected chain of coincidence, upon which Dostoevski lavishes so many pages, that builds up the murder so that it is a kind of separate being existing between Raskolnikov and his victim. As he climbs the stairs, he feels that Alyona Ivanovna ought to be ready for him, ready to be murdered, for he feels that the murder is somewhere between them, other than either, but equally accessible to both. It was in the nature of Dostoevski's insight to see always that the actor and the patient are both implicated in the deed, and that they are joined by it. The actor, in this case, has more consciousness than the patient of the implication; in *The Idiot* it is the other way round, and Myshkin, the patient, is shown as more conscious, or more representative, of the deeds that are done to him than the doers of the deeds can possibly be. In *Crime and Punishment*, it is Sonia who is perhaps the counterpart of Myshkin, for to her all deeds happen whether the doers realize it or not, and they happen, moreover, completely. It is perhaps because Raskolnikov is the other sort, the sort who requires of a deed that before it is credible or fully significant he must do it himself. He does not believe in the murder until he has done it, and not altogether even then. Constantly it slips away, a thing he realizes that he has forgotten, or a thing he has to re-enact, to emphasize, and so a thing that tends to lose its meaning except as he identifies himself with it; whereas to Sonia, once she has learned of it, once she has submitted herself to the idea of it in him, she has no doubts about it and it is entirely meaningful. Nothing herself, Sonia is able to contain everything; while Raskolnikov, who must be everything himself, can contain nothing for long. Dante would have known how to punish him, looking for a mirror through an eternal hell; but Dostoevski has rather to transform him in order to save him, or more accurately to show him as about to be saved in Sonia's eyes.

But he is not transformed for a long time, never permanently in the book; never can he leave the murder which fixed him, nor the images of which it was made: the images of stench, poverty, drunkenness, vanity, sick-hunger, lechery and intellectual debauchery, through which the murder comes to be a deed in being, with the double power of invocation and growth. At first, indeed, he forgets it for the images and the sickness which went with it, and when he wakes to it he finds that instead of feeling it behind him it has somehow got ahead of him and he is driven to catch up to it. Instead of freedom, power, completeness, he is more at loss than ever, and more incoherent, there are only "scraps and shreds of thought," suspicions, excitements, alarms, and fresh temptations to extraordinary declarations of himself. This is, of course, the first phase of the Punishment for the Crime, that having striven by the crime to reach a complete solution of his incomplete life, he should find himself not only less complete than ever and more wayward but actually perilously incoherent, with a personality on the verge of dissipation. He lives in a haunted vertigo, into which for the time he can invoke only the shrieking phantoms of rage and dread. He is in the position, so humiliating to his continuing pride, where he is completely powerless as the perfectly good man, as powerless as Sonia. There is nothing he can yet see to do for himself, and nothing any longer that he can do for others. When the police send for him about his IOU which his landlady had sold, he feels himself possessed by "a gloomy sensation of agonizing, everlasting solitude and remoteness," and knows that it will never be possible for him to appeal to anyone in any circumstance of life. There is a sense in which Dostoeski might have stopped at this point, for he had put Raskolnikov on the path at the end of which lay the meaning of his Crime as Punishment. For as in the Christian psychology no man may complete himself in deed, so the meaning of a deed can never be completed within the history of the man who enacts it. Only the judgment completes either the man, or his deed, or his meaning.

But both the deed and the meaning can continue in their course of meaningfulness. The growth of meaning is infinite. At the moment he feels his agonizing solitude form consciously within him he hears the police discuss the murder; that is, it is given to him from outside for the first time, and as not his murder, but as an object in no one's possession; at once he is driven to confess, to seize it for his own, but a combination of the fumes of paint and the pang of creation cause him to faint. When he comes to, he goes out leaving a strange impression and a potent silence behind him.

Out of that strangeness and silence grows the pursuit-game which occupies the rest of the book, for Raskolnikov, having decided that suspicions may have been roused about him from his peculiar conduct, begins playing a complicated and eccentric game, or rather a set of games. He pursues the police, eggs the police on to pursue him, and himself both pursues the murder, the acknowledgement of it, and denies it whenever he comes face to face with it. The result of all his rash, tortuous, and vain activity is that he creates such an image of the murder that at last it overwhelms him. He plays his hands so that others play to him. In the event, there is nothing for anyone to believe about him except the extraordinary reality of the murder. He could not have made more certain of his arrest and imprisonment had that been his entire object. Only he delayed it, played with it, encouraged it to develop, in order to get the full savor of it and of himself.

First he rouses unconscious suspicions in Razumihin, then in Zossim—of the doctor in whom the suspicions may have been quite conscious, for he looked at Raskolnikov "curiously" whenever there was opportunity, and especially after that scene where Raskolnikov himself first realizes the murder in a parallel and arbitrary image which brims and trembles as you look at it. It is that image which comes when Raskolnikov lies abed listening to the doctor and Razumihin talk of the murder, and how a housepainter has been mixed up in it. Nastasya, who is present, bursts out that Lizaveta was murdered, too.

"Lizaveta," murmured Raskolnikov hardly audibly.

"Lizaveta, who sold old clothes. Didn't you know her? She used to come here. She mended a shirt for you, too."

Raskolnikov turned to the wall where in the dirty, yellow paper he picked out one clumsy, white flower with brown lines on it and began examining how many petals there were in it, how many scallops in the petals and how many lines on them. He felt his arms and legs as lifeless as though they had been cut off. He did not attempt to move, but stared obstinately at the flower.

It is so that the murder is brought home by the housemaid's first mention of the other and incidental murder of Lizaveta. We feel what passed in Raskolnikov's mind, and feel it as if it passed in his face, and in his hands, too: quite as if he had plucked the scalloped petals of the clumsy white flower off the wallpaper. Razumihin, who was simple, may have seen nothing, but the doctor, looking at this dissenting soul, surely saw what Raskolnikov saw in the flower even if he could not then have named it. The blankest or the most conventional image is, as Dostoevski knew, the best to hold the deepest symbol if only there is enough tension present when it is named. It is only another instance of this device that when Raskolnikov is about to go into the bar where he meets and gives himself away to Zametov, he first sees a good many drunken women, some of forty and some of seventeen, almost all of whom "had blackened eyes." Raskolnikov, who had gone out to end *this*, as he put it to himself, reflects upon this bevy with blackened eyes and pocked cheeks, that even the worst life is precious.

"Only to live, to live and live! Life, whatever it may be! . . . How true it is! Good God, how true! Man is a vile creature! . . . And vile is he who calls him vile for that," he added a moment later.

Whereupon he proceeds to risk his life, to make it precious, by playing like Hamlet on Rosencrantz and Guildenstern, upon the suspicious nerves of Zametov the police clerk as he drank tea in a restaurant. This scene, like the two great scenes with Porfiry, and like the last scene with Svidrigaïlov, shows Raskolnikov clinging with a kind of ultimate shuddering tenacity to his original proud role of the extraordinary man, the role of Napoleon within the little man, and clinging the more desperately because in the act of playing it he sees the role is false, the role of the condemned man whose life is thereby sweet.

What else happens at the same time, the history of the growth of the Punishment along with the realization of the Crime, is of course present in these scenes, but it has been instigated in other scenes—those with his mother and sister and Luzhin and Razumihin and the Marmeladovs; and it is perfected in other scenes still, those with Sonia especially, though these scenes might well be lifeless and pointless without their counterparts with Porfiry and Svidrigaïlov. There is a synergy—a working together and back and forth—between these counterparts much as there is a synergy between the two parts, the proud, self-willed part and the meek, submissive part of Raskolnikov's character. This working together takes place, and the resultant unity is seen, not because there is any logical or organic connection between the parts, but because, quite to the contrary, the conflicting elements are dramatized in association, in parallels that, as they say, never actually meet except as opposites. The more nearly they seem to be forced into meeting, the more disparate they actually show themselves to be. The fusion, if it can be called a fusion, is in the dramatic *product* of the conflicting elements, not of the elements themselves.

It is something along these lines, I think, that the theory of the "doubles" in Dostoevski must be approached, and this whether we think of single characters or of whole books and the doubleness of the conflicts within either. Let us look at Raskolnikov, who is usually thought of as a typical Dostoevski Double. He is self-willed and will-less, he is proud and he becomes humiliated, he loves Sonia and hates her at the same moment, he is fond of Razumihin and cannot tolerate him, he is both on the edge of confession and of anathema all along, he is good to the point of giving all that he has and evil to the point of taking life; and in short there is neither certainty nor limit to any of his moods or acts; any role is dominant for the moment to another role that may at once take its place because it has been really dominant underneath. But he is not these roles in turn, he is the product of all their playing taken together. In any pair, the one may be taken as the idea of the other, and the other the reality of the idea, and the only alternation is as to which, at a given moment, is idea and which reality. The relation is rather like that between the idea of murder and the image of the white flower on the wallpaper, where we can reverse it and say it is the relation between the idea of the flower and the image of the murder. What we get is a kind of steady state precariously maintained between the conflicting elements. The balance tips, but it recovers in the act of tipping. We should feel it as we feel similar physiological states in the body—only as the disturbance and forward drive of life—were it not that the language itself and Dostoevski's taste for seeing the opposite to every presented element have together a tendency to formularize pure types, and then to ignore for the moment what does not exemplify the type. What happens is, by language and its dialectic mode, that Dostoevski's imagination arrests, for the maximum possible amount of attention, the moments when the balance does tip from love to hate, from pride to humiliation, from idea to deed, from image to tension, and by the arrest, by the attention which is bent upon the moment of arrest, we see how the one in each case fecundates the other. We seem to see deeply what they make together by seeing wilfully what they are apart.

By a little progress of this notion, we can say that Raskolnikov is balanced in turn against the other characters in this novel, and that the other characters and their stories make something with Raskolnikov which is quite different from anything found in them as types, though there would be no product of their whole conflict if there was not a great deal that was living within each type, from Razumihin to Porfiry to Svidrigaïlov to Sonia, and all the rest. As illustration, let us take first the Marmeladov family, and consider by what astonishing luck it was that Dostoevski thought of putting them into the history of Raskolnikov and the punishment of his crime. They were to have been, the whole little crowd of them, a novel all to themselves called "The Drunkards," a novel showing, no doubt, all the ills and humiliations that can come from the head of a poor family who has given over to heavy drinking. The luck is that Dostoevski had them all going, with past and present and future, when Raskolnikov happened to meet old Marmeladov in the tavern and heard his humiliating confession with such apparently inexplicable sympathy. The truth is that he has something deeply in common with him, and again that Marmeladov has something which he has not yet but which he must have. What they have in common comes out when Marmeladov says that he has *nowhere to turn* except to his sick and somewhat crazy wife. Raskolnikov sees that it is not Marmeladov the good-natured drunk that turns, but Marmeladov humiliated, on hands and knees, with his hair pulled, Marmeladov in the mud which he Raskolnikov has not yet reached, but will reach in good time. Man grows used to everything, the scoundrel, says Raskolnikov, and adds: But what if he is not a scoundrel?

The scene is something like the great scenes in Dickens, caricature by direct observation, with the difference that Dostoevski—and this is perhaps the way Dostoevski himself read Dickens—replaces zest of observation for its own sake with the severity of attention that is based upon zeal, and replaces the anguish of social consciousness with the dignity of religion. Marmeladov, like Micawber, is able to represent much beyond himself because he is something of a buffoon; he can talk and act for talking and acting's sake; and he can be honest, and let himself go, just to see what will happen; he can see himself at his worst in order to be at his best. And so he does; he produces, to show himself at his utmost, and for the sake of Raskolnikov, for the sake of this new strange novel in which he unconsciously finds himself, the character and personality of Sonia, whom

Raskolnikov needs as complement and salvation, and whom the novel needs for mechanics and plot. And not Sonia only, he also produces, by just the agency of his being, scenes in which all manner of things which bear on the novel can take place. His death, his funeral, the lyric insanity of Katerina his wife and her death-dance in the streets, all these are provided with new and enriched context by the accidental meeting in the tavern of the *distrait* Raskolnikov and the drunken buffoon Marmeladov. And not only Marmeladov himself, but each of his family, as he precipitates their fates through his drunkenness and buffoonery, add to the context of Raskolnikov's growing fate.

Together they furnish him with his own opposite. As he is the person who above all must act, they are the persons who must be acted upon. He is the criminal, and they are the victims, victims generally and all the way through in much the same way that the old pawnbroker was in Raskolnikov's eyes "ripe" to be murdered. No degradation is too great for the old drunkard who has nowhere to turn; you have only to put fresh degradation in his way and he will take it up with gusto. Katerina, too, eager to find insult in everyone's speech, in his absence or in his presence, imagines insult and injury upon herself at every opportunity. The children, even, with their illness and their rags cannot be treated except with brutality. And as for Sonia, she is not only eager and willing, she fairly demands further humiliation. By prostituting herself, this thin, bird-like creature, almost without a body, shows herself as inviting at best further depravity: for surely no one not depraved, no one not desiring to sack the *last* citadel of integrity, would have any use for her. Sonia had to come from such a family, for only out of the experience of such utter humiliation could her own perfect humility grow. As they are damned so she is blessed, by the enormous shift in significance caused by the shift of a single syllable. It is Gide, who knew his Dostoevski well, who observed that where humility opened the gates of heaven, humiliation opened those of hell. Sonia's blessedness is built upon the bottomlessness of their hell. She accepts, and makes into inner strength, a worse stage of the experience which tore them apart.

Thus, as Raskolnikov comes into contact with Marmeladov

and his wife, as he probes them with his intellect, they absorb his sense of himself into a kind of private hell, an abyss beyond soundings, quite off the continental shelf of consciousness which his intellect, however demoniac, can reach. But Sonia, and this is the secret of her personality, can no more be penetrated by Raskolnikov's intellect than her soul can be ravished through the degradation of her body. That is her attraction as a prostitute: that she cannot be prostituted in anything that she has to offer; and that is her power over Raskolnikov, the power of perfect submissiveness which in another place Dostoevski calls the greatest power in the world: it is the power that he cannot attain by any deed, but that can be attained by imitation, by suffering what she has suffered. It is the power of her suffering, the happiness of it, that not so much overcomes him as it infects or fecundates him. For he is not overcome, though it is promised that he will be; he fights back, the very feeling of her goodness, his very sense of the stigma of her faith, aggravates his pride and the intellectual structure upon which his pride is built, so that when he goes to her for comfort and strength he finds that he has to torture her, and repel her at every level. The love he feels for her is also and simultaneously hate, and there is no difference between the emotions as he feels them, only as he intellectually knows what they are. And this is an example of the profound psychological rightness of Dostoevski's judgment, for surely it takes only a pause for judgment to see that as hate or pride is the burden Raskolnikov carries so love or humility is the *burden* of Sonia's life. If she feels his burden as love and accepts it as of nature, he must feel the burden of her love as intolerable. He is indeed a kind of Prodigal Son who finds the love with which he is welcomed the very burden from which he ran away in the first place. It was not of Sonia that he made the following remark but thinking of her and just before seeing her, so it fits all the more: "Oh, if only I were alone and no one loved me and I too had never loved anyone! *Nothing of all this would have happened.*"

It will be remembered that earlier in the book Razumihin has explained to Douania that her brother is perhaps a person incapable of love. Razumihin may have meant only that Raskolnikov is a lonely fellow, but he was literally right as well; no one can be said to love who does not feel as acceptable the burden of love in return, and who does not feel, too, that in loving someone positively, he is imposing the most difficult of human burdens. Sonia knows this in herself, by intuition directed inwards as well as outwards, as a condition of her being, and it is to that double burden that she submits.

Like the crime which existed *between* Raskolnikov and the old pawnbroker, so between Sonia and Raskolnikov there exists her intuition of love, which she feels so strongly that he *must* know, that gradually by a contagion from her understanding he does know it. It is a love, this unassailable love of the unsmirchable prostitute, that has nothing to do with sex. Not that it might not have been sexual, and even might have taken the means of a kind of ultimate lechery of the spirit, and still have been within the Christian insight, but that Dostoevski was unable ever to create a character or a mood which showed more than the most superficial aspects of sexual awareness. His people were not eunuchs or in any way deprived of sex but they were born without it. It is love *manqué* that Dostoevski deals with, love *malgré-lui*; and it is for this reason perhaps that Dostoevski is able to show love as pure spiritual renunciation. That is why, too, in what was to others the romantic fancy of purity in a prostitute, he sees a kind of exorbitant and omnivorous reality: a true dramatic enactment of the idea of purity. That is why, again, he so often concerns his characters with the idea of debauching young girls, girls before puberty, in whom sex as anyone else would have understood it would not have ripened, so that the debauchery would be of the actor alone.

If these remarks help explain the character and power of Sonia who is of the character of the saint, they help with the others as well, most particularly with the riddle of Svidrigaïlov, to whom we shall come in a moment for his own sake, but whom now we shall consider in his relation with the character of Douania, Raskolnikov's sister. This young lady is painted as all abloom with normality; she and her mother belong in Dostoevski's love gallery of simple, intelligent, sincere, generous, impulsive, and dependably decent women, young and old, of whom there are samples in almost every one of his novels—as, to give but one example, Mme. Epanchin and her daughter Aglaia in *The Idiot*. Always they serve the same purpose, to act as foils or background for the extraordinary actions of distorted or driven individuals, such as Raskolnikov and Myshkin. They preserve their identity and their normal responsiveness through every form of violence and disorder; it is their normality which, by contrast, promotes the meaningfulness of the good and bad angels, the light and the dark angels, whose actions make the stories. Nothing in themselves but attractive types, they come to life in terms of the protagonists.

In *Crime and Punishment* they represent the normal conduct from which Raskolnikov departs; they represent the order of society which he tears down and envelops; it is they, their lives, to whom he gives meaning. In the same way Luzhin, the bourgeois on the make, and Lebetziatnikov the nihilist reformer, are caricatures, the one malicious and the other kindly, of normal types of eccentricity within the ordered society which produces at its extremes the super-egotist Raskolnikov and the super-reformer Sonia. But these figures gather part of their meaning from the driven, demoniac, "secret" character of Svidrigaïlov, the lecher of women and debaucher of souls: the mysterious figure whose evil is concentrated in what is asserted to be, but never shown, his intense and overweening sexuality. As an example of sexual behavior, Svidrigaïlov is incredible. Sex is Dostoevski's symbol for a diabolic, destructive power, which he can sense but cannot measure, and which he cannot otherwise name. This aspect of the Svidrigaïlov type of figure is Dostoevski's attempt to explain, to dramatize and invoke, a force which he does not seem ever to have understood but which he knows must exist. It is a lonely, awkward, proud sort of power, hovering always on the brink of suicide; it is haunted and haunting; it is the power of the "Other" thing, the other self, the dark side of the self, the substance and drive of that secret world in us which the devil creates, the power which in conventional life—the life which we mostly live—we successfully ignore, so that we tend to estimate its presence in others rather than in ourselves—as if others were our othermost selves. Thus Douania's soul had been imperilled by Svidrigaïlov's attempt to seduce her, and imperilled precisely by Svidrigaïlov's technique, which he outlines to Raskolnikov, of assaulting her through purity. He has caused her purity, not her baser emotions but her purity, somehow to desire him, and she had been rescued, in the first instance, in the nick of time: by the confusion, in Marfa Petrovna's eyes, of her purity with her lust. Raskolnikov understands well enough what the risk is—that his sister may be contaminated, that her decency may somehow come to absorb the temptation which Svidrigaïlov affords her in the new terms of his generosity. What he does not understand is the means by which the contamination, the trespass, will take place, which is by the frustration of violence on Douania's part when in the lonely room with the locked door, she tries so hard to shoot him. She is left by the desperate effort—by the fruitless tumescence of her spirit—in a very ambiguous state, which the story of Raskolnikov's Crime and Punishment did not have time to develop. One is not sure whether in that scene Douania has absorbed something from Svidrigaïlov, or whether Svidrigaïlov has absorbed what he wanted from Douania. Something has passed between them, at any rate, which leaves Svidrigaïlov either done for or contented, either vastated or fully occupied. In either case his remaining hours are justified—his visit to his little girl fiancée and his farewell present, the adventure in the hotel-room, the mouse in the bed, the five-year-old girl whose smile turns in his dream to a harlot's grin, the dream of the flood, which is to say the coming of judgment, and the suicide at dawn. We feel that the enigma of Svidrigaïlov has either been solved beyond our understanding or that it did not really exist—quite the problem of the devil. At any rate, his function has been fulfilled for everyone but Raskolnikov.

His relations to Raskolnikov have gone beyond those with the others, both in scope and intent, however much they may depend for their actuality upon the others. For Svidrigaïlov is a foil for the whole story. He comes before the crime, in a way induces the crime to come into being, is the first to perceive the crime, and in a way *finishes* the crime without (since he does not have Raskolnikov's luck in finding Sonia) reaching the punishment. He *is* Raskolnikov in simpler perspective, he is Raskolnikov's other self, a mirror of being into which Raskolnikov never quite dares to look. He is the mystery of Raskolnikov's other self. The sense of him is symbolic, as it always is with mystery. Because he is a mystery beforehand, and exhibits himself mysteriously and providentially, he gathers meaning as he goes along, but not too clearly. He has the advantage of being not well understood, the figure grasped at but not caught, whom we are always about to understand. In fact we have frequently the sense of understanding him perfectly until we stop to query what it is we understand, when we find only that he represents precisely that secret life within us which drives us into incomprehensible actions. Like the character of Stavrogin in *The Possessed*, of whom Dostoevski says in his notes that he was not *meant* to be understood, but was meant rather to be a reservoir of the portentous, the possible, the mysterious, he is the symbolic clarification of that which cannot be expressed other than symbolically. He is the promise upon which we lean, knowing that it cannot be kept. He recedes like the horizon that follows us, only when we look.

Perhaps we may say that Svidrigaïlov envelops the disorder brought about by Raskolnikov's crime by imagining a kind of order which we cannot reach but which is always about to overwhelm us. He is a symbol of the mystery of the abyss, and it is a great witness to the depth of Dostoevski's imagination that he is able to create in the flesh, with eyes too blue and flesh too youthful, such figures at will.

It is no less a test of Dostoevski's skill—not his depth but his skill—that he is able to employ the one remaining major character in the book without, as it were, creating him at all. I mean, of course, that thirty-five year old roly-poly of the disengaged intellect called Porfiry, that man whose life, as he insists to Raskolnikov, is already finished, who has no other life to live, and nothing to do with what remains to him but probe and prance intellectually. Porfiry is so much a victim of moral fatigue that he is beneath every level of being but that of intellectual buffoonery. He represents order; he understands desire, ambition, all forms of conduct, but he knows nothing of the sources and ends of conduct, except that he can catch at them, in the midst of the game of the drowning man which he plays so long and so skilfully, like so many straws that only just elude his dancing fingers. But he is unreal, except as an agency of the plot, something to make the wheels go round; he is a fancy of the pursuing intellect whom Raskolnikov must have invented had he not turned up of his own accord. As Svidrigaïlov and Sonia between them represent the under-part, and the conflict in the under-part, of Raskolnikov's secret self, so Porfiry represents the maximum possible perfection of the artificial, intellectual self under whose ministrations Raskolnikov *reasons* himself into committing his crime, and who therefore is the appropriate instrument for driving him to the point of confessing it. It is Porfiry, who has no morals and no faith, who is all the proud game of intellect, who whenever he comes to sack Raskolnikov leaves him in a state of collapse, just as it is either Svidrigaïlov or Sonia who gives him strength. Porfiry knows what he must do, and can point it out to him in the example of the peasant who came forward to take the suffering of the crime upon his guiltless shoulders, he knows all the intellect can know, and perhaps knows that it must collapse, but he cannot push Raskolnikov over the brink, because he knows it only conventionally, by rote. He understands the Crime, because he represents that against which it was committed, and knows with what it was committed, but he cannot touch the Punishment, the completion of the Crime, because it must take place in a region of the soul beyond his grasp, the region which reason, argument, all the armament of order only clutter up and from which they must be swept, the region where the assumption of guilt by all that is innocent within the self takes place through the submission of the sinful, acting self to the faithful, waiting self, which waits, in Dostoevski's primitive Christian insight, only to be created.

I think we have touched both upon the elements that go to make up the obvious and immediate impact of Raskolnikov's crime and its consequences in action, and upon the elements which as we understand them as exhibited in the various characters leave us all—not Russians, not fanatics of humiliation, not the distorted shadowy figures of Dostoevski's novel alone, but all of us without exception deeply implicated in the nature of the Crime. A word remains with which to fasten upon the nature of the Crime an indication of the nature of the Punishment. I do not know that there is a word ready to hand, for we have fallen quite out of the way of thinking in insights and images with the simple, direct intensity which was Dostoevski's second nature. We lack the anterior conviction, the conviction before we begin to think, with which Dostoevski mastered the relationship of man to God. But at least in saying that, we state Dostoevski's major and abiding theme. To punish Raskolnikov, to bring him to retribution, to atonement, Dostoevski had only to create his relationship to God, and to show at the same time how that relationship sprang from the nature of man as a creature of God quite apart from the structure of human society as an institution of men's minds. Dostoevski believed that as Christ the innocent one took upon himself the suffering of all the innocent ones in the world, and so redeemed them along with the guilty, so the individual man has in him an innocent part which must take on the suffering caused by the guilty part. As he saw it, in our crime we create our guilt. Perhaps the commonplace example of false arrest will begin to make an analogue for what he meant. Which of us, falsely arrested, would not at once begin to assess his guilt, even for the crime which brought about the false arrest? And you would assess this guilt the more clearly because you were aware of the haphazard, the hazarded, character of your innocence. Similarly, the depth of your guilt would be measured by the depth of your faith, which would then, if you had imagination enough, transform you.

It should be emphasized that it was transformation, not reformation, that Dostoevski envisaged. Reformation would have dealt with the mere guilty act against society. Transformation, through suffering, is alone able to purge the guilt of being.

Finally, we may draw some comparisons, in this search for means of clarifying the nature of Dostoevski's notion of punishment, from recent history in our own country. When Mooney was released from his generation of false imprisonment, it soon turned out that he had no symbolic dignity, but represented rather a mere miscarriage of institutional justice; and so with the Scottsboro boys; so, too, with Dreyfus in the last century, for Dreyfus had no dignity. But if we think of Sacco and Vanzetti, does there not arise within us at once a sense that their great and terrifying symbolic dignity is due to Vanzetti having assumed, with profound humility, the whole devastating guilt of the industrial society which killed him? Whether Vanzetti was innocent or guilty in law has become an irrelevant question. But the guilt which his last words and letters, his last conduct, somehow expiated, which was our guilt, remains permanently in question; for Vanzetti, like Raskolnikov, showed himself in the humiliation of his punishment, in humble relation to God.

Parody and Critique:

Mann's Doctor Faustus

[1 9 5 0]

In this country, at this time, our way of looking at our culture makes it difficult for us to look at a work of literary art which announces itself in its title, in the motto on its title page, and in the attributes of its hero as in intention a great work dealing with a very great man. We do not take to great men unless they be criminal or popular or fashionable or dead in some other way; we resent claims to maximum attention and maximum response—we like our great men to do our work for us, and we like to take up their greatness on the side, without noticing it, and without pain. The attitude is prudent, avoids risks and avoids snobbery but it leaves us at a loss before Thomas Mann's *Doctor Faustus*, the Life of the German Composer Adrian Leverkühn as told by a friend—and the sense of being at a loss is all the more acute when we see that the rest of the title page is covered by nine lines of Dante's Italian taken from the opening of the second Canto of the Inferno where Dante pauses to take his first breath in the unutterable human hell in which he found himself. Because I have now read this work three times, and have been moved variously and incongruously each time, it seems not only necessary but a good thing to risk both mistaken judgment and possibly snobbery—it seems good and necessary to take this work in its asserted role and attempt to frame the maximum response which maximum attention can initially yield to this image of greatness in our time. I have no fear I am alone in this attempt; I know of others, though they do not crowd; but first of all I have as friend and companion him who tells and meditates upon the life of this modern Faust, I mean of course the Catholic humanist, Serenus Zeitblom, that serene flower of the hellish time, and it is because of him, and so much of faith as we share—we are both humanist though not both Catholic—that I understand how to begin.

I begin with the humanist's natural questions. I ask, in order to remind myself, what the name Dr. Faustus on a modern work might mean; and I ask what Dante's Italian is doing there under the title. What have a devil myth and an invocation of the Greek Muses got to do with contemporary bourgeois humanism? (We are still bourgeois, for the time being, if we are humanists at all.) Why should a work purportedly written by a humanist go so far back for its title and its motto—so far back that in each case it touches upon forces recognized, if at all, as prior to the human? Is it the predicament of the humanist that in order to combat the inhumanities of his own day he must get succor in remote forces that must seem at least as menacing as they are propitious? Or is it rather that he feels he must refresh in himself the stream of daemonic inspiration, of hidden and inexplicable strength, in order to combat not his enemies but his own weaknesses? I think both. But let us examine into title and motto for their own sakes.

What or who is Faustus? A medieval legend, an Elizabethan incantation, a German epic, a French opera, an attribute of the arrogance of the modern or experimental man; but in all cases combining the two traditions that inhabit us from our past and trouble us as to our future, the two traditions of light and darkness. There is on the one side the tradition of reason and revelation and inspiration, and on the other side the tradition of the daemonic, the chthonic, and the magical. Somehow in the image of Faustus the two traditions are combined; the things of darkness work into the broad day; and the combining agent is the devil, who offers us the pride of mastery of both traditions. All images of Faustus have to do with the mastery of absolute knowledge followed by the loss of it altogether. The devil tempts us by offering us knowledge of the truth about ourselves which, without the power of his temptation, we

should not have the strength to bear; the knowledge refused to Adam
in Paradise. How should we put it? It is a temptation to the absolute
possession both in knowledge and of the substance of knowledge, so
that we might know both our inspiration and what keeps us going:
the knowledge both of what we love and of what we shun to think
we are. The glorious and the sensual—neither of them "reasonable"—are in this image reconciled with the humiliating and the
ascetic—which are not reasonable either. Faustus woos the Muses
with the aid of the devil, the divine with the daemonic. Goethe was
correcting nothing in the old legend when in the Second Part of his
epic the marriage of Faustus and Helen serves for the reconciliation
of the Greek and Christian worlds; he only developed the human
necessity that was there to be declared, and to be created if it was
not there. And it is on such an insight that Thomas Mann brings
out his Faustian image; but because of his particular moment in
time—our moment when so much has been taken away—he cannot proceed where Goethe left off; he has to begin behind Goethe
in Dante, and he has to try to go further back still, not only into the
old legend, but also into its roots in that country of the mind which
is neither Christian nor Greek, to the country, in Mann's own phrase,
of the naked human voice.

To do all this you have to be a little solemn and dedicated, but
you have also to be passionate and exact. You have to believe and
you have to wrestle with your belief in the flesh of the actual world
around you. You have to be a humanist, not of the renaissance but
of the bourgeois world—the bourgeois in that rebellion against both
reason and flesh which constitutes his vitality; you have to be the
bourgeois humanist seeking to rediscover, now that his order is failing, what all that turbulence was which he had put in order. You
have to see, like James Joyce in *Ulysses*, the darkness that is in the
light as well as the darkness that is all about us. You must look into
two kinds of chaos, the mere disorder and the original black. Othello, you will remember, saw both kinds at once when looking after
Desdemona in anguish of self-impalement he cried out:

> Excellent wretch! Perdition catch my soul,
> But I do love thee! and when I love thee not,
> Chaos is come again.

In short you have to deal with the devil in order to reach the dae-monic, and as a humanist you will remember that, without the human, the daemonic is the diabolic. The daemon is the indwell-ing power, or spirit, or genius in things, whether for good or evil; the daemon represents the basic conditions of human life; the devil is their corruption, the temptation of finding means of not accepting those conditions. Thus the devil in our psychology is a way-station to the daemon, providing by rebellion and denial and parody, the incentive of remorse to go further. Look in the dictionary: Diabo-lose is the slanderer, the calumniator, in Greek; in Hebrew, the tempter and spiritual enemy of mankind—offering other than human conditions. One form of Christian tragedy is in the confusion of the two, the merging of that which slanders with that which tempts; Greek and Satanic pride here touch; and it is that confusion, that equivocalness, which inhabits the Dr. Faustus of Thomas Mann. So it is that in the first chapter of that work, we find Serenus Zeit-blom, the Catholic humanist and son of the Muses, meditating the life of his friend the great musician Adrian Leverkühn, and finding that that life forces him, by its God-inflicted genius struggling with the corrupt Faustian bargain, into the further meditation of the dae-monic: in his friend's life and, above all, in his friend's music, both of which he loved with tenderness and terror. There is the whole theme of the work announced at once in terms of its title.

Now let us look at the motto or epigraph from Dante which appears under the title. The motto is an appeal to the Muses, to high Genius, to Memory, and the appeal is that of Dante, that rebel of reason and liberty against the hardening of order into violence; an appeal made between the middle age and the renaissance, between the beating of light and the spread over Europe of the odor of death. The passage is worth looking at, in itself and for Dante, and also because it is quoted to set going a Faustian work by this last product of the northern renaissance and baroque reformation; a human type so much more *aware* of the under-barbarism than the Mediterra-nean world has ever been. It is we northerners, always, who under-stand the *ground of appeal* to the resources of the Latin and Catholic spirit; we need them more. I do not say this was so for Dante's time; certainly not for Augustine's; but it is so for us. We know what is corrupted, what corrupts, and how the relation may become tolerable: we know what we must acknowledge although we do not wish to acknowledge it: the terms of an everlasting and vital predicament; and it is characteristic of our age that the acknowledgment should be attempted in works of art. And so, in the similar age of the fourteenth century, it was with Dante.

> Lo giorno se n'andava, e l'aere bruno
> togliea gli animai che sono in terra
> dalle fatiche loro; ed io sol uno
>
> m'apparecchiava a sostener la guerra
> sì del cammino e sì della pietate,
> che ritrarrà la mente che non erra.
>
> O Muse, o alto ingegno, or m'aiutate!
> O mente che scrivesti ciò ch'io vidi,
> qui si parrà la tua nobilitate.

(The day was going off, and the brown air taking the animals that are on earth from their toil; and I, one alone, was working myself up to bear the war both of the journey, and of the pity, which memory that errs not shall relate [retrace]. O Muses, O high Genius, now help us! O memory, that has inscribed what I saw, here will be shown thy nobleness.)

Half the Graeco-Christian world is here, and very nearly all that remains of it: what is human and invocably human. The twilight is there, and the task: the journey from birth to death, and also the pity of the journey seen in itself; and so the war between the pity and the journey and the war in each. Then Memory, whose daughters are the Muses, is invoked as the image of the truth—the truth of the tradition and the truth of the actual experience; memory as the high or presiding genius of man—not man himself but his nobleness, the light that shines in him. What then does it shine on? What are the grounds on which it is appealed to?

This work of Thomas Mann, this discourse of an old humanist, this serene late bloom of spirit working through the discourse, is meant to stand for the possibility of an answer. The tireless spirit remains even after the most exhausted animals are gone. This is the spirit that was always there even in the worst moment of the war of the journey and the pity when the scum of the earth in each of us— Thomas Mann's phrase for the Nazi regime—put in power the dictatorship of the scum of the earth all the more scum for the memory it soiled, the tradition it debauched.

But what was the war; what extreme form of what perennial war? It is interesting that Dante did not have to ask that question. His memory knew that answer, and knowledge of it was implicit in his genius; but for us it must be made explicit, and it troubles us almost more than the question that we are driven to ask it. It is as if, by a change in the *phase* of consciousness (which we call self-consciousness or sometimes heightened consciousness) we had acquired a new possibility, however threatened, of choice: as if we had found some new way of tragic aspiration, some new perspective of intolerable failure, to compel us to new efforts of assent and dissent. The new occasion here—the extreme form of the perennial war—is the occasion when those so nearly without mind that their memories lie, take charge, like the Nazis in Germany, of those who still live and still woo—not the folk and the mob—but the Muses.

This is not a change—only a reversal of phase. We find in control what had been the object of control. We heighten the old techniques of imagination weighted by memory with the *élan* of our fresh freedom from purpose. The forces which we tried to understand overwhelm our understanding. Yet those forces, where they still move in the human animal, still crave to be understood—still crave to acquire the nobility of memory. The long human howl, the cry of infants, the naked human voice, will be music yet: though the whole world howl before it happen, and if in the process it seem to come to destruction.

So the humanist faced with the Faustian image must believe, and that is what the passage from Dante gave Serenus Zeitblom the strength to believe while he passed through the war of the journey— the Germany of the last sixty years—and the war of the pity—the life of his friend the great German musician, Adrian Leverkühn. So, as in the first chapter we found the whole theme of the work announced in terms of Faustus, in the second chapter we find that theme repeated and strengthened, counterpointed, with another strain. Here the Faustian image is put to music, and in that music we hear the classical tongues of human reason and dignity over against that other language of tones, a language not humanistic, not reliable: both living by contradiction in human nature; the one nobility of mind, the other peril of spirit, here joined in new service to the deities of the depths. It is as if the humanist insisted that it is the function of his culture, by piety to his memory, to regulate and propitiate the entrance of the dark and uncanny into the service of the gods.

It is in the service of the gods, then, that this life of a great musician is written under the double image of a new Faustus and old Memory; and it is the role of artist—that characteristic hero of the high literature of the last seventy years—and the music he creates which press together to combine the image. So much for the statement of the theme; interpretation may come later; meanwhile we remind ourselves of the material through which it is worked and of the techniques or forms to which it takes for expression.

The material is of several kinds. There is the immediate biography of the young genius capable equally, at twenty-one, of experience, of music, and of theology. He withdraws from experience and theology and dedicates himself to the composition of music which is a further reach of both: his withdrawal is perfected after a single sexual contact which leaves a secret syphilis to combine with a hereditary migraine, and after, also, a single hallucinated interview with the devil. He is by nature one not to be touched, to be adored not loved; and he becomes by consequence of his disease and his compact with the devil free, or almost free, of the obligations that go with human contact and love, and is bound only, and almost wholly, by the special obligation to mocking laughter—which is response pure, response without sharing. That is, he can sink unimpeded into what underlies all experience—what is in the self *no matter what* is taken away: the revelation of the equivocal without any control or standard except for those of the process of revelation. Thus, having no connection with experience, except through daemonism and disease, he can afford that ruthless irresponsibility of the artist which is in the end responsibility plain, full response *away from* the truth, *under* the truth, *without* truth. In other words, he is asserted to have in fact that absolute mastery of experience which every adolescent requires himself to see as the immediate, or at least the next possibility of his own genius: surely the oldest imagined role, older than Faustus, older than Memory. In his life itself he succeeds in his withdrawal, his dedication, and secret power till near the end, when life strikes him two blows. The first blow is the murder of his one personal friend which he brings on by expressing a desire for marriage. The second is the death of his darling and beautiful nephew Nepomuk or Echo—the echo in infant form of the life he never lived. From the second he never recovered except for the moment of his last composition. Finishing that—the lamentation of Dr. Faustus—he collapses into idiocy, his work done, and the life he never lived still to be begun, if at all, by those who are to come after him.

Against the biography of Leverkühn there are three critiques: the critique of the social history of the German haut-bourgeois from 1885 to 1940, the critique of German national history in the War from 1939 to 1945, and the critique of Adrian Leverkühn's principal compositions, all told in the increasingly desperate humanistic tones of Serenus Zeitblom. Altogether, the three make a single critique of Europe as the forced sell-out. Let us say that the critique of the Nazi war is of the ambience: it is the horror in our nostrils, and it is there in the book; and saying that let us have done, for it is only the holocaust of what had been long on fire. But let us think of the critique of society over against the figures of the composer and the scholar, each further ahead of his society and deeper in it than anyone, as the artist and humanist ought to be—and each misunderstood or ignored by the society he expressed. The artist expresses what the humanist must understand: man's disobedience to his own nature. Only here in this time, 1885–1940, instead of a tension, a precarious balance, between expression and understanding, which hold society together, we find society tearing itself apart. We get expressionism and authority, not balanced or related, but identified, confused, a matter of random because of indistinguishable resort.

This we see wonderfully in the careers of the lesser characters, particularly in those of Clarissa and Inez Rodde, ending for the one in blackmail and suicide, for the other in drugs and murder, the one caused by shame and failure of talent, the other by distrust of suffering and cultivated infatuation. We see it in the aesthete who bought bad pictures and loved the beauty of bloodshed, and in the poet who wrote no poetry but invoked violence. It is in Schild-knapp, the cadging translator and anglophile, who never got his own work done; in Rudi Schwerdtfeger, the fiddler, the victim of his own coquetry. Above all it is in the discussion club of the 'twen-ties where because all the horror of the 'thirties was seen as *possible* it was adopted and wooed as a *necessity*; but it is no less in the writhing reptilian eloquence of the impresario from Paris. What we see is the moral suicide—not simple viciousness or ordinary deprav-ity—but such confusion of order with disorder—such failure of memory—as is tantamount to the moral suicide of bourgeois soci-ety. No wonder the chattering terror became the only mode, first of expression, then of action. And for final commentary there is the hideous and gratuitous death of little Echo. It is always the gratui-tous that reminds us of the essential.

There remains the third critique which is of Adrian Lever-kühn's music: *Love's Labours Lost*—a mocking opera bouffe of Renaissance Humanism; the *Gesta Romanorum*, a parody of the daemonic element in medieval Christianity; the Oratorio of the *Apocalypse*, where the howling glissando of the human voice, mov-ing from the bestial to the sublime in mocking imitation parodies the musical styles of hell, reaching finally the "inaccessibly unearthly and alien beauty of sound, filling the heart with longing without hope"; and lastly the lamentations of Dr. Faustus, written after the death of Echo, which we now see was a parody of the life of Lev-erkühn and his society. Of this last piece, here is the humanist's description:

We children of the dungeon dreamed of a hymn of exultation, a *Fidelio*, a Ninth Symphony, to celebrate the dawn of a freed Germany—freed by herself. Now only this can avail us, only this will be sung from our very souls: the *Lamentation* of the son of hell, the lament of men and God, issuing from the subjective, but always broadening out and as it were laying hold on the Cosmos; the most frightful lament ever set up on earth.

[341

So the humanist, Serenus Zeitblom; and saying that, he forces himself a little beyond his humanism: out upon the base on which humanism is built, and which it denies and shuns, avoids and rediscovers at moments of outward catastrophe or inward "breakthrough." It is always the task of humanism to break through itself *again* to reality, whether by reason or image. That is what that early humanist, Marco Lombardo, whom Dante found untying the knot of his anger in Canto XVI of the Purgatorio—that is what Marco meant when he said Man has a mind of his own.

> A maggior forza ed a miglior natura
> liberi soggiacete, e quella cria
> la mente in voi, che il ciel non ha in sua cura.

> Però, se il mondo presente disvia,
> in voi è la cagione, in voi si cheggia. . . .

("Ye lie subject, in your freedom, to a greater power and to a better nature; and that creates in you mind which the heavens [i.e. the influence of the stars, mechanical law] have not in their charge. Therefore, if the world today goeth astray, in you is the cause, in you be it sought."—Temple Classics edition.) *The Divine Comedy* is among other things a great exemplary breakthrough by reason and image to the base of the human. Adrian Leverkühn's *Lamentation of Dr. Faustus* is an image, an idol, an invocation for such a breakthrough; a supplication which, if we could only hear it, might enact itself in our contemplation. It is the human voice at the crisis of phase: at the moment of reversal or renewal: and it is in this light that the remaining comments of Serenus Zeitblom ought to be read. He is asking us to hear. To hear all modern music as lament and *lasciatemi morire*. To hear *this* putative music as Echo, "The giving back of the human voice as nature-sound, and the revelation of it *as* nature-sound . . . essentially a lament: Nature's melancholy 'Alas!' in view of man, her effort to utter his solitary state." He asks us also to hear this music as complete, as saying "nothing and everything," as creating a universal identity of the blest and the accursed, in which the freedom is so wholly expressed that it is wholly subject to the form—*a maggior forza ed a miglior natura*. The intention is again Dantesque; for it is Dante who is the most deliberate and the most complete of all poets; it is in his work that everything is taken care of, and something else besides; and so we are meant to hear the evoked music of Adrian Leverkühn—both as to the deliberateness and as to what is deliberated: the liberation of maximum expressiveness in the condition of maximum control. The *Lament* is written in twelve tones (the chromatic scale of Arnold Schoenberg) on the twelve syllables of the words "For I die as a good and as a bad Christian"—good by repentance, bad in that the devil will have his body. "It is the basis of all the music—or rather, it lies almost as key behind everything and is responsible for the identity of the most varied forms—that identity which exists between the crystalline angelic choir and the hellish yelling in the *Apocalypse* and which has now become all embracing: a formal treatment strict to the last degree, which no longer knows anything unthematic, in which the order of the basic material becomes total, and within which the idea of a fugue rather declines into an absurdity, just because there is no longer any free note." What this form controls in absolute liberation is the last change of mind—"a proud and bitter change of heart!"—in the "speaking unspokenness" of music, whereby final despair achieves a voice, and the consolation of the voice, the voice for the creature in its woe, and whereby "out of the sheerly irremediable hope might germinate . . . a hope beyond hopelessness, the transcendence of despair." . . . The end is the high G of a cello. "Then nothing more: silence, and night. But that tone which vibrates in the silence, which is no longer there, to which only the spirit hearkens, and which was the voice of mourning, is so no more. It changes its meaning: it abides as a light in the night."

That is how Serenus Zeitblom would have us hear "the most frightful lament ever set up on earth," and a little later, when before the final wail of his own voice, Leverkühn mangles and eviscerates himself in words ("one's fellow men are not meant or made to face such truth") Zeitblom makes the following observation: "Never had I felt more strongly the advantage that music, which says nothing and everything, has over the unequivocal word: yes, the saving irresponsibility of all art, compared with the bareness and baldness of

[343

unmediated revelation." And in this observation is clarified the mystery why it is music, in the absence of religion, that makes the break-through into reality tolerable as truth and viable as image. Dante would not have needed it, or would have used it—indeed he did so use it—as a compensatory weight; but this other age has need of it: "the saving irresponsibility of all art," clearest and most nearly credible in music.

It is this evoked, this putative music, its working presence to the good will of our belief, that transforms the critique and the anecdotes and the biography into something we can call a novel; of two composers whom I know, one insists he wrote Leverkühn's music and the other hears it completely; as for myself, with less skill, I hear it incompletely; but I know how everything works into what I hear and do not hear. But if the novel is governed by the music, we must emphatically remember that all the music, except the last piece, is parody and that the medium of the parody is that echo of nature the naked human voice, and that it stands in analogy and parallel everywhere to a series of critiques of individuals in their history. The notions in these words, parody, critique, and the naked human voice, taken under the image of Faustus and Dante, represent the means by which the work was composed, and also both qualify and limit the meaning—the music—which goes on when the book has stopped.

Of these three notions, the naked human voice should be familiar: its presence, real or invoked, has always worked as a great force; it is the substance of poetry so far as we can read it and of music so far as we can play it; and it is the one daemonic force in which we all have some skill at heightening ourselves, by which, in ourselves, we call on something beyond ourselves. Parody and critique as serious means to artistic purpose, especially in the novel, are relatively new, and are without rules of thumb; and what makes them interesting here is the sense that Mann was driven to employ them by a combination of the limitations of his talent and the cultural conditions of our times. Parody is the form of this novel and critique one of its developments. Let us see.

If parody is the right name for the form of this novel it cannot be unique and is not likely without a common cause; which may well be some inability to create individuals along with an unwilling-ness to resort to type in the use of the age before our own. Gide, Kafka, Joyce, Eliot, Mann—even Yeats and Proust—have none of them had the gift of creating individuals or composing in sustained narrative. Each has lacked power of objective creation; each has depended in high particular upon his own biography. Individual character reached its height with Shakespeare and Rembrandt and Tolstoi, and, if you like, Beethoven. It may be that harmony is needed to create character, vital and cultural harmony, and that in a polyphonic age only parody of character and the individual is possible to express. Private life disappears either into public life or into itself and is in either case, when expressed, only a parody of itself. But if I am right I do not see that parody is any less expressive than the epic. And I suggest that "myth" in the lauding sense we use it of Joyce and Kafka can only be a parody, so self-conscious it is, of what we mean by myth in Greek drama.

A few claimers and disclaimers as to the meanings and uses of the word are in order. Parody is something sung beside the main subject. Parody is not caricature, not satire: it is a means of treating reality so as to come short of it either on purpose or through neces-sity. Parody emphasizes mechanics, especially prescriptive mechan-ics in executive technique, and greedily fastens on the merest possibilities in the material. In our day, every man is a parody of his moral self. Parody is our ordinary means of judging men and events. Music alone parodies the rest of humane culture: which is why it frightens us and how we put up with it: we know what is parodied. Because it involves, points at, and limits, what it parodies, parody is a good name for a means of getting at material that—in our state of belief—does not submit to existing system. Parody is arduous, rigorous, and establishes relations in its own way. It makes possible the free use of dualisms—the oldest technique of Yin and Yang, Up and Down—for parody is free of single beliefs and is bent on the object.

In Mann's chapter of the corrupt bargain with the devil we have precisely an example of parody freely resorting to dualism, for here Mann parodies both his own book and the humanity the book was meant to re-discover. But I do not know that Mann parodies himself. For him parody is a way out, and he can be objective about it—as Leverkühn in his opera bouffe of *Love's Labours Lost*. He can submit all his desperate material to the arrogant, debasing parody of itself. That is the advantage of the bourgeois turned artist. It is the rebellion of the bourgeois against himself in a created self. Only the bourgeois understands Bohemia (his slipping) or needs the devil (his climbing); or at any rate, the bourgeois is in the gulf between his slipping and his pride—which is why he adapts to himself the notions of birth and breeding: that he may somehow reach irresponsibility and dishonor. He is like Pascal in this, who saw that birth and breeding save a man twenty years. And it is the devil who lets the bourgeois parody himself; the devil is always what happens to the ideal: the dishonor and irresponsibility of practice carried to an extreme.

What is the temptation to the young bourgeois composer, Leverkühn?—That the presumption of total and absolute guilt—of the sin so great mercy is impossible on it—gives absolute knowledge and with it the nearest approach to absolute redemption. It is the lust in the brain, not the lust in the flesh, that is tempted. As if, thus renouncing love, the human touch, the fraternal, and thus assuming the great human cold (that is, by deliberately parodying our inadequacies), we could somehow come on the elemental and the actual, and, however intolerable themselves, communicate through them a joyous life to those who come after: an ambition, surely, of love and touch and brotherhood. It is the temptation "within"; it has nothing of the temporal power about it. It is the right temptation for the time held to be sterile in its technics and techniques: in a time of asserted omniscience and the mechanization of crafts. Adrian Leverkühn strove for that illumination by which he could restore assent to the conditions of human life by himself, in his genius, first escaping or denying them; and to do this required a compact with the devil: at any rate a confusion between the daemonic and the diabolic. He parodied his humanity in order to find it: at once an affair of pride and force and a protean cheapening of himself: the lout, the merchant, the familiar—above all the lout—in which forms the devil made his apparitions. The parody points, terribly, at the reality, as the devil points at God; and it is one of the possibilities of the humanist in our time so to point.

It seems to be not a possibility but a necessity for the humanist to resort also to critique, to carry his critique along with him and make it a part even of his most imaginative works. Partly he does this to make present what he cannot create, partly to explain what his audience will not understand in what he has created, and partly in the effort to make up for the lack of a common background—the lack of the Great Memory which mothered the Muses—in even a small and select audience. As Shakespeare had to bed down his play about *Troilus and Cressida* with images of lechery and insurrection, a novelist like Thomas Mann has also to bed down his work with a critique of present history and character and surviving memory. If we can think of *Troilus and Cressida* as the train of its images, we can think of *Doctor Faustus* as the train of its critique; both trains are employed for the same purpose: to unite disparate elements, to order inchoate elements, and to mark the vitality of what is united and what is ordered. The image and the critique are what the works are about; and in the case of Mann this is what separates him from Fielding's Lucretian inter-chapters in *Tom Jones* and the essays on the theory of history in Tolstoi's *War and Peace*, where the critique was on a parallel intellection of the subject: In Mann's *Doctor Faustus*, as in *The Magic Mountain*, they are central to the subject and reveal it.

Thus, in *Doctor Faustus*, when we come to Leverkühn's next to last piece *The Apocalypse*, we feel the excitement of a real thing in the critique by Zeitblom which alone presents it to us. We feel all three of our themes: the artist, the humanist, the naked human voice—together with their rigid correspondences in the world of history and the world of critique—all these themes have merged, or at any rate they give voice to one another in one organized place in time. We see, or hear, in the *Apocalypse*, that the music is about all these, and so makes the one "critique" that unites the intellect in the feeling, transforms the feeling in the intellect, and makes of the whole, as Croce would say, an instance of theoretic form. Art has itself become critique.

[347

So it has with Gide: in the various journals for *The Counter-feiters*; with Joyce: in the polylingual multi-myth of *Finnegans Wake*; with Proust: in the "Place Names" and the "social history"; and, perhaps, with Kafka: in the creation and distension of a pseudo-mythical world to explain "K." It is merely because Mann is so much more explicit than these others, and wishes to make his critique stand for so much more of ordinary life in present history than they do, that he stands out as a novelist of critique, and has made more to do with it than they have. But he is not alone; and what he has done with critique, like what he has done with parody, is a reflection of the cultural conditions of the times. Granted that he intended great work, the resort to critique in the novel of the individual as humanist beyond himself was inevitable. For one thing, the horizon of the humanist had stretched enormously with the divisiveness of modern knowledges and their incongruous techniques; for another thing, even the best humanist finds his own Great Memory failing, let alone that of his audience: he must tell himself as well as his reader what he has in mind; and, for a third thing, the impulse to set the individual in his milieu, his history, and what Erich Auerbach calls his "moving background," has run out, along with its dividends, and there has been a renewal of the older impulse to create the individual in terms of his type, that is to say, in terms of the critique of the individual and his "moving background." But since the humanist here is imaginative, the critique itself must become art: which with Mann is the art of music.

There are many ways of saying it. We can think of the novel as the characteristic art of the modern individual and his world; and it may be that the world in which that individual is lodged has so changed that the art of the individual can no longer redeem the sense of the individual, nor the intellect that of the intellect. Critique would then be the last gasp: *Doctor Faustus* would then be the bonfire of the daemonic. Our great hope lies in our consciousness of terrible loss in our inability to portray the individual. Knowing the loss proves the individual still exists, we still hear his music and in the music his voice. In our sense of loss is our right to that music and our new sense that the music is somehow a critique of the reality. Critique is the mind turning to parody because it must; and music is the imperative of the turning.

Parody, then, is what art must do when it has become critique, when in it the individual becomes biography and anecdote; parody comes about because art can no longer be pious to either the journey or the pity in the old forms, and has not yet found the means to settle on new forms. Parody is a form for transition, and in the interim of transition can well lean on music for its models. If music is equivocal and is also the organization of sound, then it is the art both most apt to parody and the furthest from it. It parodies what it is and it reaches what it is through parody; as the later quartets of Bartók show more clearly than any music of Schoenberg. It reaches the naked human voice and—in that—the absolute irresponsibility of art.

Above all it is parody that rescues us from the curse—we cannot be rescued from the burden—of critique and the false escape of anecdote. It is parody that makes it possible, in such an age as ours, to seek what we must shun; makes it possible to see the elements of the substance of our ordeal not in logical or statistical but in organic opposition; and so, after the break-through, make something out of them. Parody brings us to the voice and the irresponsibility.

Let us return with all these provisional and, in all the old senses, disheartening terms to Thomas Mann's book itself. This great man and German and composer, Adrian Leverkühn, is above all a parody of the human. Standing between the dictatorship of the scum of the human race and the folk who threw up the scum; or, not standing, let us say bestriding them, Adrian Leverkühn is that parody of all the bourgeois humanist held dear which shall restore him: he is what is in the names of his principal works—*Love's Labours Lost, Gesta Romanorum, Apocalypse, Doctor Faustus.* He is that terrible parody of the bourgeois, the "break-through" by which he may yet be re-created, only in another image. Only the idol is dead. Parody is a means, no matter how hard to take still a means to touch the understanding, which might, for practical purposes, reach further than the everlasting mercy—at least when, like Leverkühn, we must pass through the daemonic to reach again the human.

[349

If that is true—if in any sense we must pass through the daemonic to reach the human—we can take that truth as the clue to *Doctor Faustus* at its most serious level: which is the level where we identify Faust and Leverkühn. Adrian Faust Leverkühn is the daemonic scapegoat for humanity. He comes to his destruction, is absorbed by the devil, precisely at the moment when he has understood the sins of mankind by re-enacting them in that mood of the mind which is both most human, in that it stirs, or touches, the deepest human places, and, also, is most removed from the human in that it touches directly upon none of the ordinary concerns of men. Faust has sold his humanity in order to come upon understanding of the force which keeps humanity alive and perennially on the edge, in the maw, of suicide. And this Faust, this Leverkühn, achieves his understanding by creating its image in the most equivocal language available to man, which is the image of music: the naked human voice. But there is no redemption here, no Christ, no Cross, only destruction. Our Christian religion has at its heart the image of a perfectly good man who takes up the evil that breaks life into his goodness, taking it to salvation in a mystery. The image of Faust as Leverkühn is not a mockery of Christ but a reversal: it works back into the conditions from which Christ is the redemption. It reminds us in its own way, and in another language, what the European Christ is for. The devil is always the other thing than God, like God; the devil is God gone to the devil; the man possessed of the devil is the man stripped of everything human except the elementally human: those very elements out of which, after each catastrophic slump to gulf-bottom, the human can be re-born, re-made, re-created.

That is why Adrian Leverkühn is cold—the coldness of the human; why he is mathematical—the sequence of the heart-beat; why he is aloof—the loneliness of the human; and it is why he is proud—because of the great human pride, the temptation to re-create himself in his own fastness. He is cold, mathematic, aloof and proud; but he is neither a good man nor a bad man. He is neither above nor below good and evil; he is both good and evil in the culture of 1900 to 1950, and being both he is apart from either. He is the image—the idol or eidolon—to which good and evil happen, and he is required to be enough deprived of ordinary humanity to meet the truth of that image: the truth which he devoted himself, with a devotion constantly on the edge of infatuation, to create. And for this devotion, this infatuation, he must be the man without God; for if he thought he had God, if he felt he were the man-God, he would have been the god who gave in to the temptations on the mountain, he would have been the god become—as Hitler and the others—the dictatorship of the scum of the earth: the debasement of the divine, or the daemonic, in the human. No; Adrian Lever-kühn is the man become the devil on behalf of the divine; the man become the devil insofar as the devil is a parody as a means of access to God: Thomas Mann's limit of human approach.

There is something absolutely irresponsible about any image which is perfectly evil, perfectly good, or perfectly apart from both; but of the three images, the human imagination in our day, having too much experience of the first, and too little of the second, can attempt to create only the third. This is no time for Cervantes to create Don Quixote; and anybody who tried would make a worse failure of the perfectly good man than Dostoevski did with that haunting failure Prince Myshkin in that great book *The Idiot*. Thomas Mann was right. In line with Cervantes and Dostoevski, he yet followed Goethe, who struggled to make the very Europe live which we wish to re-create, and like Goethe Mann chose the image of Faust as his weapon. Only in the image of Faust can Thomas Mann's understanding, lacking the everlasting mercy and the living grace, come upon "the hope beyond hopelessness, the transcendence of despair" which may yet break through to mercy and grace because they are the naked human voice itself, the voice crying in the dark always there. But the voice is the voice of the Muses.

The Charterhouse of Parma

[1 9 6 4]

One remembers that Stendhal ends this novel with its dedication: *To the Happy Few*, a phrase which some think was borrowed
from Shakespeare. Perhaps. The meaning is at any rate something
precious, which when I am reading Stendhal I seem to share: as a
kind of elation, a kind of promise; although I cannot explain it.
Stendhal had another phrase, to which Baudelaire three times adverts,
that beauty is the promise of happiness, and here is the pang that
goes with the elation: promises worth making are never kept. But let
me quote Baudelaire:

La dualité de l'art est une conséquence fatale de la dualité de l'homme.
Considérez, si cela vous plaît, la partie éternellement subsistante comme
l'âme de l'art, et l'élément variable comme son corps. C'est pourquoi Stendhal, esprit impertinent, taquin, répugnant même, mais dont les imperti-
nences provoque utilement la méditation, s'est rapproché de la vérité plus
que beaucoup d'autres, en disant que *le Beau n'est que la promesse du
bonheur.*

There is more, but I pause on the three adjectives, impertinent,
teasing (or tormenting), and repugnant for Stendhal's mind or spirit,
adjectives of which Stendhal would have been proud, whether for
himself or his heroes, and proud with a fierce pride, too: the very
pride which is *against* every form of resignation, the pride which

we do not dare permit to possess us, but which Stendhal's heroes (and half his heroines) wonderfully and rashly appropriate. It is the poetics which Aristotle did not write for the Greeks, but which Lu Chi in his *Wen Fu* did write for the Chinese and for the non-Greek parts of ourselves, and from which I ensample this: "Lay hold of the mutinous soul by sounding its secret depths, pay homage to its vital fierceness as you search for the very self: reason screened and obscured begins to creep forth, thought comes screaming, forced out from the womb" (Part II, Section O, numbers 3 and 4). This is the poetics of hysteria, also that of Stendhal.

Let us at least pretend for the length of these reflections that there is a verisimilitude in this notion.

Stendhal at once makes it easy for us to do so when he indicates that it is a high thing "to sin from motives of hatred and love," especially if in the presence of a sense of *puntiglio*, passion, and honor, with a contagion or contact of manners and hysteria. Thus the entry of the French army into Milan transformed effeminate manners into passion, caprice into violence. "To risk one's life became the fashion." *Puntiglio* is ultra-mannerly hysteria. It is naturally an explosive force, especially in a "land of crafty despotism." One wonders whether Stendhal is not making a substantive critique of *puntiglio* when he hinges this last phrase to the idea of caricature. Manners always tend to their own caricature; any given hysteria *is* a caricature of its source, whether of blindness, syphilis, or love.

Examples are almost continuous in Stendhal's opening pages. There is an activity in these chosen people which if it did not have the attractiveness of hysteria (one might say, or do, this oneself!) would be mere fret, which if it did not have the horror of *puntiglio* would be mere violence, and which if it did not have that quality of honor-in-action which goes with manners would be mere fustian: the movement of discommoded instinct—the movement, as we might say, of instinct out of place. Here is a good place to suggest that there is little question of "realism" in Stendhal, and that what we need to approach his books is a convention as remote from realism as Ben Jonson with his ballet of farce and force—as Congreve with his lilting surfaces shot with sudden piercing phrases. These men got plenty of the "real" into their works, but not in the conventions of realism. The avarice of Volpone is as real as the anger of Fabrizio, and the lovely lyric of Millamant's speeches is no less real, and no more, than Gina's manner of dealing with two of her lovers, Limercati and Canon Borda. I think these realities are close kin and the ways of conceiving them even closer, though there is little relation in the mode of treatment. Neither Jonson nor Congreve ever stuck so fast to the anecdotal as Stendhal, who, on the other hand, leaves in unaccountable and incomplete matters which neither playwright would have permitted. In Stendhal, only the emotion has its fragments tied together; its seat, source, and story never are. It is a rare thing for Stendhal to complete any scene or any action.— But, to get back to Gina and her lovers.

When Limercati thought her wish that he revenge her husband's murder absurd, her "contempt for him killed her affection," but not her ingenuity. She rekindled his affection into a fire of desperation, and for three years he wasted himself in the country, returning every other month to Milan to talk about his past favors. Meanwhile Gina conducted what was to her a false affair with a certain Conte N—. "When she had made quite sure of Limercati's despair," she told N— she did not love him, to which he made answer: "If you will be so extremely indulgent as to continue to receive me with all the distinctions accorded to a reigning lover, I may perhaps be able to find a suitable position." Gina's hysteria takes up the slack of missing reality and helps her bite her own nose off. Limercati and Conte N— use their hysterias rather to protect themselves from reality and at the same time as their only access to the coveted dream of reality which Gina had opened for them. Gina is volatile in mind, passionate in soul, as no doubt were her lovers, but note the preposterous situations she finds convenient and even necessary to keep herself going between one lover and the next. Consider Gina flinging water over the head of Ascanio to get rid of him. Or better still consider Gina climbing on a rock in the middle of Lake Como so she could "see herself assailed on all sides by raging waves." When she fell in, Fabrizio saved her, and Stendhal adds: "No doubt it is not a pleasant thing to feel oneself drowning, but the spirit of boredom, taken by surprise, was banished from the feudal castle."

[355

This is neither the caprice of Dostoevski nor the gratuitous act of Gide, but it springs from similar insight and impulse during the novelist's effort to convert behavior into manners.

Gina's treatment of Canon Borda is perhaps the best example in the first part of *The Charterhouse*, if only because, in its three or four pages, it is most nearly developed into a scene, and because in it we see clearly the combination of hysteria, manners, and honor at the delicious edge of farce. (The reader who wishes to laugh again will find the episode nearly at the end of the fifth chapter.) Neither Gina nor the Canon is deceived by the other, but each must pretend to be. After all, which of us has not been caught up in an intrigue— merely because it was *possible*—even though the real stake was quite outside the intrigue and might even be imperiled by it? A woman has only to rest her weight wholly on one leg and the thing is done, if the man has any sense of honor to his manners. Even the window shopper will sometimes break the glass. Here nothing happens, but it might. It is Stendhal at his best. Actually, all Gina wanted of the Canon was information as to what the police meant to do to Fabrizio, and as a reward to him he was to bring it to her in her box at La Scala; at quarter to 11.00 she and her friends would send everyone away, close the door, and blow out the candles. Then the Canon would come, a new aria in the opera. The time and place were chosen because "this would be the least compromising course for him." The least compromising is evidently the most conspicuous. Who will *not* see the lights go out, the doors close, who will not know that Gina is still there? Gina was the most beautiful woman in Milan, and her box the most stared at. Surely the Friends of Santa Margarita (Gina's name for the C.I.A. of the day) would not misunderstand.

In the light cast by Gina's relations with Limercati and Canon Borda, regard Fabrizio at Waterloo and at Romagnano, zenith and nadir of Fabrizio's Napoleonic period: in which he is shaped, out of which he is released upon the world. Speculation is garrulous if not endless; so a few hundred words will not be amiss before we say, like Stendhal at so many interesting places, "and so forth." In Stendhal's two large novels it is Napoleon up and down: that man as great as a man can be without virtue, that man more Stendhalian than Julien Sorel or Fabrizio del Dongo could ever be. In *The Red and the Black* it was the *Memoirs of St. Helena*; here it is Waterloo and reflections at Romagnano. There it was the myth-image of past glory. Here it is the débacle. The glory little Fabrizio had gained from his Latin genealogy plus what he had heard from his father about Napoleon gave him incentive, resolution, will, heroism—all blind, looking for a vision; and it is only the form of these which is broken down by his realization of the incongruity between Napoleon's proclamations and the muddle of his last battlefield. The force has been roused or precipitated in his characters, but only that. His ethos is not yet his fate. He is one of those who, lacking experience, resort to resolution; lacking purpose must needs be heroic; lacking choice must needs invoke will; lacking discrimination must needs lose temper. He is an early and promising member of the intellectual proletariat who now invest us. Stendhal's *La Chartreuse de Parme* is the immediate preface to Matthew Arnold's *Grande Chartreuse*, which is the more interesting since no two men could with more reason have more detested each other.

It is amazing how blank Stendhal makes Fabrizio, so blank that one suspects Stendhal's intellectual powers—so blank that one suspects a whole department of *literature*, a word which, as a lover of Stendhal but not a Beyliste, I firmly italicize. Must hope in that quarter be a form of paranoia? At any rate, Fabrizio gets glory from a genealogy and an empty mind from the Jesuits and good grades by Gina's bribery. But one should not overrate one's suspicions, which is telling without kissing. This may be what must happen in the novel of ideas. Fabrizio is the embodiment—perhaps the history—of an idea, but he cannot be said to show any instinct for ideas himself. One would not expect him to use ideas as regular weapons unless they became the medium of intrigue. One would say the same of any figure in Balzac. Novelists have not yet been forced to find or construct genuine public motives, which are not the same as those of our private chaos; a situation to which I do not object but which I think should be more generally recognized. Perhaps in Fabrizio the other sense of idea is the one at work: idea as image, as a thing seen with an eye that almost handles its sight: the idea of generosity, justice, heroism, glory, and love, something gallant as a possibility, but not at all something sacrificial or sacramental to grand action, as in Dante or Shakespeare.

Both courses of ideas are welcome; one needs only the right salutation. Consider: Fabrizio represents the ideas of ambition and career. For ambition, he is a charming figure of our common lot: which is to be one of those who have not yet (no matter how well along) found out what ambition is. He is one of those, we hopefully say, to whom, if he lives long enough, ambition *will come*, and when it comes will come as a freshet of relief in a dry season: as a solution and washing away of strains. Yet one doubts that Stendhal could have made one of his heroes live long enough for that: for such a hero would have lost, for the sake of one possibility, one genuine wager with the gods, his quickening sense of many possibilities. Without alternative games to play, he would have been merely swept along, his scream drowned in the flood.

No. In Stendhal there will always be games to play every time you open your shut eyes. Games, in Stendhal, are how you handle the incomprehensible; which is how it is we find Fabrizio playing an all-consuming game in the sudden vast waste of Waterloo: the game of pretense—the most reassuring pretense of all, the pretense that is better than truth—that one does not know what it is. If you have enough games—not cards but games—you can always play. You need no revelation, no rebirth, no permanent commitment, only a game. If he had thought of it, Stendhal would have attached to Fabrizio at Waterloo the idea of the *déraciné*. As it is, there is something of the *déraciné* in the Happy Few, those who read and plague themselves, and play the last resourceful game of inventing the games others cannot or will not play. But for Fabrizio, as for Julien, there will always be games to play. Let us look again at Waterloo where he talked by signs in order not to give away his bad French, and so of course made himself more suspicious than ever. The cloak and dagger are everywhere, so to speak, under every disguise. No wonder he did not know, this charming and ferocious boy, whether or not he had been in battle or even whether there had been a battle. At Romagnano, where he was exiled *because* he had been at Waterloo, though most of the time he rode all day, "he went three leagues on foot and wrapped himself in a mystery which he imagined to be impenetrable, in order to read the *Constitution-nel*, which he thought sublime. 'It is as fine as Alfieri and Dante!' he used often to exclaim." The curé was right who said of Fabrizio: "He is a cadet who feels himself wronged because he is not the first-born." All Fabrizio's hysterias are devoted to raising himself to the position of the first-born who is at the same time illegitimate. There is a special ambition in Stendhal: which is to *usurp* your own place, and find yourself a hero by the act of usurpation—and such fun, too! or (in Stendhal's phrase) "such delicious puerilities!" Consider, for a small example, the scene in the melancholy café at Romag-nano where Fabrizio rushes on the stranger with his dagger: we do not know with what reason and we never learn the upshot. Stendhal merely observes that he had forgotten honor "and reverted to instinct, or, more properly, to the memories of his earliest childhood." That is to say, he had reverted to behavior without manners; or, better still, pure behavior had come up on him. It is a commonplace to say that all sorts of writers and artists anticipated Freud, and indeed Freud says so himself. To me, there is perhaps less distortion of actual life in the behavior of Fabrizio than in the insights of Freud. Each mastered hysteria in a different way.

This remark must not be taken by itself. One good context is to think of hysteria—whether deliberately, spontaneously, or arbi-trarily undertaken, and whether as the result of a wound or a wish— as one of the mind's great modes of dealing with reality, whether to solicit it or to escape from it making little difference. Doubtless, like seeing visions, it is a dangerous mode, though universal and peren-nial. We are not concerned with therapy, but with the expression of experience in theoretic form (Croce's phrase for what lyric poetry gives to feelings) in novels and individual lives. The point seems to be that, as Eliot says, contradicting Arnold, mankind cannot bear very much reality. If reality strikes out at us, or if we need a modi-cum of reality for comfort and we cannot find it no matter where we look, then we respond with a heightened imitation. This is why a doctor of my acquaintance defined love as habit-hysteria. At any rate the imitation of reality in our response is often hysterical: in some sense inappropriate, incongruous, irrelevant, even self-destructive. Hysteria is never prudent. Only in great hands is it raised into final decorum, deep congruity, immediate relevance, and true creation. Your ordinary actor hams Shakespeare beyond need, your great actor finds his lines a being. Stendhal, one thinks, was not great enough; he had the impulse and the insight, but a kind of positive smallness of stature. Hence the intensity of the mere language and the "mere" action (words and acts seldom joined). Hence his heroes were boys, his heroines delicious women who never grew up either in sex or mind. Hence their hysterias were compelled to turn half to farce, half to *puntiglio*, with intrigue to keep the emotion going. That his books have been mistaken for works of rational imagination in the great sense is no fault of his; they excel in their own order. He recorded within his convention what a great many people, and these not the least lively, are actually like in their behavior, or wish they were like, or did not know, till they read Stendhal, that they might be like. Hysteria is for them the only acceptable substitute for reality because it is the only one really believed in while it lasts, really forgotten when it is gone, and really available when wanted in fresh supply. We make it for ourselves and it takes us over. I do not know that there is any other mode of imagination that for so many keeps life a continuing adventure. Surely it is related to what Lu Chi was talking about in the lines quoted at the beginning of these remarks.

Assuming that the quotation has been reread, does it not touch the quick in Stendhal? in Fabrizio? in Gina? in Mosca? Each of them is in search of reality, or of love, or of a way of getting along: each wants the reality to appear as a scream, the love to be a grand passion, the way of getting along to carry infinite risks. None of them can tolerate boredom, which is the presence of undesired reality, the condition, as Tolstoi puts it, of desiring desire. Each is unequal to his or her self-appointed task—not from incapacity of ideal, but from too much ideal, and also because the promptings of reality emerge as caprice and are regulated by an absence of good sense. As Baudelaire says, Stendhal is full of *caprice sans motif*—unless, as Baudelaire of all people must have known, the motive was to escape or prevent boredom.

Consider, with this in mind, how each of them dreads, and woos, the precipitation of reality through a word. Gina extinguishes the lights and shrieks when she learns from her maid the first sound of the word love. Fabrizio resolves never to utter the word to Gina, for then the thing between them would have a name. Mosca cannot permit himself the fatal word jealousy, though he is ravaged by that disease of love. Indeed, so curiously have these three persons constructed themselves that, had they been able on the sudden to speak simply, their simplicity would have appeared the outbreak of cynicism or hypocrisy, precisely as prudence takes for them the form of cowardice, and motive generally the form of fear. In short, being incapable of reality or love, yet desiring both, they are drawn to use the mechanism of intrigue—intrigue which is reputed to manage reality and to arrange love—to get them through their days and nights and even through their moments of crisis lest the crisis show its real nature with its name. A superb example is the last quarter of Chapter Seven where Mosca develops the jealousy he will not name in a series of unspoken soliloquies, first in the presence of the Prince his master, then alone with an anonymous letter, lastly as the *terzo incomodo* (Italian for when two is company three's a crowd) at Gina's apartments. There, she and Fabrizio are making that love which is not quite making love (the beauty which is the promise of happiness?) while he paces up and down before them, each pace a degree of madness. Suddenly he left, "calling out in a genial, intimate tone: 'Good-bye, you two!—One must avoid bloodshed,' he said to himself." And the next day he questions Gina's favorite maid. To this we may add as comment some characterized words spoken by Fabrizio but which seem to me to belong better to Mosca. Gina asks him if he wants to run away from her. " 'No,' he replied with the air of a Roman Emperor, 'but I want to act wisely.' " Nothing could have been further from Fabrizio's or Mosca's heart.

"With the air of a Roman Emperor." The Roman Emperor told everything but nobody would look at more than the statue of it. Let us think of Mosca della Rovere. It is like Mosca when we first meet him: an actor in a farce who is ashamed of the gravity of his position in the farce as a minister of state; that Mosca who said of his master, "he has fits of panic [*des accès de peur*] unworthy of a man, but these are the sole source of the favor that I enjoy"; that Mosca whose age and powdered hair made him a kind of Cassandra, hoarding in the avarice of his emotion all his anticipations of his visit to Gina in her box at the opera: only to find, as he went, that he had lost his desire, overcome by an "impulse of genuine shyness"; that Mosca looking woefully to old age "when"—I now locate the phrase I have already used—"when one is no longer capable of these delicious puerilities." Mosca, of course, is still quite young enough, but he speaks in lovable voice for those who are not. Mosca, it seems to me, has always the air of a Roman Emperor— of the thing itself, not of those hideous, eyeless statues which we cannot look at without looking away from—but he takes care to show that air as little as possible.

Instead, he uses intrigue: the entanglement of things (but not their mystery) in a manipulable form. Intrigue is the substitute for mystery in action. Intrigue is intricate like a mystification—she gave him an intriguing look. For many persons intrigue is the limit of belief; if a matter cannot be converted into intrigue, its existence is at best dubious. That in the end a given intrigue blows up, never mind: another intrigue is already on the way. And so on. We can make some comments and ask some questions. Intrigue is a formal means of transforming caprice into motive. To enter into an intrigue is the cheapest way to acquire momentum. To intrigue is to make use of manners as disguise, not as expression. With these propositions we may associate the following questions. Does intrigue control hysteria, or does it rather give hysteria opportunities? Does hysteria give intrigue something really to do, or does it rather make the hysteria real? We speak of course with reference to *The Charterhouse of Parma*, and we will come out best if our conclusions are not too firm. Intrigue is a neutral medium, a rhetoric that invites any action to an attractive lodging for the time being; then we move on. So it is with Stendhal; he moves on. These propositions and these questions (and others would have done as well or better) are dramatized and burlesqued with great local importance by Stendhal, but I do not think them (or any other frame of intrigue) central to his purpose or results. The local importance is quite enough, and critics who think otherwise have forgotten what fun intrigue is as a medium. That something else may show when the intrigue is dropped is another matter, and another matter still that what shows may have been going on all the time. Consider Chapter Thirteen, which contains the episode of Fausta: Stendhal was wrongly tempted to cut it from the novel.

We are in Bologna where (as I once read in an eighteenth-century English travel book) the women cannot help scratching themselves as they make their evening walks in the spring, and which was then as now famous for the beauty of its women and the excellence of its cooking; and when we are not in Bologna we are secretly in Parma: intrigue is the medium by which we move between, and move ahead, and move away—all in relation to a certain discovery which Fabrizio makes about himself. For here Fabrizio finds his second Waterloo in a manner even more foolhardy than he had found his first: in a sedan chair drawn by twenty thugs with torches. Where at the first Waterloo he had sought glory and had his horse taken away from him, here, with equal vanity, and with the special incentive of boredom, he had sought love and found, though he had played with ruse after ruse and pinched himself all over, that for him love did not exist. The body of a servant girl or of an actress more nearly met his 6.00 o'clock appetite than any love. He is indeed—so far—that man whose destiny it is to be lacking in one passion. So little does he have of it that he cannot even carry through the game of it to pass the time, much less to make of it a career. The hypocrisy by which honest lovers rise to their roles, or reimmerse themselves in their passions, is impossible to Fabrizio except as burlesque.

Stendhal was right to entrust the fate of Fabrizio in battle to a *vivandière*. Nothing could be fantastic enough to render glory unpalatable to a sixteen-year-old boy. Was he not right, too, in terminating the *willed hysteria* of Fabrizio's love for Fausta in a sedan chair followed by a duel as senseless and inconclusive as the fight at the bridge in the earlier episode? This Fausta, to whom Stendhal does not permit much existence, is part Siren and part Circe, but insufficiently either to hold or degrade Fabrizio. We see better than he that it is his aunt Gina alone who could accommodate him; and we see, also, why Stendhal has made Gina impossible for him to secure. Beauty is the promise of happiness.

There is something about our hero's name, Fabrizio or Fabrice, which is suggestive of the calamities that happen to him. He is a creature *made up* for the old great roles of Prelate, Soldier, and Lover, but who is yet—though placed at the heart of prestige, power, and opportunity—personally incapable of playing any of them. No wonder the omens for him are prison and crime—but always with the haunting possibility that Gina might in some impossible "yet" recreate him in her own image—at her own intensity—her own true ardency—of the force that now moves him only to affection; and even with that crime and prison must be the end. Stendhal envisages no other fate for his heroes than truncation.

It is in such considerations that we find the shape of this novel accruing—an almost unearned increment—upon the psychological clusters, deep gestures, and hysterias that eventually defeat themselves in action. Was the world so changing for Stendhal that some part of his spirit could not assent to it except through the comic repudiation of all the values which he had encouraged so to survive in himself? It is this sort of question to which he constantly makes us return.

Fabrizio, certainly, has so far taken only a comic part in his occupations: the unseemly, fearful comedy of the thing, man, spirit incongruous with itself. Things must be kept moving, kept a little fantastically beyond themselves in expression in order to be tolerable at all. If we could arrest the flux, freeze the immediate, we might be overcome by the intolerable illusion that the immediate was all. It is the awareness of this possibility that leads to Stendhalian comedy.

If we take the series hypocrite and hysterical as needing a next member might it not be histrionic? He who pretends, he who induces force beyond practicable incentive, is not he precisely histrionic— an actor playing beyond himself just so much of life as he can pretend to or invoke? Does he not then create a new sort of reality for the moment, which we rejoice in even while we do not believe in it? Or do we go a step further? Is not the histrionic the most powerfully seductive of all our native talents: our first squall of breath, our last moan or sigh? Whenever the histrionic talent has taken us over, and we have come back, we know well enough, though we do not know what it is, that we have been in touch with reality itself, and have been in procession with it: the heaviness, the light, the crying. Some of the religious call it speaking with tongues, which would never do for Stendhal, but which is something like in the ordinary world the effect of the soliloquies and the rash acts of Gina and Mosca and Fabrizio. They are histriophones.

If the notion is at all apt, we should perhaps reverse the order of our series and make it: histrionic, hysterical, hypocritical. This is, of course, an aesthetic not a prudent order, mutinous, not assenting; it is the voice of *midi-carême*, Halloween, saturnalia with *puntiglio* and a sense of honor: a sense that perfect murder would approach perfect virtue. Our civilizations are never properly ours, our proper reality shows best only in our intercalary feast days. And so forth; there are many ways that Stendhal's people make us say the same thing. . . . Considering that civilization is a tissue of surfaces we slide off and of institutions that raise or degrade us outside our proper reality, and considering that we cling in our sliding to that civilization just the same—as if could we but sit still we would be ourselves!—it is to be expected aesthetically and imperatively that we should find something *other* than that civilization, perhaps fatal to us without the civilization, to express ourselves in at least symbolic action. I cannot put it more formally. It is the willy-nilly cry of the willies within, the cry of the individual affronted in his dignity. If you would like a companion to Stendhal in this matter think of William Blake. Had it happened that way Fabrizio could have known "The Marriage of Heaven and Hell" by heart. Though he would have spoken looking in an opposite direction, the voice is much the same. Each from the proper reality cried the proper freedom.

Not that Stendhal ignored other worlds and other imprudences. It was he himself who fired off the pistol in the concert, or as he should have said in Grand Opera, for the politics are operatic, or *opéra bouffe*. This would hardly need saying if there were not critics who think that Stendhal wrote genuine political novels. The genuine is something like what you find in Tacitus, Saint-Simon, and Anthony Trollope rather than Suetonius, Stendhal, and Disraeli; though if you think of the two sets together they cast strange lights on each other. In Stendhal the truth has been taken out of the issue; there is no sense of the mangled truth in continuing purpose, and of its vitality in corruption; only the personal stake remains. It is as if political gossip were political power, where at most it may sometimes disclose it and at worst obfuscate it. Yet in politics we know there are no *unnatural* vices: the stake is common and has values superior to any principle. Machiavelli tells us this, not Stendhal.

As a novelist, he is not required to. The sense of what is at stake may be very small in a novel or play and yet stand for everything. It may be very personal as in *The Possessed* or very generalized as in *St. Joan* and in either case carry great and lasting force. But I do not believe that Stendhal's more or less unconscious convention of grand opera without music will carry his novel as politics. Perhaps he did not intend it to do so; perhaps the politics only got in in the sense that any other trade or profession might have got in: to give occupation to the hero and provide the career ladder of success and disaster. To the contrary, I think Stendhal meant to express his sense of politics to the hilt or handle: his version of what actually goes on; he was treating political behavior exactly as he treated behavior in love. In other parts of his mind he may have thought differently, but in the novelistic part this is how it was: a pattern that beset him and a patter that he practiced.

Let us remind ourselves of the terms we have been deploying: *puntiglio*, honor, rashness, hysteria, intrigue, to which we now add the politics of grand opera to follow on the histrionic. It is a vocabulary which cannot be accused of jargon, but in which every word crosses a threshold into the crackling sensibility of Stendhal.

For the operatic politics consider Chapter Fourteen. Rassi and the Marchesa Raversi have managed to get Fabrizio sentenced to twenty years *in absentia*, not so much because they hate Fabrizio, and certainly not for justice, but in the course of the contest for power, position, and prestige in the Parmesan court. Gina and Mosca together manage to abridge the sentence to twelve years by bulldozing the Prince and playing upon him generally. They believe they have secured exoneration, but the Prince fools them—as a Prince should. In these efforts Mosca is guided partly by his own struggle for power but much more by his allegiance to Gina. Gina is guided entirely by her (false) image of Fabrizio and by the impetuously grasped possibilities which bristle in front of her. Since everywhere in the Grand Duchy of Parma power takes absolute forms it takes also *small* forms, small enough to be grasped. Corruption is available, and is indeed for those anywhere near the top the only path to action. Corruption is the cement of this society; or, if not the cement, the elastic plastic adhesive which when it snaps lets crime and violence in. Thus Gina heaves her bits of power about with the magnificence of possibility and the exaltation of intrepidity which go with madness. Consider these items taken from the twenty-odd pages of this chapter of absolute but precarious politics. La Raversi is *mad with joy* at the twenty-year sentence. Gina *breaks into song* at her own intention and is *in a transport of joy* when she pretends she will leave Parma. The Prince *reigned a quarter of an hour* (by keeping Gina waiting) and knows that Gina *will make everyone believe* her own account of things if she leaves Parma. Gina, like Fabrizio, speaks *with a Roman pride* and makes her peace with Mosca *with a merry glance.* "She had acted at random and for her own immediate pleasure" and "had fully believed" her own intentions. But when her servants applaud her new decision to remain at Parma, she responds "like an actress taking a *call."* Writing the archbishop, she signs her full name because "in the eyes of the middle classes the caricature looks like beauty." Similarly, the Prince worries how to insult his minister Rassi; and Rassi (whose power lies in crime) wants prestige to guarantee his crime. And similarly the banished Raversi forges Gina's writing to bring Fabrizio to jail.

It is a magnificent scene in which no one is implicated in anything but the part played, and in which the players are monsters of vanity and rancor. The secret of their energy is indicated by Gina's phrase about herself in one of her bad moments: "I can no longer form an *exaggerated* idea of anything in the world, I can no longer love." The exaggerated idea is the prompter of most of the behavior in this book, and it is applied with the logic of passion: "The profound interest which it feels in knowing the truth does not allow it to keep up vain pretenses, while at the same time the extreme devotion that it feels to the object of its love takes from it the fear of giving offence." This was written of Clelia in love with Fabrizio;

but if you put for passion "exaggerated idea" you have the whole story. One of Clelia's own observations gives a further emphasis: "What a terrible passion love is. . . . And yet all those liars in society speak of it as a source of happiness."

Stendhal's psychology of the exaggerated idea is accurate enough, if we correctly estimate its ignorance, and is sound for its purpose within that accuracy. It provides a useable form to take care of the view and practice of life which we call burlesque: the last term we shall add to our series. The question will be how much Stendhal's burlesque is a true mode of the imagination and how much is mere puerilization: a question which is only to be asked, by no chance to be answered.

If you do not like the word burlesque, you may use *Commedia dell'Arte*, which was played on certain evenings of the week at the court of the new Prince. Only the plot was put on the boards and each player was left to fill out lines and action with whatever could be improvised or apparently improvised at the moment. I say "apparently" because there were of course occasions when one or another player made cause to fit into his role speeches already invented and even rehearsed. So, for example, did the young Prince make love to Gina, when he knew ahead that he might play the role of lover opposite her that evening. I suggest that the structure of the whole novel is like the structure of the game at Court. It is Grand Opera with the music left out, and sometimes, in the heat of the moment, with the plot left out, too. But there is always improvisation, careless or planned.

Item. When Mosca met Gina he was already married; that was careless improvisation. But when the time comes to marry Gina, the existing wife is readily forgotten, which is planned improvisation.

Item. When Fabrizio takes up preaching he has ready on the footstool in his pulpit a paper containing the prayer for the unfortunate man, which he then reads as if to Clelia in her golden chair. This is planned improvisation.

Item. The whole formula of Clelia's oath never again to see Fabrizio (of course she could be with him in the dark) is like the posted plot in the game. Granted the medium, everything follows by improvisation: by what will do at the moment, so long as only a burlesque of the sentiments is in order. Stendhal cares nothing for sentiment, everything for sensibility.

Item. Many times in Stendhal when a matter or a scene reaches the point where it would, under other hands, cry out for development, Stendhal writes his customary "and so forth." This is the black-out, the bursting into song and dance in a musical comedy. For example, the Princess' letter to Gina to the effect that she will make her Grand Mistress of her court breaks off with "and so forth" when it reaches the point of burlesque.

Item. Gina's letter of instructions to Fabrizio for his escape from jail (in Chapter Twenty) is either superb burlesque or idiocy—like the escape itself.

Item. When Gina confronts herself with the magnificence of a lonely death for the sake of that wretch, Fabrizio, it is characteristic of Stendhal to report it in private monologue. No one hears it, nothing is done with it, no one answers. Perhaps in this case, perhaps in any *one* case, Stendhal is right, but he does a similar thing everywhere in the book. These monologues, these speeches, these truncated sentiments of which this book is so full, are addressed to no one. They are the life not lived, almost the thought not thought, the act never construed. They represent either what one should have said or what one might possibly say: meanwhile knowing in blood and bones the absolute impossibility of ever saying or thinking or doing.

Ordinarily we have burlesque as an adjunct of satire (as in Jonson, or Martial, or Aristophanes): to castigate or destroy something or to protect ourselves from it in exaggerated mockery; or we have burlesque as high jinks in the lower and still playful parts of our sensibility, where we let ourselves go along favored and indecorous lines, as in slapstick, in masquerades, in games played in the dark, in fantasies of impossibility; and we have our modern burlesque with its coarse chorus and coarser skits punctuated by strip-tease with drums, where, as it ought, the bawdy approaches the obscene, and things in general get as near the sewer as the gutter can get. (There was that other form, now dead, last exemplified by the early Marx Brothers, and seen in reminiscence only now and then in

Danny Kaye.) All these are ordinary forms of burlesque, and have quite sufficiently their own meaning. Stendhal's burlesque is another thing; it neither castigates, nor destroys, nor plays with reality. Like the hysteria upon which it is founded, it is meant to get hold of reality, or, if not that, to make by improvisation from caprice a substitute for the missing reality. I do not believe in Gina's playfulness when she makes all her peasants drunk and has her reservoirs opened to flood the streets of Parma; but I do believe in the hysteria, the caprice, the improvisation, and I have a special attachment which is not the same thing as belief to the burlesque of life in which, under Stendhal's hands, this combination results.

That is, this burlesque is a pretty precious form of the actual—for many an irresistible hallucination of the actual, while it lasts. In the *Charterhouse* there is a wonderful forced-flowering of that talent for sudden explosions of almost pure behavior—for rash acts—for shots in the dark—for nightmares at noon—for fire-crackers at midnight—for practical jokes taken as the height of action—for anything done without consideration for others—the talent for all those things having fatherhood in the anarch in us we call caprice.

I suppose the great images which inhabit our literature with the vital authority of caprice are the *Tempest, Don Quixote,* and the *Brothers Karamazov*—with some good words to be said for *Pickwick Papers.* Stendhal is not in this line because of the immaturity of his sentiments and because he never explored the behavior he tapped. Note that there is no quarrel with the maturity of his emotions. Emotions are not susceptible of maturity, only of different degrees of depth, intensity, and hysteria. But going back to caprice: it is those springs in behavior which incline us to anarchy: that is to say, rebellion to tyranny, the sweet and fearful intuition of our own natures, or the immediate creation of an absolutely fresh order out of the old materials. Caprice is our unmediated recognition of the underlying chaos and our knowledge that all our orders are made out of chaos. Order is what we do with chaos, as unity is what we see in chaos. The usual fields for capricious action are love, politics, religion, war, and crime. (I speak of history, morals, daily life; and say nothing of the mathematics, symmetrical and otherwise, which make life possible.) In the works named above the caprice is from very deep levels of perception of the underhalves of our natures. In Stendhal, the caprice comes from a perception which penetrates very little, and only into the effects, of our under-nature. The underblows to him are only a sort of trade wind. For another useful comparison look a century ahead to André Gide and his gratuitous act: the mere act against, or sometimes within, society which liberates the actor from it, usually at the expense of some individual. Gide seeks after freedom as if it were a suicide that fails, and his moral stoicism is a prelude to an orgasm of the intellect. His caprice, his anarchy, is far more in what his reason does to his behavior than in what his sensuality—and the tender ache in him—does to his reason. He suffers from what strikes me as a great heresy: the belief that to *cultivate* sin gets you any nearer either to behavior or to reality. "And so forth." Well, Stendhal lies between.

Let us look at an example and have done. When Fabrizio (this known criminal, this casual murderer) became bishop-coadjutor with the succession secured, as it seems, to the archbishopric, and at the same time lost hope for the love of Clelia, he made out as near as possible to retire from the pomps and vanities of this wicked world in a wonderful huff. He wore black, went nowhere, valued nothing, put on his death face (as one puts on a smile) and was a very holy man indeed: with the sense strong in him that he owed nothing to anybody since his possessions had no value. At this time Mosca and Gina were in their chosen exile (made for the purpose of return) and Mosca called upon this innocent false-recluse for aid in the politics of Parma. Fabrizio suddenly realized rhetorically the sum of his debts to the Count and carried out the political mission faithfully and expertly. He stepped at once out of every character he had had and became a model of Richelieu or Mazarin at twenty-five. This is the caprice of Napoleonism if you like. But let us say also that it represents the conflict of capricious psychologies within the narrow frame of Stendhal's mind; he is right to mix burlesque with the serious adventure, it is the only mixture he knows, and if he can improvise fast enough it may work. We note that in Stendhal's version of the psychology of caprice, there are no committing acts—no perfidies to the self—which cannot be reversed, at least in the leading characters. Each is always free for a new dodge, another resumption without continuity or rationale; there are instead successive waves of infatuation. In the Stendhalian world, only the lesser persons, whom we see only sideways, off side, or in perspective, enjoy purpose, choice, or decision at a rational level; and it is a travesty of modern psychology to say that the heroes enjoy these qualities at a deep level. The hero's intent only unfolds itself through a succession of caprices, and his achievement (usually death or desuetude) only in the unity of accidents seen together. This is the heroism of the simple gratuitous act, the caprice of the fresh start. It is very inviting, as the wilful in us always is; but what it amounts to is submission to the goddess Fortuna. Stendhal shows that he knew this by submitting the boy Fabrizio to the care of the Abbé Blanés, the astrologer who burlesqued the future by means of the past. That the balance for Fortuna is Scientia, or knowledge earned in life, Stendhal chose not to know. Hence the emptiness of the psyche in Fabrizio (he had plenty of spirit) which led him to cultivate his infatuation for Clelia—after having *himself* made it impossible that it should come to anything but sex at midnight—by scattering *nosegays* in Clelia's *garden*. What else could he do?

It is for this reason, too, that boredom is taken to be the engine of action in the world at large. Caprice, as an invoked pattern of conduct, leads inevitably at the turn of the wheel to another boredom and so to another caprice. It was a fatal caprice, says Stendhal, that led Fabrizio to want his illegitimate son for himself. So the child died, so Clelia died, and so in a year Fabrizio himself died. Yet there is the haunting memory of capricious acts which created moments of freedom; and those moments, for all their hysteria, are a burlesque of life itself. Almost, as we see in the lives of many people, they pass for life, and their beauty is indeed a promise of happiness. To create that illusion may not make a novelist immortal but it gives him lasting life.

ACKNOWLEDGMENTS

"The Charterhouse of Parma" copyright by Kenyon College. First published in The Kenyon Review, *vol. 26, no. 1. Reprinted with permission of the author's estate and* The Kenyon Review.
"Henry James" reprinted with permission of Macmillan Publishing Co. from Literary History of the United States, *4th revised edition, edited by Robert Spiller, et al.* © *1946, 1947, 1948, 1953, 1963, 1974 by Macmillan.*
"A Critics Job of Work," "Notes on E.E. Cummings' Language," "Examples of Wallace Stevens," "New Thresholds, New Anatomies," "The Method of Marianne Moore," "The Later Poetry of W.B. Yeats," "Emily Dickinson: Notes on Prejudice and Fact," "Unappeasable and Peregrine: Behavior and the 'Four Quartests' " and "The Expense of Greatness: Three Emphases on Henry Adams" from Language as Gesture *by Richard P. Blackmur, copyright 1936 by Betty Bredemeier Davison; copyright 1940, 1951, 1952 by Richard P. Blackmur; renewed 1964 by Betty Bredemeier Davison; renewed 1968 by The First National Bank of Princeton; renewed 1979 by Elizabeth Blackmur and Helen Van Eck; renewed 1980 by Elizabeth Blackmur.*
"The Critical Prefaces of Henry James" from The Lion and the Honeycomb, *copyright* © *1955 by Richard P. Blackmur; renewed 1983 by Elizabeth Blackmur.*
"Parody and Critique: Mann's Doctor Faustus" *and "Crime and Punishment: Murder in Your Own Room" from* Eleven Essays in the European Novel, *copyright 1950, 1964 by R.P. Blackmur; renewed 1978 by Betty Bredemeier Davison.*

Published by arrangement with Harcourt Brace Jovanovich, Inc.